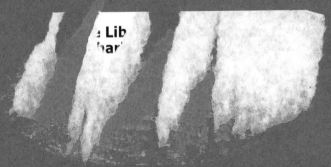

THE LEGENDARY "LUGS" BRANIGAN

Ireland's Most Famed Garda

By the same author

Georgian Dublin: Ireland's Imperilled Architectural Heritage
Dublin's Vanishing Craftsmen
Stoneybatter: Dublin's Inner Urban Village
Dublin Street Life and Lore: An Oral History
Dublin Tenement Life: An Oral History
Dublin Pub Life and Lore: An Oral History
Dublin Voices: An Oral History
Streets Broad and Narrow: Images of Vanishing Dublin
Dublin's Lost Heroines
The Bombing of Dublin's North Strand, 1941
Ireland's Arctic Siege: The Big Freeze of 1947

THE LEGENDARY "LUGS" BRANIGAN

Ireland's Most Famed Garda

KEVIN C. KEARNS ∾

Gill & Macmillan

Gill & Macmillan
Hume Avenue, Park West, Dublin 12
www.gillmacmillanbooks.ie

© Kevin C. Kearns 2014
978 07171 5939 0

Index compiled by Kate Murphy
Cartography by Keith Barrett, Design Image
Typography design by Make Communication
Print origination by O'K Graphic Design, Dublin
Printed and bound by CPI Group (UK) Ltd, CR0 4YY

This book is typeset in 11/13.5 pt Minion.

The paper used in this book comes from the wood pulp of
managed forests. For every tree felled, at least one tree is
planted, thereby renewing natural resources.

A CIP catalogue record for this book is available from the
British Library.

5 4 3 2 1

In memory of my daughter,
Megan Corrigan Kearns

CONTENTS

ACKNOWLEDGEMENTS

In the early 1970s I began my research to historically chronicle various elements of "vanishing" Dublin, as old communities and traditional customs were disappearing with bewildering swiftness. Apart from archival research, I conducted hundreds of oral history sessions with elderly Dubliners who possessed lucid memories of the "old days." My eleven books on Dublin focused largely on the period 1910–60. In tape-recording their lives I was surprised how often my respondents made reference to a garda by the name of Jim "Lugs" Branigan—though he had no direct relevance to the topic I was researching.

When I reached seventy years of age, in 2010, I found myself paging through decades of transcripts, remembering how often the name of "Lugs" had popped up, how so many Dubliners spoke of him reverentially as a "legend." Perhaps belatedly, I decided to undertake a book project on this admired garda. Who was he, what role did he actually play in people's lives? And why was he "legendary"?

I first dug out my copy of Bernard Neary's fond memoir of his friend Lugs, written a quarter of a century ago. It provided a most interesting account of various aspects of Branigan's life. What I had in mind was to write a historical-biographical book, developing a full portrait of the man. I next contacted Neary and proposed my idea. He was gracious and supportive, encouraging me to forge ahead with the undertaking. This was just the spur I needed to venture forth.

Branigan, born in 1910—exactly a century previously—had died in 1985. I would need to conduct lengthy oral history interviews with remaining family members, friends, and gardaí with whom he worked closely. By good fortune, I found that during the last twenty years of his career, especially when he commanded the famous "riot squad," established in 1964, he had personally selected the fittest, toughest guards to serve with him. Most of them were thirty or more years younger than himself. This meant that they would now be retired, in their seventies and eighties—perfect candidates for oral history. However, this meant first finding them, then hoping they would assist me with the book.

Thanks to Gerard Lovett, former general secretary of the Garda Síochána Retired Members' Association, I was put on the trail of a number of Branno's closest Garda mates. Most of them were delighted to meet me for taping sessions, eager to help in putting the "Branigan story" on the record. They in turn often put me onto a few other men. And so it went.

Meanwhile I tracked down his two sons, Alick, aged seventy-two, and Declan, sixty-eight. Both were gentlemanly, private men, not inclined to speak to annoying journalists or media types seeking a few sensational quotes about their father. Over the years they had declined many such interviews. At first I was no exception, as they politely resisted my overtures. It was only when they connected my name with some of my previous books, with which they were familiar, that they recognised me as a serious historian. An immediate warming followed, as both gladly offered to meet me and assist in any way they could.

Ultimately, it took the generous assistance of many people to make this project possible. As with all my books, Dr Mary Clark, city archivist, and her superb staff at Dublin City Library and Archive in Pearse Street were absolutely indispensable. Garda Paul Maher of the Garda Síochána Museum took time to talk to me and retrieve valuable photographs for inclusion in the book. Garda Liam Holland, liaison officer, Kevin Street Garda Station, directed me to residents in the Liberties who knew Branigan well. Similarly, Liz O'Connor of St Nicholas of Myra Heritage Centre in Francis Street put me in touch with excellent contacts, adding her own insights to the conversations. I am deeply grateful to all Jim Branigan's friends and fellow-gardaí whose oral narratives are included in this book. Their personal, first-hand and often graphic memories authenticate this work in a powerful way.

To his sons, Alick and Declan, I am most indebted. Immensely kind and generous, they discussed with great candour every subject I raised. Despite his health problems, Declan invited me to his home for many hours to share his intimate recollections, revealing much about his father's "soft side," as he liked to call it, seldom seen by the general public. Only six months after our pleasant meeting, Declan died; but his sensitive contributions to his father's legacy will live on.

I cannot thank Alick enough for all he did to assist me in myriad ways: meeting me several times, exchanging e-mail, excavating old family photographs that no-one has seen for ages, sharing personal and poignant reminiscences of his father from early childhood.

Gill & Macmillan, my publisher of the past twenty years and seven books, again transformed my manuscript into a dignified tome. My long-time friend, editor-in-chief and publisher Fergal Tobin (retired at the end of 2013) was unequivocally enthusiastic from the outset, giving me the green light. Nicki Howard, his successor, and Deirdre Nolan, commissioning editor, deftly guided it through the editorial maze. Deirdre Rennison Kunz, managing editor—my "security blanket"— again took charge of the exacting editorial process.

My sincere gratitude goes to all the staff members at Gill & Macmillan who were involved in publishing this book, especially for their patience and indulgence in putting up with a Luddite such as myself—one who still submits a two or three-inch-thick paper manuscript, typed on a small manual typewriter, then sends in original photographic prints rather than discs. Of course I like to think that they find it all rather "quaint"—but I have a suspicion that perhaps this is not so. In any case, "thank you!"

My warmest appreciation goes to my partner, Cathe Brown, who for the past eighteen years has shared my life of joys and sorrows, researching and writing, loving Dublin, and unfailingly providing support and enthusiasm for all my book projects. These would have been lonely journeys without her companionship.

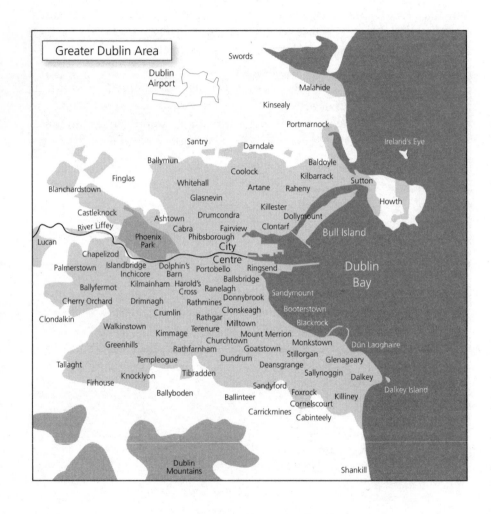

Greater Dublin Area

Swords

Dublin Airport

Malahide

Kinsealy

Portmarnock

Santry

Darndale

Ireland's Eye

Ballymun

Baldoyle

Coolock

Kilbarrack

Finglas

Whitehall

Artane

Raheny

Sutton

Blanchardstown

Glasnevin

Howth

Castleknock

Ashtown

Drumcondra

Killester

Dollymount

River Liffey

Cabra

Fairview

Clontarf

Lucan

Phoenix Park

Phibsborough

City Centre

Bull Island

Chapelizod

Palmerstown

Islandbridge

Dolphin's Barn

Portobello

Ringsend

Dublin Bay

Inchicore

Ballsbridge

Ballyfermot

Kilmainham

Harold's Cross

Ranelagh

Sandymount

Cherry Orchard

Drimnagh

Rathmines

Donnybrook

Booterstown

Clondalkin

Crumlin

Rathgar

Clonskeagh

Blackrock

Walkinstown

Kimmage

Terenure

Milltown

Mount Merrion

Greenhills

Churchtown

Monkstown

Dún Laoghaire

Rathfarnham

Goatstown

Stillorgan

Tallaght

Templeogue

Dundrum

Deansgrange

Glenageary

Firhouse

Knocklyon

Tibradden

Sallynoggin

Dalkey

Ballyboden

Sandyford

Dalkey Island

Ballinteer

Foxrock

Killiney

Cornelscourt

Carrickmines

Cabinteely

Dublin Mountains

Shankill

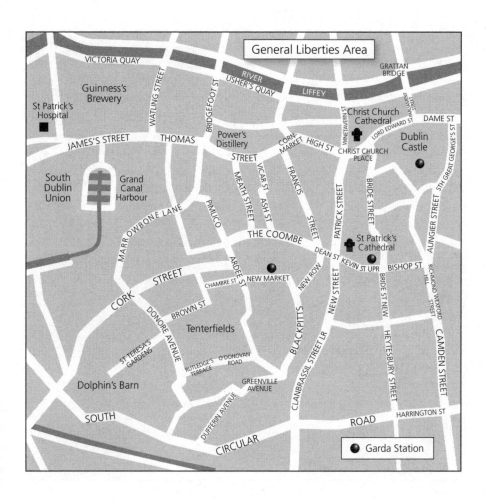

General Liberties Area

VICTORIA QUAY
RIVER
USHER'S QUAY
LIFFEY
GRATTAN BRIDGE
Guinness's Brewery
St Patrick's Hospital
WATLING STREET
BRIDGEFOOT ST
WINETAVERN ST
Christ Church Cathedral
DAME ST
LORD EDWARD ST
PARLIAMENT ST
JAMES'S STREET
THOMAS
Power's Distillery
CORN MARKET
HIGH ST
CHRIST CHURCH PLACE
Dublin Castle
STREET
MEATH STREET
VICAR ST
ASH ST
FRANCIS
STREET
PATRICK STREET
BRIDE STREET
AUNGIER STREET
STH GREAT GEORGE'S ST
South Dublin Union
Grand Canal Harbour
MARROWBONE LANE
PIMLICO
THE COOMBE
DEAN ST
KEVIN ST UPR
St Patrick's Cathedral
BISHOP ST
RICHMOND
WEXFORD STREET
HILL
CORK
STREET
ARDEE ST
CHAMBRE ST
NEW MARKET
NEW ROW
BLACKPITTS
NEW STREET
BRIDE ST NEW
CAMDEN STREET
DONORE AVENUE
BROWN ST
Tenterfields
ST TERESA'S GARDENS
RUTLEDGE'S TERRACE
O'DONOVAN ROAD
CLANBRASSIL STREET LR
HEYTESBURY STREET
Dolphin's Barn
GREENVILLE AVENUE
DUFFERIN AVENUE
SOUTH
CIRCULAR
ROAD
HARRINGTON ST

Garda Station

PROLOGUE

On Saturday 7 October 1973, at the retirement dinner for Sergeant James Branigan held at the Garda Club in Harrington Street, Dublin, Chief Superintendent Edmund Doherty, a man not given to hyperbole, rose to tell the hushed crowd: "He is one of those people who become a legend in their own time." Heads nodded.

Ireland has long cherished its legendary figures and heroes. From the realms of literature, politics, patriotism, and religion, they fill libraries and graves around the country. Most achieved their renown for great deeds or monumental achievements; they are deeply embedded in Irish history and folklore. In modern times, for an ordinary man to be acclaimed an authentic "legend" is an extraordinary story.

His origins were modest, unpromising of greatness. He was a child of the old Liberties in Dublin, his father employed in the South Dublin Union—the workhouse—in James's Street. He distinguished himself neither in school nor on the sports field. A rather shy lad, he showed no leadership qualities, preferring to be a follower. In truth, nothing about him stood out—except his ears.

At the age of fourteen he left school to take a job in the Great Southern Railways yard in Inchicore. Timid, he was seen as a sissy and was cruelly bullied by other boys, some of whom beat him up badly. Yet he steadfastly refused to fight back. Though seemingly a coward, he had the courage to return to work day after day to suffer the same punishment. He hardly seemed a candidate to become a heavyweight boxing champion, or to earn the "undisputed reputation as the country's toughest and bravest garda."[1] But he would achieve both. The stuff of legend, to be sure.

As former Chief Superintendent Michael Reid attests, Jim Branigan was a "man of many contradictions," a paradox that puzzled his own family and close friends. He would gain fame as Ireland's "most fearless" pugilistic policeman, lauded in newspaper headlines. However, the roles for which he was most loved by many city-dwellers were clandestine and unheralded in the press. It was what Reid calls his great "humanity . . . compassion" for the downtrodden souls of the city. His son Declan simply refers to it as his father's "soft side."

——

James Branigan was born in January 1910. His life would span the great events of the century—the 1916 Rising, the Civil War, the Depression, two world wars—into the age of jet travel, nuclear bombs, space exploration, and computers. In his infancy the first experimental planes were airborne for only brief spells, just above the heads of awed observers; newfangled motor cars sputtered and clunked along at five or ten miles per hour; films were still silent, not "talkies."

Yet from childhood, flickering films on the screen of the Lyric or Tivoli cinemas helped to mould his character. All children were enthralled at seeing the early "cowboy and Indian" moving pictures, sitting on the edge of their wooden seats, held in suspense as Tom Mix, Hoot Gibson or Gene Autry faced down the lowest "dirty polecat" they had ever seen. There was no higher excitement for Dublin youths than seeing the heroic sheriff of Tombstone or Dodge City lash a villain's face with his leather riding-gloves or, when necessary, resort to his "faster than greased lightning" pistol draw. When the "talkies" came in, with Gary Cooper and Randolph Scott, the action seemed even more real.

Young Jim Branigan took it more seriously than other lads. As his son Declan vouches, he comprehended the basic principles of "good versus bad," of courage, fairness, and justice, behind the exciting action scenes. The "ideology of the western sheriff rubbed off on him . . ." The *morality* of the stories made a lasting impression. He would become a lifelong aficionado of American western history and lore, seeing every film that came to Dublin and amassing a collection of books that would eventually reach the hundreds.

————

When Branigan joined the Garda Síochána in 1931 as a 21-year-old recruit, the country had only recently achieved independence from Britain. The new police force was but a few years old, attempting to create an identity separate from the old Dublin Metropolitan Police, which had been despised by many people. For recruits there was excitement in the challenges ahead; but first, young Branigan had to pass a few tests.

At nearly six feet four inches tall, he towered over most other young men taking the physical examination. But he was as lanky as a blackthorn stick, and the crucial chest measurement was much in doubt. For months before the examination he worked diligently to build up bulk where it counted most. When the day came and the measuring tape was carefully drawn around his chest, history hung in the balance. He met the requirement by a small fraction of an inch.

From the first days in training at the Garda Depot in the Phoenix Park, Dublin, he embraced the life as his true vocation, brimming with enthusiasm and confidence. There was only one hitch: he was required to learn boxing, for purposes of self-defence. On his first days in the ring he was pummelled by a tough recruit and left with a bloody nose and bruises—as well as a bruised ego in front of his new mates. By the following year he would be a member of the elite Garda Boxing Club, fighting top-notch boxers from Belfast, London, and Manchester. Later, in Berlin and Leipzig, he was pitted against Germany's pampered pugilists, who fought like gladiators to please Hitler's henchmen, sitting in the first row. They saw their prime fighters as proof of "Aryan" supremacy and expected them to win—convincingly.

In the 1930s and early 40s Branigan found himself in uniform during the era of Dublin's notorious street gangs, which battled one another savagely and often terrorised citizens. Brawling with barbaric weapons—knuckledusters, knives, razors, hatchets, chains, bayonets, and even ancient swords—they intimidated gardaí, who were outnumbered and out-armed.

The first major chapter in "Lugs" Branigan's storied career, and the foundation of his reputation and legend, was his battle to smash the reign of the gangs, dubbed "animal gangs" by the press. This he would accomplish in 1940 in the famous "Battle of Baldoyle," in which "Hannigan's army," as it was dubbed by the newspapers, made up of gang members from the Liberties, met in open warfare with their arch-enemies. Despite written and verbal threats to stay out of the court case, Branigan stood his ground and emerged as the man most responsible for ending their reign of violence and fear. The *Evening Herald* proclaimed: "Garda Branigan will always be remembered in Dublin as the man who broke the 'Animal Gangs.'"[2]

———

Each decade of his life presented new challenges, and he proved resourceful in countering them, always keeping up with the times, and up to the task.

In the post-war period Branigan developed what he called his "unorthodox" methods of law enforcement, what would become widely known as his unique practice of doling out "summary justice" on the streets of Dublin. In his training he had been taught that guards had to "use their own discretion" when faced with challenging situations, applying their judgement in deciding what action best fitted the problem at hand. As a man who eschewed conformity and rigid regulations, preferring to rely upon his own strong intuition, Branigan found that the freedom of using discretion suited him perfectly, especially as he possessed what he called his "indefinable gift," or sixth sense, which allowed him to comprehend a tense situation and decipher the social dynamics of the scene faster than anyone else.

"My father could size somebody up," explains his elder son, Alick: "get at the truth, get the answers . . . an *instinct*." His Garda colleagues found it uncanny how he could arrive in the midst of a melee, instantly detect the principal trouble-makers, and assess their intentions and threat, always able to distinguish in a flash a blowhard's bravado from the raving of a genuinely tough man who posed a real danger to others and had to be handled accordingly. Some of Branigan's fellow-gardaí claimed he knew how to "get into the brain" of those he faced. He never spent much time trying to analyse his "gift," for he was too busy applying it daily to his policing duties.

His rationale for using unorthodox methods was to thwart violence, teach trouble-makers an instant lesson, and act as a deterrent to future lawlessness. Confrontations often came down to a frontier-style showdown, or "duel," as he liked to phrase it. Through his conflicts with the animal gangs he learnt that, when faced with a mob of riotous men, if you could yank out the ringleaders and defeat them before the eyes of their followers, half the battle was won. This became his forte.

Branigan's repertoire of forceful techniques was developed by gradual experimentation on the streets of Dublin. Unlike other gardaí, he flatly refused to carry the heavy wooden baton. As his friend Garda Matt Mulhall puts it, "he didn't *need* a baton: his *fists* were his baton." With his fists he could handle any type of ruffian by administering what he variously called a "tap," "clip," "clout," or "clattering"—the latter meaning a "good hiding." In court he forthrightly told judges that in his experience "a belt on the mouth was the best medicine" for many belligerent toughs. And, when necessary, he used more powerful punches to "tone down" dangerously violent men. The judges accepted his word.

Then there were his legendary black leather gloves—to him, an indispensable weapon. He was "never without them," Alick affirms, even when off duty. These he used to lash a man's face in order to defuse his ill intentions. Whether Branigan had got the idea from Tom Mix or Gary Cooper one can only speculate; but they became astoundingly effective in dealing out different degrees of summary justice. The gloves carried a belittling, emasculating effect that took the spirit and starch out of belligerents—directly before the eyes of cronies. As Garda Con Hearty witnessed many a time, the gloves had a "demeaning effect on a thug who moments earlier had been foaming at the mouth . . . [but] now suddenly became cowed."

By the early 1950s, around the roughest streets of Dublin, "Lugs" Branigan was being referred to as "the sheriff." His word was law. He took on lawless men face to face in public showdowns. Few dared come up against him. As Garda Paddy Daly describes it, "he was like a sheriff in the Old West . . . He took over this town!" Matt Mulhall cites a typical incident when he accompanied

Branigan to a street riot in Inchicore: "A huge crowd and absolute mayhem . . .
killing one another. He just stepped out of the car, and it was *'Lugs is here!'*—
and the whole thing stopped. Just *stopped!*"

His presence sent shock waves through a disorderly crowd. The clarion
cry of *"Lugs!"* at a scene of turmoil signalled retreat, as most trouble-makers
scattered, allowing Branigan and his men to deal with the ringleaders.

———

In the mid-1950s, Dublin experienced a dramatic invasion. Two mighty
social phenomena swept across the airwaves and film screens from America
and Britain: the "youth rebellion" and the "rock-and-roll craze." Adults were
ill prepared for the transformation. Most were not only unfamiliar with
"Elvis," "Brando," "Dean", and "Little Richard" but had not yet heard the word
"teenager." All would change, like a cultural tsunami, as Bishop Cornelius
Lucey warned that he saw "signs of teenage revolt" on the horizon.

To adults the rock-and-roll craze meant "crazy," as young people's behaviour
began changing bewilderingly. Many became disrespectful, troublesome,
defiant, rebellious. Seeking their own independence and new life-style, they
collided with traditional values. Their "primitive" music and "jive" dancing
were condemned from the pulpit as degenerate and immoral, while to teenagers
like Gerry Creighton it "woke up a passion in me!" Adults were hopelessly "out
of it." They just didn't understand.

Staying out late, congregating in the street, stirring up trouble, became
commonplace. When packs of teenagers became lawless, gardaí had to restrain
them. More serious problems began when the "Teddy Boys," a subcultural
group with origins in England, appeared on the Dublin scene. At first they
struck adults as merely odd, perhaps even amusing, with their narrow
"drainpipe" trousers, swallow-tail coats, bright red, yellow, or orange shirts
and socks, and thick-soled shoes, their hair sculpted into a perfect "DA" (duck's
arse). But when they began carrying knives, razors, and sharpened steel combs,
fighting tribally among themselves and assaulting people, they became a feared
menace and a challenge for the police.

Garda Headquarters called on Branigan to lead the charge against the
general teenage "revolt" and Teddy-Boy threat. Like an anthropologist, he
delved into their culture and learnt their lingo so that he could communicate
clearly, and *fairly*, with them. He eagerly took on the challenge.

When the film *Rock Around the Clock*, with Bill Haley and his Comets, hit
Dublin's screens there was pandemonium, with rows, vandalism, and assaults
on cinema employees. Branigan was given the specific assignment of quelling
the cinema disturbances. Single-handedly, he stationed himself in the cinema

to stare down a mob of frenzied rock-and-rollers, with only his black leather gloves in his hand. By the time he finally got the madness under control he had seen the film ninety times!

Later, in February 1957, when Haley and his Comets slammed into Dublin like a meteor for their personal appearances at the Theatre Royal, Branigan and his colleagues were ready. But when "Beatlemania" erupted in the city a few years later with the arrival of the "Fab Four" at the Adelphi Cinema, a sea of teenagers swamped the gardaí, resulting in what newspapers called "one of the wildest nights" ever seen in the city.

During the 1960s Branigan was in his fifties, still remarkably fit and strong from his weekly exercise at the gym, where he continued to spar with Garda colleagues in their twenties. He was still not a man to be trifled with—as everyone knew. When a new epidemic of gangs and flick-knife assaults put people in fear, judges who were fed up with the rampant lawlessness wished aloud that flogging was still permitted. But thank God, they intimated, they still had Lugs Branigan!

In response to the increasing crime, in August 1964 the Garda Síochána launched what came to be known as the "riot squad." It was probably Branigan's creation, as he had championed the concept for years. A small, mobile force in a black Bedford van, which came to be known to gardaí as "Branno 5" and on the streets as the "Black Maria" (from the American name for a van for transporting prisoners), it patrolled the city throughout the night hours. Branigan was the leader, allowed to select his own team—men tough, intelligent, dedicated. It struck fear into "villains" (as Branigan always called them), who knew they were now within his quick grasp. He would always say that it was particularly his years as head of the riot squad that "made me notorious" as the "toughest and most fearless" policeman in the land.

———

He was most admired, however, by the women of Dublin for his role as their "guardian." As Mary Waldron (now eighty-two) says, it was an age when "men used to give *shocking* treatment to women, *banging* them . . . getting kicked." Most gardaí stayed away from what were then called "domestic disputes." Behind closed doors, men viciously battered women, leaving them bloody, bruised, with broken bones and spirits. As Declan Branigan asserts about his father, "husbands were drunk and beating the daylights out of them. He *hated* that!" Branigan himself asserted: "I cannot *stand* any man assaulting a woman! I'd give him the clatter"—a bitter taste of his own medicine, sometimes knocking him out cold on the floor. As Garda Gerald Byrne witnessed on many an occasion, "he just *saw red*—he'd use force."

His role of protecting women was a clandestine one, which did not make headlines or win him promotion within the force. But, as 82-year-old Una Shaw of Rutland Street said, every woman in Dublin knew "he was a *tough* cop, and yet behind it all he was so *humane,* so gentle," in helping those abused. As Garda John Collins pithily puts it, "women . . . oh, he was a *god* to them."

In like manner he looked after the welfare of the piteous prostitutes of Dublin's dark streets. Many had become social outcasts for no crime other than having had a baby out of wedlock, or fleeing a cruel husband. He got to know them, to learn about their backgrounds, understand their sorrowful tales. "He had a great love of the street ladies," says Garda Séamus Quinn, who saw his compassionate treatment, "but he hated and *detested* their pimps." As with battering husbands, Branigan gave abusive pimps a "clattering."

To Branigan the women were "pavement hostesses," as he considered other terms derogatory. He became first their friend, then their protector and counsellor. As one of the women confided, "many of the street girls regard Mr Branigan as a father figure." His role was kept hushed, as Garda superiors feared it could be misconstrued. Only after his retirement would the full compassionate story come out.

In the courtroom, Branigan would become as legendary as on the streets, though this also seldom made the newspapers. Yet his role in seeking justice in the courts was no less important than the summary justice he doled out on the streets. Unlike most guards, Declan says, "he loved going to court— he held centre stage!" He was adept at presenting evidence, giving testimony, questioning witnesses, offering insights and advice to judges—even recommending sentences when a judge sought his opinion. And he had a great flair for it all, recalls Garda Dan Walsh. "Jim could be very dramatic in court—a performer. Oh, yes, he was on stage." His audience was the judge, jury, solicitors, visitors, and reporters. When Garda Tony Ruane watched him in court, "it was like the theatre; better than any other show in town."

More important than his theatrics were his inestimable contributions. Michael Reid confirms: "He was in court five days a week, and his hallmark was fairness." He typically had more than four hundred cases a year—an astonishing number. He was admired more than anyone else for being unfailingly fair and egalitarian, equally respectful to all. As Paddy Daly observed, "to Jim, in court, everybody was the same . . . a prostitute, a criminal, a judge—he treated them all the same." And in court he was known for often showing his "soft side." Many a time he would speak up on behalf of a wayward youth he had dragged into custody himself, giving the judge some mitigating information and asking that the young man be given a second chance. Judges always complied. On the other hand, he showed no mercy for abusive husbands: in fact he would let a judge know if he was displeased with a light sentence.

No less important was his mentoring of young gardaí in court, often stepping forward to "rescue" them, as Tony Ruane puts it, if they were stumbling in their presentation, later instructing them about how to improve. Young guards liked to hang around court when possible to observe Lugs at first hand on stage, as novice actors would watch Laurence Olivier from the wings. It was a more valuable lesson than some they learnt in books.

―――

When Garda Jim Branigan approached the age of sixty, an "older man" by the standards of the time, he entered his "old gunfighter" years. His strength and reflexes diminished, he became less formidable and intimidating—and more vulnerable. To some old foes he became a target for revenge. The day came when Lugs had to begin looking over his shoulder.

His later years were years of some disappointment, new opportunities, enjoyable times, and inevitable decline. Through it all he remained as famously fearless and courageous as ever. As his friend Joe Kirwan, who visited him in hospital the night before he died, mused, "when they made Jim Branigan, they threw away the mould. Oh, he's a legend!"

―――

This book endeavours to present a biographical chronicle, as well as social history, of James "Lugs" Branigan, based on archival research and oral testimony gathered from his family, close friends, and Garda colleagues who served beside him in all manner of duty. Their first-hand observations and personal narratives provide an immediacy and authenticity that capture the character and "soul" of this extraordinary man, one who was so well known and acclaimed for some of his roles and yet virtually unknown for others. Hopefully, a holistic portrait will emerge.

Chapter 1

FACING LIFE AND RAILWAY BULLIES

"Dublin's toughest cop . . . was a sissy and weakling in his teens."

(*Evening Herald*, 24 JANUARY 1973)

"I had a reserved upbringing in which discipline was highly valued. No bad language or brawling was ever allowed by my father."

(GARDA JAMES BRANIGAN)

"My father *loved* western films, and books. It was the discipline of the western sheriffs . . . always the good and the bad, and mobs."

(DECLAN BRANIGAN)

"I was assaulted many times by bullies, belted and harassed. But I never retaliated . . . I would not hit back."

(GARDA JAMES BRANIGAN)

January 1910. Bookings on the *Titanic* were already being sought for its first voyage across the Atlantic two years later, from Southampton to New York. Aristocrats, business barons and social luminaries were vying for the coveted 324 first-class berths, all looking forward to the historic inaugural crossing on the world's most magnificent ship. Meanwhile from America came word that the Wright Brothers, Orville and Wilbur, had successfully kept an aeroplane aloft for more than an hour. Henry Ford's model T automobiles were rolling out of his factory nearly as fast as newspapers flying off a printing press. There were wondrous new developments in telephone communication and photography. Cinematographers in France, Italy and the United States were producing silent film "shorts" that captivated audiences. Some even predicted that "talking" pictures would soon be a reality. Awesome new weapons were also being built, catapulting armies beyond the age of cavalry and cannon.

Marvels of human ingenuity and technology seemed little short of miraculous. The new century appeared to hold limitless possibilities and pleasures. Perils as well.

In Ireland, the privileged classes may have been able to listen to Enrico Caruso and Nellie Melba on their gramophones, but impoverished tenement-dwellers were still living in the Dark Ages. Patriots and visionaries saw changes ahead, with increasing demands for the end of British rule. Dublin, as always, was the centre of speculation and political agitation.

Only a few days into the new year the *Irish Independent* published worrisome international news. An article headed "German war scare" warned of a "risk of setting Europe ablaze." Tensions were mounting throughout the Continent. In many parts of the world the "old order" was being threatened with political upheaval, militaristic rumblings, and social change. The *Irish Times*, however, reported that in Russia "a new palace in the Italian style was to be built for the Tsar at Yalta, Crimea,"[1] while in Ireland, newspapers focused on the passionately debated "home rule" question:

> Questioned about Home Rule, and the "safeguarding of the loyal minority" in Ireland, Mr. Winston Churchill said that every step would be taken to safeguard all the subjects of the Crown and effective supremacy of the Imperial Parliament. (Cheers.)[2]

––––

In Dublin, nowhere was more moored to the past than the "Liberties," the area to the south-west of the city centre. It still retained the appearance of a small country town from the late 1800s. On Thursday 6 January 1910, as dawn broke over the frigid Dublin skyline shortly before half past five, John and Ellen Branigan of James's Street were awaiting the birth of their first child. Shortly before six, in the calm of a winter's morning, their infant son entered the world and was bestowed with the fine name James Christopher Branigan—later in life to be whittled down to a four-letter moniker.

John Alick Branigan was a Co. Tipperary man, Ellen Kavanagh a strong-willed woman from Co. Kilkenny. After their marriage they made their home in the heart of the Liberties. John Branigan obtained a secure job as an official in the South Dublin Union (a union of parishes for the purpose of providing workhouses), and their home was in the grounds of the institution. It was, his grandson Declan attests, a very "respectable" position, of which "he was proud."

The South Dublin Union (now St James's Hospital) was a sprawling complex of buildings and open spaces covering nearly sixty acres. It then encompassed a workhouse, several hospitals, a nursing-home, a maternity unit that took in unmarried mothers who were rejected by other hospitals, a morgue, a convent of the Sisters of Mercy, two Catholic churches and one Church of Ireland, a bakery, schools, playgrounds, and the union officers' quarters. Enclosed within high stone walls, it stood on the Dublin cityscape as a distinct enclave, its buildings connected by a maze of streets and courtyards.

Socially, it was like a world unto itself. With more than three thousand residents—inmates, doctors, nurses, nuns, and officials—it functioned as a sort of inner-urban village with distinctive population groups. Different areas of the union contrasted dramatically with each other: the workhouse took in Dublin's impoverished, infirm and demented souls, while others were privileged. At eighty-three, Máirín Johnston, reared in the nearby tenements of Pimlico, recalled vividly the Dickensian aura of the old union. In the early 1930s she had to accompany her mother in visiting her granny and Uncle Paddy, who were patients there:

> I hated going into the place, it was so depressing . . . lots of grey stone buildings. People in the "union" part were called "paupers," while those in the hospital were "patients." Some of the paupers were on crutches or walking-sticks, shuffling around or sitting on benches . . . others in senility.

By contrast, the sequestered officers' quarters, where the Branigan family resided, was one of privilege and comfort. Residents were well housed, clothed, and fed, with medical treatment and the use of churches, schools, social amenities, and sports fields. There existed a strong sense of community and contentment. Their environment was tidy, orderly, and safe—a decent and civilised setting in early twentieth-century inner-city Dublin. Contrary, therefore, to common belief in later years, young Jim Branigan did not grow up in the rough-and-tumble streets of the Liberties, with fists flailing: instead the confines of the union provided a secure and peaceable "cocoon," where the rules of propriety were followed faithfully. Officials and their families were regarded as respectable citizens, who socialised almost exclusively with one another.

This was not typical of life within the Liberties, just beyond the high walls, where many people lived in squalid tenements, suffered poverty, hunger, and illness. While Jim Branigan and his childhood pals would play happily on their side of the barrier in bucolic green fields, in the world just beyond, in Meath Street, Thomas Street, Francis Street and Patrick Street and down along the Coombe, barefoot urchins ran wild and coped with deprivation as best they could, scrapping for food and scrapping with one another. Street children had to be tough in the unruly streets of the Liberties in those hard days, when nearly every tenement street had its amateur boxing club. Within the union, officials did not tolerate fisticuffs.

John and Ellen Branigan were appreciative of the many advantages their son had living within the union, especially good health and medical care. At this time "Dublin recorded the highest death rate of any city in the United Kingdom."[3] The reputation of the tenements as "multitudinous fever nests and death traps" was tragically well deserved. The city was also racked by a host of other illnesses, such as smallpox, diphtheria, typhoid, whooping cough, and pneumonia. Children under the age of six were particularly susceptible to illness and early death. Tuberculosis, then called "consumption," was rampant. Because children within the union were better fed, clothed, housed and medically cared for, they were considerably healthier and stronger than those only a few streets away. Though he was spared TB and other killer illnesses, Branigan did confirm later in his life that he had had double pneumonia and pleurisy in his youth, though when union children fell ill they were given the best of medical attention.

––––

As a child of five and six he was quite shy, playing around his home with a few pals and staying near his parents. Though very admiring of his father, he was closer to his mother, whom he adored. The most formative memories of his young life were focused on her. When he would accompany her on shopping and other errands he noticed that she manifested a different attitude from most other women when encountering British soldiers or later the dreaded Black and Tans. While other men and women of the Liberties seemed intimidated when passing them, typically stepping aside, she held her head high, marched straight forward. It just seemed to be in her nature not to be afraid of them. In fact to young Jim she didn't seem to fear anyone or anything. Her refusal to step aside for British uniforms made an early and lasting impression.

Among his most vivid recollections were his mother's display of courage during the 1916 Rising, when British soldiers patrolled the city's streets. Just across the road from the Branigans' house, on the other side of James's Street, lived William T. Cosgrave, a lieutenant in the Irish Volunteers. Branigan's mother was fond of him, and the fact that he occasionally brought political comrades to his house did not deter her from visiting him, despite British surveillance. During the Rising the union was occupied by the Volunteers, and at the age of six Jim saw some action when he heard gunfire, saw a British soldier wounded, then witnessed a volunteer barge into their home, poke his rifle out the window, and fire.

In his eyes, his mother's most defining act of courage was when the British army subdued the Volunteers and the Irish Citizen Army, rounded them up, and began marching them off to Kilmainham Jail, surrounded by a tight cordon of soldiers. Standing beside his mother watching it all, he saw her suddenly bolt forward and break through a gap in the British ranks to extend a handshake to her friend Cosgrave. A term he would often use to describe his mother in later years was "fearless." Thirty years later he would tell his own children bits and pieces about their grandmother, without dwelling on family history, as so many did. Yet, explains Alick, his father's admiration for his mother was unmistakable, and her influence on him conspicuous in his character:

> She was *very patriotic,* and in his childhood I know that his mother had strong inclinations towards the 1916 Rising, when things erupted here. There was some shooting around where they lived, and his mother was involved on a peripheral basis . . . A British soldier had been shot, and somebody was going to her house [for cover]. Her patriotism—presumably that carried over to him.

By the time he began school at the age of five he had two younger brothers and a sister. His brother John Alick was eighteen months younger, sister Norah three years younger, and Frank five years his junior. As children all were close. His earliest school days were spent in Basin Lane Convent School, among other children from families much like his, many of whom were already pals, and he fitted in well.

His early school years, from 1915 to 1919, saw two colossal historical events, the 1916 Rising and the First World War, which reshaped Ireland and the world beyond, though both events were largely incomprehensible to a child's mind. It is unlikely that the nuns who taught him deviated from their curriculum to discuss contemporary events with children aged five to eight, though Jim Branigan probably picked up fragments of unfolding history within his home, especially from his politically conscious mother.

In 1919, at the age of nine, he moved to James's Street Christian Brothers' School for the next six years of his education, this time being exposed to a wider range of children from different social backgrounds. Here again his school record is largely undocumented; however, from the oral history of his family we know that, by his own admission, he was a mediocre pupil. Attentive, diligent, obedient—but average in academic performance. His parents did not push him to be a scholar. He performed his tasks, behaved well, and was polite to teachers. In other words, a completely satisfactory schoolboy according to the expectations of the time.

Two features made him an unremarkable, rather introverted classmate:

he was thin, and he was shy. Reserved around others, he wasn't very good at mixing. At first he was reluctant to plunge into games and sports with others his age; but once he joined in and learnt to socialise freely he was a good playmate, respectful and fair to others, for which he was liked. While some other lads got into skirmishes, suffering a black eye or bloody nose, he refrained. His father was a disciplinarian, though not an extreme one, who lectured him against crude or "uncivilised" behaviour, meaning no brawling, vulgar language, or being disrespectful to teachers or other adults—nothing that would bring as much as a tint of shame upon the family.

An obedient son, he always kept his father's words in mind. He simply characterised it as "a reserved upbringing . . . in which discipline was valued."[4] Even as a child he thought this reasonable. He was astounded when he first saw how some children living in poor tenements beyond the Union would give lip to teachers, curse, mitch from school, rob an apple or orange, or fight with fists.

Despite his reserved manner, he was a fun-loving youngster who liked joining in all sorts of games and sports once he was accepted. He simply wasn't one of the leaders. However, once engaged in an activity he played vigorously and was quite competitive. But he was not a particularly gifted athlete. As with academic studies, he was average, but capable enough to make his contribution. He had a fondness for almost every type of sport—running, cycling, hurling, handball, rowing, football, soccer—with a special love for Gaelic sports. Even as a youth he understood that the value of sport was its physical fitness, competitiveness, and camaraderie of playing together as a team.

————

As he reached twelve or thirteen he began to explore in a limited way the "real" world of the Liberties. This part of his early education, beyond the walls of his schoolroom, was eye-opening. He learnt that other lads of his age could be sent off to a place called Artane, which he was told was a "reformatory," for merely mitching from school, snatching a banana, "scutting" or hanging on to trams or lorries, playing innocent pranks—and for as long as five years. A frightening prospect. This reinforced the wisdom of his father's principles of good behaviour in life.

In 1920 he suffered a crushing blow with the loss of his eight-year-old brother, John Alick—his best pal and closest confidant. Later in life he would seldom be able to bring himself to talk of his little brother's death; but when his own first son was born and named after him it meant a lot, as Alick recounts: "My father's brother died—and that's who *I'm* named after. Now, I never asked my father [more] about this . . . but I *should* have."

It was around this time that Jim decided to become an altar boy, apparently without coaxing from his teachers. Yet he was not known as a particularly religious boy at school. He clearly enjoyed it, because he would remain an altar boy up to the time he joined the Garda Síochána at the age of twenty-one. His dedication to this role may have caused his parents to wonder if he ever considered the priesthood. This was a logical assumption in those years—and a dream of many mothers. But his family cannot recall him ever expressing such an aspiration.

During his formative years in the Christian Brothers' school, from the ages of nine to fourteen, many of his core values were shaped. He was a keen observer of life around him, possessed unusual intuitive powers, and exhibited good sense and discipline for a lad his age. Though he did not distinguish himself academically, or athletically, during this period, he became one of those people who were liked by everyone. He was never a troublemaker—nor was he a "goody-goody." His parents had every reason to be proud of him for being the person he was.

If he had one compulsion it was trying to see every new western film that came to Dublin. This was an addiction that afflicted many other youngsters, and adults, in the period from about 1920 to the 1930s. He simply seemed to have a more serious case than others.

For children, the westerns were the greatest rage of all. From nine to nineteen, there was no better place to be than at a matinée in the local picture-house, perched on a wooden bench awaiting the first flickering images to appear on the screen. Among the early favourites were Hoot Gibson in *The Cactus Kid* (1921), Tom Mix in *The Lucky Horseshoe* (1925), and William S. Hart in *Tumbleweeds* (1925). They were packed with almost non-stop action—stagecoach robberies, Indian attacks, cattle rustling, bank heists, chases on horses. Saloon brawls, fist fights and plenty of gunslinging. Bandits, outlaws—and brave sheriffs. When the early "silents" were replaced by "talkies" the experience was even more realistic, with the sounds of gunfire, pounding horse and cattle hoofs, buffalo stampedes, fists cracking on jaws. Young Jim Branigan and his pals could listen to the intense dialogue as Gene Autry or Gary Cooper faced down a desperado: "I'm going to fill you full of lead . . . Draw!"

No-one better understood the influence of early picture shows on a youngster's mind than Robert Hartney. Born in 1892, he was hired as an usher by the Manor Picture House in Manor Street from the day it opened in 1920, showing silent films. For a charge of fourpence children lined the long benches, their heads cocked upwards:

> Most popular with children were the cowboy pictures. Oh, *great* excitement! You'd see the little faces looking up at the screen, all excited, and you could

hear them all saying, "Look out there, he's *behind* you!" If they got *too* excited or scared you had to tell them, "It's *only* a picture. It's not *real!*" So as to comfort them.

For the more astute children there were also lessons of morality to be learnt from westerns, as they typically featured heroes and villains, sheriffs and outlaws, the quest for frontier justice—basic differences between good and bad characters and the principles of right versus wrong.

Like other children, young Jim would collect jam jars, run messages and do odd jobs to collect the few pence needed to get into the next show. From the age of ten or so he developed a serious fascination with America's "Old West." According to Bernard Neary, "he always loved that period in American history . . . and as a boy he went to *every* western film shown in the Lyric Cinema,"[5] as well as frequenting other picture-houses so as not to miss a cowboy film.

The difference between the impressionable Jim and most of his pals was the manner in which certain films influenced his thinking and values. While he enjoyed the action sequences—the chases, robberies, and stampedes—nothing riveted him like the dramatic "showdown" between a sheriff or marshal and a villain, symbolising the clash between good and evil. A "lawman" had to be courageous to stare down a bullying gunslinger. The *character* of the sheriff made a lasting impression on him, one that would shape his adult life, his son Declan confirms: "He loved western films . . . I mean, it was the discipline of the western sheriffs, that this is the way it should be! That there was always the good and the bad, and mobs—and he could *differentiate.*"

In the late 1920s and 30s, when Branigan was a young man in his twenties, westerns became more sophisticated in plot and dialogue, as stars like Gary Cooper, Randolph Scott and John Wayne elevated the level of acting. These films portrayed a deeper social and moral meaning for Branigan. While he was still thrilled at seeing a sheriff with powerful punches and a "greased lightning" draw, he was even more impressed by what he stood for—and dared stand up to. Later in life it would become increasingly evident that his early comprehension of western law and justice profoundly shaped his character and principles.

———

In 1924, at the age of fourteen, he left school, and his education ended. It had been his hope to continue with his academic studies, but the reality was that his parents' finances were insufficient. "If I had my way I would have tried to further my education . . . but my parents couldn't afford it."[6] It was not easy for his father and mother to disappoint him, but he understood.

It was normal in the 1920s for inner-city youths to leave school at fourteen and seek a job. The fortunate ones might secure a seven-year apprenticeship at a trade or craft. The plum jobs were in Guinness's brewery, Jacob's biscuit factory, the distilleries and the shoemaking factories, such as Winstanley's, as well as the nicer shops around the city. But he was not interested in being confined to a factory or shop; nor did he want to become a cooper, docker, stonecarver, seaman, or building worker. He didn't quite know what he wanted to do with his life.

By fourteen he was a good few inches taller than most of his friends but as thin as a poker. His arms, shoulders and chest had not begun to fill out into manhood yet. Atop his lanky frame was a pleasing face, engaging smile, bright eyes, and a head crowned with a thick thatch of sandy-coloured hair.

And then there were his ears.

Conspicuously larger than normal, their size was accentuated by his rod-like physique. They were not only disproportionately large but protruding. They appeared as two bookends symmetrically aligned, framing his likeable boyish face. Even at some distance, on a street or playing-field, it was easy to pick him out.

In his adult years, from about the age of thirty, there would be a perception among the public that "Lugs" Branigan got his oversize ears from his boxing days; but a photograph of his school class at the age of eight or nine shows clearly the size and shape of his ears. They were an endowment of nature—not sculpted by boxing gloves.

Whether as a youngster this made him self-conscious or embarrassed or caused derision we don't know; nor whether he would have confided this to his family. That he was a rather shy child might suggest that this was so, but there is no evidence of this. It is hard to imagine that he was never subjected to hurtful remarks from other children. If so, we can only speculate about what lasting effect this might have had on him. We do know that as an adult in the Garda Síochána he was known to detest the nickname "Lugs" and would scold or punish any person daring to use it in his presence. But such transgressors were few.

At fourteen young Jim Branigan pulled off quite an accomplishment: he signed up as a trainee fitter in the old Great Southern Railways works in Inchicore. At first glance this might not seem particularly impressive; but a seven-year apprenticeship with the railway, with the promise of a steady job and a pension, was a highly coveted one.

How he managed to break into the railway world is something of a mystery. At that time the prime jobs were largely closed to outsiders, open only to relatives of railway workers. Somehow, through his parents or family friends, he must have had a good connection or recommendation to gain such a treasured position. If his apprenticeship was successful, by twenty-one his life would be set for him.

Unfortunately, straight away he found that being an apprentice fitter was far from a good fit. "I hated the dirt and the dust of the bolts and carriages,"[7] he said. Furthermore, he found it a job of repetitious drudgery, offering no mental challenge or creativity. He didn't mind the strenuous physical demands of the work, but the grimy conditions did not suit his disposition. At day's end he would straggle home looking like a begrimed coalminer.

―――――

From his first day on the job he faced a far more serious problem. He was treated as a pariah by the other workers, all from traditional railway families. They all deserved their inherited positions: he was an outcast who didn't belong. Theirs was a railway culture, with its own heritage, customs, and vernacular. To them he had stolen a job from one of their own—and they resented it.

In the 1920s railwaymen, like men in most old trades and crafts, were clannish. They tended to live near one another, drink together, mix socially together. Paddy Whelan, the son of an engine-driver, entered his job in the GSR in the same period. It was in his blood. He knew what young Jim Branigan was up against:

> Oh, railwaymen were a *tough* crowd of men, got on very well together . . . a terrible bond between railwaymen. It was their *whole life!* They were a special breed. There was nothing but railway talk.

Not only were they toughened by their hard work, but many were also boxers in their local clubs, as was Paddy Whelan.

Whoever had recommended the innocent fourteen-year-old Jim Branigan for a railway job did him no favour. Within his first hour on the job they began to verbally and physically abuse him and thereafter were relentless in their bullying. Any other sensible fourteen-year-old lad, seeing what he was up against, would not have appeared in the railway yard on the second day. Yet every day he showed up, suffered insults, taunts, and pounding. When he came home bruised and bloody on the first few days he simply told his father, "I got a bit of a hiding." "Why?" No reason.

From what little we know, his parents were sympathetic and admiring of his fortitude and his resolve not to be defeated. Did they encourage him to give it up, or to go on? It was obviously his decision to make. He stood his ground, absorbed his punishment, refused to fight back:

> I was timid as a youth. I was assaulted by bullies many times in the GSR works in Inchicore, but I never retaliated. I was belted and harassed and

often came home with my nose bleeding, but I would not hit back . . . though my mates would laugh me to scorn.[8]

Though his father was opposed to brawling, he surely would have approved of his son defending himself. He chose not to do so.

It was one of the first of many contradictions in his life that he adopted a passive attitude, completely at odds with the film heroes he so admired. What was most extraordinary about his behaviour was that he did not run away from the bullies. Though he dreaded their punches, he did not fear his tormentors. He would accept their beatings and return to work the next day to take more. This puzzled them—and his family as well. And perhaps himself. Despite the black eyes, swollen lips, cut face, there was never any crying or complaining. Perhaps "stubborn" was the best word to describe it—a term that would be applied to him by others for the next half century.

One thing was certain: there could hardly have been a more unlikely candidate to become a heavyweight boxing champion and Ireland's undisputed "toughest and most fearless garda."

Some days were better than others, as the physical abuse slackened, probably because his abusers became bored with it. What dispirited him more by this time was the job itself. After some deliberation, and consultation with his parents, he decided that rather than quit the job outright he would ask his manager if he could be shifted to a different type of work. Because of his excellent employment record it was agreed to keep him on at different tasks. Though it helped, he still intensely disliked railway work. As time passed, it became more intolerable; but he stuck it out.

His only salvation was trying to fill his off-work hours with pleasurable and meaningful activities. In his late teens he was still serving as an altar boy. And films continued to consume part of his weekends. Sport began to occupy a positive role in his life, not only for physical fitness but because it introduced him to an array of new and stimulating social relationships. He joined cycling, hurling and rowing clubs. His membership of Dublin City Harriers was especially enjoyable, as striding through the fresh air of the countryside nourished both his soul and his spirit. All his sports activities provided a wonderful camaraderie and light-heartedness, full of banter and good cheer that seemed a world away from the drudgery of the railway.

At seventeen he took on two new serious pursuits for personal betterment and to make a contribution to society. He realised that if he wanted to relinquish his railway job and hope to find a real career he would need to advance his education. Some of his friends were attending the technical schools in Parnell Square and suggested that he join them. His goal was to acquire some practical skill in accountancy and typing, which were in much demand in the business world. He could even pick up some shorthand for good measure. So, for the next three years he steadfastly headed off after work, two or three nights a week, to attend classes. In this he was also learning another valuable lesson: organisation and mental discipline.

Somehow, in 1927 he found the time to join the St John Ambulance Brigade. This required several months of training, beginning with a six-week course that included lectures by doctors as well as instructions on how to treat injuries. According to Noel Brady, who joined the brigade about the same time, "we learnt to treat wounds, bandage, control haemorrhages, treat fractures," and so on. They treated victims of accidents and human violence: people injured by motor vehicles, suffering heart attacks and seizures, work-related accidents, as well as bloody fistfights and battered women. Unknown to him at the time, his ambulance skills would serve him importantly in the years ahead.

————

His social life was quite active too between the ages of eighteen and twenty-one, with attendance at cinemas, dancehalls, pubs, and sports events at Croke Park and Lansdowne Road. And girls.

He always enjoyed the company of girls and dancing at one of his favourite dancehalls. He preferred "going out on the town" with a few pals to being in a crowd. He was tall though still lanky, nearing six feet three inches and about twelve stone, and could look striking when he went out for the night. He unabashedly referred to himself as "a natty dresser" in his younger days. A photograph of him at about twenty to twenty-two shows a young man in a well-tailored suit, crisp shirt, elegant tie, looking much like a mannequin in Clery's window. He clearly considered himself a notch above the ordinary chap, being tall, well groomed, and snappily dressed. Though he could be eye-catching to women, towering above others on the dance floor, he was still conspicuously shy—certainly no Fred Astaire. His shyness, however, may have enhanced his attractiveness to young women. And he always treated them as politely as he did his own mother.

Going out with the lads meant "fitting in." By his late teens he smoked and drank in moderation. They were costly habits, best kept to a minimum. Most of his friends were athletic-minded like himself and not given to excess. Those who would meet him after 1941, however, when he was thirty-one, would only know a man who neither smoked nor drank, and assumed he had never done so. His son Alick corrects the record: "My father actually used to smoke *and* drink! And he stopped when he got married—he just pulled down the curtain and said, 'No more!'" He had given up smoking a number of years earlier when he took up boxing.

There were a few occasions when he slightly exceeded his normal limit and found himself feeling rather mischievous—even *daring* at times. He was known for liking pranks and innocuous shenanigans. A few of his early episodes were passed down through oral history and became part of his family lore, as Alick confirms:

> He was just a bit wild when he was younger, which would have been normal—you know, being merry, and this sort of thing—in his *heyday*. There was the story that he was walking across the top of trams and buses
> . . .

This was a story he always candidly confessed to, and with some delight. And it was no quick "hop-on, hop-off" stunt but a daring, and foolish, act—the same one for which he would later admonish other youths. As he admits:

> Booze gave me Dutch courage. I would do things with drink taken that I would not do when sober. For example, I remember for a shilling bet travelling through the city on the roof of a tram.[9]

His experience of the false courage derived from drink would help him to understand later how a man's mind becomes impaired when drunk. For this he would be a more sympathetic guard. Yet his post-1940s friends would always swear with certitude, "Oh, Jim *never touched* a drink in his life!"

———

Ironically, the one sport in which young Branigan apparently had little or no interest was boxing, which was at a peak of popularity in the 1920s and 30s. Local boxing clubs had mushroomed all over the city. Many of his friends enjoyed learning the rudiments, if for no other reason than as a useful defensive skill in Dublin's tough streets.

During those halcyon years of the sport, boxing champions were the best-known, most admired athletes in the world. Some of the best boxers from Dublin's boxing clubs became good enough to go to the Golden Gloves in America and step onto the world stage—and *win*!

In Branigan's youth, international boxing had direct links with Ireland, and some of the greatest champions were of Irish heritage. From 1919 to 1926 Jack Dempsey dominated the world heavyweight championship. In 1926 Gene Tunney, another Irish-American, became world champion. Both men boasted of their Irish roots. On 17 March 1923 the boxing world turned its attention to Dublin, where the world light-heavyweight title was being contested between Mike McTigue of Ireland and "Battling Siki" of Senegal. When McTigue won the title by a decision, Irish fans were delirious. It gave a huge boost to Irish boxing.

As far as we know, Jim Branigan had no particular interest in the boxing world in his younger years. Having been pounded by bullies at the GSR yard would make this perfectly understandable if he wished to remain physically and psychologically removed from the violent sport.

One person who *was* impressed with the sport was Major-General William Murphy, commissioner of the Dublin Metropolitan Police, who set up the Garda Boxing Club in 1924. He valued all forms of athletic competition but contended that boxing could be especially beneficial for young gardaí: it kept the body fit and reflexes sharp, honed the mind to concentrate and think quickly, taught men how to defend themselves and combat violent resistance, instilled confidence and pride. Furthermore, if by good fortune the new club should breed a few champions it would surely generate favourable press coverage for the new national police force. Boxing training, he believed, should be required of all recruits.

In 1929, the year Branigan reached the age of nineteen, two classic western films were released. In *The Virginian,* Gary Cooper played a heroic figure of inner strength and resolve. He could confront a villain and stare him down with the intensity of his intentions. He didn't have to pull a gun to make his point. Cooper's great appeal was his integrity, whether in the role of cowboy, frontiersman, or lawman: here was the real thing. Branigan comprehended this.

In *The Big Trail* a new actor by the name of John Wayne sauntered onto the screen with broad shoulders, a swagger, huge fists, and a most unusual manner of slow, deliberate speech which commanded one's attention. He used his fists and his gun only when he had to. Like Cooper, he represented a thoughtful, often understated breed of hero, the type most likely to inspire young, impressionable Jim Branigan.

It was about this time also that he was captured in a family photograph standing beside his father's relations in Co. Tipperary, holding a rifle across his chest and with a string of dead rabbits dangling around his neck, looking like a Western frontiersman. He had become a competent marksman with a .22 calibre rifle and contributed significantly to the family's food supply.

1930 was to be a transformative year in his life. On his twentieth birthday he became more keenly aware of his unhappiness with work at the GSR, and of a desire to find a job that offered a future with higher purpose and satisfaction. He still could not envisage any type of truly meaningful work. He had invested six years with the railways and was nearing the end of his apprenticeship, with its promise of security and ultimately a pension. Many would have thought him a fool for even questioning his investment with the GSR.

Then, on 26 July, his mother died, while only in her forties. For a twenty-year-old it was a terrible blow. More than anyone else she had influenced his basic values and principles. He would always feel that he had inherited much of his integrity and fearlessness from her.

Life could be short and unpredictable; it should not be squandered working at a job that was boring and unsatisfying. By December he'd had enough of the railway yard. "I could stick it no more . . . I resigned the job. I began to think of my future."[10]

————

As the weeks and months passed, his unemployment bred anxiety. He may have realised that quitting the railways before he had secured a better job was foolhardy. On the other hand, he wanted to act when motivation compelled him to do so, out of worry that he might not later have the courage.

After several months without income he decided that, as a practical matter, he should at least try to find some temporary work until the right position came along. He was discouraged when even this proved difficult. He wisely continued with his technical school courses and his work with the St John Ambulance Brigade, as well as his participation with Dublin City Harriers and other sports teams. What he was seeking seemed simple enough: a job with a lofty purpose that would give meaning to his life. Turned down for one job after another, he was unemployed for a total of six months.

One afternoon he was sharing his growing worry with a team-mate who happened to be a member of the Garda Síochána. "The garda with whom I had been hurling said I would have a good chance of getting into the Garda force, because of my height." He began mulling this over in the following days. With his exceptional height he stood out like a beacon in a crowd—ideal for a garda. Strangely enough, the idea had apparently not occurred to him earlier, nor been suggested by family or friends. In considering a garda's life he found it appealing, for a number of reasons. It was a steady, respectable, decently paid job, and with a pension. Unlike a monotonous factory, shop or office job based on routine, each day would be different. It also came with challenges and the experience of working among the public. There was sure to be camaraderie among colleagues. And the Gardaí stressed physical fitness and sports.

The combination seemed to offer a stimulating way of life; and it was a position in which he could take pride. Furthermore, at six foot four he would doubtless look striking in his Garda uniform, which was no trivial consideration to Jim Branigan, an impressionable 21-year-old. He had always liked uniforms, whether police, soldiers, firemen, ambulance crews, or cinema ushers. As he would confess later in life, "the idea caught my attention . . . and I had always been fond of uniforms." Lastly, his father was supportive of his idea of applying.

However, there were some negative considerations to be weighed as well. The 1930s were a time of depression, unemployment, dire poverty, heavy drinking and brawling. Frequently gangs and mobs formed, and riots occurred. Guards still used baton charges to quell riots. There were real physical risks, and guards were regularly injured. The hours could be long, and all-night duty required.

The general image of Dublin's police force was still tarnished by its history. It had only been in 1925 that the DMP and Garda Síochána were amalgamated into a single national force. But public prejudices against the old DMP were deeply entrenched from the harsh treatment often doled out to citizens. May Hanaphy, born in 1909 in Golden Lane in the Liberties, remembers all too well:

> Now, I remember the DMP. They were very hard on men . . . I saw it myself. They'd frog-march helpless men, made them walk on their hands, into the station, holding up their feet. *Very painful* . . . a form of cruelty.

Many Dubliners perceived the police as their enemies. It was a negative image that would not be changed overnight. As Séamus Breathnach writes in his book *The Irish Police*:

> For over seven hundred years the Irish people had sought their own kind of justice, indigenous legislation, definition of freedom, equity and self-Government; above all, they sought their own police force. Now they had it.[11]

But in the early 1930s many Dubliners still regarded it as disreputable to join the police force, which was one reason why more country lads were enlisting, outnumbering recruits from Dublin itself.

Branigan was a notable exception. By virtue of his privileged youth within the compound of the South Dublin Union, he was largely spared seeing the abuses carried out by the DMP on the streets. On the contrary, during his childhood he was exposed to the police in a very positive manner. His parents had befriended several policemen who were stationed within the hospital grounds, and even socialised with them in their home. To young Jim, nothing was more natural than mixing amiably with members of the force:

> Unlike other children, I had no real fear of gardaí. This was because they were regular visitors at my parents' home . . . Often they drank tea and played twenty-five [a card game] with my parents.[12]

———

By the end of 1930 he had made up his mind. In December he found himself
filling in an application form at Kilmainham Garda Station. But it wasn't
a walk-over, as he quickly found out. If his height was in his favour, other
aspects of his physique were deficient. The station sergeant who handed him
his application form did not hesitate to bring this to his attention:

> The station sergeant said there was no reason why I should not get the
> entrance examination—but he warned me that I looked a bit skinny and
> would have to build myself up.[13]

Fortunately, the physical examination would not take place for nearly six
months. But he realised that he also faced other deficiencies. He was weak in
Irish and in maths, and would need to strengthen these if he hoped to pass the
examination. For the moment, however, he found it a simple matter to fill in
the application form. It was a single sheet, requiring no more than a few words
in answer to most questions. After his name, date of birth and address he had
to provide information on his height and weight, then questions about his
educational level, employment since leaving school, and verbal and written
command of Irish. Then followed other questions:

—Have you ever been dismissed or discharged from any employment?

—Have you ever served in any police force, foreign army, navy or in any
other Government department?

—Did you serve in the National Army?

—What is your religion?

—Have you ever been married?

—Are you in debt?

—Are you in good health? Subject to fits or any other bodily infirmity?

—Is your vision good? Do you wear glasses?

—Does insanity or other hereditary disease exist in your family or relatives?

Finally, the applicant was asked to give particulars (in a space one inch by
five inches) of why they wanted to join the force. The answer given by one of
Branigan's future friends, Garda Senan Finucane, was probably typical: "To
better myself and make a living."

Without delay, he began polishing up on his deficiencies in maths and Irish
at home. But his regimen was not well structured, and his progress was slow.
By good fortune, his father was in a position to ask a teacher and family friend,

P. T. Kelly, to tutor him. "Mr Kelly helped me brush up on my Irish and maths," which significantly improved his ability at a steady pace.

His "skinny" physique (as he called it) was a different question. It was not merely a matter of adding bulk to his slender frame but of building muscle and dimensions in the right places. This was specified by the Garda Síochána, especially the requirement to have a 42-inch chest. This was the critical statistic, and every applicant knew it. No exceptions.

Here again his father came to his assistance. A friend, Kit Madden, had been a British army instructor with an "old world" rule of discipline. He agreed to devise a rigorous training programme for lanky young Jim, aimed at building bulk and muscle. His new student gratefully accepted, though with a degree of trepidation. Madden put him through what he called "a six-months PT grind." It paid off visibly, as the exercises were professionally calibrated and regularly notched up each month. His daily regime left him exhausted but in superior physical condition. Within months, real signs of success were evident.

And so it went until June 1931, the day for his examination. After nearly seven years of railway work that he detested, at twenty-one he had found his desired role in life. And now his future was hanging in the balance by a fraction of an inch.

Chapter 2

PUTTING ON A UNIFORM AND BOXING GLOVES

"He joined—and he *loved* it from day one. He *found his vocation!* And he dedicated his whole life to that vocation."
(DECLAN BRANIGAN)

"I never saw a boxing glove until I was training at the Garda Depot at the age of twenty-one. When my father heard I was taking up boxing he sat down and broke his heart laughing."
(GARDA JAMES BRANIGAN)

In June 1931, five months after his twenty-first birthday, James Branigan was called to take his medical and written examinations to become a member of the Garda Síochána. He was more nervous about facing the tape measure than the exam questions in Irish and mathematics, though he knew that the person doing the measuring had a bit of discretion over fractions.

Mercifully, he got the results quickly. As he candidly admitted, "I passed the written exam flying . . . but my chest measurement barely reached the Garda requirements."[1] Upon hearing the positive results, his chest was so puffed up that a second measurement would probably have given him an inch to spare.

He was quick to credit Kit Madden's gruelling physique-building regimen: "I would definitely have failed the medical examination but for the special six months' course in physical exercises on chest expansion." His father deserved no less credit, for it was he who had arranged his son's special assistance with both the written and the medical exams.

On 18 June he took the pledge and officially joined the Garda Síochána— the proudest day of his life, yet one tinged with regret that his mother could not have lived a year and a half longer to see him in uniform. Unfortunately, for him and his fellow-recruits there was little time for celebrating their acceptance into the force. As Senan Finucane explained when he too joined the Guards in the thirties, "we went into training *right away*—oh, it was like the *army!*" An abrupt goodbye to civilian life as stern drill sergeants took command of their lives:

> We lived in barracks. Up at seven for drill, a long walk, in for breakfast. Boots and brass buttons had to *shine*. And a haircut every week or so. Oh, *tight*. There was never a dull moment.

Over the six-month training period, recruit life was centred on drill and decorum, together with classroom instruction. The strenuous physical training tested the young men to their limits of strength and endurance. As with soldiers in training, the Garda recruits groaned and complained at day's end when they straggled in fatigued.

Branigan was a conspicuous exception. After six months under Madden's demanding tutelage he was in superb physical form, far superior to that of his mates. He found the demands of drilling a mere walk in the park compared with Madden's military exercises. In fact while others "endured" the physical strain, he embraced it with fervour. To him, the more challenging the better. His superiors took note of his most unusual, unfailingly positive attitude.

Ironically, it was the rules regarding dress and orderliness that caused him most annoyance: the fixation on perfection in such matters as immaculate dress, shined boots, and polished brass buttons. To him, basic cleanness and tidiness were sufficient. Bedding made up in a particular way seemed senseless. Several times he received mild reprimands for not adhering to the required standards of presentation. He improved, but with subdued irritation. In uniform one had to be immaculate: boots, gloves, hair, cap, posture, and behaviour. All part of the regimentation of uniformed life. But before long, it felt natural enough.

During training, the topics of politics and religion were generally avoided. Fortunately, there was one topic that both groups passionately shared: sport. It stimulated lively and good-natured conversation and debate, which helped to break down superficial barriers. By the third month or so of training, the recruits were making lifelong friendships. Jokes crossing cultural lines became a part of their shared banter. And here Jim Branigan from the Liberties was not immune, says Garda Eddie Finucane (Senan Finucane's son):

> Most of his colleagues were from rural Ireland, and there was a discussion among the gardaí about crops and harvesting. Jim thought tomatoes were harvested from the ground, like potatoes. This created a lot of laughter from his country-born colleagues—and obviously some embarrassment for Jim.

In turn, country recruits had a lot to learn about life in the city, with its bewildering population density, frenetic street life, noise, buses and trams, tenements, and night life. Being thrown together in the Depot's living quarters in the Phoenix Park would ultimately turn out to be one of the most rewarding and memorable experiences of life for country and city lads alike.

The sense of unity forged among the Garda recruits was one of the most fundamental requisites of their shared six-month training, for in years to come they would be dependent upon one another in critical situations. For Branigan, who had been a misfit and treated like an outcast at the GSR for nearly seven years, the new feeling of "belonging" was especially gratifying. "I really enjoyed the life in the Garda," he exulted. He regarded it as his true calling in life. Declan affirms that his father "found his vocation," as surely as a doctor or a teacher. To him it was a *higher* calling, a *noble* calling. Where others may have stepped into Garda life, Jim Branigan *plunged* in with a passion. Compared with his unhappy GSR years, the Garda Síochána felt like a fraternity, a brotherhood. The Depot was his new home.

———

Garda recruits were allowed a social life and were issued a pass at weekends. Branigan's acceptance among his comrades made him more gregarious than ever before. He had always been amiable and cheerful by nature, known also for being supportive of friends in need, the first to offer a helping hand. Within the force he developed a wide circle of friends, his best pals being men like Mick Flynn, Robert Simpson, Paddy Curnane, Matt Crehan, and Tim O'Donnell. They enjoyed conversation with one another and headed out on the town together on Saturdays and Sundays.

Leave was precious—liberation from the confines and regimentation of Depot life. By bus or tram they could zip into the brightly lit city centre for an evening at a dancehall, cinema, or pub. And passes could sometimes be granted on week-nights, from 6 to 10:30, when men like Branigan could visit their families. Saturdays were always the big occasion, when there was an extended period of independence from two in the afternoon until half ten that night.

In town there was always a swirl of social activity: music, dancing and pretty women. Tall gardaí in uniform always stood out impressively. On occasion they were required to carry a cane and dress gloves, creating the appearance of a true "gentleman" garda, admired by the public. Branigan cut quite a dashing figure with his height, ramrod posture, pleasing smile, and polite manner.

Though gardaí may have appeared as a "good catch" for young women, their financial status was less than impressive. The men habitually groused about their paltry wages, an endless topic because it limited them in their life and their plans. "My pay was £2.50 in 1931," revealed Branigan. "It was *not* good money."[2] Especially galling was the fact that "twelve months before I joined the force we got £3 a week, but we were asked to forgo 50 pence to help the economy—but we never got that money back when the economy improved." Tradesmen, craftsmen, factory workers, office staff, even unskilled labourers typically earned a better wage than uniformed gardaí, who took great risks.

Nor was there any way for a garda to make a few extra shillings, because "we did not get overtime, and even when we worked on our leave day in an emergency we seldom were given a day off in lieu of it." Throughout his career, especially after he was married and had children, Branigan would use the phrase "scrimp and scrape" to describe a guard's pay problem. "I learnt to live with bad pay." Unfortunately, not all his friends could say the same. As the years progressed and they married and started families, a good number of his mates would be forced to relinquish their Garda career for a better-paying job. This problem stood out as the one nagging negative aspect of Garda life that Jim Branigan was openly displeased with.

When he did have money in his pocket the two entertainments he enjoyed most were dancing and seeing a good western film. The large, colourful cinema posters advertising such evocative titles as *Billy the Kid, The Hard Hombre, The Nevada Buckaroo* and *Cimmaron* were hard to resist. But he also joined his friends who favoured dancing at their favourite dancehalls, "so I used to dance weekly at the Ierne and the Teachers' Hall, Parnell Square." Both had a respectable clientele and were frequented by nice young women. If he met a dance partner he liked he could arrange to see her again and perhaps buy her sweets or ice cream after dancing. But he had to watch his wallet.

He and his mates enjoyed sharing a pint in their favourite pubs as well but were mindful to drink moderately. Inebriation could crash a career fast. A few pints always enlivened the conversation on Saturday nights, and sport could dominate if there was a big match on at Croke Park the next day. When the talk became more serious, the men shared their ambitions at times. Branigan found that his friends varied widely in their career goals. Some of the young trainees, only twenty to twenty-three years old, talked unabashedly of their hope to reach the upper echelons of the Garda hierarchy, some openly aspiring to become a chief superintendent, and possibly commissioner, one day.

Such thoughts did not even occur to Jim Branigan. Nor would they ever. He simply didn't see his Garda career in such a context. Though a bit of a pay increase would be nice.

———

Trainees attended classes in which every aspect of policing was taught—all the rules and regulations, methods and practices they needed to learn before they could hit the street on their own. Branigan liked the book-learning and lecture sessions of the six-month course, and did well. It was emphasised by the instructors that the young men were part of a new native Irish police force, taking over from the old DMP days. Theirs was a new model, new system, founded on different ideas from those of the past, with high expectations and responsibilities.

The DMP's methods had often been heavy-handed and discriminatory. Some said they were routinely harsh and abusive, especially towards the poorer classes. The new force was to follow a humane approach—sensitive, tolerant, and fair. Instead of being set apart from the citizens, gardaí should try to relate and interact in a friendly manner on the beat, aim to become part of the community. Recruits were informed that many people still had ill feelings towards the police and that it would take years to dispel such attitudes.

Instructors emphasised the importance of personal judgement and discretion. Policing wasn't defined in clear black-and-white terms: there was the imprecise "grey" area that called for discretionary interpretation, and action. This was a delicate matter, left to each individual. While trying to avoid the old, detested policing strategies, the new gardaí would also need to be careful not to be too lenient, too soft, as this could erode respect for law and order.

It was a fine balance. There were risks in acting too strongly, and too weakly. The term "discretion" was repeated over and over for the new recruits. In *The Irish Police*, Séamus Breathnach elucidates the inherent problems:

> How would the police use their discretion? There are guidelines for the wearing of uniforms, but not for how to intervene in a domestic dispute ... for use of departmental property, but not for whether to break up a sidewalk gathering. To use any discretion at all, where the law does not specifically state the action to be taken, is a completely subjective situation fraught with all kinds of dangers.[3]

The bedrock of discretion was common sense, fairness, and sensitivity, according to how each individual guard interpreted them. It was a thorny problem inherent in policing and one that would bedevil guards every hour on duty, every day.

No garda took the concept of discretion more seriously than Branigan. He regarded it as the very core of police work. His interpretation was generally consistent with the standard definition of the term: "individual choice or judgement ... power of free decision or latitude of choice within legal bounds."[4] It could not be conveniently codified: rather, it was a personal, rational and moral process. A person had to be guided by their own set of values and principles. Act accordingly—and hope for the best.

As it so happened, on the evening of Thursday 18 June 1931—the very day he joined the Garda Síochána—there occurred on the streets of Dublin an incident that illustrated the use of police discretion in handling a riotous scene, one that made the front pages of the city's newspapers and was surely read by Branigan and his fellow-trainees. At about eight o'clock a demonstration began assembling in the heart of the city in support of two Republican prisoners who were on hunger strike in Mountjoy Prison. The *Evening Herald* reported that "it was a very large meeting and the crowd extended from O'Connell Street all through Cathal Brugha Street to Marlborough Street." As various speakers addressed the crowd, the level of agitation arose. Additional guards were called to the scene in case the demonstration erupted into violent action; but the increased presence of uniformed gardaí only raised the hostility of the men. When the guards began ordering them to disperse it became ugly, as some of the men began hurling stones, bottles and other missiles at them.

According to reporters on the scene, the leaders of the demonstration began leading the crowd towards the North Circular Road, exhorting them "to march on to Mountjoy and, if necessary, raze the prison to the ground."[5] In response the Gardaí "put a cordon across the road and ordered the procession to stop." This infuriated the leaders, one of whom shouted that it was "time to *rush the police*,"[6] after which a hailstorm of objects was hurled at unprotected guards.

They were now faced with on-the-spot decisions. There was little doubt what the old DMP would have done. The crowd had clearly coalesced into a violent mob, as "guards were assaulted, kicked in the legs and stomach, struck on the mouth."

"It was at this point," the *Irish Independent* confirmed, "that the police ordered a baton charge."[7] These had been a hallmark of the DMP—one of the reasons they were so feared and detested. It was exactly, therefore, what the new force had hoped to avoid. But in the judgement of the gardaí on the scene it was an absolute necessity.

On 19 June the *Evening Herald* featured the incident on the front page with the heading "Story of baton charges in Dublin last night." When the case reached court the demonstration's leaders charged that the guards had severely "over-reacted . . . The public were batoned, as it seemed the police had run amok."[8] It was just the sort of publicity the Garda authorities didn't want.

The incident stirred fresh controversy over the new Garda force. In Dublin District Court, Judge Hannon, known as a fair-minded judge, having heard testimony on both sides supported the action of the guards, stating that he believed their baton charge to have been wholly justified and adding that, in his judgement, the police had certainly not "run amok."

Young Jim Branigan and his fellow-recruits knew they would soon face similar situations on the streets of Dublin, having to make their own critical decisions, using their best discretion. One thing Branigan already knew: he didn't like batons.

———

His more immediate problem had to do with using his fists. Recruits were taught the fundamental offensive and defensive techniques necessary for doing their duty, such as "master grips," disarming a person, evading kicks, and the basics of wrestling. The emphasis was on defensive techniques and restraining violent resisters. Street fighting could be utterly uncivilised, as hooligans used not only their fists but elbows, knees, feet, heads, even teeth. Drunken men routinely used their head as a lethal battering-ram, and sometimes actually bit off a foe's finger or ear, or jabbed fingers to blind him. It was a primitive form of combat, and every garda needed expertise in handling it.

A garda was also issued with a heavy wooden baton, and taught how to use it; but when—or if—to draw the baton was always his critical decision, unless ordered to do so by his superiors.

Fists were another weapon, presenting quite a different dilemma for Branigan. With the new Garda boxing policy every recruit was required to enter the ring and learn the fundamentals of the "art" of boxing. Considering his personal history with bullying pugilists and his refusal to defend himself, one can only imagine the apprehension he felt over having to climb into a boxing ring.

The rationale was that boxing added a valuable component to a garda's defensive skills: how to deflect punches, take punches, *throw* punches if necessary. Men were taught how to use footwork, move in and out, lean backward and forward. The ability to master the jab provided a garda with the ability to ward off a thug's wild swings. Branigan comprehended the concepts of boxing's defensive usefulness; he needed only to learn how to apply them in the ring, facing another man.

A good number of the recruits had experience in boxing, some being quite accomplished; others had little exposure to it. But Jim Branigan was probably the only one among them who had never engaged in a typical playground or street skirmish with his fists. Yet he had probably taken more punches than any of them. He had seen "ruggy-ups" or fights around the Liberties, but only as an observer.

Who knows what was spinning through Branigan's mind that first day when he was told to lace on the gloves. He would always say that "I never saw a boxing glove until I was training at the Garda Depot." All around him, men were eagerly slipping on the gloves, pounding them together, bursting into a bit of fancy footwork, looking unnervingly experienced.

After the preliminary instructions on boxing, sparring sessions would begin. The instructor, Tommy Maloney, told the recruits that the natural instinct would be to flail away; but the most fundamental element of real boxing, as against merely "fighting," was to restrain wild swings, to be controlled, use your head, be measured. It sounded reasonable enough.

Waiting for his debut, Branigan watched other men spar as he fidgeted. While most were obviously learners, others were clearly not. Finally, his name was called. "On the first day in the gym I was told to put on shorts and boxing gloves and get into the ring with a big, tough Offaly man my own weight."[9] His opponent had weighed in at only half a stone heavier, but he was shorter and more stocky. As the two men met tentatively in the centre of the ring, Branigan clearly seemed the weaker.

As luck would have it, his opponent was as unskilled as himself. Unluckily, he was considerably tougher and more aggressive. "Though neither of us knew how to box, he battered me around the ring." Although their gloves were padded, the blows hurt, and leather cut the skin. When not on defence he tried to throw looping punches. By the time it ended he had received a real leathering, and his face showed it. What worried him more was that his performance may have made him look weak in the eyes of his peers.

For some reason, the next day the instructor pitted him against the same man—with the same result. The third and fourth days were replicas of the first two, except that Branigan's face was now more swollen and was black and blue. On the fifth and sixth days his opponent, now supremely confident, took target practice on Branigan's body. But despite taking the beating, he remained determined and soldiered on. "I came out on the sixth consecutive day sporting bruised lips and a bleeding nose. My father jeered the hell out of me."

The following day the instructor, for some apparently good reason, threw the two mismatched opponents into the ring once again. He had probably experienced this situation enough times to bet on a positive outcome for Branigan, if not physical then perhaps psychological:

> On the seventh day I got into the ring with the same man. I was *determined* to win ... and I shut my eyes, took a wild swing and caught him full on the nose, which began to pump blood.[10]

The man lay flattened, on the canvas, stunned. It altered his outlook as well, because the next day he requested that the instructor not pair him in the ring with Branigan again. The request was granted.

It was one of those transformational incidents in a person's life. *One punch.*

A cinematic-like moment of dramatic redemption, followed by a surge of restored pride and confidence:

> It was a very important psychological step forward, for it proved that I had guts, tenacity and determination to win—and that I was far from the coward I appeared to be when working on the railway.[11]

It was a mental victory that would shape his future. From that day forward he was dedicated to improving his boxing skill, eagerly climbing into the ring each day against assorted opponents.

He now took a keen interest in both the national and the international boxing stage, particularly within the Garda Síochána, where such champions as Matt Flanagan, Ger Driscoll and Dick Hearns were idols to the other men. One day Maloney promised Branigan that if he was dedicated enough and made sufficient progress he might even be able to spar with them.

It could not have been a more propitious time for young Jim Branigan to embrace the sport of boxing, for it had assumed colossal interest throughout the world in the 1930s, even taking on political importance. As the heavyweight champions Jack Dempsey and Gene Tunney relinquished their reign, the German boxer Max Schmeling rose to win the title on the eve of Hitler's Third Reich, with its ideology of "Aryan" supremacy. Then along came Joe Louis, the "Brown Bomber" from the United States. Even non-fans could not help but be captivated by the symbolism and drama of the world boxing scene.

Though Branigan was no budding Jack Dempsey or Joe Louis—his two great idols now—he was indisputably a fast-improving young boxer under Maloney's tutelage. Dedicated and hard-working, he never seemed to tire of skipping, weight-lifting, punching the light and heavy bags, running, shadow-boxing, sparring spiritedly. His family and friends could barely believe the transformation.

Nothing showed his commitment to boxing more than his promise to Maloney only a few days after his "rebirth" in the ring: "For him I gave up smoking so that I would have better wind"—a measure of both his discipline and his fierce determination. He wondered if one day he might be good enough to receive an invitation from Maloney to join the Garda Boxing Club with the real Garda champions; it was even being mentioned in the newspapers that the elite Garda boxers might be going to the Olympic Games in Los Angeles.

By the late autumn of 1931 he had made huge progress in the ring, and Maloney now had him in sparring sessions with some of the GBC boxers, against whom he looked impressive. As Branigan put it, "I proved to be a useful boxer at the end of my training." His training ethic was peerless. Maloney's feeling was that he had real potential.

In December, with Christmas approaching, he successfully completed his six months' training and passed out as a fully fledged member of the Garda Síochána. Though he was elated, he was also nervous about his immediate future in the force, worried that he might be stationed in some small town or village—"out in the bogs," as he called it. He had seen enough of country life to know that this would be antithetical to his background as a city lad. He dreaded the possibility but knew that his posting would be the luck of the draw.

He was saved by Tommy Maloney and his dedication to boxing; for by this time his instructor recognised his potential and decided that he deserved a chance for advancement in the sport. Taking Branigan aside, he promised him two things: firstly, he would intercede on his behalf to see that he was assigned a posting in Dublin; secondly, he would offer him a chance to join the Garda Boxing Club. Branigan was delighted—and it showed.

The Christmas season seemed to him brighter than ever before, as Dublin was bejewelled with coloured lights and decorations. Along O'Connell Street, Grafton Street, Dame Street and Henry Street, carollers sang on corners as cheerful crowds passed by. Adults and children alike marvelled at the shop windows with their scenes of Santa, his reindeer, and elves in the toy workshop. Street dealers were in high spirits, but none higher than Jim Branigan.

Everything had gone his way—or so it seemed. Then came orders for his specific Dublin posting. "I was selected for the ten-man Defence Unit, composed of athletes, boxers, and footballers." It sounded like an elite unit and a prime posting. He felt honoured.

He took up the post in January 1932, within days of his twenty-second birthday. He soon discovered that it was nothing like what he had expected. His first disappointment was that he was still stationed at the Depot, so there was no change in social or geographical environment. For the most part he had mundane tasks, such as guard duty, providing an escort for senior officials, or being implanted statue-like at the entrance of court buildings. He saw these as secondary roles, "odd jobs," not real policing. He had joined the force to be a "front-line" garda, combating crime, hunting down "outlaws," maintaining law and order in the streets. He felt very much in the shadow of the major Garda force.

On occasion he was despatched outside Dublin on a temporary assignment in Cos. Mayo, Sligo, Clare, and elsewhere, "to such lonesome parts of Ireland as Bangor Erris and Crossmolina," places he had never even heard of. Here his duties often involved dealing with agrarian disputes and land feuds, problems alien to his city culture. In later years, he would confess, "as a Dublin man I was bored by agrarian feuds—and I thought I would *never* get home."

He did value one type of assignment outside Dublin as a learning experience. This was when he and a few of his stronger mates were sent to escort troublesome prisoners from provincial jails to the Dublin courts. This duty "gave me my first taste of dealing with toughs and hardened criminals," some of whom had a venomous hatred of guards. Here his self-defence training paid off against their often wild resistance. He would later meet some of these same culprits on the open streets of Dublin.

What sustained him during these early years of duty was his boxing in the Garda Boxing Club, as well as weekend passes with his pals. He longed to be "out on the beat," like most of his friends, amidst the daily swirl of the city's life. But at least as a new member of the boxing club he was focused and kept active. He was now being put in the ring with top-rank boxers, such as Willie Blackwell, Dick Hearns, Jack Driscoll—the best training he could receive. Maloney kept the pressure on, moving him up a slight notch at a time. Branigan welcomed it with zest, and came right back for more. While he by no means had the natural talent of those boxers, he exhibited the heart and determination of a champion.

In January 1932 Maloney decided it was time to test him against some outside competition. His first test bout was with a capable boxer from the RUC, against whom he was fairly matched. When he emerged victorious he felt pride in having performed so respectably, as if he had validated Maloney's faith in him. Over the coming years he would meet opponents from Britain and the Continent, dividing the wins and losses about evenly but always learning and improving. He regularly shared a few pints with his Garda mates: as he put it, "during my boxing days I used to drink a lot of beer. I would drink to celebrate a win, or drink to drown my sorrows after I lost a fight." But never to excess.

    ——

On 18 June 1932—exactly a year after the baton charge against the crowd in O'Connell Street—there amassed an even larger crowd of highly energised people. More than one million. And it was up to the Garda Síochána to maintain order and keep the peace. This time Branigan was in uniform.

The thirty-first Eucharistic Congress had been awarded to Dublin, to celebrate the 1,500th anniversary of the traditional date of St Patrick's mission to Ireland. Visitors flowed in from many countries, as distant as the United States and Australia. The event stretched from 18 June to 1 July, but the central events were scheduled for 22–26 June. The entire Garda force was called out to meet the challenge.

There were processions of church hierarchy and political potentates in a city lavishly decorated, from O'Connell Bridge to the smallest local streets. Nancy Cullen of Cook Street remembers it as the happiest time of people's lives: "It was *absolutely great!* Our little street had a beautiful altar and light bulbs on a wire. And an old-fashioned gramophone, and we'd all be singing." High Mass was held in the Phoenix Park on 26 June, attended by more than a million people. John McCormack sang, and his voice was carried throughout the city by an elaborate system of loudspeakers so that everyone could share in the event.

For Branigan and his fellow-gardaí it was like a huge military operation, with guards posted at strategic points all over Dublin—not so much to control the crowd as to assist them: to events, accommodation, medical facilities, and amenities. The crowds were so huge that camps had to be set up in Cabra and Artane to help provide shelter for people. To make the job of the Gardaí more difficult, they were days of sweltering heat. On their feet all day, some suffered from dehydration and even heat-stroke. Young, fit guards like Branigan held up the best.

————

By September 1935 he was due for rotation and was finally transferred out of the Depot to a new post in Irishtown. At first he was pleased with the new setting and more interesting policing duties: walking the beat, meeting local people, handling problems on the street. But before long a problem emerged that changed his attitude towards his new position.

He had to work under a station sergeant known for his brusque manner, insensitivity, and often offensive treatment of men under him. It was ironic that Branigan, at this early stage, should encounter a garda with whom he clashed in personality and principles, for throughout his 43-year career he would get along exceedingly well with every other member of the force. No-one was more likeable or more easily befriended.

By December, after only three months, he felt dispirited at having to work under such an unkind, domineering station sergeant. Then, by a bit of good luck, his destiny took a turn for the better. As he liked to tell the story, one day when he was out on duty he was stopped by Major-General Murphy, who asked him about his black eye. When he explained that he got it boxing with the Garda Boxing Club, a discussion of boxing ensued. When Murphy learnt that Branigan loved being a guard but was less than happy at his post, he offered to arrange a transfer for him.

In January 1936, having turned twenty-six, he was gleefully transferred to New Market Garda Station in the Liberties. He was "home." Here he would begin his legendary career. Once again, his involvement in boxing had saved him.

He had now been boxing for five years and was a bona-fide member of the

Garda Boxing Club, bigger, stronger, more skilled by far than at twenty-one or twenty-two, good enough in fact to be part of the Garda Boxing Club's travelling team when they visited other countries. He now weighed about fifteen stone, moving up in the boxing division to the light-heavyweight and heavyweight ranks, facing the "goliaths" of the sport. The difference now was that while Branigan always tried to outmanoeuvre and outpoint his opponent, the man facing him was often seeking to knock him out, unleashing powerful punches aimed at his head. He was in a different league now, and knew it.

When the Garda boxers were pitted against those from the North or Britain it was generally a well-matched tournament, and they got to know one another over the years. However, when Irish boxers ventured further afield the opponents could be unknown, and the pairings sometimes conspicuously unfair. Nonetheless, always determined, he never backed off, putting up the best performance he could. He was still winning about half his bouts, always on points. However, he was sometimes taking a leathering from a clearly superior opponent. But *never* being knocked out. In this he took enormous pride.

In the mid-thirties the Garda Boxing Club took a giant stride upwards in the European boxing realm by arranging some tournaments with the German clubs. German boxing was at its zenith at this time, with Max Schmeling having held the world heavyweight championship and inspiring young German boxers. Furthermore, the 1936 Olympic Games were looming in Germany, and Hitler expected his boxers to dominate, to showcase German superiority. German boxers were treated like treasured thoroughbreds, pampered and trained in the best of facilities by gifted instructors. They were glorified to a point where the hierarchy of the Third Reich would show up for their bouts, to sit in ringside seats and applaud them as they defeated their opponents. They had every imaginable training advantage available to them and were fed the best of meals.

When German boxers travelled to other countries for experience they moderated their power. Conversely, when at home in Germany before the Nazi leaders they unleashed their "killer instinct," always seeking a knock-out. Nonetheless, even in Ireland, when Branigan first faced a visiting team of German boxers, he could tell they were highly skilled, superbly conditioned—a different breed from what he had known. Some were so good that they might as well have been professionals.

What he didn't yet know was that before long he would be travelling to Germany to fight the leading German boxing princes, on their home soil and in front of Hitler's highest-ranking military and political leaders.

Chapter 3 ～

| ON THE LIBERTIES BEAT

"The magic of the Liberties itself, it fascinated me. It held me in its spell . . . the sounds, banter, laughter . . . the little shops."

(ÉAMONN MAC THOMÁIS)

"At the old New Market Garda Station in the Coombe I did ordinary beat work around the streets. Slowly but surely I got to know and understand the thug, the street fighter, the petty criminal—and how to cope with him."

(GARDA JIM BRANIGAN)

"He *loved* the Liberties. And he took a personal interest in the lives of the people. Every second person in the street would stop and talk . . . he was so well known. And it helped him in the execution of his duties."

(DECLAN BRANIGAN)

Of all the posts in Ireland, none could have been more fitting, or made him happier. New Market is in the heart of the Liberties. Born and reared a Liberties lad, he was a native on the streets. At home.

The Liberties, as defined by Elgy Gillespie in *The Liberties of Dublin*, is "in its broadest sense . . . concentrated upon the older parts of Dublin 8, roughly bounded by the Castle, the Quays, St James's Gate and Blackpitts."[1] It was a part of Dublin distinguished by its ancient history, rich culture, and old customs.

In the ninth century the Norsemen made this area south of the Liffey important for seafaring and trading activities. The French Huguenots arrived in the late 1600s with their silk-weaving looms, and by 1784 the quarter known as the Liberties was thriving as a centre of weaving.

About this time "serious rioting was of frequent occurrence between the Ormonde Boys, or butchers of Ormond Market, and the 'Liberties Boys,' tailors and weavers of the Coombe."[2] On some occasions as many as a thousand combatants were engaged in fierce fighting, while "businesses were suspended, shops closed, peaceful citizens confined to their houses."

Following the Great Famine of 1845–52, desperate refugees from the worst-affected counties flowed into the city, seeking relief and sustenance. Many gravitated towards the Liberties, where Irish was widely spoken and old ways retained. Here the brewing industry prospered, especially Guinness's, and a scattering of small factories, shops and trades that offered work.

Throughout the latter part of the 1800s and well into the 1900s the Liberties retained its geographical, historical and cultural identity and separateness. It became known for its rural or "village" character, an enclave in the expanding capital city. Well into the first half of the twentieth century old customs and traditions were faithfully followed. Many Liberties residents still wore shawls, smoked clay pipes, relied on home cures, held traditional wakes. Many Dubliners from the "modern" parts of the city viewed the area as a charming anachronism, enjoying a ramble around Meath Street, Thomas Street, Patrick Street and Francis Street, especially on a Friday or Saturday, when street life was most exuberant. It was an excursion into a simpler past age.

In the mid-1930s, when Garda Jim Branigan began his Liberties beat, the area was little changed from the turn of the century. Houses were a fascinating mixture of Georgian, Victorian, artisans' dwellings, tenement houses, and even small stone cottages down back lanes. Most streets were narrow and cobblestoned and lit with gas lamps. Shops were small and family-owned, with the proprietor living in the quarters above. Credit was still given to regular customers. Small huckster shops and local pubs were a ubiquitous feature, with a loyal clientele. Streets were lined with the stalls of women dealers, while tuggers, carters and horse-drawn vehicles were a common part of the scene.

It was often said by residents that theirs was a "world apart," and indeed it was. So provincial was it that most people seldom ventured out into other parts of the city; there were still elderly residents in the 1950s and 60s who vouched that they had *never* been to Grafton Street or St Stephen's Green, a mere fifteen-minute walk away. (The author verified a few such cases still existing in the 1980s.) To the mind of most Liberties residents there was no need to go outside their realm, as theirs was a self-sufficient community, possessing all the needs of life: grocers, pubs, churches, chemists, banks, doctors' offices, schools, pawnbrokers, cinemas, newsagents. And Garda stations. And undertakers for their final journey.

The people with whom Branigan would daily mix—and come to love— were mostly the working class. The better-off were tradesmen, craftsmen, shopkeepers, with publicans atop the social hierarchy. People here possessed a strong work ethic, moral character, family loyalty, and pride in heritage. Their roots ran deep in the same street, many living in the same house in which they, and even their parents, were born. And they were religious. As Patrick O'Leary, a chemist in Thomas Street for nearly fifty years, saw it, "religion was their anchor."

Through all life's troubles and hardships, says Lorcán Ó Diolúin, "these people, even when they were stricken, they never lost their dignity."[3] And indeed life in the Liberties could be fraught with misery and sorrows. Their tradition of sharing and caring for one another was the core of community life. "We're all family here," many of the women liked to say.

––––

But all was not idyllic. The Liberties had its dark, almost Dickensian side as well. For there were countless squalid tenement houses in which the poor struggled and suffered terribly. In 1936, Branigan's first year on the beat, the *Irish Press* published an acclaimed three-week exposé of the city's decrepit tenements under the title "Dublin's slum evil." Many of the fetid, inhumane hovels the reporters visited were in the Liberties, declared "unfit for human habitation" by inspectors. The worst cases revealed hunger, poverty, poor clothing, sickness, despair. This is what Branigan's Garda mate Senan Finucane found when he was first assigned to the Liberties beat with him:

> My first impression of the Liberties was the tenements. Down in Francis Street and the Coombe they were the *worst*. A lot of hardship, diseases, fevers, slop buckets . . . the most horrible places.

Unemployment was widespread, intemperance prevalent, evictions common. Typical family sizes in the tenements were six to ten children; twelve to fifteen was not uncommon, and a few mothers had twenty, though not all lived. And yet it generally fell to the women to somehow provide for their family. With so many men unemployed, explains Lar Redmond, "it fell to the lioness of the pride to provide for the large brood."[4] The women worked as street dealers, domestic servants, tuggers, factory workers, hotel maids, cleaning women in offices—whatever it took to keep a roof over their head and a crust of bread on the table.

As Garda Branigan and Garda Finucane would find as they walked their Liberties beat, despite the appalling hardship most people were cheerful and buoyant in spirit. As another garda, Paddy Casey, observed, "they were *extraordinarily happy* for people who were so savagely poor." Sidney Davies, writing in his book *Dublin Types* in 1918, also marvelled at the "unruffled cheerfulness and good humour" of the Liberties poor. When Lar Redmond lived in the Liberties he attributed it to their "great sense of belonging to a close-knit community . . . and hearts were more kindly then."[5] Branigan would come to agree.

Judging by their exuberant social life, people in the Liberties were the happiest in Ireland. Outsiders acclaimed it time and again when visiting them. "They hadn't much, but they were happy with their lot," Finucane found. "Oh, great pride, and very good-natured . . . I liked walking the beat, to talk to them, mix with them." He and Branigan found it exhilarating—every day. Others felt the same, expressing it in their own way. Éamonn Mac Thomáis wrote that he was always "fascinated . . . with the *magic* of the Liberties,"[6] while Lar Redmond exulted, "it was like heaven" to be among the people there.

Jim Branigan had the great good fortune to have been assigned there as a young man, to walk the beat there every day. Here he learnt to feel the very pulse of the community. And in the 1930s and 40s the Liberties was in full flower. A kaleidoscope of human movement, colour, sounds, sights, smells. Stimulating, captivating. Nothing more so than the cries of the dealers: "Fresh fish!" "Apples and oranges!" "Coal blocks!" all amidst their matchless banter, gossip, and earthy wit. Streets teemed with hordes of children shouting, laughing, daring a bit of devilment, enlivened by the appearance of balladeers, buskers, organ-grinders, bringing music and song to the scene. And in the centre of the social whirlwind was Garda Jim Branigan, trying to absorb it all.

———

His first morning on the beat began in perfect calm and quiet. Nothing stirring, the only sound that of his boots on the pavement. It was nearing dawn on a cold January morning, when most people were still wrapped up in their beds. Having left New Market station after grabbing a cup of tea, he was strolling at a leisurely pace, feeling pride in finally being a garda out on his own beat. Making his early morning rounds, he encountered the lamplighter putting out his lamps. Then he heard the milkman's clattering as he passed by and waved. The "clop, clop, clop" of his horse's hooves would become one of his favourite sounds, a rhythmic cadence that rose and faded pleasantly.

Scanning the dim streetscape before him, he failed for a moment to gaze downwards and nearly stumbled over a large object. He found himself standing over a body. Not a drunken man, but a corpse.

Just the two of them there. It was highly unnerving. As he would later tell an *Evening Herald* reporter, "as a young cop, my *first* day on duty in the Coombe, at 6 a.m. in the morning, I tripped over a dead man in the street."[7]

For a novice it was understandably alarming. But, as he would learn with the years, it was not unknown for a guard to happen upon a body in the streets. In the darkness of night the figures of drunken men were commonplace. A dead body could be the result of accident, heart attack, or foul play; which of these he often could not discern on the spot. Anyway, that was not his job: the coroner would determine the cause of death.

On this morning, the discovery of his first body, he quickly returned to New Market station, informed the sergeant in charge, then returned to the scene to await the ambulance to take the body away, proceeding thereafter on his first morning's rounds already feeling a bit experienced.

It would be a contradiction that through his long Garda career he didn't fear the living but could be frightened of the dead. His son Alick reveals that he always had an aversion to being around death. His father once told him about a case in which he and several other gardaí had to enter the crypts of Christ Church in search of a suspect in hiding: "He said to me that he thought it was a very scary place to be, among the dead . . . you know, bones and skulls."

Nor did he like having to go to the morgue to identify a body laid out on a slab. Seeing bodies dragged out of the river or canal was nearly as unsettling. He just didn't like *being around* dead bodies, explains Alick. "He had to watch over bodies for a number of hours [on occasion], and he didn't fancy that. I don't know if he was afraid of death . . . or maybe just the thought of it."

———

Only a short time later he experienced an even more traumatic incident on his beat, one that he would recall as "the most chilling experience I ever had." It began miles from the Liberties, in the dark of night, when a pregnant woman realised that the moment of birth was nearing. She and her husband had set out urgently for the Coombe Hospital, one of Dublin's three maternity hospitals. They made it most of the way, until she sagged down to the ground in Thomas Street. It was not yet dawn as they frantically stared up and down the street for help.

Along came Garda Branigan, a 26-year-old unmarried man, having lived a fairly sheltered life—by his own admission—and knowing frighteningly little about childbirth. Suddenly he was confronted with an urgent situation, shocking him, which demanded his immediate action:

> I had to deliver a baby at 6 a.m. . . . to act as a midwife to a woman who was walking to the Coombe Hospital to have the baby. But she found she could wait no longer. I was *terrified*. I was a young garda . . . and did not understand those things.[8]

The woman and her husband both looked to him in a frantic plea for help. His mind was racing. During the first few moments his eyes were darting up and down Thomas Street in search of a woman who might help. *Any* woman.

Meanwhile the frantic husband was telling him how they had walked three miles from their home to reach this point. Finding clarity of mind, he took control without further delay:

> I ordered her to sit in a shop doorway, and sent her husband to phone for an ambulance. While he was away the good woman gave birth. She had a boy. They both lived. It took me days to recover from the shock of delivering her.[9]

Ironically, oral testimony from his fellow-gardaí who served with him describe him as absolutely "fearless" and "unruffled" through the most harrowing, dangerous situations. While he may not have exhibited a Hemingway-type "grace under pressure," he did thereafter take pride in having summoned enough calmness and courage to carry out his duty. Cold corpses and newborn babies. Life and death. All part of his Liberties beat.

Normally, his daily routine was quite pleasant, at least during the mornings and afternoons. His day always began with visits to the famous women dealers of the Liberties. "All characters," it was often said. And to him, all friends, which Mary Barnwell can attest personally. Three generations of women dealers in her family, including herself, knew and loved "Mr Branigan." Back in the 1940s and 50s, when Liberties residents bought most of their food from street markets, scores of dealers lined the streets. Most, with unemployed or under-employed husbands, worked from dawn to dusk to support their large families. They were the real backbone of Liberties society. Branigan delighted in beginning his mornings by wading through the crowds of dealers, pausing to engage in chat and repartee, pick up the latest news and gossip, of which there was never a shortage. There was nothing the women didn't know about what was going on in their Liberties. In later years they would become an important source of information for him.

By all accounts, the dealers adored Garda Branigan from his earliest days on the beat. He would become not only their friend but their confidant, counsellor and protector—what some would come to call their "guardian" garda.

Mary Barnwell knew him from her childhood days in the 1930s, when she helped her mother with her stall:

> He was a great friend of my mother's—oh, yes, and *her* mother's too! He'd always buy fruit off my mother. He'd speak to *all* the women dealers, chit-chat. He had a great nature. I never saw him in bad humour. And if they had a problem, they could mention that to him, and he'd help them out. Oh, he was very obliging. A *proper gentleman*. All the dealers *loved* him!

———

The Liberties was long famed for its galaxy of colourful characters, variously described as "curious," "amusing," "eccentric," and "bizarre." Most local people simply referred to them fondly as "one of our characters." As Bill Kelly affirms, "characters there were in plenty . . . The streets were thronged with them."[10] They undeniably provided a daily element of unpredictability and sometimes humour for everyone around. Éamonn Mac Thomáis contends that "these old characters . . . without them there'd have been no Liberties."[11]

The more famous ones were wonderfully eccentric and idiosyncratic. Most were completely innocuous, bringing only smiles and good humour. Others, however, could be boisterous and bellicose; a few could become aggressive and even dangerous. But all were "adopted" by the Liberties residents as their own, and here they felt safe. This was partly, explains Lar Redmond, because "the coppers kept an eye on them, and they were gentle."[12] No-one watched over them more protectively than Jim Branigan.

As he made his daily rounds he enjoyed their quirkiness and antics as much as anyone. Over time he got to know each one, at least as well as possible. He learnt bits about their background and "condition," became a sympathetic friend. The more renowned ones were inevitably given fitting nicknames, the following being some of the better known:

Damn-the-Weather	Doco No-Toes
Hairy Lemon	Johnny One-Match
Jembo No-Toes	Love, Joy, and Peace
Johnny Forty-Coats	The Bird Flanagan
Mary All-Papers	The Toucher Doyle
Mad Mary	Cyclone Warren
Shell-Shock Joe	The Professor

Like everyone else, Garda Branigan had his favourites. Among those for whom he had the greatest sympathy were First World War veterans who were victims of exploding shells or mustard gas. In the 1930s Paddy Mooney, who lived in Whitefriars' Street, felt great compassion for "a lot of men who came back shell-shocked." Some were given to fits of madness in the open streets. One man, he recalls—"Christ Almighty, it was terrible looking at him . . . He'd go mad and start bashing the metal rails with his fists . . . blood gushing out of him."

By contrast, others were joyful. "Love, Joy, and Peace" was a small, well-dressed man with a quiet, professorial demeanour who traipsed around carrying a piece of chalk with which he would draw a shamrock on the footpath, writing "love," "joy" and "peace" on the three leaves. "Mary All-Papers" was a tiny woman who carried an old shopping-bag full of papers of every description, wearing several coats and an old battered hat. To Lar Redmond, "Damn-the-Weather" was one of the most memorable. A short, blocky man wearing a peaked cap, he would be walking quietly along Meath Street or Thomas Street until suddenly, "like the report of a rifle shot," he would smash his hands together and roar "Damn the weather!" startling women and children around him.

"Bang-Bang" probably achieved the greatest notoriety, being the source of endless frights throughout the city. Walking the streets or hopping on and off buses and trams, entering shops or coming up behind people, always with his big key aimed like an imaginary gun, he would shout *"Bang!"* in an extremely loud voice. His victims would sometimes laugh or feign being hit; but Máirín Johnston remembers her childhood days in Pimlico in the 1930s and 40s when she and her young friends were "terrified of Bang-Bang . . . and his demands for hugs and kisses." The girls would run away, emitting "hysterical screams."[13]

Branigan placed his protective cloak over the street characters, making it clear that anyone who abused them would be punished—by *him*. There could be a fine line between teasing, taunting, and tormenting, but violators would learn the boundaries, as he doled out warnings or punishments. When any of the characters ran foul of the law he would be there in court to speak on their behalf. He was the one who could provide the judge with the specifics of their unfortunate background, which often had a mitigating effect on his decision.

From his first day on duty at New Market, Branigan didn't have to go far to encounter one of the great local characters, for he was one of his own Garda colleagues. A corpulent garda, he too had an evocative nickname, "Swally-the-Pig," given him by the children of the Liberties, who were engaged in an endless cat-and-mouse game with him. As Máirín Johnston recalls, he was a source of excitement and drama for her and her pals in Pimlico:

> A figure of fun and fear in our youth . . . he was of enormous proportions, with a belly the size of a Guinness barrel and a face like a full moon in a fog. He was "public enemy number 1."[14]

He was constantly chasing children for various violations, such as playing in the streets. His globular shape and lumbering manner could be highly deceptive, for, as local children learnt, he was surprisingly swift on his feet when motivated to sprint after them. When he caught repeat offenders in his clutches he could give them a smack on the ear or have them brought before the Children's Court. Their parents could be fined two shillings and sixpence—a lot of money in those days.

For Branigan he was a valuable colleague when trouble arose on the streets or in a pub: huge, strong, and swift. Branigan, a six foot four boxer, and Swally, with his "big fat head stuck in a tall helmet, and on his belt a black leather case with a truncheon," arrived at the scene of a row as a most intimidating pair of policemen. On raucous Saturday nights Swally was worth his weight in gold.

————

On Saturday mornings the streets were suffused with good cheer and friendly exchanges. Everyone loved Saturdays, the most enjoyable day of the week. About six in the morning would be heard the sound of country carts on cobblestones, loaded with turf or vegetables. When they began their haggling with dealers over price, the Liberties took on a fair-day atmosphere. By mid-morning it was "all hustle and bustle and a wonderful air of excitement and gaiety," Máirín Johnston wrote, "as street dealers sang out their wares and good humour was all around." Children, off school, were racing wildly and shouting. Before long the organ-grinders and lavender man showed up. The community gradually took on a carnival atmosphere.

Declan Branigan recalls how, when he was a young lad, his father would take him into the Liberties on a Saturday: "for me it was an *adventure*. He was so well known . . . Every second person in the street would stop and talk." On Saturday, nothing in all Dublin was more lively than wandering around the streets of the Liberties.

At the end of the day, however, Saturday night loomed. It was as if the curtain had fallen on the first act, then was drawn up again to reveal a dramatically different stage: different lighting, sounds, mood, social behaviour. And featured performers.

Garda James Branigan's reputation would largely be built on Saturday night episodes, Dublin's peak period of social activity, and disorder. Máirín Johnston describes the dramatic transformation: "As Saturday night wore on the pubs filled up, the hooleys began and the 'ruggy-ups' erupted."[15] Fuelled by drinking, good fun could turn to nasty behaviour. Arguments began, rows flared up, and brawling could break out. Sometimes, if not quickly quelled by Branigan and his colleagues, it could deteriorate into rioting. Like other inner-city areas, the Liberties had its respectable pubs as well as its rough-and-ready ones. Everyone knew the difference, especially the local gardaí. One problem for the police was that many residents looked on Saturday night brawls as exciting free entertainment, and were in no hurry to contact the Garda station to have it broken up. Golden Lane, where May Hanaphy grew up, was among the most notorious:

On Saturday night it'd be *murder!* Oh, *always* fighting! Golden Lane was known as the "four corners of hell," 'cause there was a pub on each corner. At a ruggy-up they'd say, "Here's the police!" And the police had whistles.

Having to confront drunken fighters, many of whom had boxing experience in local clubs, always carried risks for the gardaí, and injuries were common. They had orders to use their baton only if absolutely necessary, and never on the head. From the day Jim Branigan put on his uniform he was instinctively disinclined to use his baton. As it would turn out, during forty-three years as a guard he never once did so.

To Branigan the most distressing feature of Saturday nights was not the rows in pubs but the abuse habitually inflicted by drunken men behind closed doors, against their wives, children, or in-laws. In those days domestic violence was commonly regarded as a personal issue within families, not a matter for the gardaí. Whether it was verbal, emotional or physical abuse, a garda seldom intruded to halt the violence. It was largely a matter of "discretion"—and most guards wanted no part of it. They would rather be called to stop a brawl among men than be drawn into a messy "domestic" crime behind closed doors. As Senan Finucane candidly verifies, back in those days "in family rows guards wouldn't interfere in nine cases out of ten."

Garda Branigan would become the highly notable exception, respected as the garda who could never tolerate a man striking a woman.

———

During the mid and later 1930s, when he was still single, he continued to enjoy socialising with his friends when he was off duty. Going out on the town to his favourite dancehalls and films was something to look forward to, as a diversion from his long and often stressful duties. Dublin's ubiquitous dancehalls were the best place for single men and women to meet and form relationships, often leading to romance and marriage. This was certainly the hope of Ellen Ebbs and her pals from the sewing factory who regularly attended their three favourite venues: the "Pally" (Palace) in Parnell Square, La Scala (later the Capitol) in Prince's Street, and the Workmen's Club on the quays. "There were *loads* of dancehalls all around. We'd meet fellas . . . and they'd buy us some minerals or ice cream afterwards." When off-duty guards showed up, looking tall, poised, clean-cut, they never failed to catch the attention of young women in every corner. And they knew it.

By 1936 cinema attendance in Dublin was greater than ever. Hollywood was producing an array of films for every taste—comedies, thrillers, mysteries, romance, westerns. In the depressed thirties, films were the best form of escape for people. Lar Redmond saw evidence of this around the Liberties, where "the unemployed stood on street corners penniless, but somehow they managed to scrape the price of the cinema together . . . where they could forget for a little while the grim world around them." Their favourite picture-houses, less costly than the luxurious city-centre cinemas, were the Fountain (later the Lyric) in James's Street, the Tivoli in Francis Street, the "Core" (Inchicore), the "Broad" (Broadway) in Manor Street, the "Mayro" (the Lyceum in Mary Street), the "Feeno" (Phoenix) on Ellis Quay, the Rialto, and the Leinster at Dolphin's Barn. At day's end even weary women dealers enjoyed entering a picture-house with a bottle of Guinness and bag of pig's feet hidden beneath their shawl. As John J. Dunne states, because of people's magnetic attraction to films, Dublin "gained the reputation of being among the most cinema-conscious cities in the world."[16] For many avid filmgoers it became an addiction. As Dunne contends, "Dublin went to the pictures with a frequency born of compulsion."[17] Cinemas were packed, having to turn patrons away. This created a problem for Branigan and his fellow-gardaí, as it generated a thriving black market for tickets. They were ordered to try to stamp out the illicit activity.

For Branigan personally, 1936 was a banner year for classic Westerns featuring heroic characters. Most notable were John Wayne in *Two-Fisted Law*, Randolph Scott in the role of *Frontier Marshal*, and *The Plainsman* starring Gary Cooper. All serious adult films with mature plots and dialogue, stressing law and order, toughness, courage, and the morality of a man's character. To Branigan, Cooper and Wayne epitomised the rugged individualism of the Western lawman and hero.

————

Despite the demands of his Liberties beat, Branigan remained a dedicated member of the Garda Boxing Club. At twenty-six he possessed boundless energy and required minimal sleep. His passion for the sport was greater than ever. In 1936 he was in his boxing prime, sparring with the best men on the team. His enthusiasm for the sport may also have been boosted by the huge worldwide attention that year on an international heavyweight fight. The German boxer Max Schmeling, who had held the title from 1930 to 1932, was making a comeback. On 19 June in New York he confidently entered the ring to face an upstart by the name of Joe Louis, a Black American with an enormous following. With Hitler on the brink of his quest, the political and social symbolism of the event was glaringly evident.

Branigan and his Garda boxing mates were especially attentive to top-rate German boxers, groomed to maximum performance level, as they were now facing them more often in tournaments. When Schmeling knocked out the "Brown Bomber" in a stunning twelve-round victory he returned to Germany a hero, and the Nazis used the event as a propaganda tool for white supremacy.

By the autumn of 1936 Branigan had been boxing for almost five years and had nearly seventy-five official bouts under his belt, of which he had won about half. Some of his losses were a close shave, on points, in which he had looked impressive against some excellent opponents. However, his most challenging experience was serious sparring against Dick Hearns, the brightest star of the Garda Boxing Club, whom Branigan called "one of the greatest ever produced by the Gardaí"—good enough to become the Irish light-heavyweight champion. He and Hearns had become friends, and the latter always tested him to his limits in their sparring matches. By late in the year "I had been his sparring partner for three months," said Branigan. "I boxed him almost every night and picked up every trick he had."[18] This gave him great confidence, to the point where, as he put it, "I was won over on the idea of becoming a champion."

In November 1936 he got his chance. On a night when film devotees were flocking to the Capitol Cinema in Prince's Street to see *Rose Marie*, starring Nelson Eddy and Jeanette MacDonald, the finals of the Leinster boxing championship were being held in Portobello Gymnasium. There was a full slate of bouts, stretching into the later hours, drawing a packed crowd and press coverage. There were some well-known top-class boxers contesting for championships, especially in the lighter divisions. Popular boxers such as Tommy Kelly were always exciting to watch and were assured of colourful coverage in the newspapers.

By comparison, Branigan was a relative unknown, who had fought his way into contention for the Leinster heavyweight championship by winning his previous bouts on points against generally mediocre opponents. On 6 November 1936 the fight card read: "James C. Branigan of the GBC versus Tom Penny of St Andrews."

By the time the heavyweight contest was announced, some fans had departed, and the newspaper men were looking tired, if not uninterested. Into the ring stepped Jim Branigan and Tom Penny. The men were quite evenly matched. In physique, Branigan was the taller, Penny the broader. Both were superbly fit, and determined to make the most of their opportunity to shine. They had only three three-minute rounds in which to prove who would be champion.

At the opening bell both men were cautious in their strategy. Seeking to score on points rather than a knock-out. Their styles were not exciting, yet they were competitive in trying to outmanoeuvre one another and slip in some solid punches, though they did little damage. Branigan had had plenty of spirited matches that were far more exciting, but never one in which the stakes were so high.

At the end of what was a comparatively lacklustre championship match,

the two men exchanged friendly words as the final bell sounded. It's likely that no-one in the crowd would have been willing to bet much on how the decision might go, it seemed so close—including the two boxers, who stood in suspense. Then the referee raised Branigan's arm and announced him as the new Leinster heavyweight champion.

On 7 November the *Irish Times* praised the performances of several new champions in the lighter ranks, particularly Tommy Kelly's "truly splendid win" and J. Foley's "best performance of the night." About the heavyweight championship it pithily stated:

J. Branigan (Garda) beat T. Penny (St Andrews) on points.

Of all Jim Branigan's achievements over the years, capturing the Leinster heavyweight championship received the most measly press coverage.

————

Not that it probably bothered him. Momentary praise was not what mattered: it would be the mantle of "heavyweight boxing champion" that he would wear for his remaining days. He would always carry it modestly, never boasting of it, though others often did so on his behalf. As the years passed, the prestige of the title would grow in the public's mind. It would eventually be largely forgotten that he had won the championship in a three-round contest over a mediocre opponent, and on points.

Many would come to assume that he had become champion in a bruising match, out-slugging a tough opponent, if not knocking him cold. For this was the "Lugs" they knew.

One might wonder if any of the bullies in the GSR yards who had unmercifully pummelled him for years were in the Portobello Gymnasium crowd that night to see him climb out of the ring as heavyweight boxing champion.

Chapter 4 ～

| THE "ANIMAL GANG" ERA

"With the animal gangs, you *had* to fight your way on the street. And if you wouldn't, they'd *kill* you!"

(GARDA JOHN MURPHY)

"He got his reputation from fighting. If there was a row he'd *go in* with them. And they were *hard,* them fellas—they could *fight.*"

(JOHN JOE KENNEDY, FORMER GANG MEMBER
OF THE 1930s and 40s)

"I waged a private war against the gangs. It was a battle between me and them. If I saw a street fight involving gangs I used to steel myself and wade into the middle of them."

(GARDA JIM BRANIGAN)

"Garda Branigan will always be remembered in Dublin as the man who broke the Animal Gangs which terrorised the city."

(*Evening Herald,* JANUARY 1973)

On 7 November 1936, the day after Branigan won his Leinster heavyweight boxing title, the *Saturday Herald* published an article headed "Hooligan activities in Dublin," which both the public and police surely found disquieting.

It reported on the rise of gangs around the city, and how they were becoming bolder in their acts of theft, vandalism, and violence. Some gangs fought only against one another, while others, comprising tough "blackguards," roamed the streets to carry out acts of "wanton, senseless destruction . . . intimidating householders" by smashing their windows and threatening them.[1] Assaults on innocent citizens were taking place in the open streets. It had reached a point where "citizens are terrorised" by "these ruffians." The newspaper queried:

> It's a disgrace to any civilised community . . . all this done by a hooligan element. Is Dublin to remain helpless before this conduct?[2]

Citizens were asking the same question. Were the Gardaí and courts not able to protect them from the increasing criminality?

The appearance of gangs had been reported in the press for the previous two or three years. The largest and most dangerous were armed with barbaric weapons, used primarily, though not exclusively, against one another. And if any garda dared interfere they risked serious injury.

On 24 September 1934 the *Irish Times* headed an article on page 1: "Dublin charges: We are the animal gang." In court, the gang members defiantly proclaimed themselves to be "animal" gangs.[3]

The name arose from a dispute between newspaper-sellers and Republicans over the price to be charged for *An Phoblacht* and *Republican Congress*. On 12 September a crowd of newsboys marched to the offices of the Republican Congress in Frederick Lane and a violent brawl ensued, during which Frank Ryan, the editor of *Republican Congress,* declared that those involved were "little better than animals." The name "animal gang" was coined by newspapers, applied first to the newsboys and then to the hooligan gangs that operated in Dublin, some of which took up the name themselves.

A month later, in October, gangs from Townsend Street and North Cumberland Street made the news for their savage fighting. In Dublin District Court, Judge Little declared that the gang members "have no regard for the law or the basic principles of Christianity."[4]

By the time Jim Branigan put on his Garda uniform, the gang problem was expanding throughout the city. There now existed in Dublin what was being called a "gang culture," a breeding-ground for gangs proliferating throughout the inner city. It was becoming so bad that in some districts the Fire Brigade ambulances had to "carry axes with them for fear of encountering the gangs."[5] When several members were brought to court and were sentenced to a month in prison "there was some cheering in court." It was a small victory, considering what lay ahead.

Like all gardaí, Branigan was distressed by the growth of violent gangs. He had been especially frustrated in his early years, when he could do nothing about it, for he had mostly been posted like a sentry outside court buildings or as part of an escort for national or foreign officials, while the "real" policing was being carried out by other guards on genuine "active" duty. With the gang problem increasingly in the news, he was aching to get in on the action, confident that he could perform an important role.

——

The origin of Dublin's infamous gangs may be traced to a number of factors that conspired together in the early 1930s. This period has sometimes been called the "hungry thirties," when times were hard and spirits crushed, years of economic depression, unemployment, and poverty, which created idleness, boredom, and frustration, leading for many to disenchantment with society and a distrust of government and the political system. Including a dislike for the police and courts.

Unemployed men, young and old, bored and frustrated, gravitated towards street corners. They passed the time engaging in chat and repartee, commiserating and grousing. Here arose the seeds of the gangs' formation, ordinarily starting out as a form of innocuous "social club"—a "hierarchy" formed, with leaders and followers. Gradually, a gang culture would evolve. Different groups of men formed naturally along the lines of shared district and personal interests. While most of the men were harmless, others were tough and prone to misbehaviour.

Stephen Mooney grew up in Pimlico and remembers well: "You'd see the gangs hovering around, and you didn't go down around them, because they were *tough* guys. If they saw me with money they'd stop me and take the money off me."

Members were generally between eighteen and thirty-five. The gangs mostly took their names from the streets where they lived, some of the most notorious being those from Townsend Street, Gardiner Street, Stafford Street, Corporation Street, Foley Street, North King Street, Wolfe Tone Street, Waterford Street, and Sheriff Street. Around the Liberties the gangs from Ash Street, the Coombe and Marrowbone Lane were the most famous. Pride in "home" street made them very territorial in defending their turf against intruders. Some gangs, however, were more creative, such as the "Tigers" and the "Hawks' Nest Gang."

Gangs typically ranged in size from about twenty to as many as fifty. They normally had a loose social hierarchy of leaders and followers, with the older, tougher men emerging as leaders. In some districts, however, local criminal families could exert influence and gain control over the gangs, using them for their illicit activities. As with all gangs, there was a strong feeling of collective identity and bonding, a sense of brotherhood or "family," a loyalty to one another and a unified force against their rivals.

The gangs could be easily spotted, because, as Paddy Mooney (Stephen's brother) relates, the gangs "were *always* in groups . . . Oh, you'd keep your distance—and a very respectable distance." Some of them adopted a distinctive style of dress, some as simple as wearing a common type of cap, neckerchief, or shirt, or just a cap worn at a certain angle. John Joe Kennedy, a young member of the Ash Street gang in the 1930s and 40s, describes the dress of one of their hated rival gangs:

> They wore these black shirts with white ivory buttons. Oh, you could spot them a *mile away!* And they used to carry blades sewn into the beak of their caps. They used to take it off and give you a crack across the face with it. It was like a knife—oh, very dangerous.

This naturally led to different gangs engaging in an "arms race." By the end of his career Garda Branigan would amass a veritable museum collection of gang weapons: knives, knuckledusters, iron bars, hatchets, picks, razors, chains, saws, swords, and bayonets—all capable of bashing a foe's head or carving up his body. And doing the same to a garda.

————

When gangs clashed, residents were eye witnesses of the awful savagery. In the 1930s Mary Corbally lived in Corporation Street, in the famous Monto district, and brawls took place only a few feet below her tenement window. "I had a ringside seat . . . The animal gangs fighting and killing each other."

Their rivalries were bitter, and wild fighting was often fuelled by drink. Every gang wanted to establish a reputation for being tougher than their foes. "Most of the animal gangs around here," says Johnny Campbell, "were all dockers—the toughest men in Dublin," who mostly fought when they were unemployed.

Sometimes their skirmishes turned into real battles that lasted for hours and even days. Paddy Mooney recalls a prolonged battle royal around his Liberties tenement area:

> This fella I knew, they beat him into bits, and it led to a battle that lasted day after day. There was *hundreds* of fellas fighting all around Pimlico, Marrowbone Lane . . . knives, chains, forks of bicycles. People and shops had to put up their shutters.

His brother Stephen continues the tale:

> The animal gangs *battered* one another with chains, razors, bars, knives. Oh, yeah, they even had *bayonets*. Tommo Flynn, he led this one gang, and he found a sword, rotten with rust, it was like King Arthur's sword! And, by God, I'll tell you, he split many a skull with it!

After every encounter the gangs would be intent on settling the score later; thus their warfare continued from one battle to the next. Arch-enemies would carry out unexpected invasions of another's territory to catch them off guard.

One afternoon John Joe Kennedy and his Ash Street gang were enjoying a matinée at their local picture-house when a surprise attack occurred: "We were at the Tivoli, and a whole crowd from Stafford Street came over." His gang didn't have their weapons with them, so they had to use what they had, "fighting with fists, boots, knuckledusters, *anything* you had to defend yourself. Oh, you had to be tough to survive." Very often, when he and his mates would have to hike over to the Labour Exchange in Gardiner Street to collect their dole, the Gardiner Street and Corporation Street gangs lay in wait for them on their own turf. "We'd go over and we'd *get a hiding*."

In this world of violence, a garda had only his whistle and baton, and efforts to "suppress the new gang culture" met with little success.[6] Outnumbered and out-armed, guards were understandably intimidated by gangs who showed blatantly that they had no respect for police uniforms. The "pack mentality" of the gangs gave them collective strength. "The police were *afraid* of them—I *seen* that!" Timmy Kirwan vouches. "Oh, now and again they'd go against the animal gangs—but they always lost. Oh, they'd leave them alone . . . When there was gang warfare they wouldn't interfere." Occasionally a few brave guards would dare to take on gang members, says Kirwan. "Oh, policemen *would* get in rows . . . I was in a fight myself, fighting police." But too often they got the worst of it. Johnny Campbell tells how gang members were very savvy about handling a garda if he drew his baton on them:

> This man, Johnny—a policeman took out his baton and hit him. But he *knew* what to do—he took the guard's baton and kept twisting . . . *twisting* . . . around the guard's hand. And stopped the circulation of blood going through him. *Then* the garda was on the ground and your man murdered him, gave him an awful beating.

A small squad of local gardaí were no match for the gangs. As Séamus Breathnach documents in *The Irish Police*, there were "hundreds of assaulted gardaí" in this period.

In the 1930s gardaí were reluctant to engage in combat with gangs for another practical reason: they were not well protected by the injury laws. As Breathnach explains:

> Policemen got a raw deal from the legislation regarding compensation for injuries sustained. In effect, before a garda had a claim for full compensation he had either to be killed or maimed.[7]

The fact that a garda might be "beaten black-and-blue didn't account for anything," so long as he was not maimed. This meant suffering permanent disability. Consequently, "hundreds" of guards severely beaten in their duty found they had no claim to compensation.

In one illustrative case, Garda James Foley was beaten and kicked so viciously that his jaw was fractured and he was left in a thoroughly smashed condition, to the extent that even a year later he was only fit to perform light duties. Yet his claim for compensation was dismissed by the Dublin Circuit Court; only on appeal to the High Court later was he given a paltry £300. What message did this send to other gardaí out on the beat?

These were some of the harsh realities facing young Jim Branigan when he joined the Garda Síochána in the early 1930s. With gardaí who were understandably afraid of them, and lenient judges in the courts, it was no wonder that criminal gangs were in their heyday.

———

Meanwhile Branigan was honing his boxing skill, emboldened by his title of "heavyweight champion." He was now a goliath of a man, about six feet four inches tall and tipping the scale at nearly sixteen stone. Garda Paddy Daly, who would see him use his size to advantage when he later served with him, says: "Jim was a *huge* big man . . . with *big hands*." As Tony Ruane more descriptively puts it, "he had hands like shovels, like big forks . . . you know, like King Kong."

In peak physical condition, he was mastering both the offensive and the defensive skills of boxing, agile in movement and possessing quick reflexes. With a long reach and good jab he could usually keep opponents at bay.

In the period 1935–7 he boxed in numerous tournaments against RUC and British opponents as well as Continental Europeans. He especially welcomed facing the German boxers, who were so highly skilled that they pushed him to his limits. Win or lose, he was always certain to improve against them. At a tournament in Tipperary arranged between the Garda club and the German police he was matched with an opponent named Rosenfeldt, the German cruiserweight champion. Stronger and more seasoned, Rosenfeldt won on points, but Branigan was pleased to have held his own so well, learning a few new techniques in the process.

———

It was not until 1936, when Branigan was transferred to New Market Garda Station in the Liberties, that he had his first direct contact with local gangs. This happened to be the time when they were flexing their muscles, acting toughest, and daring to carry out more serious lawless acts. While the gangs had previously fought, mostly among themselves, they were now venturing into new illicit activities within the community, causing great alarm.

This transformation was caused in significant part by the influence of films now showing regularly in the cinemas. Hollywood's new genre of crime films was having a verifiable impact on some elements of both American and European audiences. The phenomenon was studied during the 1930s and 40s by sociologists and other academics, who had abundant evidence of the effect of crime films on criminal groups in large cities in America and Europe and now in Dublin. It would even be verified that American crime films influenced not only gang members but some of Nazi Germany's propaganda officials. Dublin's unsophisticated gangs were highly susceptible to influence by what they saw on the screen at their picture-houses.

In the early 1930s a number of blockbuster crime films awed audiences with their cunning and ruthless gangsters and their raw violence, as well as their criminal strategies for exploiting people for profit. Among them were *Little Caesar,* starring Edward G. Robinson as the feared killer Rico Bandello—a flimsy disguise for "Scarface" Al Capone. *Public Enemy,* featuring James Cagney as "an Irish-American street punk," exploded onto the screen, the story of a gangster who tried to make it big in the world of organised crime, followed by a host of similar films with Humphrey Bogart and George Raft. These films had an aura of reality, as they so closely replicated the lives of actual American criminals who were at that time making the daily headlines—Al Capone, John Dillinger, "Lucky" Luciano, "Machine Gun Kelly," "Pretty Boy" Floyd. The press—and now films—made their criminal exploits seem enthralling and rewarding. Gangsters seemed beyond the reach of the law, making the police look inept and bungling and the courts incompetent in dealing with them.

Gangsters were glorified on the screen, and their profitable crimes made to seem easily copied. These included extortion, robbery, gambling, protection rackets, and "fixing" horse races and boxing matches. Their rewards were lavish—sleek cars, grand houses, diamond rings and watches, swanky attire and, with their fedora worn at a jaunty angle, silk-clad molls on each arm—all achieved by the gangsters being "smarter and tougher" than the police, and willing to take chances. Best of all, gangsters enjoyed fame and celebrity for the crimes they flaunted. As Lee Horsley describes them:

> Movie gangsters such as Cagney and Robinson were heroes of dynamic gesture, strutting, snarling and posturing, possessing a blatant anarchic appeal . . . with emphasis on action and violence . . . wily and tough and law-defying.[8]

For Dublin's gangs, not only great entertainment but inspiration.

Meanwhile in Berlin, Hitler's minister of propaganda, Josef Goebbels, as well as leaders of the Gestapo, Stormtroopers, and ss, became aficionados of American gangster films, inspired to use some of the tactics they saw on the screen. In his superb history book *In the Garden of the Beasts*, Erik Larson documents the influence of such films on Nazi tactics during the 1930s, confirming "a deliberate effort to generate a kind of daily suspense, copied from American cinema and thrillers that helped keep people in line."[9]

To John Joe Kennedy and his fellow-gangsters, lessons learnt on the screen seemed simple enough; maybe they too could imitate some of the gangster activities of Cagney and Bogart. They began by acting the role of American gangsters—in manner, lingo, body language, facial expressions, tossing around phrases like "You mugs," "Squealers are rats," "That guy's a sucker!" and "those crummy, flat-footed coppers." They packed the Tivoli, Rialto and Mayro night after night, seeing some films over and over, learning all the dialogue. Adults around the Liberties were witness to their new gangster persona—and didn't like it. Lar Redmond's mother loathed the films, considering them a dangerous influence on local youth and men; to her "the pictures were a pernicious and diabolical influence."[10]

It was only a matter of time before some of Dublin's gangs would try to copy the criminal activities so smoothly pulled off by screen gangsters. The most logical were the protection racket, extortion, and illicit money-lending. Paddy Mooney saw it all unfold around him at first hand between about 1932 and 1945. To him the socio-psychological impact of the films on local gangs was perfectly evident:

> You must appreciate that at that time the gangster films were coming out of America, and they'd [local gangs] think, "*Oh,* that's something *we* could operate here!" So, animal gangs got involved in racketeering. They'd go out and terrorise a neighbourhood. They threatened to burn shops and stop people going into them if there wasn't a sum of money paid—oh, the protection racket was *going.* They all liked to be tough guys . . . Ah, sure they were all "gangsters."

In pubs they could be overheard plotting their "new business," telling one another to "clam up," as Cagney would say, if they talked too loud. Cagney became the favourite gangster archetype. He proved to the gangs that you didn't have to be big to be tough. Some fellas exhibited perfect imitations of his swagger, snarl, and speech. Loan-sharking, bribery, meddling with betting were among their new enterprises. Sometimes their strategy was to leave their own community largely alone and venture into other districts to carry out their illegal activities. Which, of course, brought them into conflict with opposing gangs.

The Gardaí were inevitably drawn into their expanded criminal activities of threatening and exploiting citizens and shopkeepers. However, as loan-sharking, bribery, extortion and the protection racket were essentially clandestine, "behind-the-scenes" activities, there was usually little a garda could do. If he happened upon gang members actually threatening or using strong-arm tactics on a person, he risked injury by interfering. The Gardaí were in a real quandary over how to cope with the growing gang activity in Dublin.

In 1936 Branigan finally entered the scene. His previous experience in breaking up brawls had largely involved trying to separate drunken bowsies. But once he was stationed at New Market, the local gangs became his personal problem, one he was not about to ignore:

> When I came to the area first, they were rough—and you *had* to be rough *with them*. They'd give you a chance to fight—and if you didn't, they hit. I got a few clips. [But] I got a chance to fight and I *took* it.[11]

Once out on the beat, at the age of twenty-six, he knew the local Liberties gangs would test him. He would also soon learn of their particular moral, or cultural, code of courage and fairness. One thing he instinctively knew from his first day on the beat was that, when confronted by gang members, he could not back down or show a hint of cowardice. That would be the ultimate mistake for a young garda. This is confirmed by Garda John Murphy, who says flatly: "With the animal gangs, you *had* to fight your way on the street. And if you wouldn't, they'd *kill* you. But he was a heavyweight champion, which stood to him. Tough, *tough*." They knew who he was. And *what* he was. Yet he was still just one garda.

Despite their lawlessness, gangs had respect for a man's courage, and fairness. But it was a form of respect that had to be *earned*. Stephen Mooney cites a memorable case of a gang member from the Liberties who tangled with a foe from a rival gang:

> The Mayro cinema was a borderline cinema for two animal gangs. Now there was this fella, Charlie, with a head like a bucket and good with his fists. He went to the Mayro, and the north-side gang seen him, and there was a battle royal took place. Oh, they nearly *killed* him! Well, Charlie, he went over *again*, by *himself*, with a chain—and he just *lashed* into them. And the north-side gang thought it was *great*! 'Cause he was *unafraid*! Charlie then was a hero! And he became like a mediator between the gangs when there was rows.

Gangs both disliked and distrusted most gardaí: they were generally seen as the "enemy." When gangs and gardaí clashed, the latter often went in with batons flying and asked questions later. Yet, as Branigan admitted, "they had no fear of a man because he is a garda."[12] Nonetheless, as in many gangster films, they recognised a difference between "good cops" and "bad cops." A "good cop" could be one who simply gave them a "fair shake" in life.

Despite Branigan's reputation as a boxing champion, which gang members admired, to gain their real respect he would eventually have to earn his "street credentials," which were quite different from those in the ring. His first physical encounters with gangs are not documented, but they most probably occurred in 1936, his first full year on the beat. They may have involved facing several men on a street corner, or having to contend with a larger gang row. Years later, in retrospect, he shared his feelings about these dangerous early confrontations:

> If I saw a street fight involving gangs, I used to steel myself and walk into the middle of them . . . sailed into a battle between thugs and disarmed them of such horrific weapons as knives, razor blades, knuckledusters and axes. I didn't consider myself brave . . . in fact, I always had a feeling of tension in the pit of my stomach. But I went in just the same—it was *my job*.[13]

And never with his baton drawn—for, as his friend Garda Matt Mulhall repeatedly said, "His fists were his baton—and he knew how to use them." For gang members, seeing a garda plunge into their midst, apparently without fear, was quite a revelation. Of this they took close notice.

As a member of the Ash Street gang with whom Branigan would often clash over the years, John Joe Kennedy saw him close up in street fights, "and he'd fight the best of them, *hard* fellas." He was willing to fight them in the open street, on *their* terms, either bare-knuckle or with his black leather gloves on.

From her tenement window in Meath Street, Bridie Chambers often saw him taking on gang members: "Lugs Branigan was the *head man* around here. A fine, big strong man, and he'd have a go with *anybody*—he'd box them. Everybody had respect for him." Tommy Lowry, born in Mercer Street in 1929, often watched Branigan daring to stand up to multiple gang members:

> I have memories of Jim when there was trouble here with the animal gangs—and Jim was only a young man in New Market station then. But Jim Branigan was worth a *hundred policemen!* Because they had *respect* for him!

Inter-gang battles were the wildest and most risky. One of Branigan's greatest assets was his ability to detect the ringleaders in gangs, even amidst the chaos of a row. Throughout the years this quick perception would be indispensable in quelling riots and rows. Once he spotted the main ringleaders he headed straight for them, without hesitation. Paddy Mooney witnessed this fearlessness:

> The animal gangs, dozens and dozens of them, always had something in their hands. . . . knives, chains. But Branigan, he was *unafraid!* If there was a hundred of them there, he wouldn't be a bit impressed by them—I actually witnessed this now. He beat a lot of them, and he was responsible for bringing a lot of them to court. But he was *unafraid*—I'll say that much for him.

In this period probably the two most renowned street fighters in the city were Spike McCormack from Gardiner Street and "Joe-Boy" Collins in the Liberties. However, Bernard Neary would proclaim that by the end of his career Jim "Lugs" Branigan was "the greatest street-fighter this city has ever seen." Though this may be disputed, there was no-one more fearless. He would inevitably suffer his share of injuries, rarely agreeing to hospital treatment. As he would one day come to say about his countless street battles, "I have 'war scars' to prove it."

―――

Nothing so enhanced his reputation for courage and sheer toughness—and gained the respect of the criminal gangs—as his confrontations with Travellers. This is a little-known aspect of his Garda career, one not mentioned in the newspapers or officially documented. It was during the 1930s and 40s that the traditional trades and crafts of the Travelling community were being made obsolete. They had lived a nomadic life, making circuits around the country in their horse-drawn caravans, providing useful services to rural people: tinsmithing, horse-dealing, doing seasonal farm labour, repairing fences and barns. They occupied a beneficial niche in rural life. As this role was rendered obsolete they gravitated towards towns and cities, settling in encampments on waste ground for a more sedentary life. Here they turned to scrap-collecting, performing odd jobs and, too often, begging. Some of the men created problems by drinking heavily and fighting. In many communities they were treated as pariahs.

Several Traveller families settled on waste ground around the Liberties, especially during the harsh winter months. For the most part there was an "apartheid" system between local residents and Travellers, and most shops and pubs barred them. They travelled around collecting scrap metal, clothing and rags to sell to the local ragmen. On Saturdays they often meandered into Meath Street and Thomas Street to shop at dealers' stalls and to drink at the few pubs that would admit them. It was then that the trouble could ignite.

Travellers were known to be the best bare-knuckle fighters in Ireland. For centuries they had inter-clan contests to select the "king" of bare-knuckle fighting. Young Traveller lads aspired to be good with their fists. Local gang members wanted nothing to do with them when it came to fist fights; and for local gardaí they posed a dreaded problem when drinking and brawling. While there was much open prejudice and discrimination against Travellers by the settled community, and by gardaí as well, Branigan made every effort to treat them fairly and with equality.

Jack Roche grew up in Meath Street, helping his father in the family's popular vegetable shop. On Saturdays he watched Travellers bring in bundles of rags to sell to Harry Sive, the ragman, just across the street. Once they got paid they headed directly for a certain pub. Soon afterwards, trouble would erupt. Tossed out of the pub, they fought on the street. If other guards were on duty that day they would customarily let them punch it out, until all were sprawled on the ground. Interfering would only have placed themselves at risk.

Some local people saw this as great entertainment. But when Branigan was on duty things were different:

> Now, when the Itinerants would get paid I'd see the fights. And *then* Jim would come into action! Several of them fighting, but that *didn't matter* to Jim—he'd go in and give them a few digs and clatter . . . And he'd sort out the whole matter. They held him in *great* respect.

Even more dangerous was having to enter their encampment to bring a few men down to the Garda station. This happened from time to time when one was accused of theft or some disorderly act requiring the station sergeant to order his men to "bring him in." The intrusion of uniformed gardaí in a Traveller camp only strained relations further between the two factions. At such times Jim Branigan often did the unthinkable: he volunteered to march in alone and bring out the suspects. Carrying no baton. He was exercising his discretion, as he saw it. But how could his station sergeant have granted him such permission?

John Joe Kennedy and his gang mates never ceased being amazed at seeing Branigan assume a lone-guard role against errant Travellers, on their own turf:

> He got his reputation from fighting the likes of the Tinkers, going in and out. There used to be a couple of old yards, and there was about ten caravans there. And the minute rows started he would be up there—like a shot! He'd come by *himself!* And he'd go in! Most of them were chimney sweeps, like the Wards, and we used to see them fight. And they were *hard,* they could *fight*—all bare-knuckle. But it was *fair* fighting. But Branigan,

he was tough and *feared nothing*. If there was a mob—he'd go *right* in, digging and digging. And he could *take it,* he could take the punishment. So he'd go in and give them two warnings: "*Stop!* Or *else!*" And he'd walk in between them . . . Oh, he'd fight the best of them.

As with the local gangs, Travellers abided by a code of respect for a man's courage and fairness in a fight. After the dust settled they usually accompanied him to the Garda station without a problem.

———

As his reputation throughout the city grew, many people had begun calling him "Lugs." He not merely disliked it, affirms his friend Garda Séamus Quinn, but "he *detested* the name 'Lugs.'" By now, in the midst of his boxing career, it was assumed by most people that his large ears were the result of pounding by leather gloves. They had not known him as a child, nor seen his early photograph, which clearly proved otherwise.

The origin of the nickname remains disputed. According to one story he was given it by an unsavoury member of a criminal family, and it was for this reason that he loathed it.[14] However, Tommy Lowry claims he was being called "Lugs" before his Garda days. Childhood playmates may have given him the name; or the railway yard bullies may well have taunted him with the derisive term. His surviving children are not able to trace the origin.

What *is* known is that, from the day he put on his Garda uniform at the age of twenty-one, he would not tolerate being called "Lugs" by anyone, be they strangers, friends, fellow-gardaí, even superiors. People therefore variously called him "Jim," "Mr Branigan," "Garda Branigan"; later his fellow-gardaí would call him "Branno." Dare anyone let slip with a "How'ya, Lugs," and they were admonished on the spot with a stern scolding, or even a "clip"—his term for a smack. Even if a kindly granny mistakenly uttered his nickname, she too was promptly corrected. Children who knew no better, having heard it used commonly by people not in his presence, might well hail him as "Lugs," or even "Mr Lugs." The scolding they received depended on their age.

It was natural enough that so many Dubliners would refer to him as Lugs Branigan, as the words fit together phonetically so well; but respectful reporters never put it in print. And, as far as is known, it was not used in his boxing world of the 1930s, when ring nicknames were common. As the years went by he was known to almost everyone as Lugs Branigan—but safely out of earshot.

———

By 1937, with nearly ninety bouts to his credit and roughly a fifty-fifty record of wins and losses, he was a valued member of the Garda Boxing Club. Though not one of the team's top-echelon boxers, he was good enough to be included on their trips to foreign countries for tournaments. By this stage he had learnt something about himself in the ring: he did not possess a fighter's "killer instinct." A pugilist learns this only by being pitted against opponents who do possess it. This was evident in some of his matches against Continental Europeans, particularly Germans. It had never been his motivation to severely beat an opponent in order to gain a knock-out: instead he enjoyed the skill of the sport that resulted in a win on points. To him, boxing was more like a chess match than a back-alley brawl. He thought of it as a "civilised" contest. In fact he didn't even want to hurt his opponent. This he attributed to an early bout he had about 1932 or 33, when he was starting out:

> I broke a fellow's jaw with a blow one night . . . and it affected me. I felt terribly sorry for it, and could see no point in trying to punish or maim anybody. I think this incident was always present in my mind when I boxed.[15]

Many of the men he was now facing in 1937 were clearly not of that mind. They were "sluggers," not interested in fancy footwork or artful jabs leading to a win on points. "Hitler's fighters" always seemed hungry for knock-outs, and the faster the better.

In late 1937 the Garda Boxing Club announced that it would be making a trip to Germany the following year to participate in a big international tournament. It was to be the club's first trip to the Continent, and Branigan was thrilled to be going. It was an honour—and an opportunity to enhance his stature. Garda boxers could show off Ireland's boxing talent, and take in sightseeing trips as well.

Pre-war Germany was hailed by some people as a miracle of revival and modernisation. The esteemed *Irish Times* published a lengthy article headed "Germany under Adolph Hitler: Some attractive features of the new regime":

> The Germans were down and out, had lost confidence in themselves . . . had no hope of revival. Now all that has disappeared. There is no doubt whatever that Adolph Hitler has done some great things for the German people.
>
> Germany was a second, or even third rate power . . . Now she is one of the strongest countries in the world.[16]

On 4 January 1938, two days before Branigan's twenty-eighth birthday, the Garda Boxing Club embarked on its sea voyage to Germany, brimming with enthusiasm and confidence. Neither Branigan nor the others were seasoned travellers, and they suffered from seasickness and insomnia. When they reached Germany they shuffled off the ship weak and wobbly. Inexplicably, whoever had arranged their itinerary had them scheduled to fight that very night—in a matter of hours.

On the evening of Thursday 7 January, after three days at sea, the Irish boxers were escorted into Berlin's magnificent Sports Palace. They had never seen anything like it before, and for a few moments it made them forget how debilitated they felt. The Sports Palace was crammed to capacity for the boxing tournament, which featured contestants from a number of European countries, all of whom were top-rate selections. Major sports events in Germany always drew elite figures from the government, military, business, and entertainment. On this evening, in the prime front seats, were many of Hitler's top officers, wealthy industrialists, and foreign diplomats. Most conspicuous were Rudolf Hess, Deputy Führer to Hitler and one of his most loyal henchmen. Close by was Albert Speer, Hitler's favoured architect as well as minister of armaments and war production. Both men were Nazi royalty, and treated as such.

When Jim Branigan stepped into the ring he glanced over at the opposite corner to size up his opponent, a highly touted Danish boxer named Nielson, who was well rested and eager to swing away. He knew virtually nothing about Nielson—nor would it have made much difference. At the sound of the bell he gamely summoned strength from some inner source and determinedly stepped forward. Seasickness had left him feeling limp. His power was obviously lacking as he took hard punches to his already weak stomach. It would be a three-round bout of pure torture.

In the early seconds of the first round he managed to land a few harmless punches, then faded fast as he lost stamina. His opponent, sensing the advantage, pounded away relentlessly. From that point on it was a matter of sheer willpower to survive being knocked out, as the *Irish Times* reported:

> In the light heavyweight class Branigan met the Danish boxer, Nielson, and though he scored at close range in the first round, could not last the pace against a strong and fast opponent.
>
> In the third round, the Irishman went down, but was up again before the count exceeded two. The Dane, however, then drove him into the corner with merciless blows and the referee stopped the fight.[17]

He had lost on a "technical knock-out"—not a *real* knock-out. His record was intact. Nor did his Garda mates fighting that night fare any better, as "all four Irish boxers lost in their respective categories."

At the end of the evening a spokesman for the Irish squad was eager to explain to Reuters: "We are making our first trip to the Continent and we are not very satisfied with our showing,"[18] hastening to add that the arduous sea voyage had made the boxers ill, sapping their strength and stamina. He cited two by name who had clearly not been in top condition: "Branigan and Kerry were tired after their journey and fought under their usual form." Dick Hearns, representing the team, stepped forward to bluntly tell the *Irish Times*: "The boxers had to fight on the same day they landed—after three and a half days' sea voyage!"[19]

Branigan refused to offer any excuses. He was not one to use excuses in his life. But he was clearly embarrassed by his poor performance and hoped to redeem himself in his next bout, in Leipzig three days later. In the meantime he would hope to regain his appetite, get some decent sleep, and renew his strength, as well as doing some sightseeing.

Travelling through Germany, and especially Berlin, the Irish boxers could not but be awed by the modernity and prosperity they saw. Bustling cities with stately, towering buildings, streamlined roads, modern automated factories, sophisticated shops. A people proud and confident in their attitude. Patriotic, with flags everywhere. A country functioning at full throttle, employment booming, population well dressed. Branigan was especially impressed by the physical fitness and spirit of German youth. Everywhere he went, without fail, he saw young lads and girls dressed in crisp uniforms, marching spiritedly, with bright eyes and exuding ambition. Well fed, well groomed, athletic-looking, as if they physically worked out every day—which they did, he learnt. In fact there was a fitness programme for the entire nation, sponsored by the government. Sports were emphasised because they taught discipline, order, competition and unity. To Branigan, it seemed a utopia.

His trip to Germany made a positive and lasting impression on him, something he would talk about admiringly for years to come, despite the war that was about to break out.

———

On the night of 10 January, in Leipzig, Garda Branigan's opportunity for redemption in the ring arrived. What knowledge he had of his opponent, a German champion named Pietsch, we do not know. Probably not much.

In Germany, Pietsch was widely known as an aggressive boxer and "knock-out artist," intent on destroying his opponent in the shortest possible time, to make the best impression on those watching him. To Pietsch, winning on points or by a technical knock-out was always a disappointment. He had been groomed as a sort of German gladiator, capable of putting other boxers on the canvas within seconds. His knock-out record was important to him.

Did he know that his Irish opponent had never been knocked out in nearly ninety fights? And that his record of having never been knocked out was just as important to him?

The bouts were taking place in Leipzig Zoo before a wildly enthusiastic crowd. As always, some Nazi royalty began to enter, with their usual entourage. Some people in the crowd stood up to see one figure in particular—who was hard to miss. In all his magisterial splendour, attired in his white uniform, in strutted Field-Marshal Hermann Göring, waving imperiously to the crowd. At nearly eighteen stone, he had a girth befitting his domineering and gregarious character. He had been a First World War flying ace and was a renowned sportsman and competitor. He liked blood sports, including boxing. Seated not far away was Josef Goebbels, the minister of propaganda, a fierce anti-Semite who was instrumental in forging the "final solution," leading to the Holocaust.

Into this charged setting stepped the young garda from Dublin, ready for his three-round match. Having rested, and regained some appetite, he felt decidedly better than in Berlin three days before yet far from his full strength, eager to at least put on a better performance and retrieve his pride.

Pietsch possessed a wicked hook. Branigan liked to get in close during the first round, mix it up, placing himself within perfect range. Within seconds of the opening bell he felt a jolting, numbing right hook, which dropped him. By instinct, he pushed hard with his gloves and rose from the canvas. There were still nearly nine minutes of fighting remaining.

The sudden blow, like an explosive piston, had been so devastating, both physically and psychologically, that he must have realised he was in for a survival struggle. If he could put up a defence and land a few punches he might make it through. His paramount determination was to go the distance.

Three times he went down in the first round. Blows to the body weakened him, causing his head to drop, framing the target for another hook.

Three more times he went down in the second round. To everyone's astonishment, he kept rising groggily from the canvas, finding his equilibrium, then standing his ground or lunging forward. Each time Pietsch, the referee and spectators expected him not to make it—all probably hoping, for Branigan's sake, that he would be unable to climb to his feet for further punishment.

The contest was not halted, though it was clearly over. Could Pietsch add another knock-out to his record?

In the final round Branigan was dropped three more times, collapsing hard. By this time it was apparent that the Irishman had won huge admiration from the German crowd—from no-one, probably, more than Pietsch himself.

Finally, with only thirty seconds remaining, the referee stepped between the two men and halted the bout, whereupon there erupted a thunderous applause. By all accounts of both German and Irish reporters, it was as much—if not more—for the Irish policeman as for the German champion.

In one of the most remarkable contradictions of his contradictory life, Jim Branigan, by officially losing on a "technical knock-out," had in fact won, in what he would come to regard as the greatest and most memorable "victory" in his boxing career. Because he had not been "knocked out," his record was intact.

Thanks to both the Irish and the German press, he returned home days later victorious, his feat having been lauded by reporters who wrote of the admiration of the crowd for the Irishman's raw courage. Some German newspapers had lavished as much praise on Branigan as on Pietsch. At home it was seen as a tribute not only to the Garda Boxing Club but to Ireland. And it earned him a new title, "Battling Branigan"—one that would stick for life.

The ultimate irony was that if he had actually won the fight in a conventional manner it would have made little lasting impression on the press and public as the years passed. But having survived *nine knock-downs,* in a weakened state, at the hands of the German gladiator—each time refusing to accept defeat and rising from the canvas—he gained lasting admiration and respect. For it had been more about *character* than boxing skill. And *this* everyone remembered.

Back home and out on his daily beat he was hailed by friends and strangers with congratulations, handshakes, and pats on the back. It had given even greater meaning to his "fearlessness," and greatly enhanced his reputation. Even some gang members stopped him in the street to offer their congratulations.

Thirty-five years later, upon reflection, he shared his sentiments about the experience with the *Evening Herald*:

> I became known as a man who could soak up punishment, for I was never knocked out. And I have the distinction of being knocked down nine times inside of three rounds and still staying on my feet.[20]

———

In 1939, with his thirtieth birthday approaching, he continued boxing, though perhaps not with the same zeal after nearly ten years in the ring. His pattern of social life remained much the same, his favourite pastimes still being attending dances, cinemas, and sports events. But his close group of friends was shrinking, as some of the lads got married and had children and their family life now came first. Now nearly thirty, he had been giving more serious thought to his domestic future as well—if ever he found the right partner in life. While he seemed open to the prospect of marrying, he didn't feel any sense of urgency.

One day in the summer of 1939 "Battling Branigan" was given bad news by the Garda Boxing Club's doctor, the hardest blow he had received in all his boxing days. By now he had amassed a record of nearly 140 boxing matches, still splitting the wins and losses—not to mention the countless rounds of serious sparring over a decade, always taking on tougher opponents with more powerful punches each year, and always taking pride in being the fighter who "could absorb punishment," as he phrased it.

The club's doctor had been keeping a close eye on Branigan, probably more so than the boxer realised. At twenty-nine he was undeniably in excellent physical condition, having apparently weathered thousands of hard blows. Nonetheless the doctor detected signs he didn't like. While he admired Branigan's determination and his willingness to "soak up" punishment to keep his "no knock-out" record intact, the doctor knew it was a mistake, realising that Branigan would never be a "quitter." It was unlikely that he was ready to throw in the towel on his boxing career. The decision was entirely in the hands of the doctor.

Branigan may have seen the blow coming. Not one to beat around the bush, the doctor told him straight out that he was concerned about possible brain damage, and as a precaution wanted him to put an end to his boxing career. How Branigan reacted to this news we don't know, but he apparently put up no resistance, respectful of the doctor's authority.

Some years later, telling a journalist how he had always been a "glutton for punishment" in the ring, he admitted that the "doctor ordered him to quit fighting," flat out:

> I had to retire prematurely because I was taking too much punishment. The Garda doctor told me that this was bad, and too many blows to the head could cause brain damage.[21]

There was no more concise—or convincing—way to put it. However, Branigan's choice of the term "premature" suggests that he had had every intention of continuing fighting for some years to come.

Even after complying with the doctor's order to terminate his boxing career, he continued his standard boxing regimen in the gym, doing calisthenics, weight-lifting, skipping, punching the light and heavy bags, even engaging in light sparring sessions with boxers younger than himself.

Then, in yet another contradiction in his life, "it was when I gave up fighting that I developed a *big punch*—I worked at strengthening my punching on the bags, and weight-lifting." Yet he never offered his rationale for this puzzling decision. Did he foresee a practical purpose for it?

———

As the decade ended he felt satisfaction in his first ten years as a garda. He had won the respect of Dubliners, established a reputation not only for courage and fearlessness but for fairness, and had made real progress in controlling the criminal gangs, at least those on his turf around the Liberties:

> I waged a sort of private war against the gangs . . . In my years in the old New Market station I made considerable headway in cleaning the streets of gang warfare.[22]

Considering that he had often acted as a sort of one-man battalion, it was quite an accomplishment. The toughest of the gang members even admitted to admiring him.

But he would soon find that the gang era in Dublin was far from over, for what the newspapers would call gang "battles" were yet to come. And he would play a leading role in finally breaking their reign.

Chapter 5 ∾

| THE "BATTLE OF BALDOYLE"

"The 'Animal Gangs' had their last fling in the 'Battle of Baldoyle'."

> (*Evening Herald*, 22 JANUARY 1973)

"In the 'Battle of Baldoyle' the rioting was led by 'Hannigan's Army,' recruited from the Coombe. The 'troops' had knuckledusters, a sword, a dagger, a butcher's knife. Guards saw the crowd run in all directions."

> (*Irish Times*, 20 NOVEMBER 1940)

"I knew there was a rumble on. I saw a bunch of them apparently conspiring on the corner. They were all villains with the animal gang. My suspicions were already aroused."

> (GARDA JIM BRANIGAN)

The 1940s dawned ominously. Beyond Ireland's shores a world war was looming, and the Government declared a state of national emergency. Germany was about to march into neighbouring countries, unleashing its terrible war machine and revealing its true intentions throughout the continent.

As people fled, fought, and died, neutral Ireland essentially went about its life as usual. There were, of course, inconveniences, such as the rationing of tea, cigarettes, and petrol. Such luxuries as bananas and oranges would vanish from the markets. A black-out would be imposed at night. The Air-Raid Precautions Act provided for the protection of people and property from injury or damage in the event of attack from the air—which no-one really worried about. Nonetheless air-raid sirens were installed, a warden service was established, and flimsy above-ground concrete bomb shelters built, known derisively as "hat boxes."

For Branigan and his fellow-gardaí, the war meant trying to thwart the flourishing black market in rationed items, enforcing the black-out, inspecting bomb shelters, and assisting in air-raid drills.

Those who closely followed news of the war were inclined to give thanks for their privileged neutral status, which spared them the horrors of warfare. On 10 May 1940 Dubliners picked up their *Evening Herald* to read the chilling headline:

> Hitler leading his army—Germans swoop on Holland, Belgium and Luxembourg.[1]

"In a series of lightning strikes in a single night," the German army had successfully invaded all three countries. It was worrying for Irish people to see how other small countries were so suddenly and easily conquered. Those who were politically astute realised that Ireland's neutrality would be honoured only so long as Hitler wished. German forces had also bombed several French cities and launched air strikes on some British bases in France. Incendiary bombs were even dropped at Chilham, near Canterbury.

The fall of France in May 1940 stunned Irish people, as it did the rest of the world. On 14 May the *Irish Independent's* headline reported the bad news: "Germans continue fierce onslaught: Allies retire."[2] The article went on to describe how "in a great battle . . . huge German forces were hurled against British, French, Belgian and Dutch troops . . . Thousands of tanks in action."

It was scarcely two years since Jim Branigan had been in Germany as a guest, given lavish treatment and sightseeing tours of Berlin, Leipzig, and other areas. He had been greatly impressed with the dynamic new Germany. Now Hitler and his Third Reich, led by some of those who had sat at the ringside for his boxing matches, were seen as a menace to freedom and civilisation.

———

Meanwhile, as Europeans were fighting for survival, lawlessness in Dublin was increasing. Though Garda Branigan had made headway in reining in gang activity on his turf, other gangs were still carrying out their clashes. It was made worse by the fact that they were now taking some of their skirmishes into the public arena, at dancehalls and sports events, amidst huge crowds, putting innocent people at risk.

On 23 March 1940, in what the *Irish Times* headlined "Dublin football venue onslaught," a row broke out at a match between Mountain View and St Stephen's United in the Junior Combination Cup. In the midst of the match the "Ash Street animal gang tangled with their cross-Liffey rivals, the Stafford Street gang . . . as blood was spilled on the terraces of the Dublin football ground."[3] Spectators scrambled to get clear of the fighting.

On 24 March the *Irish Press* reported: "Batons drawn at Dublin football match," this one between St James's Gate and Cork United at the Iveagh Grounds in Crumlin. There were more than twenty thousand spectators in attendance when brawling erupted, and a number of people were "knocked down and trampled on in a mad stampede" that followed.[4] Two days later, following a melee at Drumcondra soccer grounds, nine youths were charged with attempted murder. On 28 March "gardaí were rushed to Donnybrook" to quell a bloody fight between "rival gangs who came into conflict."[5] Peaceful citizens were becoming fearful of attending their favourite sports events.

The pervasive lawlessness and violence could break out anywhere. On the night of Saturday 11 May 1940 the manager of the Olympia Theatre called the Gardaí to report that two men on entering had refused to pay for their tickets. Within minutes Garda Fitzgerald arrived, confronted the men, and asked them to leave. They assaulted him without hesitation, as described by a witness:

> One man attacked him, punching him about the head with clenched fists ... When he slipped down both men punched him in the head. His nose began to bleed and he got a black eye ... His tunic was saturated in blood.[6]

No patrons stepped forward to aid the fallen garda. When several more gardaí arrived the two men were arrested. One was found to have an iron bar in his hand.

The blatant disregard for the law and disrespect for the guards was a mounting problem. Policemen were not only beaten but murdered. In the early 1940s the "rate of murdered policemen had reached a threatening scale, six men being killed between 1940 and 1942."[7]

Some of the crimes were "big-time" jobs. One Monday morning in the open streets of Dublin there was a daring robbery. As described by the *Evening Herald*, it was like a dramatic scene straight out of an explosive James Cagney film:

> A terrific gun-battle took place in Holles Street this morning when armed men attacked two police officers conveying State mail ... Two machine-guns opened fire from the cars as the Guards shot it out with attackers.[8]

Dublin's streets rang with the "rat-tat-tat" of machine-gun fire and screeching tyres of the getaway car in their high-speed escape. The increasing violence by gangs and criminals was becoming a "menace which appeared to threaten the very fabric of Irish society."[9]

———

On 13 May 1940 people in Dublin were in high spirits, enjoying an early burst of summer weather that "has brought out flimsy frocks, open-necked shirts, light sandals and bathing costumes," wrote the *Evening Herald*:

> Into the open air this morning from homes in every part of the city the first great trek of holiday makers . . . young men and women on bicycles, hikers, fathers with fishing rods . . .[10]

Sports enthusiasts were delighted with the onset of warm weather, as many matches as well as horse and greyhound races were scheduled. In particular, the Baldoyle Races were always one of the most popular sports events of the season. On Monday 13 May things got off to a great start. "The overflowing attendance made for an exciting day," wrote the *Irish Independent*.[11]

Tuesday promised to be even better. Racing aficionados scanning the "Baldoyle Selections" in the *Irish Independent* learnt that there were some unusually good races shaping up, such as the Williamstown Plate for two-year-olds, while the Claremont Plate had an array of "good class stayers in the card."[12] The "ladies of fashion" would also be in competitive spirit on Tuesday, as it was their day to show off their style, all hoping to be photographed for the next day's newspapers. With the prospect of glorious weather, the *Irish Independent* promised:

> The racing at Baldoyle to-day will not wane in interest.[13]

———

In the early morning of 14 May, Garda Jim Branigan expected an uneventful day ahead. In fact it promised to be unusually quiet, as many of the local gang members were sure to be out at the Baldoyle Races for most of the day. He left New Market Garda Station to begin his day's rounds. By now he knew almost every living soul along his way, and all about them—at least, what he needed to know. He had made it his business to learn a lot about the local gang members and their background and habits.

As he walked along the Coombe, everything seemed normal. The usual dogs barked at the morning milkman and his horse-drawn cart. Then he began to feel that something was slightly "out of its natural order." That was the best way he would be able to describe it later. "Looking back now after years . . . I *know* I was gifted with some indefinable magic or psychology . . ."[14] Says Alick: "My father could *realise* if something 'wasn't quite right'—an *instinct*." Declan elaborates:

> He had *great foresight*. He had this *feel* . . . that he could *see* that something was *wrong*! Feel the presence of wrongdoing. My father always got to know what was *going* to happen . . . He'd know that something was going down, and he could pre-empt!

Garda Dan Walsh simply says, "He just *had something* there . . . that you can't put your finger on." Garda Gerald Byrne often marvelled at him as well. "I *studied* him . . . I'd watch Branigan . . . The touch . . . a certain *way* he had. He was very, very good. *Absolutely.*" Retired Chief Superintendent Michael Reid ultimately concluded that "he was *intuitive*" at an astonishing level, and was able to sense and decipher things that others missed.

Whatever it was, it was definitely working in the early morning of 14 May 1940. The trouble was that, while it placed him on high alert, raising his curiosity and suspicions, it provided no answers. At least not yet. If something was indeed out of natural synchronisation in his Liberties he would watch for some palpable signs.

As he continued on his beat down the Coombe and up Meath Street it wasn't long before the first sign appeared. He knew that local residents were creatures of habit, especially the early-morning people, like market dealers, delivery men, carters, shopkeepers. Most never varied their schedule by more than a minute. And so it immediately caught his attention when he spotted some figures who were *never* out on the street so early in the morning.

Unemployed men had no use for early-morning hours. Strangely enough, on this morning there were a few of them shuffling along the pavement, looking out of place in the rising sun. Not long afterwards he spotted a few more of their pals traipsing along in the same direction. They met at a corner, stood around with hands in pockets, and began chatting. Pubs, their usual first destination of the day, were not open yet, which made their behaviour all the more curious. Branigan decided to be patient and not approach them yet.

Gradually, more men ambled along and congregated at a few street corners. At this point Branigan was convinced that his intuition was valid:

> The streets had been quiet when I came on duty earlier in the morning. But when I saw crowds of men gathering at street corners all around my beat I *sensed* we were in for a rough day. I recognised them all, and they were all villains, many of whom had connections with the animal gangs. I was determined there would be no trouble in *my* area.[15]

He remembered hearing over the past week some faint whispers among dealers about "some trouble on," but nothing to act on. Could this somehow be related? Around mid-morning he decided it was time to find out. Men were now clustered at the corners of Meath Street and Francis Street as well as the Coombe. They ranged in age from about eighteen or nineteen, like John Joe Kennedy, to their mid-thirties. Some were known hardchaws, toughs, others merely followers.

As he approached the first group he assumed they would be secretive, perhaps hostile towards his intrusion. It was best, he decided, to be assertive but not accusing. "I pushed in among them. 'I hope you are not going to start any trouble today, lads,' I growled in my toughest tone."[16] To his surprise, they were congenial, in "gay form." This immediately furthered his suspicions, as they were acting out of character. He knew when interrogating suspects that deviations in normal behaviour, social demeanour or speech were often telling signs. "They chatted me up and dallied in conversation, as if to prove there was to be no 'bull' [fight] today."

The façade didn't fool him. "I was having none of their sweet talk." One thing was perfectly clear: the men were waiting for something to happen. His intuition now strongly told him it was a major "rumble," as he put it. But where, and at what hour?

———

A few streets away he encountered another "bunch of thugs congregating . . . apparently conspiring." They too were falsely affable. This time he would probe more deeply. He picked out a young man he knew fairly well, an unemployed labourer named Murphy. He was a good target, as he was "sporting a heavy blackthorn stick, which I suspected was not going to be used as a walking aid." Branigan turned his full six foot four frame to Murphy and, remarking that his walking-stick looked more like a war club, asked him where he was going with it. "To a wedding," Murphy replied, drawing smiles from his mates. Not amused at this flippant answer, Branigan asked Murphy once again, more sternly. This time he replied that he had a sore leg from a kick, that the blackthorn was for support. Branigan promptly told Murphy to pull up his trouser leg and show him, but there was no mark of any injury. No-one was smiling now.

Ruffled, Murphy then blurted out that there would be "no trouble here," adding that "we're going out to the country," which further piqued Branigan's curiosity. He snatched the blackthorn from Murphy and, in his most commanding voice, warned the group that if they started any trouble in the Liberties he would haul the whole lot of them in. Then "I searched them all. They were all clean."

About midday he was walking along Ash Street, trying to work out the plot behind it all, when he happened to notice a woman friend standing in the doorway of her tenement, looking "strained and tense." He paused to reassure her that there would be no outbreak of violence in her area that day. Without hesitation she blurted out: "They're going to have a bull at the races—and somebody is going to be killed!"[17]

He knew she was not one to speak of such serious matters without having reliable sources. But beyond that revelation she could not fill in the specifics of where, when, or with whom. He took the woman to be credible, as "I learned to give credence to such people who could read the signs . . . I learned that the most casual snatch of conversation can lead to the cracking of a crime."[18]

By one o'clock or so the mystery was deepening. The men were now all drinking liberally and becoming quite boisterous. "My suspicions were aroused, as all the villains had drink taken—and I knew they could not pay for it." He was now getting plenty of signs, but they were still not fitting together.

Just then he spotted Garda Tony Fahy, a colleague from New Market station who had come on duty, heading his way. Fahy confirmed that he too had picked up the unusual signals but was just as baffled as Branigan about their larger meaning. The two guards agreed to carry out a joint surveillance during the rest of the day and evening, checking periodically with one another to compare observations.

But first he needed to return quickly to New Market and report his suspicions to Station Sergeant Joe Reidy. Reidy was not one who indulged in unsubstantiated "hunches" that wasted his time and led nowhere. He could be impatient with young guards who took up his time with trivial matters. But he was a respected, professional policeman, loyal to his men. Branigan condensed his information, now supported by Fahy, and presented it. Reidy listened. Then he turned and began paging through a newspaper to find the schedules of race meetings for that day. The big Baldoyle races were on.

Reidy promptly made a phone call to his friend Sergeant Cox in Howth. This message was immediately forwarded to Superintendent Cronin of Howth, who was in charge of the Garda detail that day at the racecourse. A possibility of gang warfare in such a crowded public venue was taken seriously, for, if not controlled, it could have dire consequences.

By mid-afternoon out at Baldoyle the social scene was unfolding. People enjoyed showing up before the big races to socialise, to share a drink or hot tips. The "Women's Representative" for the *Irish Independent* and her photographer had to arrive early to watch the women coming through the gate. In her column the next day she would set the scene: "The course looked pretty with its white railings and green grass, and the sea shimmering at the back of the stands . . . another delightful day."[19]

———

Back in the Liberties, things were becoming more mysterious by the minute. Branigan had returned to the Coombe, where he had last seen a large group of men drinking. His primary task now was to find out where the drink was coming from. Suspicion led him first to Carroll's pub in the Coombe. Sure enough, Patrick Carroll verified, they were fuelling up in his pub, putting away one pint after another. And Branigan was quite right: they were not paying for their own drink. Carroll liked Branigan and was fully co-operative. He knew as well as Branigan that something out of the ordinary was going on. Some extremely generous person was spending a small fortune on drink for his "friends." Branigan asked Carroll if he knew who was doling out the pound notes for the free booze. The publican identified the man with the pocket full of cash as Jamesie Winters. But he knew it wasn't really *his* money either. To Branigan this meant there must be a "mastermind" behind it all.

Then Carroll volunteered some further information, which he would later share with an *Irish Times* reporter. According to the publican, there were now more than twenty men in the group, drinking heavily and clearly "on for trouble" of some sort. Furthermore, he noticed that "nine or ten of them seemed to have something under their coats."[20] Branigan deduced that there was indeed to be a "rumble," and the pub was being used as a staging area. However, the battle site was still not known; but he felt certain it was most likely to be Baldoyle racecourse.

For the time being, as the men were not in any violation of the law, he could only maintain his surveillance around Carroll's pub and begin making notes of all he had thus far observed, as well as all the conversations he had had with different sources. People would sometimes be surprised to learn that the tough Lugs Branigan, heavyweight boxing champion, also happened to be one of the most meticulous note-takers among the entire Garda force. His attention to recording details would many times prove of crucial importance in court cases.

Meanwhile Garda Fahy was carrying out his part of their joint surveillance. He had been observing Jamesie Winters conferring with another man, George Hannigan, one of the most prosperous, and notorious, bookies in the city. He followed the two men as they drifted over to the Coombe Hospital and into the lobby and continued to "conspire," as he regarded it. When Hannigan noticed Fahy observing him he promptly walked over to the guard and proceeded to inform him that he was going to have to phone for a taxi, as he had "lost" his own car the previous day. He didn't explain why he couldn't recall where he had misplaced a car.

It struck Fahy as very odd that Hannigan would feel obliged to share this bit of information with him. As he didn't seem to be asking the guard to help him find his car, Fahy volunteered to assist him. Could Hannigan give him the registration number, and any other particulars? But Hannigan instantly declined, saying he would find the car himself.

To Fahy, it sounded suspiciously as if he were trying to establish an alibi of some sort. But for what?

The Hannigan family was known to everyone in the Liberties, famed and feared by many. "Ma" Hannigan, who owned a greengrocer's shop in Meath Street, was the powerful matriarch of a large family, which included seven sons. They all faithfully followed her orders, and profited from doing so. It was well known that the Hannigans had their hands in all sorts of nefarious activities. The little shop was their headquarters. Branigan knew George Hannigan well as one of the "corrupt bookmakers who abounded in the city at that time and always brought a retinue of muscle men with them" to carry out their misdeeds, especially at racecourses.[21] Some of the local gangs were controlled by corrupt bookies and racketeers, who exploited them for their own purposes. They also profited from illicit money-lending, extortion, and various intimidation schemes, cleverly using local gangs as their puppets.

As Stephen Mooney explains, Ma Hannigan and her boys were shrewd and ruthless:

> Ma Hannigan, a money-lender—she was responsible for the formation of an animal gang. She was tough, she wielded the power . . . They were all *vicious bastards* . . . She sought out the *tough* guys who were unemployed, who would do *anything* to get money. And they ventured into the protection racket and money-lending. So she'd get the heavies, and they'd beat up a husband, beat up the wife, they'd *wreck* the house . . . of anyone that owed them money. And she'd put it to them [her thugs] that if she could shake a few heads the rest would pay up! Vicious animals!

They regarded themselves as untouchable, according to Mooney, because if a shopkeeper or resident "reported them to the police, there was no way the police could do anything—because it was all *under threat.*" So long as the bosses were safely ensconced behind the scene while their hirelings did the dirty work, they were clear.

If the Liberties had a "Little Caesar" character it was indisputably George Hannigan. He wore tailored suits and drove a big car—in a community in which almost no-one owned a car in those days. He had an imperious, smug persona that rubbed Branigan and his Garda colleagues up the wrong way, conveying an attitude that he was untouchable. No-one in the Liberties would dare to cross the Hannigans. The only people who would dare cross them were other, equally ruthless bookies.

When Fahy told Branigan how George Hannigan had politely approached him in the hospital lobby to volunteer his story about his lost car, the two guards shared their bewilderment about the meaning of it all. But neither doubted that the motive was there for the finding.

———

By early afternoon Branigan was stretching his powers of perception in an effort to fit some of the pieces of the puzzle together. He knew that Jamesie Winters worked for Ma Hannigan in her grocery shop but also as an organiser for her other activities. He was given the money and instructions to carry out Hannigan's schemes. Branigan could see now that he was a central figure in this caper, as he was the one directly conspiring with Hannigan, then going back across the street to Carroll's pub to check on his hirelings. He kept slapping pound notes on the pub counter to keep John Joe and his pals happy and primed for their "action," soon to come.

As Branigan was standing outside Carroll's pub, keeping watch and adding to his notes, along came two other men, named Craven and Curtis, who also worked for Ma Hannigan and George. Into the pub they went to join the others. The mob was growing.

At the same time, over in the lobby of the Coombe Hospital, Thomas Lowry, a furnace man going about his work, was approached by Hannigan, who asked him if he would order several taxis on the phone "for his business." Upon their arrival, the taxi men would be informed of their destination and paid fully in advance.

Within a few minutes, five or six taxis pulled up. Winters popped into Carroll's pub and shouted to the men that their taxis were waiting. The men gulped down their last drinks and left in twos and threes. As an additional incentive to do their job well, Winters would give each man some money for his own betting—for they were all going out for a day at the races.

As the two dozen or more boozy men began piling into the taxis, another man who had been in the pub, by the name of Joe Brown, was asked by Winters if he would like to join them. When Brown saw the inebriated condition of the other men, however, and that they were now armed with weapons, he knew that trouble was ahead and declined the offer.

The men fumbled and fell into the taxis, bellowing with laughter, all ready to get to the racecourse. Then, like a convoy of drunken conquistadors, they pulled away, making all sorts of racket. It was now about half past two in the afternoon. Neither Kennedy nor his fellow-adventurers knew exactly what their "mission" was.

In part, they were going out to settle a score with one of their arch-enemies, the Gardiner Street gang, with whom they had had a recent skirmish at another venue. As Kennedy recalls it, "See, there were a crowd of us went down to Shelbourne Park, and the *whole* of the north side was there—and they *hated* us." Badly outnumbered that day, the Gardiner Street bunch gave them a sound whipping. "Oh, the crowd stopped it . . . but we said, 'We'll finish this in Baldoyle!'"

As the taxis rumbled towards Baldoyle, the occupants may have been thinking of simple personal revenge. They were not yet aware of George Hannigan's more lofty motive against a bitter rival bookie. Kennedy's recollection of the event years later sums up his perceptions at the time:

> The Hannigans was throwing beer into us. And the next thing we were all three-quartered [drunk] and the taxis was called—so we went down to Baldoyle to finish this row. About twenty of us, against the north side. We were *drunk* . . . didn't know any better. Oh, we all had the false spirit in us!

The *Irish Times* would describe it rather differently, in military parlance:

> The party in the taxis was "Hannigan's Army," which was recruited from the Coombe. The "Chief of Staff" who mobilised the "troops" and gave them directions was Winters.[22]

The drink-sodden "soldiers" would be the last to realise they were meant to be part of an invasion force. In due course it would all come out in court: how Hannigan's motive for the expedition was also vengeance, but of a different sort.

The Gardiner Street gang were also being used as troops by his bookie rival to carry out his dirty deeds. This bookmaker had pulled off a double-cross on Hannigan—and he was not about to get away with it. By giving his Gardiner Street lackeys, including one of his assistants, a good thrashing at Baldoyle, Hannigan would send him a clear message and reassert his pre-eminence.

No sooner had the taxis with his militia rounded the corner at the Coombe, headed for Baldoyle, than another taxi pulled up, into which climbed a passenger dressed in a tailored suit, accompanied by his accomplice. Hannigan and Winters were driven off. The brave "general" and his "chief of staff," as they would become known in the newspapers, had sent their troops ahead of them to the battlefield.

———

By all reports it was a spectacular day out at Baldoyle racecourse. Among the spectators was a colleague of Branigan's, Garda Pat McGillion, enjoying his day off duty. Also ambling slowly among the racegoers were Superintendent Cronin and his guards, who, thanks to Branigan, had been alerted to the possibility of a gang flare-up of some sort. They were concentrating mostly on the big ring, scanning spectators, seeing nothing out of the ordinary. Because of the size of the crowd, they could not see very well what might be taking place in the outside ring. But all appeared normal.

"Backers enjoyed all the luck of a thoroughly enjoyable afternoon's racing," wrote one newspaper. The Claremont Plate was about to get under way as the crowd's anticipation rose. With the popular jockey E. M. Quirke riding "Walter Merry," it was sure to be a good race.

Shortly after the race began, with an awful suddenness a deep collective groan erupted from the crowd. At first, Superintendent Cronin and his men may have feared it was an outbreak of trouble; but within seconds all eyes were fixed on the same point on the racecourse, and a hush fell over the spectators. As stewards and trainers raced towards the spot, people stood in suspense. Some doctors from the stands were seen rushing towards the site. Those with binoculars got a glimpse of what had happened, as described by a sports reporter with the *Irish Independent*:

> The field had only covered a couple of furlongs when "Walter Merry" crashed into the rails and was killed instantly. The horse had badly staked himself.[23]

It was a shocking and gruesome sight. Two doctors examined the jockey, who was unconscious. They agreed that he should be taken immediately to St Vincent's Hospital in St Stephen's Green.

————

As the tragedy was unfolding at the racecourse, Hannigan's "soldiers of misfortune" were in their taxis, blabbing like fools, boasting about how they were going to exact revenge upon the rival gang, in the process revealing their plans for the taxi-drivers to hear. In John Joe Kennedy's taxi he and his cohorts, fortified by their false courage, were spouting their bravado like eejits, as he would later put it. According to the *Evening Mail*, one driver clearly heard his passengers say "they were going to have a fight with another gang . . . going to give the Gardiner Street gang a hiding . . . There was going to be a 'bull' between them."[24]

As the crowd's frayed nerves following the accident were gradually calmed before racing resumed, several taxis rolled through the gates. Within minutes, however, the bumbling passengers were drawing attention to themselves for their boisterous, raucous behaviour. Minutes later another taxi pulled up and two men got out, exchanged a few parting words, then went their separate ways. Winters joined his troops, while Hannigan casually walked over to miraculously find his lost car conveniently parked nearby. He drove it a short distance to a vantage point from which he could see the race grounds, but well out of sight himself. And there he sat in comfort and security—or so he believed. As Branigan would later encapsulate it:

> Having recruited his army from the Coombe, mobilised them in Carroll's

pub, and transported them by taxi, the bookmaker, like a true general, was sitting in a motor car behind the people's stands in a place of safety.[25]

At that moment Branigan was back at New Market station conferring with Garda Fahy and Station Sergeant Reidy. Reidy was impressed with the detailed accounts Branigan had recorded—names, numbers, times, verbatim conversations, important facts such as finding out that Hannigan had paid one of the taxi-drivers in full to cover the cost for all. Yet none of the guards knew what to expect next. They would have to await word from Baldoyle, if there was indeed anything to report.

With many members of the gang gone, the Liberties scene returned to its afternoon normality.

––––––

Winters' mob milled about among the crowd at Baldoyle, weapons barely concealed beneath their jackets. Unknown to them, the Gardiner Street gang had arrived earlier, bringing with them their ultimate weapon in the person of the feared Spike McCormack, the champion boxer and street fighter, equal to any ten men in an all-out brawl. As a middleweight boxing champion, McCormack was beyond being an actual member of the gang; but, as his son John confirms, he was easily led when bribed with drink—a fact well known to his good friend Jim Branigan. McCormack had been recruited by the Gardiner Street gang to join them at Baldoyle for the afternoon but brought no weapon: he didn't need one. Explains John: "He was *bred* to fight; the man was a pit bull! Barrel chest, big arms, big knuckles—and his *left hook*! Oh, he could *fight!*" Few men would be foolish enough to face him. He gave the Gardiner Street gang a great physical and psychological advantage in any clashes.

Kennedy believed his Liberties gang to be well armed. "Oh, we had walking-sticks, knives, knuckledusters, lead pipes . . . and a French bayonet!—you know, a bamboo cane and a snake head on the top, and when you pressed the snake's head a blade shot out." The Gardiner Street men had a similar arsenal, including some chains and hatchets.

The flashpoint came the instant the two gangs spotted one another. Like wild animals, they tore into each other with fists and weapons flying. Within seconds, blood was splattering on stunned spectators caught in the melee. John Joe Kennedy was flailing away as mindlessly as his mates:

The row started in the last race, and people started to run—*running everywhere!* Twenty of us against the *whole* north side—Spike McCormack and all. We all had weapons . . . and there was *murder*.

It erupted suddenly and violently, creating a scene of complete pandemonium.

The sounds of people shouting, shrieking and crying were heard everywhere. Panicking spectators, confused and disoriented, ran in every direction, pushing and tumbling over one another. A perfectly positioned *Irish Independent* reporter captured the terror and chaos all around him:

> The fracas occurred during the betting on the last race and took place in the outside ring when a large party of men, divided into opposing groups, began fighting. Weapons included butcher's knives, swords, spears, daggers, iron piping.
>
> The sight of the swaying mass of men brandishing their weapons caused a stampede among race-goers . . . Men and women dashed for safety and several bookmaker's stands were knocked down in the rush . . . A number of women fainted and received first-aid.[26]

"All the Guards in the immediate vicinity at once rushed into the mass of fighting men," reported the paper, as "Supt. Cronin and other guards on duty in the Big Ring hurried to the scene." It took precious minutes for them to force their way through the stampeding crowd to the battle scene, ducking flying bottles as they drew closer. One guard was immediately despatched to send for reinforcements.

Jamesie Winters, armed with a large butcher's knife, promptly attacked a rival named Daniel Towell from Killarney Street, a bookmaker's assistant apparently working for Hannigan's rival. "I saw Jamesie Winters rush at me with a big knife," Towell would later say, though he had no idea at the time why he was being attacked.[27] Then, as he was assaulting Towell, Winters himself was suddenly set upon, becoming a victim. He suffered a wicked blow to his head, from which blood gushed. Near Winters was Murphy—minus his blackthorn stick, confiscated by Branigan, but who had found another weapon. "The row started and it was all digging one another," said Murphy. "There were bottles and sticks and bars . . . I saw Jamesie Winters and his head was bleeding."

By now there were an estimated forty to fifty combatants in the bloody battle, scattered widely. A number of victims already strewn about the ground bleeding were calling out for help. Pat McGillion, the off-duty garda, made his way towards the scene of butchery, unprotected. No sooner had he reached the epicentre of the fighting than he was knocked down by the stampeding masses, as "women screamed with terror" around him.[28] Lifting himself from the ground, he saw a man, later identified as Towell, "walking backwards trying to defend himself against a man [Winters] with a butcher's knife in his hand." It was only seconds later that Winters was smashed in the head, and McGillion heard him cry out, "Get a doctor! Get a priest!"

As Hannigan sat safely in his car, straining to see what he could, his "chief of staff" was sure he was dying. And might well have died. When Garda Thomas McGann came upon him he was seriously injured but still gripping his large "bacon knife smeared with blood." He pleaded with him: "Guard, save me, I'm dying!"[29] His left hand and face were covered with blood. When Superintendent Cronin reached Winters he concluded the same, describing him as "weak and lying on the grass, face covered in blood, hair dishevelled." However, he judged Towell to be in more serious danger of death, with a deep knife wound through his body, "on the ground . . . He thought he was dying." Cronin shouted towards the crowd in the grandstand to have a doctor sent down at once.

Another guard, Sergeant Michael Spellman, arrived to apprehend Murphy, "his hands bloody and in an excited and angry mood, muttering . . ." He had apparently been struck dumb by some weapon. By this time almost all the combatants had suffered injuries of some sort, having been stabbed, punched, beaten with some weapon, or hit by a bottle. If they were not knocked cold, or on the ground writhing in pain, most were stumbling around wounded in a half-conscious state.

A man named Donoghue had "a bad cut on the left side of the forehead," while another, Boyd, had a serious "cut on the back of his head." Many of the injuries were lacerations to the head, which bled freely.

A combatant named Kinsella from Lower Kevin Street had different wounds. He was at the numbers board when he received "a belt of a large wood beam" on the shoulder, and then "a stab in my left leg—it went right through and out the back." He heard screams from the nearby crowd, saw his assailant fleeing, then "I walked a hundred yards and fell to the ground."

Amidst this chaos, many racegoers were struck and cut by flying bottles and other missiles, while confused gang members mistook some bystanders for enemies and attacked them with weapons, to their utter amazement. One spectator, Patrick Doyle, an employee of Dublin United Tramways Company, told of seeing an innocent man being beaten viciously as blood splattered all over his clothing. With such havoc it was difficult for gardaí to distinguish attackers from defenders, gang members from spectators. Injured gang members and innocent racegoers were sometimes stuffed into ambulances side by side. The pandemonium also allowed other members of the gangs to escape the scene—at least those who still had the necessary mobility.

By chance, during the height of the pitched battle Garda McGillion glanced over in exactly the right direction, at exactly the right moment, to clearly spot "George Hannigan seated in his bookmaker's car when the trouble was on,"[30] peering out, straining to see what he could—a positive identification more important than he could have realised at the time. The "general" was safely detached from the fury and bloodshed, listening to the uproar from the race grounds, anxiously awaiting Winters' report from the front.

As gang members had become dispersed throughout the grounds, still skirmishing in twos and threes and fours, it took a while for the gardaí to completely quell the warfare. By now word had reached New Market, where Branigan, Fahy and Reidy, as well as other guards on duty, could only try to imagine what had taken place. But Superintendent Cronin promptly affirmed that it could have been far worse had it not been for the early alert of gang warfare raised by Branigan and Fahy, which allowed him to have extra guards on duty and vigilant.

But Branigan's day was not over yet.

––––

Out at Baldoyle racecourse, Superintendent Cronin supervised the final rounding up of combatants, and the ambulance crews taking victims to hospital. An unknown number of gang members had escaped the scene.

Unnoticed by Cronin and the other guards, a tense-looking man in a black car was slowly pulling out the gates, heading back to the Liberties. He could wait no longer for Jamesie Winters' battle report. The next morning's newspapers would tell him all he needed to know.

As the last guards left the scene, groundkeepers combed a field of broken bottles, bloodstains, and a scattering of abandoned weapons missed by the police. Thousands of racegoers were making their way home, still stunned by what they had experienced, beginning with the sad death of the racehorse and injury to its jockey, followed by horrific gang warfare. As they talked of these events, most had probably forgotten the most exciting race of the day, the Clonard Hurdle, described by the sports reporters as barely "won by a neck— by a horse named 'Gang Smasher'."

By evening, Branigan had received a full report on the debacle at Baldoyle. It was considerably worse than he had expected. When the names of those apprehended were phoned to New Market station, those from the Liberties matched his list. It was now up to him to track down those who got away. He would have to act quickly, within twenty-four or thirty-six hours, as he knew that some might try to flee to England—a common practice for criminals wanted in Ireland.

Not long afterwards Branigan received a further urgent report. Rumours were going around that some of the gang members who were licking their wounds were determined to meet again the same night to settle the score— again. Gardaí throughout the city were placed on alert. According to an *Irish Press* reporter, there were "fears that the clash at Baldoyle" might have repercussions in a few hours' time at Harold's Cross greyhound track, and "special precautions were taken by scores of gardaí" posted on the scene.[31]

This force was under the command of Inspector Maher, who was determined to defuse any gang trouble brewing at the track. A reporter from the *Irish Independent* who was rushed out to the track noticed that "some excitement was caused when a number of young men assembled" in agitated mood outside the enclosure and had to be dispersed by the gardaí.[32] But it proved to be a false alarm.

Inside the track, all was going peacefully until, just before the last race, a man in the reserved enclosure, Patrick Shaw, was struck on the head and knocked unconscious. The attack was so swift that spectators were unable to intervene, and the assailants, after a scuffle with some men near the railings, made good their escape. Nothing further occurred, and the man was given first aid and sent home.

Elsewhere around the city, however, between ten and twelve o'clock, trouble was still simmering. The *Irish Press* confirmed that "late at night scrimmages between the rival parties" flared up in the Coombe and a few other areas but were "quickly dealt with by the gardaí who patrolled the streets in large numbers."[33] Throughout the night small bands of gang members and their followers roamed the streets, seeking more trouble. But gardaí, out in force, batons in hand, discouraged them from acting. Branigan was already out on the hunt for fugitives.

At midnight, two gang members lay in the Mater Hospital close to death. Another man, having returned home to the Liberties in his "lost" car, probably did not sleep well that night, awaiting the next morning's papers to find out exactly what had happened at Baldoyle, as he had still heard nothing from his now missing "chief of staff."

―――――

On the morning of 15 May, Branigan was up before five o'clock, having had little sleep. He was eager to set about his task of corralling the gang members still at large. "When I reported for duty the following morning at six o'clock a written directive detailed me to meet Detective-Inspector John King, Superintendent Cronin and the other gardaí to round up the suspects and bring them in."[34] Little did they know that he was well ahead of the directive. He knew the missing gang members' names, where they lived, and all about their backgrounds.

One of his first acts would be to contact the taxi-drivers who had taken Hannigan's "troops" out to Baldoyle. For this he pulled out his notebook. "As I had taken notes of the taxi car numbers, we were able to pull the drivers in for questioning."

Scores of Dubliners were up earlier than usual in anticipation of reading all about Baldoyle. Many people had heard morsels of what had happened and were hungry for the full story. When the first morning editions hit the streets they were snatched up within minutes. Enticed by the sensational headlines, all Dublin was soon buzzing with the news of what was being called the "Battle of Baldoyle." The headlines competed for attention:

Irish Times:

"The Battle of Baldoyle"

"Attacked at racecourse"

"Baldoyle Races riot"

Irish Press:

"Rival gang clash described"

"Surgeon says men lucky to survive"

Irish Independent:

"Fracas at race meeting"

Evening Herald:

"Stab right through man's body"

There was no need to dramatise or embellish: the horrid events spoke for themselves. An estimated forty to sixty men armed with knives, hatchets, swords, and chains, slicing and smashing each other; more than twenty serious injuries, and two combatants near death. Reporters had no compunction about providing the gruesome details.

To Dubliners, this was not merely one more gang clash in the streets, or at a late-night dancehall: this took place in the midst of the Baldoyle Races, in mid-afternoon, among throngs of decent citizens. What had happened was nothing short of a national shame. It could not be tolerated.

After people scoured the morning papers they awaited the evening ones, which were sure to have fresh news. Meanwhile Branigan was focused like a laser on finding the culprits. As he put it, "I *hounded* them," as well as their families and friends. When he carried out an investigation no-one dared hold out on him. He had his ways of getting accurate information. "His eyes, they'd sort of bore through you when he was asking you questions," says his son Alick. His determination as an investigator matched that in the boxing ring: he was relentless. Declan explains: "Oh, very persistent! He'd follow up . . . see it through to the end. And solve the crime." Everyone in the Liberties knew he was on the trail of the remaining Baldoyle combatants.

Within forty-eight hours he had them all rounded up. "Every man whom I had seen at the street corners was taken into custody," he reported. "Only those who could give an alibi that they were not at the races, or in the area of the stabbings, were released."

Both the Garda Síochána and the judges wanted an iron-clad case this time. Therefore, in questioning the suspects they whittled the number down to those against whom they felt they had irrefutable evidence and reliable eye-witnesses. After exhaustive interrogation by Branigan and other guards, these were charged and held until they could have their day in court.

"We were left with twelve," Branigan counted. He looked forward to seeing them again.

———

Outraged citizens were anxious for the trial of the Baldoyle gangsters to get under way, but they would have to wait some six months. It was to be a big trial, a landmark one, and it was decided that it would not proceed until all was in proper order. Branigan and other gardaí had many investigations to conduct, while the prosecution knew it would have to secure hard evidence to prove conspiracy. The public hoped that this time it would lead to severe sentencing for the guilty and so serve as a deterrent to such crime in the future.

To those directly involved in the case it was apparent that Garda Jim Branigan's scrupulously gathered evidence and testimony would be a linchpin for the prosecution. His small notebook contained all the crucial facts behind the incident. It would be damning to the person whom he called the "well-heeled bigshot" behind the crime, the "mastermind" who tried to remain a clandestine figure, safely operating behind the scene.

For the mastermind, Jim Branigan had done his detective work too well, compiling irrefutable evidence against George Hannigan. Now Hannigan needed to get him "out of the picture," keep him out of the witness box. The young guard should be an easy mark. (That's what Pietsch had thought.)

Branigan was relatively inexperienced in matters of covert intimidation by criminal figures. His duties were dealing with street thugs and bowsies out in the open. Shrewd strategies of manipulation and intimidation were as yet little known to him. This case would prove to be a learning experience for him:

A taste of the power wielded by those who inspired fear in these gougers and thugs was experienced by me when, before the trial, attempts were made to persuade me to keep my mouth shut during the trial.[35]

First came the anonymous threatening letters, telling him explicitly what would happen to him if he did not remain silent during the trial. He read all the letters, then dutifully handed them over to his superiors.

Next came the disguised phone calls reiterating the same threatening message, but more forcefully, with a human voice. He listened, took notes, gave them to his superintendent.

When these faceless threats failed, the criminal behind them tried a more resourceful tactic. Branigan was surprised when he received "the offer of a blank cheque in return for my silence."[36] Attempted bribery was not unknown to the Gardaí, as to any police force—and doubtless was successful in some instances. Whoever made this offer surely knew that gardaí received poor pay and might be very susceptible to such a tempting financial gift in exchange for the favour of silence. But not the son of John and Ellen Branigan.

The threats by letter and phone, and the offer of a bribe, had exactly the opposite effect to the one intended: they made Branigan more determined to testify and to expose the criminal attempting to intimidate him—a person who despatched minions to carry out his dirty deeds. More than anger, Branigan felt insulted.

Last came the most insidious scheme to remove him from the case—the only one that worried him, because it was beyond his control. The mind behind it calculated that this attempt probably had a good chance of success. This shrewd effort, Branigan admitted, was "even more startling: an attempt to have me removed from New Market to Dún Laoghaire station 'for my own safety.'"[37] Presumably this had come in the form of a letter to his superiors. Worried that it might be successful, he decided on a pre-emptive measure. He promptly informed his senior officer that he would not accept such a transfer "without *first* having an interview with the commissioner himself." He awaited the outcome, but no transfer notice ever came.

Of the attempts to blot him out of the Baldoyle case he simply said: "Needless to say, they were all to no avail." He was sure he knew exactly who was behind it all. Working harder now than ever, he continued to carry out interrogations to fortify his findings. Other guards on the case also worked diligently on their preparations.

As 1940 neared its end, the war continued, and hardships in Ireland worsened. The *Irish Times* reminded readers that "once again Christmas is in the air," encouraging them to embrace the holiday spirit to offset war worries and rationing:

> The Christmas season this year will be a symbol of "carrying on" . . . to strengthen our defences against the gloom and depression whose ugly heads rear menacingly at us.[38]

As usual, the city was festooned with lights and decorations. If people were not quite as jolly as usual, most at least got into the Christmas spirit. Filmgoers at the Bohemian in Phibsborough could enjoy watching Mickey Rooney and Judy Garland—that unbeatable duo—in *Andy Hardy Meets Debutante*. But the film drawing the biggest crowds was the one at the Grand Central in O'Connell Street, where Spencer Tracy and Mickey Rooney were starring in the poignant *Boys' Town*.

Many people, however, believed that the most dramatic show in Dublin would be the one opening soon at the Central Criminal Court in Green Street.

On Tuesday 19 November, slightly more than six months after the now famous "Battle of Baldoyle," Mr Justice Martin Maguire entered the court at 10 a.m. and officially opened the long-awaited case. Before him was a packed room of participants and observers. Looking down, he saw twelve men seated in the dock, conspicuously uncomfortable. Though there had been many more combatants in the bloody battle, the number had been pruned down to an even dozen against whom solid evidence had been gathered. Some of their names had been splashed in the newspapers so often that they were now familiar to everyone in Dublin: George Hannigan, James "Jamesie" Winters, Daniel "Chick" Towell, Patrick Kinsella, and P. Murphy, along with seven lesser-known men—two of whom, amazingly, were wearing army uniforms. Some newspapers conveniently consolidated the twelve men, referring to them as "Hannigan and his henchmen"—an apt portrayal.

The twelve defendants probably wished they were facing a different judge. Maguire was known to be a man of the highest integrity, intelligence, and fairness—and a *tough* judge. He deplored criminals who preyed upon and terrorised citizens. Many Dubliners were now hoping he would be the one to finally break the riotous reign of the city's vicious gangs. However, this was by no means a certainty, as Hannigan had hired a powerful defence team, headed by the well-known barrister Felix Sherry. The eleven other defendants shared the services of Desmond Bell.

The prosecution was led by Joseph McCarthy, along with P. J. McEnerny and G. Murnaghan. McCarthy, a man of considerable intellectual and oratorical skills, would later become a Circuit Court judge. He was masterful at addressing jurors and framing evidence in comprehensive and compelling terms. Equally important, he was credible and likeable. His two associates were also top-notch barristers who had done their homework assiduously over the past six months.

The twelve men faced eight charges of "conspiracy to assemble riotously" and with "intent to cause grievous bodily harm . . . to maim and disfigure."

Addressing the jury, McCarthy laid out his case with precision:

The evidence will show that an organised body of men under the influence and control of one or more men determined to defy the law and wreak their will by violence against those who might oppose them . . . to do it with violence, inflicted by knives and bottles and such other weapons.[39]

Furthermore, as the *Evening Mail* reported, "the allegation was made that a Dublin bookmaker was the leader of a gang 'which determined to defy the law'."[40] McCarthy stressed that these charges "were very grave indeed."

Eleven of the defendants no doubt understood the charges of "riotous conduct" and "intent to do bodily harm" but may not have fully comprehended the legal term "conspiracy." George Hannigan understood it perfectly. McCarthy specifically identified him:

The evidence will establish that the prime mover in the conspiracy was Hannigan, who is a bookmaker, and that all the other men are to some extent his creatures, carrying out his plan.[41]

After the charges were read, the defendants were asked how they wished to plead. All twelve replied, "Not guilty."

————

Before Dr Henry Barniville of the Mater Hospital was called on to testify about the injuries, a large table was set up for the purpose of displaying for the jury (and the audience) the savage weapons used by the gangs: wicked knives, bayonets, hatchets, chains, razors, iron bars—weapons that really conveyed the feeling of a gang "war." The physical display had a discernible effect upon the jury.

Dr Barniville was now ready to tell how these weapons were used on the human body, for it was he who had first treated Towell and Kinsella when they were brought to the Mater Hospital with severe wounds. It was he who had saved their lives.

His clinical descriptions of the wounds were both graphic and gruesome. He told how Towell had been admitted with a stab wound in his chest, his breathing laboured, freely spitting blood, and with deep cuts on his scalp. The weapon that had caused the chest wound had actually passed through the body, making an exit hole, having travelled a distance of fifteen or sixteen inches. It must have taken considerable strength, he said, for the assailant to drive the blade right through till it emerged at his back. The surgeon determined that the width of the entrance wound was about 1½ inches. It had pierced the left lung and the sac in which the heart lay. Towell, he affirmed, was "in great danger" for ten days, and his recovery was "almost miraculous."

Kinsella had been in similarly serious condition, he testified. He had a wound 2½ inches below the groin caused by an instrument at least eight inches long, and an exit wound. He believed it had been made by "either the rusty bayonet or curved knife." He proceeded to describe the wounds inflicted on other victims who had been similarly butchered.

Towell's and Kinsella's lives were saved, the *Evening Mail* wrote, "only by the superhuman skill of the best surgical talent that could be obtained in Dublin."[42] Far better than they deserved, many Dubliners doubtless thought. The *Irish Independent* made the point that both men had been in such grave condition at first that it was doubtful whether they would live—which would mean that the Gardaí could well have had two murders on their hands.[43]

Next followed the procession of witnesses for the prosecution. The guards who had been on the scene gave first-hand testimony, identifying the accused. Garda Thomas McGann told how he had caught Winters with a bloody bacon knife in his hand as he pleaded with him to "save me, I'm dying!" Superintendent Cronin, who had witnessed as much as anyone, identified all those gang members whom he had positively seen carrying out riotous acts and assault. Garda Pat McGillion, who had been off duty, gave detailed accounts of the battles raging around him and how innocent spectators were struck with flying bottles.

Throughout the unfolding testimony, "General" Hannigan, as he was now commonly called by the the press and the public, seemed rather confident that his name was not being specifically mentioned by any of the witnesses. No-one had pinned him to the battle scene.

As expected, Garda Jim Branigan's elaborate testimony and detailed evidence proved crucial. With precision, he laid out a blueprint of the day's events preceding the Baldoyle debacle, from the early morning until the taxis were out of sight in mid-afternoon. Everything fitted the pattern: the peculiar behaviour, conversational exchanges, drinking binge. The publican Patrick Carroll was called upon to verify Branigan's observations and state his conclusion that the men in his pub were clearly "looking for trouble," and that their drink was being paid for by Winters, who was obviously getting it from a different person. And, added Carroll, he could see weapons beneath their jackets.

Garda Tony Fahy gave his report of encountering Hannigan in the hospital lobby and hearing his lame alibi about the "lost car," then calling for the taxis. Taxi-drivers then filled in the story, directly quoting their blustering passengers as they boasted how they were going to give a hiding to their Gardiner Street rivals, that a real "bull" was on at Baldoyle.

It took a good deal of courage for men like Carroll and the taxi-drivers to enter the witness box directly in front of Hannigan and the gang members and present testimony that was so damaging to them. They knew this; but neither did they want to let Garda Branigan down.

Though Hannigan must have been growing a bit nervous at this point, at least no-one had been able to place him at the scene of the crime. Then Garda McGillion revealed his discovery: the sighting of George Hannigan at Baldoyle racecourse, hidden in his big car, straining to see all the action. As a guard stationed in the Liberties who knew Hannigan, McGillion gave the court a positive identification. Hannigan slouched slightly in his chair.

—

As the defendants all pleaded "not guilty," they were given the opportunity to testify on their own behalf. All declined. In the case of Towell this was unexpected, as he had indicated to the police that he intended to testify against the assailant who had plunged the knife clear through his body. When he had been rushed to hospital, at death's door, he told a garda: "It was James Winters . . . I saw him rush at me with a big knife." His anger at being attacked by the Liberties gang was furthered by his belief that it was a "pay-back" for having "scabbed" during a strike in a bacon factory in Francis Street six years earlier. In working-class culture, such betrayals are never forgotten—or forgiven.

He saw his testimony as his chance for revenge. Days later, however, when it was time to leave hospital, he refused to sign a statement to that effect for the gardaí. He had had a change of heart. For Branigan it was a learning experience to sit in court and see the flat refusal of all gang members to speak a word against their enemies, or to implicate Hannigan in the slightest way. He clearly saw what was behind their silence:

> This was my first real experience of the Mafia's cardinal rule of "Omerta," or silence. This, in gangster lingo, means that only death and trouble awaits the canary who "sings." It was fear, because if they spilled the beans about the Baldoyle job they would pay, whether or not they were convicted.[44]

In defence of his eleven mute clients, Desmond Bell tried to dismiss the preponderance of testimony against them and "submitted that there was no evidence to show that a conspiracy had started in the Coombe," despite Branigan's evidence. Felix Sherry then rose with an air of practised confidence to tell the court that "there was no evidence given which would make it necessary for George Hannigan to get into the witness box to explain."[45] He then elaborated his point to the judge and jury, as recorded by the *Irish Times*:

> Mr. Sherry said that if he called Mr. Hannigan as a witness, and if the other eleven men had been called, the jury would be there until this day week . . . There is not sufficient evidence for the jury's consideration and it would

only mean a waste of their time and the Court's time to place him in the witness box.[46]

He fooled neither judge nor jury. Armed with all the incriminating evidence they needed, the prosecutors framed their case by closely following Branigan's detailed blueprint. As promised at the outset, they convincingly established that the "prime mover" in the conspiracy was George Hannigan, who had clearly exploited his "creatures carrying out his plans." Summing up, McCarthy drew upon a historical analogy:

> The party in the taxis constitutes "Hannigan's Army," recruited in the Coombe, mobilised in a licensed house, transported by taxis, armed with weapons. Primed and fortified by drink, they were the equivalent of the "four and twenty fighting men and a couple of stout gossoons" of Slattery's Mounted Foot, immortalised by Percy French.[47]

Turning to the jury, he referred to Murphy's cute reply to Branigan that morning about "going to a wedding" with his blackthorn stick. "If he had said, 'We contemplate a funeral,' he would have been nearer the truth!"

––––

On 23 November, after five days of testimony and closing arguments, it was Mr Justice Maguire's turn to give the jury their instructions. Reiterating many facts of the case, he raised questions to be considered. He voiced his displeasure that, because of the defendants' right not to testify, the motives behind the bloody battle at Baldoyle remained unknown. As he put it, "there is a lot in the case that requires explanation and has not been explained—matters that the accused men alone could explain." He told the jury that Towell and Kinsella, the most seriously injured men, "gave as much as they got—or tried to do so," and this should be kept in mind.

He particularly emphasised that if "Hannigan ordered the taxis, he assumed responsibility forthwith for them," as they were sent from the Coombe to Baldoyle crammed with drunken armed men on a mission for him.

Concluding his comments to the jury, he told them that "what happened at Baldoyle can only be described as an audacious outrage on the community." Yet, he added, they were to "consider the case calmly and quietly."

The jury retired at 1:30 p.m., the judge having addressed them for three-and-a-half hours. As the *Evening Mail* declared, "the final chapter in the story of the 'Battle of Baldoyle' began."

––––

The public, having devoured every morsel of the case in the newspapers, now anxiously awaited the verdict. As, no doubt, did the families of the accused. During the days of deliberation some Dubliners may have noticed the irony in the Gaiety Theatre's presentation that week emblazoned over its doors: *Trial by Jury.*

With the arrival of December, still no verdict had been reached. Some people wondered if this favoured the defence. Reporters were becoming tired of twiddling their thumbs.

Then word came. The jury was returning. Everyone scrambled back into the courtroom and sat in silence. Hannigan and his henchmen were visibly nervous. Branigan sat ramrod-straight. Dublin's newspaper presses were ready to whir. In their offices, editors and writers were waiting to spring into action.

When the jury's verdict of "Guilty" was read aloud, one might have wondered why it had taken so long. Gasps were heard among family members. The reaction of the accused was, curiously, not mentioned in newspaper reports.

At this point the prisoners—no longer the "accused"—were allowed to have someone speak on their behalf, and several did so. Lieutenant P. J. O'Connor stepped forward to state that the two men in uniform had been "of very good conduct in the army and were likely to make efficient soldiers," given the chance. Rev. John McLoughlin rose to say that he thought one of the other men "would make a good citizen," and promised to take an interest in his future. Felix Sherry stood up staunchly to speak on behalf of his client, George Hannigan—and his family—for he felt there were some pertinent facts the judge should know. He first attested that Hannigan had held a bookmaker's licence for nearly ten years, and there had been no previous complaints against him. Dare anyone lodge a complaint against him? Neither Maguire nor Branigan seemed surprised to hear this.

He also wanted Mr Justice Maguire to know that Mr Hannigan, in his early thirties, already had six children, the eldest of whom was a girl of ten. Sherry called him a good family man, whose wife and children needed him at home. And during the past six months, between the Baldoyle incident and the trial, they had endured stress and emotional upset. As Sherry phrased it, "the sufferings his wife and children have undergone and will undergo are indescribable."[48]

Mr Justice Maguire now had a few words of his own to share. Firstly, he stated his belief that three of the men "were duped into the affair by other people, whose responsibility for drawing them in is very great." He could show them some leniency. Then he exonerated one of the men whom the jury had found not guilty for lack of convincing evidence. This meant he would be sentencing only eleven men. In reality they had all been "duped" into participation by being fuelled with free drink and "false courage." Nonetheless they had to be held accountable for their heinous acts. After all, the jury had found them guilty of riotous conduct, intent to do bodily harm, and conspiracy. The judge told the defendants they were fortunate they were not before him on murder charges.

As the *Evening Herald* reported, Mr Justice Maguire seemed perfectly "satisfied that Hannigan and Winters were equally responsible," beyond any reasonable doubt. He was particularly chagrined over their apparent lack of remorse and the still unexplained motives behind it all:

> It was a matter of deep regret to him that up to that moment there had been no apology or expression of regret for the outrageous offence perpetrated at Baldoyle.[49]

It was time for sentencing. A hush fell over the courtroom. To three of the men, apparently those who he believed had been "duped" into participation, Maguire handed down a sentence of twelve months, to be suspended on "giving an understanding to be of good behaviour for twelve months." Branigan intended to see that this promise was kept.

This light sentencing may have given the other defendants a glimmer of hope. If so, it was fleeting. The next three men heard their sentences of four years' penal servitude. At this point muffled sobbing was heard in the courtroom. An *Irish Times* reporter captured the moment: "Two women fainted in the public gallery while the sentences were being imposed."[50] They were assisted out of the courtroom, their identities not revealed. One may assume they were the mothers or wives of the prisoners.

The next three men were given sentences of five years' penal servitude.

This left only Hannigan and his "chief of staff," Jamesie Winters. History does not tell us whether Ma Hannigan and George's wife were in the courtroom, or Winters' family, but it's a reasonable assumption that they were. Mr Justice Maguire read out their sentence in a clear voice: "Seven years' penal servitude."

With these words, those present in the courtroom felt a "swoosh" of air as reporters rushed for the door. A crowd waiting outside the court building got the news within seconds and scurried off to disperse it around the city. Later, people would hover around the news-stands waiting for the evening papers with the full story. Vendors would enjoy a bonanza. The newspapers didn't disappoint, as their headlines blared the big news:

Evening Mail:
> "Dublin bookie and henchmen get penal servitude"
> "Seven years for Hannigan: Cold-blooded crimes"

Evening Herald:

> "Men sentenced—Women collapse in court"

No judge had handed out such stiff sentences before for gang crimes. Over the following days Mr Justice Maguire was praised for his wisdom and his resolve, and there was something of a celebratory mood in Dublin. These harsh sentences were seen as a significant deterrent to future gang battles.

In the aftermath of the court case Jim Branigan and several other guards involved received commendation for their superb work. It was only some years later that Branigan would reveal that he had worked out what had so puzzled Mr Justice Maguire: the real motive behind it all. In fact he already had most of the answer at the time of the trial but knew it could not be entered as evidence, because it could not be proved. But ultimately, Branigan was confident he had uncovered Hannigan's prime motive:

> As far as can be ascertained, the south-side animal gang vendetta at Baldoyle was an act of revenge on behalf of the south city bookmaker who was the victim of "hedging." It was known [to some gardaí] before the trial—though it never emerged in "evidence" that the "Battle of Baldoyle" took place over the "hedging" of a bet.[51]

What had occurred, he explained, was that an equally powerful, unscrupulous bookmaker rival had placed a large bet on a "dead cert" but would not hand over the cash. Thus, when the horse won, the south-city bookie duly paid out the winnings. However, Branigan stated, "if the horse had *lost* he would *not get paid any money at all!*"

Hedging a bet was a grievous sin among Dublin's bookies, an act that demanded forcible retaliation. As the bookie routinely used the Gardiner Street gang as his "troops" for misdeeds, just as Hannigan did with the Liberties gangs, a good thrashing would teach the whole bunch a lesson, including one of the bookie's assistants. But as this could not be proved, to have introduced it in court would only have muddied the waters for the prosecutors.

The "Battle of Baldoyle" case elevated Branigan's reputation to a new level, beyond merely being tough in the ring and on the street. As the *Evening Herald* later wrote, it "won him the reputation of being a fearless cop," who could not be intimidated or manipulated by Dublin's underground racketeers. It established him as a masterful detective and interrogator and "set him on the trail of gang-busting" for the next thirty-three years.

———

Fifty years after he was sentenced for his role in the Baldoyle battle, John Joe Kennedy was asked by the author about his emotions in the courtroom that day. In the 1990s a genial grandfather in his seventies, still living near Ash Street, he first drew a momentary blank. Well, he recollected, his mind seemed numb when hearing the judge's words. None of the lads, he said, had expected so severe a sentence. After another pause he confided:

> We all done imprisonment. I got four years. It was reckoned that it was the harshest sentence ever for a gang war.

He was right about that. Yet he showed not a hint of recrimination against the prosecution, Mr Justice Maguire, or his lifelong friend Jim Branigan. Indeed they had put his life on the right track. To Lugs especially he says, "Fair play."

Chapter 6 ～

WAR, WEDDING, AND THE
TOLKA PARK RUMBLE

"At a fight between rival gangs at a football match at Tolka Park wild scenes ensued . . . A number on both sides wounded."

(*Irish Times,* 23 MARCH 1942)

"Spectators and officials were put in terror and fled from the grounds . . . One man was so seriously injured that he was thought dead."

(*Evening Herald,* 23 JUNE 1942)

"Jim Branigan played a prominent part in the battle of Tolka Park between rival animal gangs . . . after some considerable detective work."

(BERNARD NEARY)

"My mother . . . Their paths crossed on his beat. It was obviously love."

(ALICK BRANIGAN)

The year 1941 began promisingly for Garda Jim Branigan. It was unprecedented in the Garda Síochána for a guard, at the age of thirty-one, to have achieved a national reputation as a boxing champion, ace detective, fearless street fighter, and tamer of vicious gangs. Lauded in the press, he was becoming famous and, quite unknown to him at the time, was well on his way to legendary status.

No longer boxing, he now had more free time to think of his future, of eventual marriage and a family. If the right young woman should come along. Unfortunately, the early 1940s were a woeful time for young couples to contemplate getting married. Life was uncertain, and hardship assured. Ominous news from the European war fronts told of German troops on the march, with little opposition. Though Ireland supposedly had the security of its neutrality, many Irish people were shocked when France and the Low Countries fell so quickly. If Hitler eyed Ireland, life could be shattered.

An event on 4 January, two days before Branigan's birthday, made Dubliners even more fearful. At 3:55 a.m. the gardaí sleeping in Kevin Street barracks were roused suddenly from their beds by a loud explosion. Close by, a low-flying aircraft had dropped a high-explosive bomb on a residential street of red-brick houses in Donore Terrace, demolishing two houses, injuring twenty-four residents, and rendering forty families homeless. Gardaí were called from all surrounding stations for crowd control and rescue work, as well as keeping the roads open for the fire brigade and ambulances.

By the next day, it was determined that they were German bombs. Leaving people extremely jittery.

In what the Government called the "highly unlikely" event of an air raid, Dubliners were told they should use the concrete bomb shelters now sprouting like mushrooms around the city, the flimsy "hen houses" or "hat boxes," as people called them, more of a joke than a comfort. Air-raid sirens were installed on the sides of buildings, and tested periodically. Their shrill wail pierced the tenements, upsetting the elderly and causing dogs to howl in harmony. Street lamps were now being cowled to darken the streets at night as a defence against air raids—and making it more difficult for guards to patrol effectively.

Daily life was becoming more difficult. Increasing shortages of essential items meant that rationing had to be tightened, including tea, cocoa, candles, flour, paraffin oil, petrol, tyres, and bananas. The tea ration was reduced from one ounce per person per week to half an ounce. The minister for supplies also announced that cocoa rations would have to be cut to half the amount of the previous year. Men groused endlessly about the difficulty in getting cigarettes and pipe tobacco.

Meanwhile, despite the deterrent effect of the sentences handed down to the Baldoyle combatants, a number of gangs were still on the prowl, though now on a more local level. As before, most conflicts were triggered by rivalry over betting, money-lending, or the protection racket. Pitch-and-toss, a game of gambling by tossing coins, was becoming very lucrative, and gambling at the "toss schools" increased sharply.

Gangs were still getting into feuds and skirmishes, and when clashes occurred between rival gangs they always vowed revenge. Sometimes the chosen site was again a public sports venue. Branigan had gained considerable control over the gangs in his Liberties, but the same could not be said of other districts. Nor could he prevent the Ash Street gang or Coombe gang from straying elsewhere in the city to carry out retaliations.

———

But in early 1941 Branigan was more interested in romance than in tangling with gangs. The previous summer, about two months after the Baldoyle episode, he had met Elizabeth Armstrong—known to family and friends as Elsie. Not in uniform at the time, he was on a short-term plain-clothes assignment. As Alick recounts, "my mother worked in the office of Kelly's timber merchants in Thomas Street. This was part of my father's beat, and somehow their paths crossed—and the rest, as they say is *history!*" There was a labour dispute at the timber merchant's, and he was posted there to make sure no violence erupted.

A few days after his posting he was introduced to Miss Armstrong and a few other women as they left the building at midday for their lunch. It was the most casual of meetings, yet one that struck both very favourably.

Shortly thereafter he mustered the confidence to ask out the refined and attractive Miss Armstrong, and thus began their courtship. They enjoyed all the traditional things young couples did in those days: walks, dancing, cinema, visits to the Phoenix Park and the zoo, linking arms while eating an ice-cream cone and strolling along. And *talking.* The simplest of pleasures. He found she had a great love of, and talent for, music. As her sister Dorothy recalls, "she *loved* music, especially the music of the time, like in Fred Astaire [films], and she went to dances in parochial halls, from 8 p.m. to 11 p.m." When they attended the cinema, Jim and Elsie easily combined their fondness for westerns and musicals. He was happy to watch Ginger Rogers sing and dance, she to see John Wayne ride the range, six-shooters blazing.

They seemed a perfect match. Except for one hitch: she was a Protestant, a devout member of Donore Presbyterian Church. He was a devout Catholic. In those days it was no small problem to be resolved.

Her family were fervent Presbyterians. As Dorothy reveals, Elsie was also active in church affairs. "She taught in Sunday school and played the hymns on the harmonium, exceptionally well, and sang in the church choir every Sunday. She also learnt to play the organ. And she attended the national school there."

Jim's reservations regarding marriage had to do not with love or religion but with money. In the early 1940s a garda's wages were paltry, barely enough for a single man to subsist on. His married friends often complained about the hardship of trying to support a wife, and then children, on only a few pounds a week. As a matter of pride as well as practicality, it was important to him to be a good provider.

How Jim and Elsie eventually managed to work out the delicate matter of difference of religion we don't know; but it was surely not without considerable sacrifice within the Armstrong family. The outcome was that Elsie agreed to convert to Catholicism.

It would have been wholly against Branigan's character to have exerted pressure on her to do so. Conversely, it would have been wholly consistent with Elsie's strong sense of independence to make her own decisions in life. This decision, for a young woman in 1941 to relinquish her church and adopt her husband's faith, was an act of great courage as well as love. But Elsie would always be known as a strong-willed woman who made her own decisions in life, after she reasoned everything out. According to Alick, his father understood with sympathy the nature of her dilemma, and knew it constituted a great sacrifice. As Alick sums it up:

> So she had her religious instruction, and then we were all brought up as Catholics—that was the rule at the time. That was *fine* with her anyway; it was *obviously love*—or she wouldn't have gone through all of that! You know, just to get hooked.

Twelve days before their wedding the war exploded on their doorstep. On 14 and 15 April the German air force attacked Belfast in a fierce surprise air raid, as "waves of planes rained bombs," destroying buildings, setting the city on fire, and killing and injuring scores of people.[1] With Belfast ablaze, the Taoiseach, Éamon de Valera, made the decision to despatch a number of Dublin Fire Brigade units across the border on a humanitarian mission to help put out fires and save lives. He knew this was technically a violation of the country's neutrality. A hasty—and risky—move.

By 17 April more than three thousand refugees from the North had poured south into Dublin, looking like bedraggled evacuees from war-torn Europe. The Gardaí were instructed to assist them in every way possible, directing them to night shelters, the Red Cross, medical facilities, and sources of food, and to try and calm and comfort them.

On 25 April, at the Gresham Hotel, de Valera delivered a chilling address in which he stated his fear that Dublin might soon be the target of German bombs, and that an evacuation plan had to be devised right away.[2]

On the morning of Jim and Elsie's wedding the *Irish Independent* warned of dire days ahead. The British air force had just carried out a successful raid on the German naval bases at Kiel and Wilhelmshaven, striking shipyards in which warships and submarines were being built. Retaliation was certain. Meanwhile Athens Radio announced that "the Battle of Greece is hastening to its climax . . . A heartbreaking tragedy is approaching."[3]

Amidst these uncertainties, on the morning of Saturday 26 April, at St

Audoën's Church in High Street, a joyful wedding took place, attended by a small number of family and friends. They were truly a striking couple, he in his formal wedding attire, she in a tailored white jacket and skirt with matching hat and corsage, both wearing happy smiles outside the church in an after-wedding photograph.

The priest who joined them together was the legendary Father John "Flash" Kavanagh. Only a year older than Branigan, he too had already achieved renown throughout the city as a priest who "flashed" through the Mass in record time—typically fifteen to eighteen minutes; others swear even faster. He was known as well for his gregarious, flamboyant personality and his taste for a zestful social life. He was friendly with such stars as Jimmy O'Dea and Cecil Sheridan and relished the parties and stage performances that went with it all.

Everyone knew that "Father Flash" was unabashedly fond of a jar and would regularly dart directly from the altar to the pub, in full priestly regalia. John Preston, a docker who befriended him in their regular pub, the Deer's Head in Parnell Street, witnessed this many times:

> He used to do ten o'clock Mass, because the pubs opened at half ten, and he'd be *in there* at half ten—in a *flash!* He'd drink pints and small ones—all according to the collection that morning! You'd see him there in the mornings, in his red vestments, in a little back snug—that was his berth.

For Jim Branigan, marriage meant immediate change. "I had £4 a week when I got married. So I gave up the booze—I couldn't *afford* it."[4] Though he had been only a moderate drinker, he enjoyed it, and it took considerable willpower to give it up completely. Between them the newly-weds had just enough savings to make a payment on a small semi-detached house, 135 Drimnagh Road. Removed from the congested core of the city, with its noise, traffic, hubbub, they enjoyed a rather countrified atmosphere of open space and fresh air. An unexpected pleasure of married life, he found, was Elsie's fondness for cooking. According to Declan, his mother was *"very* talented. She loved doing home cooking and baking. She did *everything.* Oh, he loved her food." He also admired her ability to stretch his modest wage. "Money wasn't plentiful," says Declan, "but there was *always* a dinner on the table."

It was a good marriage. By the end of their first year together Elsie was pregnant and Jim exuberant about having a child.

———

It was in this same period that he developed a friendship with Senan Finucane, who became a regular "sidekick," sharing duty and risks over the next twenty

years. For Finucane, coming from a farming family and the lush fields of
Co. Clare to the tenemented Liberties—having never before even been in
Dublin—was like landing on an alien planet. Branigan mentored him through
the transition. He explained to him about city culture, introduced him to
dealers, shopkeepers, and residents, and gave him crisp profiles of local thugs
and hooligans, who always liked to "size up" a new recruit on the beat.

From his first day he admitted to being awed by Branigan and came to
respect him more than any other man in the force. In addition to Branigan's
tough, fearless character he was impressed by his kind and humanitarian
nature. People around the Liberties took an immediate liking to Finucane
as well. A top-notch garda, he was smart, perceptive, fair-minded, and tough
when he needed to be.

The two guards would often share the wartime duties of inspecting bomb
shelters, enforcing the black-out, trying to prevent black-market activities,
assisting evacuees from the North. Inspecting air-raid shelters could be a
nasty task. Many soon became "cesspools," as local people called them, used
as havens for dossers and drunks or as toilets, rubbish dumps, and places to
dump dead dogs and cats. The two guards sometimes encountered couples
coupling, beatings in progress, even dead bodies.

Branigan and Finucane were also on the look-out for wartime crooks.
What appeared to be a small bag of precious tea might be hawked around the
streets by some scoundrel who had cleverly spread a thin layer of tea on top of
the sawdust beneath. Similarly, men could be duped into thinking they were
buying a nice pouch of tobacco for their pipe.

Scarcely a month after Jim and Elsie were married, on 31 May, the Whit
holiday weekend, at 2:05 a.m. on a gloriously clear, starry night, there was a
thunderous explosion in Dublin. The earth quaked as the sky turned a fiery
red. Tremors were felt as far away as Enniskerry and Mullingar. A German
bomber had dropped a monstrous 500-pound bomb on North Strand Road,
causing appalling destruction and loss of life. "There was pandemonium,"
wrote the *Irish Times*. "There were shrieks and cries of people who rushed to
the street."[5] "Fear seized an entire city," wrote Pádraic O'Farrell.[6]

Garda Finucane was sleeping in Kevin Street barracks when the entire
building shook. Branigan was at home in Drimnagh Road. All city gardaí were
ordered to the site immediately. With no buses or trams running in the middle
of the night, this meant cycling or walking miles for many men. Finucane
recalls being rudely roused by the bomb:

> An awful explosion! We were called in—"Everybody out, get to the scene
> of the bomb!" The whole of Dublin went over to see—it was just the same
> as O'Connell Street during the day on a Saturday.

As he and his colleagues headed over to the North Strand at a trot, they passed throngs of panicking citizens. They arrived at a horrifying scene: houses and shops blown to smithereens, more than forty people killed, about a hundred seriously injured. Thousands would be rendered homeless. Hospitals and morgues filled within hours.

Branigan would have arrived some time later, along with thousands of men from the army and Local Defence Force (LDF) and air-raid wardens. The gardaí first set up a cordon, managed crowd control, tried to keep the streets clear for the fire brigade and ambulances, to calm terrified people who feared that another bomb might fall at any moment, though they had the same worry themselves.

Manning the cordons in such close proximity to the rescue operations, even men as toughened as Branigan and Finucane were shaken by what they saw. "People were working with their bare hands, taking out bodies all bloody," says Finucane ". . . pieces of legs, hands . . . a head maybe. A *terrible* sight!" Because of his training in the St John Ambulance Brigade, and his boxing experience, Branigan was never bothered as much by the sight of blood as his fellow-gardaí. Yet he could only have been sickened by the awful mutilation of bodies, which even distressed doctors and nurses.

Amidst the chaos of the calamity, guards had to stand on duty for ten to fourteen hours in the sweltering heat of the following day, with little food or water. Some became ill themselves. Two days later, in its editorial headed "The Dublin bombing," the *Irish Press* wrote that "this awful tragedy has also had its noble side," citing the bravery and loyalty to duty of Dublin's gardaí, firemen, LDF and air-raid wardens.[7] Under great duress and at personal risk they had exhibited "gallantry, kindliness and noble actions."

On the Sunday morning, before all the dust had even settled at the North Strand, another tragedy struck in the heart of Branigan's Liberties, only a few streets from Kevin Street Garda Station. Shortly after 10 a.m. Garda Patrick O'Connor, a colleague of Branigan's and Finucane's, heard the crash of falling masonry and saw a huge cloud of dust rising. He raced down the street to see what had happened. Two decrepit tenement houses in Old Bride Street had suddenly collapsed as the occupants were having their breakfast and preparing to leave for Mass. The buildings had presumably been shaken and destabilised by the huge blast over on the North Strand. A young mother, her six-month old baby and an elderly man had been killed. With all the gardaí from Kevin Street and New Market called to the site, Branigan would have been assisting local residents within the hour.

Over the following days Dubliners were jittery, their nerves frayed, worried about more bombs falling. Everyone wanted to know whether the German bombing had been accidental or intentional—a question that would never be answered with absolute certainty. For Jim and Elsie Branigan, their first few weeks of married life could hardly have been more tense and dramatic.

That same week the *Irish Times* published a troubling article critical of some judges and senior Garda officers. It was stated that "some District Justices were not holding their courts" as often as they should, "on the grounds of the small amount of petrol that was allowed them." Some threatened that if they did not get more petrol they "would not attend the courts" at all. Others groused that if their courts were not "put in the proper state of repair they would refuse to sit in them."

To exacerbate matters, the newspaper revealed that, according to the minister for justice, Gerry Boland, it was "unfortunately true that there were senior Garda officers who were unfit to hold their posts," with the result that the "gardaí and the general public were seriously affected by it." Though no specific details of incompetence were cited, or names mentioned, it was a shocking revelation. For Branigan and other lower-level gardaí it was harmful to morale to learn about judges and senior Garda officers who were not performing to the highest standards while they risked their welfare on the streets, endeavouring to keep the peace. Furthermore, Branigan and his fellow-gardaí knew that suspects they arrested might simply be released by a malfunctioning court system.

On 28 June, de Valera issued a message to the nation about Ireland's need to defend itself against aggressors. The next day's *Sunday Independent* published the full text about the very real "perils of war" lurking just beyond Irish shores.[8] People must avoid "complacency" and be ready to evacuate, de Valera warned. Dublin had become a city on the edge.

———

By the spring of 1942 Branigan and Finucane, as well as their colleagues stationed in the Liberties, faced a growing problem: the toss schools. Pitch-and-toss had been around in Dublin for centuries, usually considered an innocuous way of passing the time for bored men. Various games of betting for ha'pennies, pennies or shillings were part of the very culture of the city. Says Finucane: "Men'd sit down in the street and play cards to pass the time. That was harmless—only small stakes." As part of his childhood in Pimlico, recalls Stephen Mooney, "you started gambling about the age of six, pitching up to the wall with your ha'pennies and pennies. Then you graduated to card games and toss schools, which involved you in more money."

Around the Liberties people gambled in tenement halls by candlelight or "on street corners under gas lamps—where we could watch for the police. And then you'd bee-line it!" As long as the stakes were low, Branigan didn't much worry about it. In fact watching some of the more colourful operators was considered part of the street entertainment in the Liberties. Máirín Johnston remembers one of the most flamboyant characters, with the exotic name "Sartire," who put on great performances with his toss school:

> Sartire was a big, powerful man, wore a large hound's tooth tweed cap, a sports jacket with loud large check squares, plus-fours, and multicoloured diamond-patterned knee socks.
>
> Like a ringmaster in a circus, he stormed about the centre of the toss school wielding a short dray driver's whip, and would use this mercilessly to enlarge the circle . . . He roared out the results for the fellas at the back of the crowd.[9]

Even Branigan, who sometimes had to step in and stop him, found him one of the most fascinating characters on his beat.

Toss schools were traditionally held on Sunday. No game of chance was simpler. Two ha'pennies were placed on a stick about the width of the coins and four or five inches long and tossed in the air. Two heads won and two harps lost; a head and a harp meant tossing over again.

For Branigan, the problem arose when the stakes became high enough to create social problems or to trigger violence among gangs. During the war years the popularity of toss schools, and the amounts being wagered, rose significantly. Then, Finucane confirms, "wives would complain [to us] that their husbands were losing all their money . . . all their wages," leaving mothers with no money for rent, food, or fuel, sometimes leading to eviction. By 1942 the problem was making the front pages of some newspapers. Local gangs and other hooligans were rivalling one another to get in on the growing profits.

On the afternoon of Sunday 29 March, reported the *Evening Herald*, "six men who had their own toss school decided to carry out a 'commando raid' on a rival toss school."[10] The attackers swept down upon their rivals, "brandishing a knife," grabbing the money and fleeing. Then the "commando group . . . flushed with victory," decided to carry out yet another attack on a different toss school. This time, however, they "made a mistake," as the twenty or more men they took on "were of sterner stuff" and vigorously fought back, with knives and knuckledusters, stabbing two of the defenders.[11]

As some of the participants were from the Liberties, Branigan was despatched to investigate the incident and bring in the guilty men. In court, Judge Conor Maguire said he took a "very serious view" of toss schools. When a solicitor for the defendants argued that the "game" was "as old as the city itself—and came here with the Danes," Maguire replied tersely that they were nonetheless unlawful. He declared that it was shameful that they had gone on so long "unhampered throughout the country." He wanted the police in Dublin to eradicate them.[12]

Branigan knew that his efforts to halt toss schools would be met with resistance and clever ploys to outwit him. When he, Finucane and other guards began cracking down, they found that some stakes were far higher than they had realised. In some cases, says Finucane, a small fortune was being wagered on the street:

> At a toss school there might be sixty or eighty men and the place full of silver, half crowns . . . often a hundred, or maybe two hundred pounds on the ground. A *lot* of money! Oh, I often saw buckets of money. So emotions were high.

To a garda making £4 or £5 a week, £100 on the ground certainly looked like a fortune. It was no surprise to Branigan and Finucane that "a row often started at a toss school." Éamonn Mac Thomáis once saw a man first lose all his money and then, in desperation, bet—and lose—his pony and trap, which he needed for his livelihood.[13] Máirín Johnston recalls the coalman in her area who gambled away his dray full of coal, and then "the unfortunate man went completely out of his mind and tried to commit suicide."[14]

When old gang rivalries were revived over the toss schools, leading to the renewal of violent clashes, Branigan and the Liberties gardaí made it a priority. They organised squads of police to sweep in on the major toss schools and apprehend the organisers. John McCormack remembers that if gangs from the Liberties tried to invade the Gardiner Street gang's area, the local gangs unleashed his father, Spike, on them. "Oh, he *cleared up* the toss school when the south-side fellas tried to move in!"

A toss school could be set up, then disbanded, in seconds if the police were spotted. And the organisers always had look-outs. This resulted in a continuous "cops and robbers" struggle between the two groups. Garda John Murphy, who was later a member of one of Branigan's teams cracking down on the toss schools, recalls the high excitement in the action:

> In Ship Street, on Sunday mornings, we often raided. We'd come in suddenly from *that* side—and *this* side. They'd *run like hell!* And then they'd be gone. *Grown* men. And they'd leave the money there . . . and we'd give it to charity.

Gradually, Branigan and his commandos reduced the most troublesome toss schools around the Liberties, but they could never eliminate them entirely.

Meantime, war worries were mounting. Because of its proximity to the expanding war front, the *Irish Press* warned, "Ireland is a suburb of a city on fire—it would be foolish to think we are not in danger."[15] A headline in the *Sunday Independent* proclaimed: "Time of the greatest danger to our nation— War crisis near."[16]

Many families had another problem in March 1942 when they read in the *Irish Times* a despatch from Reuters that confirmed their fear of military induction for relatives in the United States.[17] The same week the *Irish Press* military correspondent wrote that "the Japanese war machine has achieved remarkable success in its efforts at dominance in the South-western Pacific."[18] Japan was now confidently turning its attention to the "capture and occupation of Australia," where many Irish people had family and friends.

The tightening of rations and general austerity became an irritation even to mild-mannered citizens. Grumbling became a favourite national pastime. The shortage of coal was a critical problem, and sugar and soap were also rationed. Motorists were expressing their "annoyance and dissatisfaction" with the prospect of an "impending ban on private motoring."[19] The black market in petrol and other products was already taking up more of Branigan's time. Cyclists suffered a blow when the Minister for Supplies announced in the spring that they were to face a severe shortage of tyres and tubes. Because of petrol shortages and reduced hours for buses there was now a sea of cyclists in Dublin getting to and from work. What were they to do if their tyres gave out?

Particularly noticeable was the dramatic return of the horse to Dublin streets. With petrol and motoring shrinking, jarveys and carters experienced a grand reincarnation, with their services now in great demand. Along O'Connell Street up to two hundred horses could be seen at a time, giving Dublin the smell of a country town. Throughout the city, down at the docks, along the quays and back lanes, thousands of horses were being worked hard in haulage and passenger transport, with the result that on 21 March it was announced that the country's blacksmiths "are seriously threatened by a severe shortage of horseshoes."[20]

———

It was some time in late March that Stephen Mooney picked up the first rumours of a "rumble" between the local Ash Street gang and the Stafford Street gang—a particularly tough bunch. As usual, it stemmed from competition and territorial disputes over profitable activities. In this case it seemed to be a feud over toss schools and the protection racket. "The protection rackets were running and it [rivalry] was coming to a head," Mooney says, "and the two animal gangs met in Tolka Park—and there was a *battle royal* there." It was what the Gardaí, courts and public had feared: the re-emergence of a Baldoyle-type clash at a public venue.

Branigan first got wind of some sort of gang trouble around mid-March, but no specific information, nothing he could translate into pre-emptive action. He put up his antennae to see if he could get any further signals, especially from the women dealers, who knew everything going on in the community. Then he and his sidekick Finucane made some enquiries at a few of the pubs around the Liberties frequented by local gangs. "The pub was a mine of information," says Finucane, "where we would get *loads* of news, *all* sorts."

In the meantime Branigan was reasoning things out. He felt confident that the older, more mature gang members around his Liberties, and probably elsewhere, had learnt a lesson from the harsh sentences doled out to the Baldoyle participants. They didn't want to end up behind bars, especially the older men who had wives and children. Conversely, the younger, more reckless gang members seemed to be still up for a rumble, especially when under the influence of drink. Branigan therefore decided that it was the younger men he should especially keep his eye on. He would observe their behaviour, collect bits of talk here and there. As with Baldoyle, he was determined that no trouble would take place on *his* turf.

By about 20 March he had indeed picked up more gossip and tips, leading him to suspect a confrontation "probably soon," at a soccer match, perhaps in Drumcondra; at least, that was the word floating around. Checking the schedules, he found that a big match was coming up on 22 March at Tolka Park in Drumcondra between St Stephen's and Mountview in the semi-final of the Junior Combination Cup. His intuition also told him that this was a very likely site for such a skirmish. He would share his suspicions with his superiors, so that they could alert the Drumcondra gardaí.

Sure enough, about midday on Sunday 22 March, what newspapers would call an Ash Street "commando squad" of "about 15 to 20 men," aged between eighteen and twenty-six, embarked on their foolhardy mission.[21] Though primed with drink, they were not drunk. As match time approached, an enthusiastic crowd streamed along Richmond Road into Tolka Park and settled into place as the players completed their warm-up. Among the spectators were the Stafford Street gang, who had entered as paying patrons but bearing hidden arms. No-one noticed.

Meanwhile, fancying themselves an elite expeditionary force, a number of the Ash Street raiders commandeered several boats moored some distance up the Tolka River on the side of the pitch opposite Richmond Road and began silently rowing towards their destination. A few other men crossed the river by wading in chest-deep water. All were feeling exhilaration over their military-style manoeuvre. They had shrewdly planned their attack for the second half of the match, when the Stafford Street bunch would be lulled into thinking the rumble was no longer on.

Upon successfully landing surreptitiously at the site, the boatmen quickly "scaled the partition, mixing with the spectators."[22] As they were scrambling over the partitions their comrades barged through the gates, overpowering stunned attendants. This action constituted an effective two-pronged attack.

Within seconds, wrote an *Irish Times* reporter at the scene, "a wild scene ensued."[23] "A full-scale invasion was launched," the *Evening Herald* reported, "armed with all kinds of weapons and in a few minutes pitched battle was under way. Spectators beat a hasty retreat and left the ground to the belligerents."[24] Knives, crowbars, flagpoles, rusty swords, iron bars and legs of chairs were used, as bottles flew in all directions.

At first the players, referee, linesmen and groundsmen tried to halt the fighting. But this quickly proved futile, and highly dangerous. According to one groundsman, John Flaherty, "at first 15 or 16 people took part in the riot ... This number increased as a running riot and fight followed."[25] Before long it was more like thirty to forty wild brawlers. Gardaí at the scene rushed them with batons drawn but had to call for reinforcements immediately. It didn't take long for injured men to litter the ground. Two men, a man named Kelly from Stafford Street and one named Leonard from Little Mary Street, were quickly struck down and rushed off to the Mater Hospital as more ambulances were arriving, their bells clanging. Kelly had suffered serious injuries to the head and back, Leonard wounds to the head and left eye.

An *Evening Herald* reporter brave enough to remain and cover the story portrayed the violence:

> One man fell to the ground bleeding profusely from the head and was carried to the pavilion by some players ... Another man was struck and *flung over* the partition into the river, where he was rescued by companions ... One participant was about to strike a man on the head with a crowbar when he himself was felled by a blow from another man with a flag pole, which broke in two.[26]

People were jostled or knocked down in the stampede. At the outset, most spectators probably thought the affray was a scuffle between rival supporters, but when the blood began to flow they guessed otherwise. "Everything was in confusion as spectators and officials were put in terror and fled, the match being completely abandoned."[27] Anyone who placed themselves in the way of the wicked weapons was in grave danger. "Scenes were unbelievable," declared one newspaper, with "a bayonet being wielded by one man as the blade flashed

1. James's Street School, fourth class, 1920. Branigan is third from left, third row. The small picture clearly shows his distinctive feature as a ten-year-old. (*Courtesy of Alick Branigan*)

2. Family photo from 1927. From left: father, brother Frank, mother, sister Nora, Jim. (*Courtesy of Alick Branigan*)

3. Holding rifle and rabbits with Kavanagh cousins in Co. Kilkenny, c. 1928–9. (*Courtesy of Alick Branigan*)

4. Formal photo, c. 1930. (*Courtesy of Alick Branigan*)

5. Posted outside Kilmainham District Court for the famous Nurse Cadden trial of 1939. (*Courtesy of Garda Paul Maher*)

6. Proudly in uniform during posting to Irishtown Garda Station, Dublin, 1935. (*Courtesy of Garda Paul Maher*)

7. Garda Jim Branigan, mid-1930s. (*Courtesy of Garda Paul Maher*)

Three Jim Branigans

8. First cousin Jim on left and uncle Jim, who lived to be 103 years old, on right, c. early 1930s. (*Courtesy of Jim Branigan*)

9. With brother Frank and Kavanagh cousins, c. early 1930s. (*Courtesy of Alick Branigan*)

10. Christmas card greeting, c. early 1930s. (*Courtesy of Alick Branigan*)

11. Garda Boxing Club, 1939. Branigan is at far right, standing. (*Courtesy of Garda Paul Maher*)

12. Leinster heavyweight boxing champion, 1937.
(*Courtesy of Alick Branigan*)

13. Garda Boxing Club, c. 1935. Branigan is at far left and his instructor, Tommy Maloney, third from left. (*Courtesy of Garda Paul Maher*)

14. Branigan in "swanky" civilian attire with Garda Boxing Club instructor Tommy Maloney, mid-1930s. (*Courtesy of Alick Branigan*)

15. Pugilistic posturing with unidentified opponent, mid-1930s. (*Courtesy of Alick Branigan*)

16. On holiday in the Isle of Man with unidentified friend, mid-1930s. (*Courtesy of John Farrell*)

17. With two good friends, Matt Crehan (*left*) and Tim O'Donnell (*centre*), early 1930s. (*Courtesy of Garda Paul Maher*)

18. With Henry Tiller, Norwegian middleweight boxing champion and Olympic finalist, 1936. (*Courtesy of Alick Branigan*)

19. In the famous "Battle of Baldoyle," May 1940, Branigan played a leading role in breaking the reign of the notorious gangs that terrorised Dublin.

20. Wedding day, 26 April 1941. *From left*: John Montgomery, Norah Branigan, Elizabeth (Elsie) and Jim. (*Courtesy of Alick Branigan*)

21. Branigan's close friend and sidekick for twenty years, Senan Finucane Sr (*left*), and Con Carmody, c. early 1940s. (*Courtesy of Garda Senan Finucane Jr*)

22. With the Lord Mayor of Dublin, Alfie Byrne (*centre*), and boxing officials, early 1930s. (*Courtesy of Garda Paul Maher*)

23. Elsie with Declan (in arms), Alick, and Helen, 1949. (*Courtesy of Alick Branigan*)

24. Jim and Elsie (far right), with Kavanagh cousins at Dublin Zoo, c. 1950. (*Courtesy of Alick Branigan*)

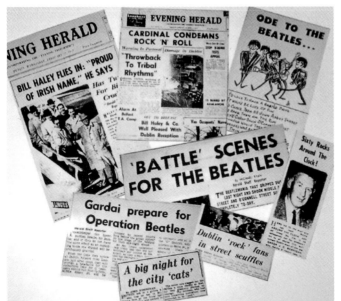

25. Rock and roll fuelled Dublin's 'youth rebellion' in the 1950s and 60s. The Beatles' appearance at the Adelphi Cinema kept two hundred gardaí busy with teenage rioting.

26. The Beatles arriving at Dublin Airport on 7 November 1963 for their performance at the Adelphi Cinema. (© *Irish Photo Archive*)

27. Bill Haley and his Comets, whose record and film *Rock Around the Clock* ignited the rock-and-roll craze and led Branigan to become known as the "Rock and Roll Cop" in newspapers in the 1950s. (*Courtesy of Paddy Daly*)

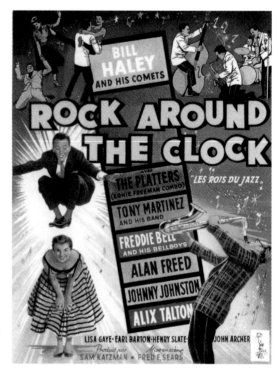

28. Enticing *Rock Around the Clock* poster, French version. (© *Pictorial Press Ltd/Alamy*)

in the sun."[28] An official came upon one fallen combatant "so seriously injured he was thought dead."

As at Baldoyle, bystanders and Good Samaritans got caught in the melee and were injured. One spectator, Thomas Fitzgerald, told how "a row started, and a couple of men started chasing me, and I got a blow on the head, fell to the ground, and was kicked." James O'Brien recounted how he was chased for no reason and "had to jump over a twenty-foot wall to get out of the grounds." One Good Samaritan, Michael Boylan, described "a state of terror on the grounds," seeing a man being beaten and kicked. When he went to assist the man a gang member stabbed him twice in the arm, which later required an operation.

———

According to the *Irish Times*, the "fight lasted for some time," with more guards arriving and struggling to quell the violence without being injured themselves. Amidst the pandemonium it was easy for gang members to escape without being apprehended or identified. As most spectators had fled, there were few reliable witnesses to question.

After it was all over, reported the *Evening Herald*, "the police are making inquiries into the affair, but so far there have been no arrests." This may have puzzled the public, as the fracas took place in full view; but, because of the bewilderment and frenzy of spectators seeking to flee, it was understandable. It meant that the suspects would have to be rounded up.

As Stephen Mooney recalls, because of Branigan's renowned success in dealing with gangs since the mid-1930s, he was logically *the* man called upon to get the job done:

> After the gangs met in Tolka Park, the court said, "I want those fellas brought in—and *that's it*, we'll deal with them in court!" So Lugs Branigan, he was instructed to go out and *bring them in*.

The next morning, Monday 23 March, the papers once again noted the striking juxtaposition of war news and that of gang battles in Dublin. Readers were left to interpret the disgrace of it. On the front page of the *Irish Times* were the following stories:

"Fierce fighting round Kharkov"

"Fight at football ground"

The *Evening Herald* printed the headline:

"Battle at Tolka Park followed 'invasion' in commandeered boats"

Adjacent to this headline were reports headed "Bitter fighting in Donets region" and "Many vessels sunk in Mediterranean."

Ten days later Branigan had rounded up his Liberties suspects, and gardaí in other districts brought in their local combatants. On 1 April, in Dublin District Court, nine defendants appeared before Judge Lennon charged with riotous assembly, assault, and wounding with intent to cause grievous bodily harm. Detective-Sergeant King stepped forward to tell Judge Lennon that the release of prisoners before their trial "might hamper inquiries, and the prisoners might also interfere with witnesses."[29] Garda Branigan fully concurred. The judge denied their request for bail.

In the interim Branigan and other gardaí involved in the case dug for evidence. While they knew it had been motivated by competition over various racketeering ventures, it would be virtually impossible to prove conspiracy in this case. They did, however, gather solid evidence of participation in the Tolka Park rumble, thanks to co-operative witnesses. When Branigan began the interrogation process in the quest for evidence in a case, people were inclined to open up to him—and to be honest in doing so. No-one wanted to let him down, or get on the wrong side of him.

In mid-June the Tolka Park case opened before Mr Justice Conor Maguire in the Central Criminal Court. The prosecutor, P. J. McEnerny (who also had a role in the Baldoyle case), opened by stating that the case was "a very serious one," in which stabbings and beatings had caused injuries that could easily have led to death. One by one the witnesses—spectators, players, linesmen, referee, attendants—were called to present their testimony, sealing the fate of the defendants. Dr Corcoran, staff surgeon at the Mater Hospital, revealed that John Kelly's wound on the back and the left loin was five inches deep, probably inflicted by a "bayonet-type weapon."[30] Asked by McEnery, "Could it have caused death?" the surgeon replied, "It could."

Not surprisingly, the accused men refused to give evidence. For the defence, Trant McCarthy conveyed their claim of innocence, despite the preponderance of evidence against them. McEnery responded: "If the men in the dock went to enjoy themselves at a football match, why did they bring knives and bayonets with them?"

On Monday 22 June, Mr Justice Maguire expressed his displeasure that the "origins of the enmity" between the gangs had not been revealed. However, he felt certain that it had to do with a "plan to get back on those other men," thus reflecting the typical gang-style revenge mentality.[31] As he prepared to hand down the sentences he stated that, because of the volume of evidence before him, presented by Branigan, other guards, and witnesses, he "could not have come to any other decision." Asserting that he "must put a stop to gang warfare" in Dublin, he sentenced the men to eighteen months' imprisonment with hard labour. *Hard labour.* That was something they could understand.

He then left them with an even more sobering thought. "The charges were very serious and could merit a sentence of penal servitude for life."[32] This time a lasting impression would be left on most of Dublin's gangsters.

Chapter 7 ~

"A SHERIFF IN TOWN"

"He was like a sheriff in the Old West . . . It was like he rode into town and took over!"

(GARDA PADDY DALY)

"He was a big fella, like John Wayne . . . He'd walk along with a bit of a sway in his shoulders, like a sheriff—that's what Lugs was. The reputation was there. Oh, he cleaned up the city!"

(NOEL HUGHES, AGE 76)

"Breaking up rows became my speciality. My method was a little unorthodox. I always had leather gloves out on the beat. A thug, I might give him a few clips, or a good hiding from me, and send him home."

(GARDA JIM BRANIGAN)

"He was feared by even hardened thugs. He would *flick* his leather gloves across their face, and it had a demeaning effect. A thug who moments earlier had been foaming at the mouth would suddenly become cowed."

(GARDA CON HEARTY)

By the late 1940s and early 50s the analogy of Lugs Branigan as a "sheriff" on the lawless streets of Dublin was becoming evident. In the public's perception, his image and growing reputation perfectly fitted the role.

During the war years he and Elsie began their family. In January 1942 she gave birth to a son, Alick, delighting his proud father. On 27 June 1943 his daughter Helen was born. While having children greatly enriched his life, it also brought new financial burdens and responsibilities, as well as a keener awareness of the high-risk nature of his job. Wartime rationing made their life even more difficult.

On Tuesday 8 May 1945 Dublin experienced an outburst of unbridled joy. The large headline in the *Irish Independent* told the story: "Surrender by Germany." It brought cheers and tears throughout Ireland. When people heard the news they burst from their homes, offices, shops, spilling out into the streets to celebrate. Especially in Dublin, where the fear of being bombed had been the greatest. The *Irish Times* wrote:

> Dubliners' reaction to the stoppage of hostilities found expression in the parading of the principal streets by thousands of people who felt relief from the five years' strain too much to keep them in their normal occupations and recreations. Main thoroughfares were clogged.

Gardaí were called out for crowd control and keeping the streets clear. It was the happiest crowd-control duty Garda Branigan and Garda Finucane had ever been assigned. They were thrilled to be among the vast throngs on such a historic, memorable day. Many uniformed guards were getting hearty pats on the back, as if they were returning soldiers. Branigan and Finucane felt little need to "control" the crowd, allowing them to let loose in their own ways. With great delight, recalls Finucane, they stood watching all the whistling, hugging, prancing around:

> It was a scene of joy everywhere. *Everybody* was delighted. They prayed, especially the women, saying, "Thank God it's over! Now we'll be able to get a bit of coal, tea, candles, sugar." It was a weight taken off their shoulders.

As the two young guards strolled through the dense crowds of the Liberties, along Thomas Street, Meath Street, Patrick Street, all was a sea of deliriously happy humanity. Drink flowed in every pub. A day they would always remember.

The *Irish Independent* noted that the war had lasted for 2,094 days, or 526 longer than the First World War. Many families could now look forward to relatives returning home from the British forces and war factories. And everyone felt sure that "better times" were just ahead, that shortages of tea, petrol, cocoa, cigarettes, sugar, candles, coal, tobacco, paraffin oil, stockings— the whole lot—would end soon and become just a bad memory. Unfortunately, when this did not materialise immediately disillusionment set in, as well as disenchantment with the Government, spelling new problems for Branigan and his fellow-gardaí, who had the responsibility for keeping Dublin's streets peaceful.

In the post-war period, food and fuel remained in short supply, unemployment high, job prospects few. Times remained tough. On 25 July

1946, when Jim and Elsie's second son, Declan, was born, the joy of the occasion was tempered by the realisation of more financial strain for a family of five.

———

Two years after the ending of the war, living conditions were still more difficult than anyone would have imagined. Food and fuel in particular were desperately short. Then, in 1947, the country was struck by an unprecedented natural calamity: the most brutal winter in its recorded history. And as Britain was experiencing the same freakish weather, it had no coal to export to Ireland.

On 19 January, Ireland was hit by an arctic siege that originated in Siberia and gripped the country until mid-March. The polar conditions dropped temperatures to −14°C, brought five major blizzards, snowdrifts of five to nine feet in Dublin and up to fifteen or twenty feet around the country. Dublin was paralysed, with vehicular and pedestrian traffic halted. With only wet turf to burn, many people, especially in the tenements, were forced to strip their homes of wood and to burn furniture. Food was running precariously short, and Dublin's death rate nearly trebled. People in the city were actually dying from cold and hunger.

It was all a great strain for Dublin gardaí. With telephone, telegraph and electricity lines down much of the time, the Garda, fire brigade and ambulance services often could not be contacted in emergencies. Citizens—hungry, freezing and frightened—straggled into Garda stations pleading for help that guards could not provide. Branigan, Finucane and their colleagues in New Market and Kevin Street risked frostbite trying to make their rounds in sub-freezing streets.

To frighten people further, at 10:27 a.m. on Sunday 26 January a bizarre natural event struck Dublin. Suddenly, the earth and buildings trembled, as crockery and utensils jingled and jitterbugged. It was a queer, quivering sensation that unnerved people. Many tenement-dwellers heard their decrepit buildings creak and crack.

Residents flocked to Garda and fire stations to ask what had happened. They could get no answers. According to the seismograph at Rathfarnham Castle, a fairly strong earthquake had hit.

The freak arctic weather finally subsided in the middle of March, and life slowly returned to normal in Dublin. Branigan resumed his usual rounds, listening to all the stories of horror from local residents. And learning that many of the elderly and frail had died during the previous three months.

Ironically, the summer of 1947 was one of the most glorious on record. Abundant sunshine and record temperatures prevailed for most of July and August. Uniformed guards perspired, wishing they had tropical attire.

Everyone wanted to be outside, heading to the seaside, engaging in cycling, hiking, gardening. Including Jim Branigan of Drimnagh Road.

———

For the Branigan family at 135 Drimnagh Road, life seemed idyllic. He had a wonderful wife, three lovely healthy children, a comfortable home, a nice little plot of land. And pets galore. Often he was met by the aroma of a fresh apple tart when he walked through the door. Alick remembers his father *"always being in good spirits."* And sometimes in good voice as well. "I used to hear him singing 'The Moon Behind the Hill,' or humming." Around bedtime he liked to make up silly songs for the children. "Like this song: 'In the shade of the old apple tree—where Alick got stung by a bee!'—you know, childhood songs."

His love of gardening and animals played an important part in his life, providing relaxation and diversion to balance the stressful demands of his police duties. By the time Alick was six or seven he had him digging around in the garden with him. The young lad liked to see his father unwinding in what he calls "just a small suburban garden," where he grew potatoes, cabbage, and onions. A city man by birth, he took pride in his ability to cultivate the soil. And his small crop helped provide food for Elsie's kitchen.

He especially enjoyed having animals around him and in the house. "He was *mad* about animals," recalls Alick: "ducks and rabbits and even a goat at one time"—adding hesitatingly, "which we *ate* eventually." In Declan's memory, "there were *always* animals in the house . . . He reared dogs, pups, and chickens. The neighbours three doors down had a cow!" Drimnagh Road had a bit of country atmosphere and scent, which Garda Branigan found a pleasant contrast to the smoke and fumes of the city centre.

His greatest passion was his dogs and birds. His two alsatians were members of the family and treated as such. They faithfully met him on his arrival home each day—and protected his family when he was away, an important role, as he did occasionally receive anonymous threats from "gougers" with whom he had dealt.

Budgies were a pride and joy as well, and he became expert in breeding them. He would dote on his little friends, making certain they were kept healthy and well fed. He frequently talked to his Garda mates about his budgies, often adding, "Oh, you must come out and see them now." A good few friends took him up on the offer and had to smile when they saw the mighty Lugs Branigan with what they called his *"huge"* hands tenderly cupping a little budgie in his palm. They liked seeing this quite different side of their friend Jim Branigan. It became routine for him to say to his fellow-gardaí at the end of a day's duty that it was time to go home now and "tend to the animals and birds."

From a young age, Declan understood how healthy it was for his father to engage in these pastimes. "He *needed* these outlets. The job could be stressful. It was a release, a relief, to come home to his little hobbies . . . the budgies, the hens, his dogs. And the plots."

He also made sure there was ample time for reading the newspapers, listening to the wireless, and reading his growing collection of books on American western history and lore. These remained his favourite subjects—supplemented, of course, by western films, which brought the action to life. If anything, his fascination with American frontier sheriffs, marshals and Indian chiefs increased as he grew older and better comprehended their complex characters. He so admired some of the famous Indian chiefs that he named his two alsatians "Geronimo" and "Cochise."

———

If life in Drimnagh Road seemed serene, the outside world was just the opposite. In the post-war years, Europe and North America seemed to be plunging forward with startling change and new developments. In some ways the new concepts and technology appeared altogether futuristic: towering skyscrapers, huge automated factories, jet planes, glass-and-steel office buildings, high-powered cars, dazzling department stores, cinemas, sports stadiums, motorways.

But Ireland remained a land of old buildings, old factories, old institutions, old pubs. As Fergal Tobin explains in his insightful book *The Best of Decades: Ireland in the 1960s,* Ireland changed so imperceptibly that even at the end of the 1950s "an emigrant returning to the Republic of Ireland in the late fifties after thirty years abroad would have had few recognition problems."[1] Everything still appeared old and dingy, comfortably in place. There were still few cars, no shopping centres or supermarkets, no national television station.

More comprehensible to most Dubliners was the article by John D. Sheridan about "The passing of the tramcar." He soulfully lamented the loss of something so "majestic," which glided gracefully along its tracks, noting wistfully: "I grew up with tramcars . . . and I hate to see them go."[2] So too did Jim Branigan. As he did not drive, he was dependent on buses and trams for his transport around the city.

———

When the war ended, Branigan and Finucane had their hands full with men returning from Britain who often could not re-adjust to civilian and family life. Alcoholism and domestic violence were commonplace. When a husband returned home to discover that his wife had been keeping company with another man in his absence, all hell could break loose. Family rows could be triggered by all sorts of conflicts. In one case Branigan was summoned when a man just back from England became furious when he found that his sister was in a relationship with a man of whom he disapproved. He was particularly aggrieved as he "had never had any kind of interview" with her suitor. One night at about half eleven he gained the support of two friends. The three men barged into his sister's boy-friend's home and attacked him with a knife, after which they stabbed his invalid brother and knocked his mother to the floor. When Branigan arrived, the *Evening Herald* reported, he found "blood splattered about and several men wounded."[3]

One Sunday evening at about eight o'clock he was called to a flat in St Teresa's Gardens, where a fight was reported. A man named Mullen lived in the flat with his wife and two children. Suddenly there was a hammering on the door and two irate men broke in, shouting, "Come out, Jimmy! We're going to finish you this time!" Before Mullen could even grab his coal shovel to defend himself he was knifed by the two men. The assailants, a 49-year-old man and his 21-year-old son, were seeking vengeance for some unknown reason. Before Branigan could respond to the call the "two men decamped on a bicycle, the older man being carried on the cross-bar by his son." When Branigan showed up at the scene and got the story he knew that the two men could not get far on a wobbly bicycle. He quickly caught up with them and hauled them to the Garda station.

Spending his time dealing with a man angry over his sister's choice of boy-friend, or chasing two drunken men on a bicycle, were not exactly what Jim Branigan had in mind when he joined the Garda Síochána.

More exhilarating were pub raids. In the late 1940s and early 50s, when times were tough even for publicans, many complained of declining profits. This prompted some to try a few tricks at out-competing their neighbouring publicans by devious and even illegal means. Most commonly they cheated by breaking the law regulating opening hours. This could be done by keeping regulars on their premises during the "holy hour" (when they were required to close for at least an hour on Sundays) or after closing time at night. When competing publicans learnt of their trickery they notified the Gardaí and demanded that they put a halt to it. If this violation was repeated, a publican could lose his licence.

Publicans could conceal patrons late at night by bolting the door, turning off lights and operating by candlelight with curtains drawn, and ordering the privileged men to pledge silence. Patrons could drink away till the wee hours of the morning. For local gardaí, seeing men staggering home intoxicated early on a Sunday morning was a dead give-away. The most resourceful publicans even devised a system of secret knocks that allowed men to enter by a back or side door at all hours. Some were even let in and out through windows.

When complaints came in from competing publicans or distraught wives, Garda superintendents would order surveillance for the purpose of organising a plain-clothes raid on a pub. Branigan, Finucane and their station colleagues enjoyed the challenge of a good pub raid, in which about six or eight guards would seek to outwit a clever publican and, with lightning speed, catch him in the act.

> Oh, we used to break the code knock—and to their great surprise! People could be sneaky in keeping out of sight, and it's *amazing* how *quiet* they could be—maybe thirty or forty people. One time we went in with the right code—and we'd come *quick*—and they were jumping all over the place! *Out* the back door and over the wall. They would run and maybe a dozen of them made an escape. *Great* excitement!

Many escapers, of course, ran into the open arms of waiting guards. When Branigan commanded one of the raids on a pub it was a satisfying victory when all went according to plan. But sometimes he was called to a pub for exactly the opposite reason: the publican was having difficulty in getting people *out*. This occurred one Saturday night in the early 1950s at Joseph Cody's establishment at 49 Patrick Street, where he and his wife lived above the pub. At closing time all the patrons obediently departed, with the exception of a man named Kelly, who became belligerent when Cody asked him to leave. Suddenly he attacked Cody and "beat him, blackening his eyes, kicking him and breaking his teeth."[4]

It was apparently his wife who called the Garda station for help. Branigan, along with Garda Grehan and Garda Shannon, was despatched to the scene, arriving shortly before midnight. Finding the doors bolted, Branigan ordered the other two to step back and then "pounded and kicked at the front door," but it was too sturdy. Thinking quickly, he told the guards to climb the drainpipe and try to gain entry through an upper window, as he stayed posted by the door. The manoeuvre worked, and Grehan and Shannon got inside to find Cody bleeding profusely, his attacker still standing there in a drunken state.

In court, Judge Mangan called it an "unmerciful beating." He allowed Branigan to cross-examine Kelly. When the defendant was asked about the "amount of drink he had taken" he boastfully replied that he "could drink thirty pints in a day."[5] Which hardly helped his case. Describing the beating in court, Cody accused Kelly of being a "gouger." Judge Mangan commended Branigan and the other two guards on their quick action, and sentenced Kelly to four months' imprisonment.

For Garda Jim Branigan, 1950 marked the beginning of a significant transition. He was now forty years old, "middle-aged" by the standards of the day, and had been in uniform for twenty years, a seasoned, highly respected guard. On 1 December 1950 he was rewarded for his superior performance over two decades with a new assignment: the Prevention and Detection of Street Nuisances Unit. If any garda had a proven expertise in handling Dublin's "street nuisances" it was Branigan. Now this would be his full-time role.

However, it meant he would have to shed his uniform for plain clothes from now on—which, surprisingly, he said he didn't mind.

His new assignment also meant he would no longer be restricted to his Liberties beat but would enjoy freedom to cover the entire city in a patrol car with a driver. He would now be dealing with the toughest men from around the docks and quays. His expanded territory and new mobility was liberating, offering fresh scenery and challenges. He felt it to be regenerating at the age of forty, exciting in its prospects.

It also meant shifting from the old New Market station over to Kevin Street, which was a Garda "action centre" in the city. In the early 1950s a new crop of young gardaí would be coming out of the Depot, men young enough to be his sons. He thoroughly enjoyed mixing with this new generation of youthful gardaí, especially those who had an interest in boxing. He would always claim that engaging in close friendship with, and working beside, younger guards was a critical factor in keeping him young and spry himself. Furthermore, it kept him informed of the life and culture of Dublin youth. Which he would soon find he needed.

He settled happily into Kevin Street station, which would be his Garda home for the remainder of his career. As his sidekick Senan Finucane was already in the same station, they would continue to work together for twenty years.

Once ensconced in the station, Branigan became disturbed by the decrepit, dangerous tenement dwellings of the district: rickety buildings with rotten floors, stairs and bannisters, leaking roofs, cracked walls and ceilings, where the poorest of the poor were crammed together—sometimes eighty to a hundred people in one dwelling—having to use slop buckets and outdoor toilets that overflowed, suffering all kinds of fevers and diseases. It distressed Branigan to see such squalor and suffering directly beside him. At about the time he moved in, recalls Finucane, "in the back of Kevin Street there was an old tenement house that collapsed, and there were two killed."

On 1 September 1954 several tenement houses in Kevin Street, only yards from the Garda station, were on the very brink of collapse, as four families fled them to sleep out in the open street. They told an *Evening Herald* reporter that they were "afraid to stay in the houses . . . The walls were creaking so badly that it was feared they would fall in."[6] Annie Murphy, who lived at number 43 with her two young children, stated that the walls of her house were already "crumbling so badly that a nail could not be driven through them" to hang a picture. Next door, Mary Slevin pointed to the spot in her sloping floor where she had fallen through two years earlier. All residents confirmed that their rooms were "infested with rats."

Seeing these tragedies being played out each day just beside his Garda station had a profound effect on Branigan. They sensitised him to the culture of poverty and the appalling injustice of the city's policies. He had direct exposure to the shocking condition of "haves and have-nots" in Dublin society. To him it was immoral and unconscionable. Every chance he got to speak on behalf of the poor to members of the city council or the Dáil, he documented their plight and argued for action to rehouse them in a safe environment.

————

His duty now was dealing with "street nuisances." This embraced myriad disorders, crimes, and characters—in fact it was largely left to his judgement to decide what constituted a "street nuisance." He appreciated having this latitude: it got back again to the original question of a garda's personal "discretion."

The task was not merely to identify a street nuisance but how to deal with it. And therein lay Branigan's uniqueness. For his policing methods would not conform to the conventional ones used by most other guards. The old "baton charge" days were on the way out. Citizens in the 1950s had better-defined rights. If seriously mistreated by a guard they could lodge a complaint or bring it up in court, though many poorer citizens still feared doing so. Branigan's dislike of batons was well known to his colleagues. Nor did he need a baton, as he had his two fists. However, in the 1950s, with the local street gangs gone, he could no longer rely on his fists and boxing skill to take on "villains" when challenged. He would need to devise new methods of force befitting the changing times.

The early 1950s were a period of high unemployment, emigration, and disenchantment, which bred hopelessness, even despair. Thousands of men and women could find no jobs and no place in society. To exacerbate the problem, many of the traditional trades and crafts were becoming obsolete, such as coopers, stone-carvers, shoemakers, farriers, saddlers, signwriters. Machinery and containerisation at the docks were making dockers redundant. It was all bewildering, soul-destroying. Unemployed men collected their dole and shuffled back and forth between pub and betting-shop.

As Branigan's new assignment was the prevention as well as detection of street nuisances, this often meant having to use pre-emptive measures for defusing disorder. Orders to gardaí were to prevent clusters of men at street corners from expanding and becoming volatile. This was a touchy challenge, as they were ordinarily good-natured men simply gathering to pass the time by chatting and seeking companionship. As Branigan's fellow-garda John Murphy explains, "if there was a crowd of fellas standing at a corner and a guard came up and gave them a few pushes [to move them on], well, they *accepted* that. And walked away." But some groups would not passively accept a guard's interference.

On 21 July 1950, at 10:30 p.m., there occurred an incident that illustrated how mob violence could be ignited by a moderate conflict that expanded and spread like wildfire. During July there had been some sort of dispute among docker factions that had festered for weeks. On the 21st, in Sheriff Street, it erupted into a bloody brawl among dockers, with coal shovels, hatchets, iron bars, and heavy stones. At first about fifty men were fighting when the Gardaí received the call to quell it. By the time they arrived the fight had spread to nearby Emerald Street, now involving supporting mobs on both sides. By this time, according to the *Evening Herald*, "200 to 300 people took part in the melee ... as the crowd gathered around the gardaí and became hostile."[7] About a dozen guards were forced to draw their batons to protect themselves from a hostile mob of dockers, the toughest men in Dublin.

During the summer of 1952 Branigan was kept busy with street violence in his own Liberties. It began in May and June when unruly mobs began gathering on weekends in the streets around a number of popular pubs. The situation became so intolerable that Inspector J. V. McManus was finally "compelled to put a Sergeant and three Guards on duty in the Patrick Street area to deal with disorderly scenes."[8] Shortly afterwards he was forced to put more guards on duty in New Street and Dean Street as well. It was beginning to look like a militarised zone.

As the summer progressed, the wild fighting worsened. Inspector McManus became more infuriated when "two Guards had been seriously assaulted." The inspector himself had been attacked on one occasion. McManus was of the opinion that the "unfortunate situation" was caused in part by "too many public houses in the locality." In close proximity to one another, they formed a natural magnetic core to which drinking men gravitated. On summer weekends, as each pub overflowed with patrons, they spilled out into the streets, sometimes becoming disorderly and belligerent. The only consolation, stated McManus, was that the area was "within a stone's throw of Kevin Street station and the Guards had not far to bring the offenders."[9]

Saturday 5 June 1952 was a balmy summer evening as the usual clusters of men took their pints outside the pubs to chat and banter. At about half past nine a dispute arose outside one of the pubs. Others heard the hubbub and trotted over to see a "ruggy-up" forming. Tempers flared, blows were exchanged, and a real fight broke out. The guards on duty quickly called for reinforcements.

Branigan had promised Inspector McManus that he'd keep a closer eye on the most troublesome pubs on Saturday night. Within minutes he arrived on the scene, with Garda Crown and Garda Tarpey at his side. By this time the various pub crowds had coalesced into an amorphous mob of hundreds. Residents were leaning out their tenement windows to watch the action. Immediately, the cry "Lugs is here!" went up.

He thrust forward, working his way towards the men he knew to be ringleaders and habitual street fighters. One of his primary targets was "Joe-Boy" Collins. A skilled boxer and feared street pugilist, he was as tough as they come, a ferocious slugger who never hesitated to take on several foes at a time. Yet, like Spike McCormack, he was liked and respected within his community. Branigan knew that if he could get Joe-Boy, with whom he had a civil relationship, under control, many others would depart.

As he was nearing his objective he caught sight of "two men, one of whom had his face covered in blood," driving off in a car in the direction of Christ Church Place. Then Branigan, Crown and Tarpey "saw P. Fitzgerald in an aggressive attitude," causing him to determine that Fitzgerald and Collins had probably been the ones "aiming blows" at the two bloodied men in the car.[10]

As news of Branigan's arrival rippled through the crowd, men began to disperse. First, both Collins and Fitzgerald ceased fighting when confronted by Branigan, whom they liked and respected. But they didn't like other guards. Branigan told Crown and Tarpey and another guard named Stack to place Collins, Fitzgerald and some other arrested men in patrol cars, as he went about quelling other disturbances. But once Branigan was out of sight, Joe-Boy and Fitzgerald again became belligerent with the guards. Joe-Boy blurted out indignantly to Tarpey: "Do you know *who I am?*" while Fitzgerald defiantly snarled at Garda Crown, "You won't *** take me! Let me have a go at him!"[11] When finally shoved into the patrol car, Collins took a poke at Garda Stack, while Fitzgerald struck at Tarpey. Both guards had to watch out for head butts and kicks.

On Monday morning, when the brawlers appeared in court, Judge Mangan stated: "It is a disgrace to the locality that such conditions should exist here at weekends. The Guards have enough to do without wasting their time on such brawls."[12]

For Lugs Branigan, however, breaking up such nasty mobs was now his regular daily assignment. In this he was not envied by his fellow-guards.

———

Realising that his future would be in dealing with street mobs, and smaller groups of gougers, hooligans, and thugs, Branigan reasoned that his methods of policing had to be changed. As he would put it, when "I was assigned full-time to 'street nuisances,' breaking up rows became my speciality. My method of dealing with rows was a little unorthodox."[13] Quite an understatement.

The origins of this unorthodoxy are uncertain. It was probably in the period 1950–52 that Garda Branigan's iconic black leather gloves came into prominence, as well as his practice of offering a choice to those whom he confronted. Both would become an integral feature of his reputation—and legend. In fact they came to define his image.

Back in the gang days of the 1930s and 40s some said he *wore* the gloves, to protect his boxing fists when he took on gang members in the streets. There was also the myth, as he called it, "that I always wore leather gloves on the beat not to mark the face of a thug who might get a good hiding from me . . . This is not true."[14] Another story, quite absurd, was that he wore knuckledusters beneath his gloves when fighting gangs and ruffians (though it may have *felt* so to his opponents).

Quite another matter is speculation about when he began carrying his black leather gloves, using them as a potent physical and psychological weapon. About this, nothing is known for certain. What is known is that by the early 1950s he was never seen *wearing* the gloves. Instead, he carried them with him at all times. Alick remembers: "He *always* carried them, the leather gloves, rolled up. *Very* sturdy ones."

Did he first use the thick gloves as a weapon by intent or by accidental discovery? It could well have been either. But there had to have been a first time when he unleashed them across the face of some troublemaker as a means of intimidation or deterrence. This may have been no more than a sudden impulse; but its effect on the recipient obviously made a lasting impression upon Branigan. He found that it had an emotional and psychological effect more potent than a physical punch. A tough man who was bellowing with bravado on the street in front of his followers could receive a sharp lash from Branigan's gloves and find himself stunned, humiliated, feeling emasculated before the crowd.

As Garda Con Hearty witnessed many a time, the most aggressive and bellicose thug, raging and "foaming at the mouth" in a street confrontation, "would suddenly become cowed" upon feeling the lash of Lugs's gloves. No punch could so effectively deflate bullies and blowhards. When he would "flick it across the face of an opponent," says Hearty, "it had a demeaning effect." Branigan discovered that, better than a baton or fists, his gloves carried *insult*.

Once he saw the effectiveness of his gloves, he used them again. And again. "That was his weapon," asserts Declan. "Just a *flick*." He learnt to use his gloves artfully, in a measured manner, with varying degrees of force to fit the circumstances. He became adept at delivering anything from a "sting" to a jolting "crack" that could stun a man as effectively as a jab in the boxing ring, leaving his ears ringing, eyes blurred, and face crimson. Working beside Branigan, Mulhall saw the magic of his gloves countless times. "His black gloves, he had them *rolled up*, and now some people said, 'Oh, he had marbles in the fingers . . .' and all that." Billy Byrne says that some fellas he knew around the Liberties who felt the wallop of the gloves used to say that he had ball bearings in the gloves—apparently an apt description of what it felt like to be lashed.

Over the years he perfected his delivery. He used a square stance, directly facing a man, with the gloves always in his right hand, in a cocked position for triggering. Because of his height advantage of about five to eight inches over most men, his arms were at the right level for a quick, snapping horizontal swing towards the face. "His gloves were *very* effective," says Alick. "I mean, a slap with that would waken somebody up!" Eventually he could almost calibrate the intensity of force he needed to execute the act. An insolent lad might receive a light wisp, as if to brush away a bothersome bee. Yet for many youths even such an "introductory" slap was well remembered for its message.

By the period 1953–4 most city residents knew about "Lugs and his gloves." He appeared to have a sort of theatrical talent in using them that people remembered. He became lightning-fast with his lash, as quick as Tom Mix and Bat Masterson on the draw. Everyone agreed it was a memorable sight to see.

He clasped the gloves in his hand even when off duty. They became almost a natural appendage to his arm. Guards who knew and worked with him from the mid-fifties vouch that they *never* saw him without his black leather gloves. Eventually he became so strongly associated with the gloves that when troublemakers were confronted by him they tended to keep their eyes nervously fixed on his right hand, wondering whether they were going to be used. Though they were usually not: the mere fear of them being unleashed was an effective deterrent to their resistance.

————

In conjunction with his gloves, Branigan developed another unorthodox method of policing. This too probably evolved over time as he realised its effectiveness. When he encountered miscreants of any sort who appeared inclined to resist or give him trouble he would offer them a choice—or issue an ultimatum—before he would take physical action or apprehend them. He regarded this as the fairest possible approach.

There were variations on his phrasing. Around her part of Dolphin's Barn, Bridie Colgan says, "he had a saying if they were set to give him trouble, or were resisting arrest. Lugs would spell out the options: If you don't want to take your chances in court, you can fight me *here and now!*" Sometimes it was abbreviated: "Fight me here—or take your chances in court." His ultimatums were just as brief and direct: "I would grab a gouger and say, *'Clear off,* go home *now!*—or I'll shove you in a cell.'"[15] As Branigan never bluffed, it didn't take most people long to decide about taking his choice or following his ultimatum.

When their decision was a peaceful one, no force was needed; if not, he acted. When a lash with his gloves was not sufficient for the severity of the situation, he was willing to use his open hand or bare fists, though he was always reluctant to do so until absolutely necessary. Rather than engaging in actual fisticuffs, as he had to do with the old gangs, he relied on a single well-aimed "clip" or "clout," as he called them. He preferred these terms to "punch" or "blow," which he did not want to have to use in court. But the judges would all come to know exactly what each term meant.

"Clips" and "clouts" were ordinarily used for defensive purposes, to protect himself, his fellow-gardaí or others from injury from a violent resister. A clip was a type of quick, crisp jab or punch to calm and constrain a man. Quite often this had to be administered when trying to control a wild-acting hooligan in a patrol car on the way to the Garda station. A drunken bowsie who was trying to kick, head-butt or bite could injure a guard quite severely. Branigan would not put up with it.

A "clout" was a more forceful punch, of varying force, used to disable a dangerous man. Because of his boxing expertise, Branigan could calculate the power of the punch required.

And sometimes he needed to deliver a "clattering," which to him meant a good and well-deserved "hiding." Clatterings were mostly reserved for vicious beasts of battering husbands who habitually abused their wives and family members, or bullies who beat up others, especially women—men who understood nothing but a fist on the jaw or power punch in the gut. In some cases they had to be knocked unconscious on the spot.

John Collins worked beside Branigan and saw his full repertoire of clips, clouts, and clatterings. "He'd *hit* you, hit some gouger, give him a couple of clips. But in all the time I spent with him I never saw him abuse anyone."

Branigan's various forceful methods of dealing with Dublin's array of villains all came under the general rubric of "summary justice," for which he would become well known, a type of "street justice" approved by the judges in Dublin's courts.

Sometimes he could be quite creative, and highly unorthodox, in doling out justice. One memorable example was passed down by oral tradition from Senan Finucane to his son, Garda Senan Finucane Jr, a case that understandably never made the newspapers or official Garda records.

One day it was brought to Branigan's attention that a woman in the Liberties was having a problem with the milk bottles left out at night for the milkman to collect the next morning. However, during the night someone had been urinating in them. After several such incidents the milkman had to inform her apologetically that he could no longer provide her with service.

Branigan took a personal interest in the case of the contaminated bottles. To him, it legitimately fitted under "street nuisances." He devised a plan to personally nab the culprit, though it might take some time and patience. Senan Finucane Jr relates: "Lugs hid himself in the garden of the householder for a number of hours each night." Nothing happened the first two nights, but on the third night "Lugs caught the man while urinating in the milk bottles."

In keeping with his practice of offering offenders a choice, he gave the man two options: he could take him to court, or "Lugs told the gouger that he could drink the urine he had put in the bottle." Branigan awaited his agonising deliberation. "The gouger accepted the latter—and needless to say, the householder had no more problems."

————

With "breaking up rows" now his speciality, his strategy in confronting crowds and mobs would be the opposite of the old DMP. Their tactic had been to amass in large numbers and mount a baton charge, indiscriminately swinging away against all those in the crowd. In sharp contrast, Branigan's method was a selective one, deliberately targeting those whipping up the mob. This meant having to "wade in," as he liked to put it, to reach his targets—a risky act for any garda. Declan recalls his father once explaining to him his method:

> With mobs, he always said to me, "If you get into trouble, go for the one that's doing all the talking! If you can get *rid* of him, you lose half the others." That was his theory when a row or mob developed—so he'd go *straight* into the middle, to who was the *cause* of the problem—and eliminate it. And he didn't fear anything, or *anybody.*

When a mob was building up to an explosive point, removing the ringleaders was like pulling the burning fuse from a stick of dynamite. That was always Branigan's contention. His role, after all, was the prevention as well as quelling of street disorders. He would stress that "my main role has always been that of deterrent."[16] And because of his feared reputation it was a role he could fill better than any other garda. A favourite saying of the guards who worked with him was "Oh, his reputation *always* preceded him!"

"Lugs is here!" became the clarion cry among troublesome crowds on the city's streets.

It was at about this stage of his career, in the mid-fifties, when he was forty-five years of age, that Tony Ruane says that Branigan was perceived as "a law unto himself." Branigan thrived on "showdowns." In his childhood days at the Lyric and Tivoli he had watched Tom Mix walk slowly, purposefully towards a gunslinger for a decisive "draw." It was his *character* that made such an indelible impression on Branigan. "The ideology of the western character rubbed off on him, in his mind," says Declan—"the *discipline* of sheriffs." Now a real lawman himself, he had showdowns with thugs in Dublin's streets and dancehalls. And it was hardly coincidence that he liked to call them "duels." There was no doubt he relished the challenge of it, the exhilaration. To him, one-on-one confrontations were the epitome of a lawman's character.

To those who witnessed Branigan's showdowns over the years, his coolness and resolve were particularly remarkable. "No roaring or shouting," states Alick: "he just *dug in*—and you took the consequences. He had no regard for what it might do to himself." As Neary depicts it, "he took off his coat and offered a hardchaw an option—to fight him or be taken to the station."[17] On those occasions when his challenge was taken up he "folded up his tunic and duelled" with the man. Since, as Con Hearty confirms, "he was feared by even the most hardened thugs," this did not occur often.

If some Dubliners saw comparisons between western film sheriffs and Garda "Lugs" Branigan, so be it. It is not a subject his Garda mates ever remember him discussing. And never did he play up to such a role, which would have been entirely out of character for him.

In one of his confrontations with a bellicose bully, Branigan showed a rare side of himself. It began outside the Bleeding Horse pub in Camden Street when a mob of men outside became unruly. When Branigan arrived on the scene he spotted one of the ringleaders bellowing, flaunting his toughness. True to form, Branigan plunged through the crowd to face him in a duel-like stance. Obviously in a jocular frame of mind, he faced the man at close range, then "stuck out his chest and said to the thug, 'Bump up against that and die happy'!"[18] Clint Eastwood himself could not have delivered a better line.

Matt Mulhall was on duty with Branigan for years, and to him the sheriff analogy was not mere hyperbole. Both his reputation and his image were now known throughout the city. Perhaps no other Dubliner was so immediately recognisable in a crowd or at a distance as Lugs Branigan. And his sudden presence on the scene of disorder elicited fear among trouble-makers. This was never better illustrated, relates Mulhall, than the time they were summoned to a riot in Inchicore:

> I have this recollection of him when we went to this riot in Inchicore. And when we arrived, everyone was out in the streets *killing* one another. You'd want to see it—*absolute mayhem!* I don't know how many fights were going on, right in the middle of the road, and a *huge* crowd all around. And he just *stepped* out of the car and then it was "*Lugs is here!*" And the *whole thing stopped!* Just *stopped.* The rows in the street, *everything* stopped. Oh, you'd have to be present to see it.

Though Branigan went largely unchallenged out in the open, he could be a target of retaliation carried out clandestinely. As more miscreants felt the lash of his glove, there were those bent on revenge. From time to time he or his family would receive threatening phone calls or letters at home in Drimnagh Road. Most were no more than cowardly idle threats. But, with a wife and three children, he took each seriously. As he once confided, "if anybody came to my house to interfere with my family I would kill them. I have no gun, but I would not like to be in the culprit's shoes when I caught him."[19]

One evening in 1953 or 54, after he had had a confrontation with some mob, he was on duty and his family were at home. Alick was about twelve and Declan seven. The tranquillity of the home was suddenly broken by a sharp sound of shattered glass in the front room. Elsie, fearing they were disgruntled men seeking revenge, quickly sent her three children to a safe place. Declan recalls:

> Our windows came in. A gang of them were throwing stones. I remember my mother putting myself and Alick under the stairs to protect us. They were men who were unemployed . . . on the corner of the streets, and decided to do something [in revenge].

Since there had been previous attempts, Elsie was "concerned about the safety of her family . . . knowing there was an element out there that could bring retribution—and, at times, *tried,*" says Declan. But never before had there been such a bold attempt. For her and the children it was a frightening experience.

When Branigan was called home following the incident he calmly told his family not to worry. He showed no anger, just concern. He assured them he would find the culprits, and that it was not likely to happen again. "He had an *idea* who did it," tells Declan. "He always had a suspicion of who was involved."

He would handle it. "He boarded up the windows and got the glass repaired." It never happened again.

———

By the mid-fifties Alick and Declan were old enough to accompany their father to Croke Park on Sunday afternoons, to share his love of sport. He explained to them his view that sports teach the values of co-operation, competition, and physical fitness. Says Declan, "He felt that if you were involved in sports you weren't going to get into trouble. So he would bring me to Croke Park *every* Sunday . . . hurling or football—he *loved* GAA sports."

Sunday afternoons became a special time for the three of them to share. With money forever tight, he spent virtually nothing on himself, especially as he didn't smoke, drink, or gamble, as most men did. But buying three tickets for a match was a worthwhile investment. Spending Sunday afternoons happily at Croke Park with his two sons was a great joy in his life, as well as a nice break from his Garda duty. Yet always on his lap lay his black leather gloves.

Everywhere the lads went with their father, especially at Croke Park, they saw his popularity and the aura of respect around him, as there was always a cascade of greetings. "How'ya, Mr Branigan!" "Good afternoon, Guard Branigan." *Never* "Lugs." Declan felt proud. "He was so well known, I was aware of how famous he was."

At home, finances were strained and stretched. As a model husband, he faithfully handed over his wage packet to Elsie to handle the family budgeting, and she seemed to work miracles with the modest amount she had to work with. Food, shelter, fuel and clothing gobbled up most of it. His gardening was going so well that he wanted to expand his vegetable crop, which would cost a few shillings but would be worth it, he felt. At the back of the Iveagh Gardens there were cottages and half an acre or an acre of ground, explains Alick; "so he'd rent so much of that off a person that owned the ground . . . and he had another one up in Ballymount Lane." It turned out to be a good investment for the extra food it brought to the table. But the real benefit, Alick saw, was that "he got *away* from things . . . to get into the garden and forget about everything."

It was about this time that he and Elsie decided on an idea for supplementing his income. "Oh, times were tough," recalls Alick, "so we had lodgers, boarders, and this was a way of making a few bob." Some of his other Garda friends were doing the same thing. Branigan was often required to work beyond his normal hours but never received monetary compensation for his efforts. "A garda's life is difficult . . . and we did not get overtime." There was no way for him to bring in additional pay. Taking in lodgers was sensible, though it demanded some sacrifices on the part of everyone. Apart from adding congestion to their home and losing some privacy, Elsie had to assume the additional burden of cooking, cleaning and caring for the guests. But she did so without complaint. Though lodgers made space in the house tighter, they were generally pleasant company.

As they were adjusting to lodgers, things in the Branigan household unexpectedly became more strained. His ageing father's health was failing, and there seemed to be no answer but to bring him into their house. Everyone agreed, and he was settled comfortably and cared for lovingly, though Alick concedes that it wasn't easy. "His father had the front room downstairs . . . but things were tough." Even the dogs found their space more confined than they may have liked.

————

In his new assignment of dealing with street nuisances, Garda Branigan experienced a variety of odd, amusing and sometimes bizarre cases, all of which enlivened his job and challenged him to devise new solutions for unexpected problems.

On 17 November 1952 he and his partner Garda Fleming were called at about 10 p.m. to the scene of a fight in Harcourt Road. A man named Fox was waiting for the bus to take him home when he was approached and assaulted by a drunken man named Devine. Devine mistook him for a foe and struck him a hard blow, knocking him back against a pebble-dashed wall. When Branigan arrived, Fox told him that Devine then "pulled out the stump of a bottle and struck me in the right ear." When Branigan tried to clean the blood from his ear to examine it he described it as looking like "a mangled chunk of meat."[20] He and Garda Fleming took the victim to the Adelaide Hospital in Peter Street, where Dr H. G. Knox cleaned the wound, only to "discover that about one inch and a quarter of the ear was missing."[21]

As the rest of Dublin slept, Garda Branigan and Garda Fleming returned to the scene and began crawling around on the ground with their torches in search of the missing piece of Fox's ear. On 18 December, before Judge Fitzpatrick in the District Court, Branigan explained how he and Fleming had "spent some time in Harcourt Street looking for the missing portion" of the ear—but with no luck. Where could it have gone, in the middle of the night? Could a dog, cat or rat have stolen the evidence? It was too unpleasant for contemplation. Next day's *Evening Herald* headlined the story: "Guards sought piece of man's ear," adding one more story to the growing Branigan legend.

A constant annoyance to Branigan during this period was the unscrupulous conmen who pulled off various scams along the streets, always preying upon gullible or elderly victims. Especially shrewd were the glib, fast-talking "three-card-trick merchants," and those with their "shell games." These sleight-of-hand crooks lured people along the street to gamble on finding the hidden shell or queen card after they were shuffled around. Such men were fast and elusive, carrying a small collapsible table that they could fold up and hide beneath their coat as they dashed away from the police.

Though it was a comparatively small crime, Branigan knew that the men who flourished in his Liberties district imposed real misery on many a poor housewife hoping to win a few extra shillings for her family. What particularly galled him was that time after time these robbers, when caught, were simply released by the court to prey upon others. In one notable case in 1954 the *Evening Herald* wrote about a slick operator named Mahoney who had been "arrested for being caught at it again—after 17 convictions."[22] When nabbed by Branigan, they were good candidates for a lash of the gloves, which was far more effective a deterrent than the court's routine treatment.

––––

On the otherwise peaceful night of 7 August 1954 there came a call to Branigan: "He's at it again!" There was no need to provide any details, other than his whereabouts on this night. The culprit was the easiest one in all Dublin for Branigan to catch. After all, he had been at his same crime for nearly sixteen years, since 1938. Though he was harmless to ordinary people on the street, he was a real menace to the city's shopkeepers. For Branigan, he had become a giant nuisance.

J. Dolan, aged fifty-four, of no fixed address, had an irresistible fetish—his life's avocation, to hear him talk of it. He was enamoured with the sound of a large glass window shattering at close range. Music to his ears. While gardaí knew exactly how he executed his act, they could never predict when or where he might strike next. Nor did he: it was when the mood came over him, he always said in court. However, it was not a random, spontaneous performance to his mind, more an artistic venture. With deliberation, he selected only the best targets. He would position himself six to eight feet away to gain the best acoustic quality, aim for the centre, and loft his missile with the full force of a cricketer, anticipating instant gratification. Then he would remain happily *in situ*, admiring his accomplishment.

It never occurred to him to rob the shop: he was no crook. Nor would he ever deny the crime; in fact he may well have been offended had anyone else claimed the credit. On this particular night, a Saturday, Garda Branigan arrived at Merchants' Quay, where he "found the defendant standing beside the window, which was broken. Inside the window was a large stone." This time, however, "Tosser" Dolan missed part of his own show; for, as Branigan was documenting the evidence, he turned back towards Dolan only to find the defendant "out cold from drink."

On 12 August, when he appeared before Judge Fitzgerald, a reporter from the *Evening Herald* was on hand to cover the continuing saga of Dolan, the Dublin window-slayer:

> He told Guard Branigan that he liked to hear the crash of glass . . . his favourite sound. One could hit a man and there would be no sound . . . but there was a lovely noise when he broke plate glass.[23]

Few in the court would dispute the logic of that. But Judge Fitzpatrick was by now fed up with Dolan's shenanigans, so costly to shopkeepers. Branigan added to the judge's displeasure with Dolan by informing him that he had done some research into his history and found that he had smashed the very same shop window once previously. Citing his record of destruction dating back to 1938, Judge Fitzgerald sentenced Mr Dolan, of no fixed address, to a very fixed address for the next six months—with hard labour.

———

"Street nuisances" came in many forms, even that of friends. Says John McCormack of his father and Branigan, "Spike and Lugs were *great* friends," but they sometimes found themselves on opposite sides of the law.

In his boxing days in the 1930s Spike McCormack became the Irish middleweight champion. He lived at number 7 Seán MacDermott Street, at the corner of Gardiner Street, had thirteen children and a devoted wife. Killane's pub on the corner was his local. He became one of the city's folk heroes, loved by virtually all who knew him, gregarious and generous. However, he was also a gargantuan drinker. John swears he could "easily" put away twenty to thirty pints in a day—but:

> He was a *dangerous* man when he had whiskey—and was very easily led. He once said to me, "John, when someone gives me a whiskey I change into another person."

When his boxing days faded in the 1940s he began habitually fighting in the street. He gained a reputation as the undisputed best "street fighter" in memory. John relates: "In 1954 he was always fighting on the street—and the police took him in," time after time. It became a serious problem for local gardaí, who dared not get in the way of his iron fists. For Branigan, it was a sad thing to see his friend become a serious street nuisance, for which he, unfortunately, was now responsible.

A recurring problem for local guards, and now for Branigan, was that some of Spike's cronies at Killane's would deliberately fuel him with whiskey in order to prod him into taking on a policeman or two they may have disliked. John often discussed this problem with Branigan, who understood its seriousness:

> Jim once said to me, "John, the people of the inner city here want a fighter who can come out and fight the policemen—and Spike'd come out and do it, if they fed him whiskey. I've *seen* him fighting policemen—and a policeman had no chance against your father."

As Branigan now patrolled the whole city, he tried to keep a watchful eye on Spike. Apart from Spike's wife, Lugs was the only one he would listen to. But even for Branigan, when Spike was "mad" on whiskey it was like taking on a wild bull.

Spike's arch-enemies were the three Corbally brothers, all powerful men and seasoned street fighters. The origin of this enmity was some vague feud dating from an earlier generation, but they were determined to keep the ancient feud red-hot. The McCormack-Corbally Saturday-night brawls were vicious and bloody like no others. As John sums it up, "the Corballys *hated* Spike's guts—*really!* And my father had this vendetta against them . . . and he'd *never* let it go."

In his memoir *It's a Long Way from Penny Apples,* Bill Cullen, who lived close by in Summer Hill, tells how he was a regular observer of their famous street clashes and how only Jim Branigan could hope to separate them. Their battles usually took place out in the street in front of Killane's pub, where all the traffic would be halted for what some people called the best free entertainment in Dublin. Time and again Branigan warned local guards not to get directly in the way of their flying fists, and not to use batons if at all possible. Their fights involved no finesse or fancy footwork: just power punches at close quarters, until they dropped like a sack of potatoes. Because of Spike's devastating left hook, he was usually the last man standing. But not always.

It was a primitive scene, painful to watch. As Bill Cullen recounts, the Guards were always eventually called, and the crowd roared, "Here come the rozzers!" But no-one paid much attention. One night, according to Cullen, "ten policemen broke through the crowd, their batons poking anyone who didn't move out of the way."[24] But it wasn't until the cry rang out, *"It's Lugs Branigan!"* that the crowd began parting like the Red Sea, as he strode towards Spike and the Corballys. He barged between the warriors and *ordered* a halt. *At once.* They dropped their arms and staggered backwards. Never would they take a swing at Branigan.

The scenario was played over and over, like a local pageant. Sometimes Branigan showed up, other times not. There was no permanent solution. As Spike grew older, Branigan would become ever more worried about his welfare when tough, braggart "young guns" around the city would start preying upon the famous Spike to gain a quick reputation for themselves. It was a problem that one day Lugs Branigan himself would have to cope with.

———

By the mid-1950s Garda Jim Branigan was regarded as an encyclopaedia of knowledge about Dublin and its underworld. After a quarter of a century in the streets he had dealt with every species of villain in the city's rough fabric. Garda superintendents, social workers, judges and solicitors all sought his advice. And followed it.

He had accumulated a litany of street lingo and names for all the types of culprits and characters with whom he dealt. Despite his work with the lowest elements of Dublin's street life and underworld, who freely spouted foul language, Branigan was known as a man who never used profanities. "Whatever my enemies may say about me," he would say, "they will admit that obscenities and vulgarities were never uttered by me."[25] He attributed this to his upbringing: "No bad language was ever allowed by my father." It was one of the many reasons why Mary Barnwell and other dealers in the Liberties always referred to "Mr Branigan" as "a *real* gentleman."

His Garda mates had plenty of colourful names for various miscreants— but not in front of him. Instead he accumulated an impressive litany for identifying all sorts of troublemakers, a sampling of which follows:

> Hooligans, rowdies, messers, hoodlums, bullies, racketeers, thugs, scoundrels, gangsters, ruffians, gougers, mobsters, rats, blackguards, wasters, hardchaws, villains, bowsies.

To Branigan, the simplest terms best identified those who carried out the most heinous acts: wife-beater, rapist, child-molester. He believed in calling evil by its correct name. For their egregious sins he showed no mercy.

As his fellow-gardaí, judges and solicitors would learn, each term had a distinct meaning for him. A "hooligan" was not the same as a "hoodlum." Nor was a "rowdy" necessarily a "ruffian." His classification carried some subtle differentiations. For utilitarian purposes he used "gouger," "thug" and "hooligans" most often. "Villains" nicely covered the whole lot.

His lexicon was soon to be expanded, to include odd-sounding terms he had never heard before: "rock-and-rollers," "Teddy Boys," "skinheads," "mods," "rockers," "Beatlemaniacs." Before long, he would get to know them all intimately.

Chapter 8 ~

THE "ROCK-AND-ROLL COP" AND THE TEDDY BOYS

"He is known among many as the 'Rock n' Roll Cop' . . . 'terror of the Teddy Boys,' because almost single-handedly he has stopped most of the Teddy Boy nonsense in Dublin inspired by 'rock n' roll' films."

(*Evening Press*, 4 JULY 1958)

"The image the news headlines project of the modern teenager is . . . of a rocking, rolling, drinking, trouble-making, loose-living person going to the devil and obviously succeeding."

(CORNELIUS LUCEY, BISHOP OF CORK, *Irish Press*, 18 APRIL 1967)

"Oh, I *loved* rock and roll! It was a *revolution*, a new era. My father wasn't a music man, but I was—I lived for it."

(DECLAN BRANIGAN)

1955

Dublin youth were restless.

The city was dreary, colourless, lifeless. Old-fashioned and stagnant. Dirty rain-slicked streets leading to nowhere. Except from one dingy pub or betting office to another. No roads leading "out" or "up" for listless youth. Only a few honky-tonk game parlours or billiards joints. Fish-and-chip shops. Greasy.

Gerry Creighton, a teenager in the fifties, recalls Dublin as "a very depressive place. *Boring!* Young men had no jobs and even less prospect of work . . . They'd stand around corners, play cards, have toss schools." The drabness was stifling, as if a heavy stench of "sameness" and rot blanketed the streets and buildings. Youth inherited the old, shabby, hand-me-down culture of their parents' generation. Lads had their father's type of haircut, clothing, shoes, mannerisms, life outlook. Girls accepted their mother's subordinate role, maternal burdens, hairstyle, dress. It was *expected* that youth would conform to their parents' culture, follow the same life-style and traditions. Remain "in line," obedient, respectful. Unimaginative. Trapped. *Bloody bored!*

In the mid-fifties their only means of escape, other than emigration, was to walk through the doors of a big cinema featuring the films that showed what American journalists and sociologists were calling the "youth revolution"— exuberant teenagers unshackled from the past, embracing "liberation," creating their own new culture. To Irish youth, a fantasy world.

America's youth rebellion exploded in the period 1953–5. It was a transformational social event, manifested most blatantly by their "shocking" new music, dancing, dress, and language. And their so-called "rebellious" spirit. And the catalyst for it all was something called "rock and roll".

Irish parents had listened to John McCormack, Bing Crosby, Frank Sinatra, had sung and danced to the music from films starring Nelson Eddy and Jeanette MacDonald, Fred Astaire and Ginger Rogers. But that was no longer their children's music. On the "teen scene" there burst a radically new type of singer: Elvis Presley, Buddy Holly, Jerry Lee Lewis, Bill Haley, Chuck Berry, Little Richard. And on the screen, in place of Cary Grant, James Stewart, Clark Gable, Bette Davis and Katharine Hepburn a startling new genre of films appeared: Marlon Brando in his leather jacket astride a motorcycle, snarling in *The Wild One*, James Dean, the quintessential rebel, in *Rebel Without a Cause*, teenagers erupting violently against the adult world in *Blackboard Jungle*.

To many American parents it was shocking, irreverent, even immoral— and a bit frightening. To teenagers it was ecstatically, defiantly *liberating*. With unbridled exuberance they embraced the new culture as their own. The British quickly spawned their own versions of the new music and teenage idols, with Cliff Richard, Tommy Steele, Eddie Cochran. British youth did not merely mimic Americans but created their unique versions of teenage rebels.

The origins of the Irish youth revolution were subtle and seemingly innocuous. It began over the radio waves and in the cinemas. Every adult had their favourite radio programmes, to which they listened faithfully. There was an impressive variety from which to choose: news, comedy, drama, and almost every type of music, from traditional and classical to show tunes. But nothing for youngsters.

Then, from about 1955, a new station was heard, picked up from a distant country, circumventing international broadcasting conventions. Among Dublin's teenagers it became an instant rage. Parents didn't know quite what to make of it. As a young teenager, Gerry Creighton was swept away by the new music, which would profoundly change his life:

All of a sudden the youth in Dublin could tune in Radio Luxembourg, 208 medium wave, each Sunday night and listen to the "top twenty." Elvis *burst* on the scene with "Heartbreak Hotel" and Bill Haley's "Rock Around the Clock."

The problem for Creighton and countless other teenagers was that Sunday evening was devoted to their parents' favourite radio programmes. Though most Irish households by now owned a radio, they ordinarily had only one. Like others in the same predicament, Creighton had to be resourceful in working out a solution so as never to miss *his* programme. By the best of luck, just beside him was a neighbour who toddled out on Sunday nights to his local pub, like clockwork. At just the right hour. "So I used to go next door to the Boltons' house to hear Luxembourg Radio, because Mr Bolton went out for a drink on Sunday night." It worked perfectly, so long as Mr Bolton didn't decide to take the pledge.

Most Dublin youths were not so fortunate. The new competition for use of the radio on Sunday evenings marked, in part, the beginning of the inter-generation struggle between parents and their children, ultimately to become known as the "generation gap."

Out in Drimnagh Road it didn't take long for Alick, Declan and Helen Branigan to lay claim to their Radio Luxembourg listening time. Besides their parents, boarders also had their favourite Sunday-evening programmes; but it seemed only fair that the children should have *their* one evening a week. While many other parents criticised, if not condemned, the new music from the outset, Jim and Elsie tried to keep an open mind, while admitting that they did not understand its appeal.

But to most Irish people, Radio Luxembourg was an undesirable foreign influence on their children. As Declan remembers, "Radio Luxembourg was *anathema* to people who were against all that, 'cause the station promoted that kind of music." Before long he and Alick, like many other young people, were addicted to rock-and-roll music. They saved up every shilling to buy records of their favourites to play at home on their record-player. Throughout the house the sound blared for hours at a time but at a volume that did not disturb the lodgers or their grandfather, whose health was deteriorating. With their sensitive ears, we do not know what Cochise and Geronimo thought of it.

Declan became totally immersed in the new music. "Oh, I loved rock and roll," he says, recalling the era as "the best time in my life." More importantly, he understood that a teenage upheaval was occurring: "it was a *revolution*, a new era." Alick was hooked as well, and could listen to his favourite, Buddy Holly, all day—and sometimes did. "Rock-and-roll music—I was *very much* into that . . . I can remember singing 'Peggy Sue'; and I liked the Everly Brothers."

Sometimes his father, when he came home from a hard day of duty, could hear the familiar thumping of "Peggy Sue" as he approached his house. He never objected. Thanks to his own children, he was coming to understand the emerging world of rock and roll better each day. But at this stage he hardly expected a revolution ahead.

––––

For Garda Branigan, 1955 began with a bang. Just after midnight, as New Year's Eve crowds were still partying and parading the streets, he was called to the Olympic Ballroom in Pleasants Street. Several young men, angry at having been denied admission, decided to set off "slap-bangs" at the entrance. Branigan arrested the culprits, confiscated their fireworks, and took them to the station.

As these arrests took place within the first few minutes of the new year, he was credited on the Garda record with having made the first charge of 1955. At the time he thought nothing of it; on reflection, however, he decided that he rather liked the honour, even if it was really meaningless. So every year thereafter, just as a lark, he decided to make something of a contest out of it: to see which garda would capture the first honour.

Chuckling, Declan confides that his father knew exactly how to win the honour year after year, even if it took a bit of innocent conniving, and stalling. Every New Year's Eve at midnight a huge throng of merrymakers, many fuelled with drink, gathered beneath the huge bells of Christ Church Cathedral, awaiting their mighty toll. Invariably there were those few who overdid their revelry by disturbing the peace: fighting, throwing a bottle, or the like. He positioned himself strategically and with his superior height scanned the crowd, ready to pounce at midnight and take his "trophy" to the station. However, Declan reveals, if by chance he had to apprehend a person a minute or two *before* midnight, he might have to be held for a few moments before being arrested and taken to the station.

Whatever the strategy behind it, his "first arrest" record over the years became an eccentric footnote to his legend.

––––

The year 1955 also became a cultural landmark in Ireland's youth revolution. This was when the rock-and-roll craze really hit. The music, adults began to realise, was the catalyst for teenage revolt—against old values, old beliefs, and traditional culture. For it was generating new types of behaviour, dress, dancing, language, basic values. Adults tended to see it as not only a cultural revolution but a moral one as well. It was difficult for older generations to comprehend. Or tolerate.

To Irish teenagers, it was all about the *"beat."* What adults didn't understand was that the new music *impassioned* teenagers, compelled them to sing, shout, dance, gyrate. To writhe and act wildly. It was all about *expression, freedom, release* of youthful emotions. Casting off the stuffy inhibitions of their parents' culture.

Angeline Kearns, who grew up in Irishtown, was seventeen in 1955. She too was glued to her Radio Luxembourg programme. "As the airwaves blasted out the new music the young loved it."[1] To parents, Elvis Presley, Jerry Lee Lewis and Bill Haley were "primitives," in their music and their mannerisms. This was just what Irish youngsters craved, says Gerry Creighton. "After years of hearing Bing Crosby and Nelson Eddy and old Irish recordings, Elvis gave me goosebumps; it woke up a *passion* in me!"

Bing Crosby, America's leading crooner and an Irish favourite, saw it differently. In fact he so abhorred the new rock-and-roll music that he felt obliged to speak out against it before a US Senate hearing. At just the time that Irish teenagers were rejoicing in the beat, he told Senate members: "Much of the music now popular is '*trash.*' It just galls me to see how much trash is on our radio and television screens."[2] Of course the more their music was condemned by adults the more American, British and Irish teenagers coveted it as their *own.*

At first Dublin's respectable dancehalls and ballrooms banned the "trashy" music, which would draw undesirable youths and drive away adult patrons. In rebellion, the teenagers began opening their own small "beat clubs" in niches around the city, often in basements. Local rock-and-roll bands formed, some better than others, as the sales of guitars in the city rocketed—and, much to the chagrin of parents, of drums. As the beat clubs proliferated around the city, Dublin teenagers came to feel they were "with it." By late 1955 there were dozens of singing idols in America and Britain, individuals and groups. Irish youths knew the words to every one of their songs.

Dublin was really beginning to rock.

——

If parents denounced the "screaming" voices and the lyrics, and singers gyrating, they were appalled at the wild dancing that rock-and-roll music inspired. Teenagers called it "jive," or "jiving." It was more a spontaneous bodily expression of the music itself. Everyone could have their own style. Sometimes the teenagers seemed to be gyrating in fits or spasms. It had a primitive or "jungle-istic" look about it. Some parents felt it was sexually suggestive—or plain "dirty." Priests called it "depraved." To teenagers it was merely an irresistible impulse stirred by the music.

What parents objected to most vehemently was that the "free-expression" dancing appeared to be not only sexually licentious but possibly arousing. Angeline Kearns didn't deny it. She and her pals at the knitwear factory in Rathmines could hardly wait to get to their favourite beat club, the Claro, which she described as "a hole in the wall" but supposedly had Dublin's first real rock-and-roll band. And it drew plenty of appealing lads with whom to dance:

> Hearing "Blue Suede Shoes" and "Rock Around the Clock" made our young blood bubble . . . The sound of 'Rock n' Roll' from America stirred me, filled me with deep emotion. [But] I never let my emotions take over, especially those that clicked and throbbed between my legs.[3]

Precisely what Irish parents and priests feared.

In adopting America's rock-and-roll culture, Irish youth now had to *look* the part as well. They pored over their favourite music idols in photo magazines, studying the dress of American teenagers. Irish teenagers wanted to look exactly like them. They believed that to be authentic "rock-and-rollers" you had to look the part, from hairstyle to shoes. Boys began growing their hair long, oiling it, sweeping it back so as to imitate the Elvis or Tony Curtis look that made girls swoon. With tight black trousers, with shirt collar up, the right belt and jacket, they were "cool," like their American counterparts. Some lads spent hours perfecting their "DA" (duck's arse) hairstyle and were never without their comb.

For girls like Angeline Kearns, "in poodle skirts we were American lookalikes . . . and myself and my friends also favoured a black, tight skirt, slit up the leg, a yellow or black turtle-neck jumper and a wide black plastic belt around the waist."[4] Many girls liked wearing tight, revealing jumpers, and skirts that swirled high enough to set a lad's heart thumping.

Lastly was the new rock-and-roll lingo. Teenagers were now "cool," "hip," while their parents were hopelessly "square." Dublin teenagers were now "making the scene," "doing their own thing." Adults simply didn't "*dig* the scene"—they were "nowhere."

When "cool" Dublin teenagers tried to mix with adults, the chemistry simply didn't work, as Creighton once experienced. He was about sixteen or seventeen and had a good job at Dublin Zoo, helping with the children's pony rides and other tasks. He was well regarded for the quality of his work. In December the zoo's Christmas dance was approaching, and he was excited about taking his girl-friend. Like himself, she loved to dance to the rock-and-roll beat. "I brought a girl to the dance because she was a great jiver," he said. Though no rock-and-roll songs were played, after a few traditional numbers the band played a tune with a zingy beat to it, and he and his girl-friend automatically broke into jive dancing before the mature crowd. "Mr Supple, the head keeper, came over to me and told me to *sit down*, that I was behaving like a native from primitive Africa—that if I wanted to dance I should do a nice waltz."

Branigan was gradually taking in Dublin's new rock-and-roll scene. As he patrolled the city he heard the sound from the various small beat clubs, saw excited teenagers in their "cool" attire on the streets in small groups. Though some were boisterous late at night, he did not perceive them as "street nuisances": in fact they added a lively and colourful new element to the city's streetscape. He and his partners often smiled at them when they passed in their patrol car.

His familiarity with teenagers and rock and roll continued at home. He was now quite attuned to the music and to some of the lingo. His children were always respectful, and his daughter, Helen, was now seriously considering becoming a nun. Alick, however, with a slight smile says that he was more interested in growing his hair long like his rock-and-roll idols. He was in the process of doing it, without declaration, wondering when his father might notice it, and mention it. "The haircut—I grew my hair longer, and [eventually] he used to be sort of slagging me for that, you know," but not really in a critical manner.

When Branigan came to realise that the teenage era was not likely to fade fast—as many adults had hoped—he decided that he should try to learn more about the emerging culture, as it might help him on the streets. Sometimes he would ask his children questions for enlightenment. Sometimes they didn't have the answers, and he would need to begin establishing direct contact with some of the more transformed teenagers out on the streets.

———

Trouble began when behaviour changed. Many parents were finding that their children were becoming "distant," detached from normal family life: staying out till all hours, not telling them what they were doing, or spending all their time at home in their room rather than mixing with the family. And incessantly listening to "that" music. Some were becoming cheeky, disrespectful. Their church attendance was declining. At the same time they seemed obsessively attentive to dress and hairstyle, achieving the "right look," living "in a world of their own," as many parents put it.

Parental worries increased when sexual conduct became more liberal, resulting for some girls in unwanted pregnancy. In the 1950s for a girl there was no greater sin. Commonly condemned, even disowned, by their own families, many were forced to go to England for an abortion, while if they remained and kept their child they were shackled with a lifelong reputation as "loose" or immoral.

Many adults blamed all the degenerate behaviour and the decline in values directly on the "invasion" of rock and roll from abroad. While parents tried to work it out, sociologists and journalists analysed it "intellectually." At the outset even the term "teenager" was new to most Irish adults. Adolescents had always simply been called "youths," "lads," "girls," "youngsters." One adult wrote a letter to the *Evening Herald* expressing his opinion that while the new "teenagerism," as he called it, was indeed a strange social phenomenon, to him it also had a positive aspect, as it appeared to make young people more "happy, carefree and nonchalant" than their parents' generation.[5] He felt they should not be criticised for their exuberant liberation—unless they became disorderly.

Strict moralists were far more harsh, arguing that the new music and culture were primitive, a pestilence to be eradicated in order to "save Ireland's children." There was an outcry against teenagers, who now acted in a rude and disrespectful manner in cinemas, restaurants, shops, and streets. In packs they could act as if they were utterly oblivious of the adult world. Mothers mostly lamented the loss of the close bond they had always enjoyed with their sons and daughters. What in the world was happening?

Plenty of critics felt they knew, some in exalted positions from which to speak with force. While parents might speak of the teenage rebellion as a "problem" or "puzzle," some priests put it in more grievous terms. From the pulpit they began bringing up rock and roll in their sermons, lambasting it as a "curse," a "plague," a "sin." Sociologists liked to refer to it as a "social phenomenon," which hardly helped parents understand it any better.

Some of the most damning criticism came from members of the Catholic Church, who wrote letters to newspapers in order to reach the widest audience. Bishop Cornelius Lucey of Cork wrote to the *Irish Press*, conceding that the emerging image of rock-and-rollers was that of a "rocking, rolling, drinking, troublemaking, loose-living person going to the devil." And he admitted to seeing some unmistakable "signs of teenage revolt." However, he did not agree with those critics who condemned "our teenagers as a wicked and lascivious generation" and stressed that, so far, there were no signs of "general lawlessness."[6]

Throwing fuel on the fire, the *Evening Herald* published an article headed "Tribal rhythms," quoting the Archbishop of Chicago, Cardinal Samuel Stritch, in his denunciation of rock-and-roll music in Catholic youth centres. He condemned the music and dancing as primitive, "a throwback to tribalism [that] cannot be tolerated for Catholic youths." The newspaper made it a front-page article:

In some of our high schools and recreation centres dancing and music are permitted which should bring the blush of shame to Catholic educators. When they stoop to such things as 'rock n' roll' rhythms, they are failing seriously in their duty. God grant that this word will have the effect of banning such things in Catholic recreation.[7]

In October 1955 one letter-writer thought he had a simple enough solution. To his mind, better parental control at home was the answer: "It seems to me that Irish Catholic parents today are losing all sense of responsibility regarding the upbringing of their children."[8] If parents were not so lax and permissive, teenage rowdiness and rebellion could be easily controlled. Which doubtless caused many readers to wonder whether he was a parent with teenage children.

While most teenagers simply ignored criticism of the new music and life-style, a few fought back. One teenage girl sent a letter of rebuttal to the *Evening Herald,* which published it under the heading "Outraged youth":

Sir,—I am completely outraged by the letter of contempt for youth of to-day . . . His attitude to beat groups is all wrong. They are by no means 'vulgar, unwashed tramps or guitar-strangling hyenas!'[9]

It was undeniable, however, that many teenagers were now staying out till all hours, some of them drinking and "running wild," sometimes getting into skirmishes.

Garda Jim Branigan, an avid newspaper-reader, was following the controversy closely. He was receiving more complaints about street disorders, loud beat clubs, and a disrespect for the law. However, he regarded teenage rock-and-rollers as a serious "street nuisance" only if they threatened the peace and order of the city. And he was watchful.

———

Teenage "rock-and-rollers," be they American, British, Irish, or other, were for the most part well-behaved young people, enjoying their new music and freedom of expression. Measured according to their parents' values, they may have been considered permissive and irreverent, even disrespectful at times; but most were orderly and lawful.

In Britain, by contrast, a different breed of rebellious youth was emerging. Most were disfranchised teenagers from poorer families who began organising in loose social groups in the period 1954–5. Rabidly anti-establishment, they sought to create their own identity and culture. Breaking sharply from their parents' stifling generation, with what they saw as its dull outlook on life, they set out to gain attention by dressing in a flamboyant style and behaving outlandishly. They began dressing in the "Edwardian" style, of the era of King

Edward II (1901–10), in long jackets with velvet collars and cuffs, but with extremely narrow "drainpipe" trousers, and shirts of bright yellow, orange, red and purple with narrow ties. Their hair was long, oiled, and combed back on the sides to form a perfect "DA."

At first, seen in small groups along London's streets, they were perceived as exotic, even amusing. Eventually the press needed a term to describe these gangs, whose numbers increased each day, and the name "Teddy Boys," after King Edward II, was created.[10] The term first appeared in print in September 1953 in the *Daily Express*.

Their innocuous image was short-lived. As the gangs became territorial and competitive they began carrying knives, razors, and chains, which led to violence. When fighting and stabbings occurred, public fears arose. Before long the Teddy Boys came to be regarded as a menace on British streets.

Garda Branigan in Dublin read all about Britain's Teddy Boys in the newspapers. As he was periodically despatched to London to bring back prisoners, he may also have seen them in the streets. What he knew about them he didn't like; and he didn't want them in Dublin. But he probably suspected that sooner or later some Irish youths would imitate them. To him their look was acceptable, but not their violent behaviour.

Sure enough, by the summer of 1955 strollers along O'Connell Street and Grafton Street were startled to catch their first glimpse of the Irish version of the Teddy Boys, aping their British counterparts and their style of dress and mannerisms. Gerry Creighton recalls the first flock of "Teds" he spotted:

> The Teds wore sobby-sole shoes, thick crepe, and the thickness gave them extra height. Their "drapes"—clothes—were expensive; women's colours of pink and yellow. And fourteen-inch bottoms on their trousers. Their socks were bright yellow, red, pink, which would show when they walked; shirt collars up at the back, and "slim Jim" ties.

To pedestrians and motorists, the colourful, dandyish exhibitionists were an entertaining sight. Compared with ordinary Dubliners they looked like a parade of circus clowns. Children and grannies alike had to smile. There was no doubt that their multi-hued appearance enlivened an otherwise grey streetscape. But many adults did not approve of them at all. "Teds were looked upon as *freaks* of nature to older generations, such as my father," says Creighton. "They were considered immoral." As they strutted down the street like prissy peacocks, some older people were stopped in their tracks, gawking at them.

At first most adults simply didn't know how to judge them. Were they merely exhibitionists, harmless dandies? Or dangerous gangs? Some people thought they might be a cult. Sociologists hastened to label them a "subculture"— whatever that meant!

Branigan and the Gardaí took a special interest in assessing them. The Teddy Boys always roamed in groups, often cocky and arrogant around other people. As their numbers grew they gathered at beat clubs, ballrooms, cinemas, and fish-and-chip shops, and their presence could drive away other patrons. Branigan knew a good few of them and found their transformation into "Teddys" fascinating, and worrisome.

Most Irish Teddy Boys were between fifteen and nineteen, with a few in their early twenties. The majority had some type of employment, which allowed them to save money for their clothes and shoes. After all, their outfit was their identity. This was convenient for gardaí, as it made them readily identifiable in the street or in a crowd.

What worried Branigan from the outset was that they travelled in packs. He was all too familiar with the "pack mentality" from his early "animal gang" days. Showing off and rowdyism could easily lead to disorder; but as long as they were law-abiding he would not judge them negatively.

As Dublin's Teddy Boys expanded in numbers it became apparent that not all cliques were alike in behaviour. Some were becoming aggressive, seeking to intimidate others whom they encountered, either in the street or at public venues. Other Teddys were obviously harmless, just relishing their offbeat role and the attention they were drawing to themselves.

Around Noel Hughes's part of the city there were those who liked to pretend they were tough. "A lot of the Teddy Boys *thought* they were hard men, but only one out of ten could handle himself. The rest were gangs of little pups who deliberately looked for trouble."

One evening in 1956 a tough-acting nineteen-year-old named Dunphy was arrested by Garda Seán Connell. Just as he was becoming abusive and resisting arrest, by chance along came Garda Branigan in a patrol car, who saw the struggle taking place. Then, as the newspapers reported it, "he went to the assistance of Connell and took control." When he appeared in court before Judge Mangan, Dunphy sourly stated that he "wished he was the size of Guard J. C. Branigan, the former boxer, who arrested him."[11] Teddys liked to "talk big" and "act big" when *en masse,* but most, as Hughes put it, were "pups," playing their group role. On their own they were no threat.

Like London's Teddy Boys, there were groups in Dublin that began feuding with one another, skirmishing at dancehalls, cafés, and cinemas. Conflicts led to the carrying of weapons. This dramatically changed their status: in Branigan's book, it qualified them as a "street nuisance."

The popularity of two American films, *Blackboard Jungle* and *The Wild One,* had an influence on Teddy-Boy subcultural behaviour. "When 'Blackboard Jungle' arrived on the scene," Gerry Creighton recalls, "the picture-houses were packed every night, and the sale of flick-knives boomed!"

This type of knife—easily concealed and quickly opened—became the weapon of choice. But the teds were given credit for fashioning their own customised weapon: a metal comb with the handle sharpened into a deadly blade. Many carried razors as well. Once it became known that Dublin's Teddy Boys were arming themselves with weapons and fighting, various establishments began banning them.

When innocent citizens began to be assaulted by Teddy Boys, public fears rose. One of the first incidents to make the newspapers and alert the public to the threat occurred in mid-1955, described by the *Evening Herald* in an article with the alarming heading "Vicious assault in Teddy Boy style." A fifteen-year-old boy was walking by himself along a footpath when a pack of Teddys stopped him to make some threatening remarks, after which they "struck and kicked him brutally."[12] By the time a garda arrived the youth was in "a pool of blood about 14 by 20 inches on the footpath." When the case came before Judge MacCarthy he was particularly angry because the savage attack was wholly unprovoked on an innocent young lad. "Here was a vicious assault on a smaller boy," he said, "committed by blackguards in a brutal Teddy-Boy fashion."[13] The attackers were sentenced to a month's imprisonment.

People began writing letters to the newspapers to share their own fearful observations. A correspondent using the name "Boiling Blood" wrote:

> Sir,—Recently I had the experience of seeing a young girl being kicked by a Dublin Teddy Boy. It makes me wonder what kind of "scum" is being reared in our city.
>
> I appeal to all Irishmen to put a stop to this once and for all, so that our mothers, sisters and daughters may walk the street without fear.[14]

Similar incidents began appearing in the papers with unsettling regularity. The public perception of Teddy Boys was no longer that of freaky, offbeat teenagers dressed in amusing gaudy outfits: they were now seen as dangerous.

Branigan felt that the Teddys relished the attention they were now getting in the press, portraying them as tough. It fed right into their craving to be noticed: to them it felt like becoming famous. Noticed and *notorious*. Now different groups of Teddys were vying for notoriety. This was seen in the manner in which some bands strutted down the pavement, marching like Hitler's Stormtroopers, clearly to intimidate people in their path. It was at this point that Branigan felt the Teddy Boys needed taming.

———

Branigan now made it his business to get to the scene of any Teddy-Boy trouble, especially as many were becoming belligerent when confronted by guards.

They taunted the police, ignored their orders, even pelted them with objects.

One of the most publicised incidents took place on the night of Saturday 4 June 1955 in what the press would dub the "Battle of Dolphin's Barn." Teddy Boys had been congregating in the area and causing disturbances over the previous weeks, and local residents were worried. Between eleven and midnight Garda J. Duffy and Garda P. Carney were on duty when they heard a loud crash of glass. As they went to investigate they saw "a large number of youths coming towards them ... of the Teddy-Boy class." They were met with "insulting words and behaviour," which they found very threatening, as reported by the *Evening Press*:

> The two guards grabbed two of them ... and there was a terrific struggle, with the defendants calling out for assistance. A crowd of 300 gathered, many of them hostile, as stones and bricks were thrown.[15]

Garda Duffy and Garda Carney fought to hold on to two tough nineteen-year-olds while trying to protect themselves from the flying stones and bottles.

When another colleague, Garda Foster, showed up he saw the two hooligans fighting "like wild animals." The three guards struggled to restrain them as they thrashed, punched, and kicked, all the while under a hail of missiles. They felt they had no choice but to draw their batons; but this only further inflamed the crowd's anger. Being outnumbered by about 300 to 3, they needed reinforcements. When one of the guards desperately put in the call, he specifically requested that Branigan be notified.

Branigan had been handling bellicose, tough-acting Teddy Boys with relative ease, as they were perfect candidates for his glove-lash. Most of the troublesome Teddys, he found, were young street thugs, rather than pugilists, some just scrawny juveniles dressed for their role. As Branigan's colleague John Collins saw it, "the Teddy Boys had their big swallow-tail coats and suede shoes, *thick-soled*—you know, five foot trying to be *six-foot!*" Acting the hardchaw, they would raise a row, then curse the gardaí when they showed up and resisted arrest, often forcibly.

But they feared Lugs Branigan: "*All* the Teddys knew me by name."[16]

And when a melee broke out he was the last one they wanted to see. As Dan Walsh relates, the Teddys had learnt the purpose of the leather gloves he always carried:

> I remember he'd get a group of Teddy Boys, and if they were up to no good he'd have to use his gloves. And if some might be inclined to give him a bit of cheek he'd *slap* them with the gloves. And that was enough.

An insolent Teddy-Boy leader would instantly turn meek with the flick of his wrist. Some actually broke into tears—right before their followers. Seldom did he have to resort to a "clip," but it was always in reserve.

On the night of 4 June at Dolphin's Barn several other gardaí showed up to assist before Branigan arrived, which made the mob more riotous. But when Branigan screeched up in a patrol car with his driver the cry went up, *"Lugs is here!"* The reaction, says John Collins, was predictable. "When a crowd of Teddy Boys would see him *coming,* they were *gone!* That was it!" Knowing how Lugs would plunge into a crowd, they began to disperse without hesitation. The remaining Teddys were restrained and shoved into patrol cars to be taken off to the station.

In court Judge Mangan stated that those who "threw stones at them [gardaí] are beneath contempt . . . are not decent citizens."[17] With a crowd of nearly three hundred agitated participants there could have been many serious injuries on both sides. Branigan was credited both by his superiors and by the press with having quickly quelled the mob, ending the "Battle of Dolphin's Barn" before more casualties occurred.

Three days later, on 7 June, the privileged young men of Trinity College decided, for some summer fun, to mock the Teddy Boys. Noting that "topicality is the first test of a revue," the Trinity Players' 1955 frolic was called "completely up to date." As a reporter for the *Evening Herald* wrote in his review, one of the "best sketches was a skit on the Teddy Boys with the verses set to the tune of 'Teddy Bears' Picnic.'" Derision was not the type of attention the Teddy Boys were seeking. For the Trinity Players it was perhaps fortunate that there were no Teddys in the audience.

———

On 14 August 1955 a controversial incident occurred at the Four Provinces Ballroom in Harcourt Street, more important for its legal ramifications than for its physical violence. The *Evening Herald's* front-page story had the curious heading "Trousers width led to row," with the equally odd subheading "Nineteen inches would have got him in."

It began earlier in the summer when the management of the ballroom had trouble with Teddy Boys, who were causing disturbances and rows. Doormen were given orders to be on the watch and to bar youths *appearing* to be trouble-makers of the Teddy-Boy type. On this night a doorman, Edward Boyne, spotted a Teddy-Boy type, by the name of Power, identified by his drainpipe trousers, long jacket, and hairstyle, whom he judged to be a "hardchaw." Boyne confronted him, saying he could be admitted only "if he had more cloth in his trousers." Power was furious, but departed. The next day Power caught up with Boyne out on the street, exchanged words, then viciously kicked and head-butted him.

It seemed to be an insignificant dispute between two men. However, when it reached Judge McCarthy's court in October the full ramifications became apparent. In effect, the management of the ballroom had taken it upon themselves to screen and to reject certain patrons on the seemingly superficial grounds of dress.

Because of his experience with the Teddy Boys as well as ballroom managers, Garda Branigan was called upon to assume an important role in the case. At the trial it was agreed that Power had broken no laws at the ballroom entrance. Nor had he created even a mild disturbance. Yet he ended up being charged with assault upon Boyne. The question was whether this had resulted from having been treated unfairly and being discriminated against. Had there been serious provocation?

The doorman testified that he was acting on orders not to admit "youths wearing narrow trousers." He was then asked, "If the defendant had been wearing trousers which were nineteen inches wide, would he have been admitted?" Boyne was uncertain, but he thought so; at which point Judge McCarthy hypothesised that "apparently there has grown up in Dublin some moral censorship in regard to dress . . . [but] the people employed to operate the censorship are not sartorial experts."[18] Which further muddied the issue.

Garda Branigan, allowed to question the defendant, found himself in a difficult position, as he understood both sides of the case: a manager's right to keep his premises safe and a patron's right to dress as he liked. Judge McCarthy also seemed understanding, perhaps even sympathetic, to both sides. The viewpoints were indeed conflicting. It was a perplexing legal and moral issue, but not one that could be resolved in his court. His responsibility was to rule on the assault charges.

After hearing all the testimony, he asked Garda Branigan for his experienced opinion on the case. Any insight or advice would be welcome.

At this point in his career, with twenty-five years of experience on which to draw, it was common for judges to call on Branigan's wisdom towards the end of a case. Branigan asserted that "Power had not been in trouble before, and is a member of a respectable family."[19] Judges always gave great weight to such endorsements. McCarthy agreed that Power seemed like a "decent youth." He was let off with a warning, and everyone seemed satisfied. At least for the moment.

But the question of discrimination and barring would continue to bedevil managements, the Gardaí and the courts for some time to come.

————

Throughout the summer of 1955 the *Evening Herald* reported that Teddy Boys were causing trouble every weekend at the Theatre Royal in Hawkins Street.[20] It was a highly popular theatre and cinema, and a bad press could hurt its business. By autumn the Teddy Boys' regular rows had become a serious problem, placing members of the staff at risk and driving away the clientele.

On the evening of 25 September a horde of Teddy Boys, "their hair combed in the Tony Curtis style . . . wearing narrow trousers and gaudy coloured shirts," made their way into the theatre. Before long an usher reported to her superior, James Byrne, that they were causing a disturbance with their noise and behaviour. Dutifully, he went down to inform them politely that they would have to cease their misconduct, as it was disturbing other patrons. Without warning, "a group of fifty ganged up on him." One nineteen-year-old named Sheridan and six companions assaulted Byrne, saying, "We'll do this so-and-so in!"[21] They struck him several times and split his lip. The management immediately summoned the gardaí, and Sergeant Sherlock showed up first to halt the disorder.

The next day, when the newspapers wrote about a "gang of fifty" Teddy Boys attacking an usher at the Theatre Royal, it increased the wariness about attending cinemas. Some people wrote to newspapers suggesting the quixotic idea of placing a guard at all the city's picture-houses and dancehalls.

Gardaí were now regularly being summoned to ballroom doors, where conflicts arose over the attire of Teddy-Boys when they were denied admission. Some turned violent. In October 1955 at the Palm Court Ballroom in Aungier Street a hot-headed Teddy Boy named Kelly and several of his pals showed up in full regalia. Spotting possible trouble, the proprietor, Solly White, met them at the entrance and flatly refused to let them in, on the grounds that they "were wearing soppy-soled shoes [and] tight trousers and that they were Teddy Boys,"[22] declaring that he had the right to bar them on those grounds.

In turn, Kelly and his fellow-Teddys argued that they had a right to wear whatever style of clothes they liked. Using foul language, they formed a line outside the entrance and would not allow anyone else in or out. Kelly then shouted out to White that if he came outside he would knife him. That was when Branigan was called.

On arrival, Branigan recognised Kelly from a number of previous convictions for assault. He knew he posed a real threat to White, being quite capable of using his knife. When Kelly likewise recognised Branigan, he wisely put up no resistance.

In court, Judge Mangan found Kelly guilty and fined him. But the quandary over Teddy-Boy dress and banning rights was no closer to a resolution.

By the end of 1955 Branigan had learnt much about the Teddy-Boy subculture. However, as he well knew, the majority of Teddys were merely harmless show-offs, enjoying their fling on Dublin's stage. It was the small minority of hooligans who were capturing the bad press and alarming people.

Surprisingly, some of his knowledge was gained from young Garda recruits just joining the force in the fifties. Not only were they in touch with youth life-styles but some had worn Teddy-Boy clothes themselves. Among them was Tony Ruane, who, at twenty, was twenty-five years younger than Branigan. He would soon become a top-flight Garda boxer who came to know "Branno" well. When he joined up he was in a good position to further Branigan's education about the surging rock-and-roll craze and the emergence of Teddy Boys—for he showed up at the Garda Depot looking like one of them:

> I wore Teddy-Boy clothes myself! Some recruits had hair down as far as their waist! And all these drainpipe trousers . . . [They] marched us down to the barber, and there was a bale of hair there—like a *sheep-shearing*.

Through his continuing involvement in Garda boxing, Branigan kept close contact with the younger generation of recruits. This turned out to be of great value to him in keeping informed about Dublin youth throughout the 1950s and 60s. It helped him to fully comprehend the psyche of rebellious teenagers of that era. As he explained it:

> In the fifties, the attitudes and talk and jokes of the young [gardaí] helped me to understand the Teddy Boys . . . and later it was the "mods and rockers" . . . and even the "skinheads." I'd hear the younger person's point of view.[23]

It all helped Branigan to prepare for serving in court as an "interpreter" between teenagers and the judge and jury.

He could now usually differentiate between the innocuous, fun-loving Teddys and the vicious, threatening ones. One such bunch, recalls Matthew Fagan, liked to attend the Tivoli picture-house in Francis Street and then hang out across the street at an ice-cream parlour called Johnny Ray's, where they often caused trouble. They began jiving wildly to the music and causing mayhem. They also carried, and used, weapons, as Branigan knew. "He didn't like *those* Teddy Boys *at all*," says Fagan, "with chains on their shoes. And some carried blades . . . And he knew them all." Many a time he saw Branigan storm in through the door, and "he'd pick out the ones he didn't like . . . and just *bashed* them" if they didn't comply immediately with his order to leave.

His problem with certain Teddy-Boy factions was complicated by what the newspapers began calling "Teddy-Girl gangs," who followed their boy-friends. They cut their hair short, dressed as rock-and-rollers, and went to places where they could jive to the music on jukeboxes. Sometimes they insisted that the music be cranked up to deafening levels. As one journalist reported, local residents "were put through a nerve-racking experience, between the teenagers and the rock-and-roll jukebox music."[24] It was a delicate situation. And when arrested, some girls retaliated by cursing, kicking, scratching, and screaming. Teddy *Boys* could be easier to handle.

———

The *Irish Independent* gave front-page coverage to an article headed "Pontiff's Pity for Teddy Boys," in which the Pope expressed his feelings about "lost" youth, who had drifted from their Catholic values into an existential abyss: "The unhappy faces of Teddy Boys and Mods and Rockers reveal profound piteous drama," he lamented.[25] He saw their music and life-style as a youthful tragedy.

Ironically, as more people were clamouring for a Garda crackdown on teenage lawlessness and other forms of street crime, the commissioner, Daniel Costigan, addressed the new gardaí at their passing-out parade in the Phoenix Park with a different message. He implored them to be patient and courteous when dealing with all members of the public. It should be an age of civility, he told them: "don't be too quick to bring people to court for minor offences when you're satisfied that advice and caution will secure observance of the law."[26]

In his opinion the courts were being clogged up with cases that might have been better resolved on the street with the right psychology. He recommended that, rather than using a gruff voice, they should say "Excuse me" or "If you please" when dealing with troublesome people, as this would "get much better results." He had obviously never been out on night patrol with Jim Branigan.

Yet neither the commissioner, his superintendents nor judges were about to admonish Lugs Branigan for his now well-known "unorthodox"—and highly effective—brand of summary justice. As Dan Walsh observed, "I travelled with him, and when stopping rowdy groups of youths they realised who they were talking to. Having seen the famous black gloves, they decided this was not a man to be *trifled* with." Commissioner Costigan had no better deterrent to crime on Dublin's streets than Garda James Branigan.

———

When 1956 rolled around, the beat that rocked America also rocked Dublin. And with its thumping rhythm, "Rock Around the Clock" became the anthem of the rock-and-roll era, embodying the sound of the teenage revolution itself. Young people listened to it incessantly, its primal beat programmed into their brains. It was hypnotic—the very *soul* of rock and roll.

"Rock Around the Clock" was the creation of Bill Haley and his Comets, who packed American concerts, electrifying audiences with their spectacular performance. When they made their film of *Rock Around the Clock,* encapsulating the spirit of the rock-and-roll movement itself, youngsters in American cinemas "went wild," wrote the newspapers. Television news showed masses of hyperventilating teenagers on a rampage after seeing the film. The stories made headlines throughout America.

In early 1956, when Irish rock-and-roll fans learnt that Haley's film would soon be coming to Dublin, they were ecstatic.

Branigan braced himself.

————

The film was scheduled to open on 13 June 1956 at the Carlton in O'Connell Street. By coincidence, another youth rebellion film was showing that week at the Adelphi in Middle Abbey Street, with James Dean in *Rebel Without a Cause.* Older generations could see a Gina Lollobrigida comedy at the Corinthian in Eden Quay, or attend the production of *Harvey* at the Gaiety Theatre with Milo O'Shea. Never had the "generation gap" been more apparent.

As show time at the Carlton approached, every teenager in Dublin envied those fortunate enough to secure tickets. Scores of others milled about the streets around the cinema, hoping to pick up some of the atmosphere, to at least be part of the "scene."

In America some audiences had turned riotous, causing destruction in and around the cinemas. In preparation for such disorderly behaviour a number of gardaí were posted around the Carlton for the first night's showing. Though the teenagers in attendance periodically erupted in loud singing, clapping, and some jiving in the aisles, there was no behaviour that was beyond the control of the staff.

A few nights after the Carlton's first showing, cliques of Teddy Boys and other teenage troublemakers, some fuelled by drink, began "going berserk" to the beat of the music. One reporter wrote of seeing "wildly cavorting bodies" engaged in uncontrolled jiving and fighting, throwing missiles and tearing out seats.[27] The rowdies, using vulgar language and threatening the ushers, caused the management to turn up the lights and halt the film—which incited worse rioting. Gardaí had to be rushed in to quell the disorder. When such incidents gained attention through the press, it only encouraged other lawless teenagers to become copycats at later showings. It became the fashion to run wild when watching *Rock Around the Clock.*

Enter Lugs Branigan.

After consulting cinema managers, the Garda authorities devised a plan. In late June, Branigan was called in and informed that he was being assigned to a new, and unique, duty. He was to act as a one-man strike force against cinema rioters.

The rationale was that, with his reputation and his experience in handling youthful miscreants, he could serve as the ultimate deterrent to hooligans during the showing of *Rock Around the Clock*. They had seen him quell street riots with his mere presence. Though he was an avid filmgoer himself, this film was not exactly Branigan's cup of tea. But he understood the importance of his role.

At first he acted as an observer, to see at what points the film ignited "craziness," causing teenagers to burst into wild gyrations and become destructive. This was easy enough. As he described his early observations, "the antics of the 'rock n' roll' mad girls screaming in the aisles, and shouting, usually led to fights in the cinemas. During these fights seats would be ripped and property damaged."[28] As some of the most electrifying scenes came at the end of the film, he realised he would have to remain and endure the entire showing. Time after time.

To be an effective deterrent he would need to make his presence conspicuous from the moment the teenagers streamed through the doors. He held his black leather gloves in plain sight, sometimes tapping them as tough teenagers passed by him. He then strolled the aisles, casting direct looks at those he perceived to be potential troublemakers. Every youth in the cinema knew Lugs—and wanted no part of him.

Nonetheless there were instances when a Teddy Boy or other rowdy teenager, usually having drink taken, would cause a disturbance or act in an insolent manner towards him. He taught them a quick lesson with his gloves, which was immediately instructional for the rest of the audience. This strategy was so successful that, at least at first, he seldom had to arrest anyone in the cinema.

The daily showings of the film greatly popularised rock-and-roll lingo in Dublin. On 16 June the *Evening Herald* published an article headed "Dig This, You Cats!" as a sort of crash course to familiarise adults with the teenage dialect now heard even in their own home.[29] Seeing the film over and over again, listening to the chatter of the teenagers, Branigan was an expert rock-and-roll linguist. He knew all about "hep cats" and "daddyos" and "see you later, alligator."

Though he was remarkably effective as a sole deterrent to trouble in Dublin's larger cinemas, when the film began to be distributed to smaller local picture-houses the real trouble arose. Lugs Branigan could only be in one cinema at a time.

As it turned out, teenagers were far more inclined to misbehave and riot in their own local picture-houses. On 30 July, at a showing of the film at the Star Cinema in Crumlin, a band of rowdy Teddy Boys raised a terrible row; "missiles were thrown, including a heavy iron bar, and damage done to seats and glass was broken." It all began when they jumped out of their seats and began jiving wildly in the aisles. One of them was an eighteen-year-old private in the army. In court, Judge Ó Riain accused them of "behaving in a riotous manner by *jiving* in the cinema."[30] It was noted that he used one of their own terms.

Their only defence was that they *couldn't* just "sit there" passively during the big beat scenes: they *had* to rise and jive. It was just a natural response to the stimulus of rock-and-roll music. That's what rock and roll was all about! The judge, doubtless feeling helpless at this point, fined them 20 shillings (£1) and issued a warning against further disorderly conduct in cinemas.

Ironically, as cinemas around the country were crammed with teenagers rocking to Haley's film, it was banned in parts of the North. When managers of cinemas in Cos. Down and Armagh refused to show it, teenagers desperate to see the controversial film swarmed south. The *Evening Herald* reported that they "travelled by bus, car, cycle and even motor-boat."[31]

Branigan, who now placed himself at those cinemas he thought most likely to explode, found that no two rock-and-roll riots were ever the same. The worst ones were where Teddys and other rowdies spilled *out* of the cinema, carrying their trouble with them into the streets, where it was difficult for the police to restrain them. So long as they were constrained *within* a cinema, they knew they could be trapped by Branigan or other guards; but breaking loose outside could mean serious trouble. This happened on 16 November 1956 at the Mary Street Cinema during the showing of Haley's film. Many in the crowd had already seen it umpteen times and were just waiting for the right scenes as a signal to erupt. Branigan was not present at that particular cinema that night—but would soon be called.

In a packed house, about three-quarters of the way through the film some teenagers began to "sing and shout." The management, in an effort to halt the disturbance before it got worse, made a tactical mistake: at about ten o'clock they stopped the show completely. As one newspaper wrote, "this caused considerable resentment," which further incensed teenagers already at fever pitch, inciting them to vandalism. They began to tear the backs from the upholstered seats. After seriously damaging about forty seats, the angry crowd pushed outside into the street and began throwing missiles and breaking windows.

By the time Branigan could reach the scene, "the crowd appeared to be completely out of control, and a knife was thrown at one of the guards." Seeing

Branigan, they began dispersing down Henry Street, and traffic was stopped at Nelson's Pillar in O'Connell Street. Many then crossed over to North Earl Street. Along the way, some scuffles broke out between Teddy Boys and guards. In their wake was left a trail of broken windows.

By the end of 1956 Branigan must have been wishing he had never heard the beat of *Rock Around the Clock*. But he was hardly finished.

––––

The year 1957 began sorrowfully for Branigan with the death of his father in late January, at the age of eighty-one. He had lived with the family for years, which made his loss all the more poignant. After the premature loss of Branigan's mother in 1930, when he was only twenty years old, his father had assumed an especially large role in his life. By all accounts they had a close and mutually supportive relationship. His father had always been helpful and wise, instilling in him the best of values, and proud of his son. He would be much missed in the Branigan home in Drimnagh Road. At the funeral, Declan noticed his father containing his emotions.

––––

"He's *comin'*! He's *comin'*!"

It wasn't Elvis; but it was about the next-best thing: Bill Haley and his Comets, the maestros of *Rock Around the Clock*, to appear in Dublin—in person. The *Irish Press* called Haley the "Rock-and-Roll King." Dublin's rock-and-rollers were ecstatic. As the city's hep cats counted the day till his arrival, Branigan again braced himself.

At about 10 a.m. on 27 February a crowd of happy, giddy teenagers began gathering at Dublin Airport. Shortly after midday they spotted the Aer Lingus plane slowly descending, with Bill Haley and his Comets aboard. "There was a flutter of excitement on the public balcony," noted one reporter assigned to capture the atmosphere of the event. After the plane's door was opened they all came out and halted on the steps so that photographers could get some pictures of them waving and smiling.

Once inside the terminal, Haley was genial as he met waiting reporters and politely answered all their questions. A press reception was held later in the afternoon at the Gresham Hotel, where they were staying. When asked by the *Evening Herald's* dance correspondent, who wrote under the name "Tempo," about the celebrated "kiss curl" on his forehead, Haley answered candidly, "It's just a gimmick, ma'am."

By the time the reception ended, several hundred excited teenagers, including cliques of Teddy Boys in their regalia, had assembled at the taxi rank opposite the Gresham in O'Connell Street, chanting "We want Haley!" When they broke into the song "See You Later, Alligator," it all seemed like innocent fun. The gardaí on hand hoped it would remain that way.

Meanwhile Branigan was busy behind the scenes. He was in consultation with the Theatre Royal's manager, Phil Donoghue, and his staff about co-ordinating the strategy for Haley's stage appearances. Donoghue was immensely grateful for Branigan's assistance. They knew that while the performance was going on inside the theatre there were sure to be thousands of excited young people out in the streets.

"Tempo" also trekked over to the Theatre Royal in Hawkins Street to ask Donoghue about his preparations for the onslaught, now only hours away. She asked what the management would do "if there is an epidemic of rock (jiving, singing, shouting) in the aisles?" Donoghue answered confidently, "Use diplomatic measures." Pressed to be more specific, he replied jocularly, "We'll go among them with long-handled mallets!"[32]

For the first performance of the evening, Branigan, in plain clothes, and a contingent of uniformed gardaí covered the area around the theatre. He probably posted himself around the entrance for immediate recognition, and also for quick response outside on the street. He detected that the atmosphere was suffused not only with excitement but also with a certain edginess. He found this quite different from the first showings of Haley's film: this time, he surmised, the city's teenagers knew there were to be only two performances, limited to a number of lucky ticket-holders. This left out thousands of loyal fans of Haley's, who still wanted somehow to be part of "the scene" and in the hope of at least *seeing* him and his Comets in person.

The crowd began gathering hours in advance. By the time the envied ticket-holders were allowed entry to the theatre, "nearly a thousand young rock n' rollers thronged Poolbeg Street outside." More were steadily flowing in from adjacent streets. They were in good spirits, laughing, singing, dancing. Among them were clusters of Teddy Boys. Guards stood back and watched in amusement. Inside the theatre an *Irish Press* reporter was stationed in the lobby, observing that the girls were "glamorously togged out as if going to a big hop . . . dressed like the rock n' rollers in colour pictures in the magazines," with lacquered hair, brilliant blouses, and tight black skirts—"oh, yes, and *perfume*."[33]

Among the crowd taking their seats was sixteen-year-old Paddy Daly, a bona-fide rock-and-roller and Haley fan who in a few years' time would join the Gardaí and later work beside Branigan in dealing with troublesome youths. "Oh, I was *at* the concert. I was a *big* Bill Haley fan—and *still am!*" (in 2011 whipping out an autographed photograph of Haley to prove it). He remembers how he and the others were jumpy with excitement in anticipation of seeing the show—not to cause trouble. The last thing he and his friends wanted was for some boozed-up Teddy Boys to trigger a disturbance that would deprive them of their experience.

When the curtain finally went up and Haley and his Comets burst onto the stage, a reporter from the *Irish Press* wrote that there was a "prolonged '*whoop!*' as he rocked away." In his article, headed "A Big Night for the City Cats," he described how Haley's fans really got into it:

> The cooler cats clapped out the rhythms . . . Devotees "sent," hunched in their seats, jerked their heads, then leaned back panting, mouth agape in a strangled grin, eyes glassy and staring. Things got livelier for "See you later, Alligator" and "Rock Around the Clock."[34]

For the most part the fans were well behaved. At the conclusion, all the reporter could hear was "a great cawing sound all around me . . . 'rawk, rawk, rawk.'" Then, swept up in the throng, "we went out into Hawkins Street where all the real leppin' was being done." Apart from some minor skirmishes and several arrests for disorderly conduct, the night ended peacefully—much to the relief of Branigan, his fellow-gardaí, and the theatre staff.

For Haley's second performance, by half past eight the next night there were nearly two thousand fans packed into Poolbeg Street. This crowd was discernibly more edgy than the night before. The guards detected it right away.

Below Haley's dressing-room window they chanted madly, "We want Haley!" as if beseeching a blessing from the Vatican balcony. But there was now a "demanding" tone to it. Haley responded, appearing at his window and waving to the crowd. After a few minutes he withdrew, and gardaí pushed the fans back into Hawkins Street and Tara Street. It seemed to appease them, for the moment at least.

Then, surprisingly, just as the guards seemed to be in control of the streets, Haley *again* popped his head out the window for his adoring fans, causing the crowds to charge back, much to the annoyance of the gardaí. They "attempted to keep the shouting crowds out of the street, but they surged through their ranks."[35] Haley would later say that "what pleased us most" was looking out the window of his dressing-room and seeing so many thousands of his fans "gathered in a solid block"—which was what most distressed Branigan and his colleagues. They knew that a compressed mass of emotionally fired-up teenagers could become volcanic, highly susceptible to mob mentality and mass hysteria. Things could quickly get out of hand.

Once again the sight of Branigan at the entrance of the theatre apparently served as a deterrent to trouble inside. However, it was of no value to the guards facing masses of agitated youths outside on the street.

At about ten o'clock tensions rose and disorder broke out. "There were fights in the crowd, as people were pushed about," the *Irish Press* reported. "There were scuffles between gardaí and youths."[36] As usual, Teddy Boys and individual hooligans were the primary provocateurs. Bottles and other objects flew through the air, and the sound of shattering glass was heard. Windows were broken in O'Connell Street when a mob, "many in Teddy Boy clothes, rushed up and down the street," acting wild and threatening and carrying out acts of vandalism. When "young girls fainted in the screaming, tightly packed crowd," one reporter said, gardaí tried to reach and assist them. Like a stampede that shifted back and forth, people were knocked down and trampled on. Crying was heard as injuries occurred. In adjacent streets, rowdy boys went along thumping their fists on cars, frightening passengers.

At this point in the chaos it is not possible to pinpoint Branigan; but it is logical to assume that when he was informed of the pandemonium outside in the streets he would have immediately rushed to the assistance of his fellow-gardaí and doubtless, in his usual manner, sought to "wade into" the riotous mass. However, this time he faced a sea of thousands of delirious teenagers, the majority of whom were simply excited youngsters caught up in the frenzy. Teddy Boys who were misbehaving would have been his primary target, but reaching them and dealing with them was nearly impossible.

It must have been an unprecedented realisation for him that his presence and reputation exerted no power over the massive crowd. The thousands of frenzied teenagers were essentially oblivious of Lugs Branigan. Amidst the mass hysteria of some rock-and-rollers, young people rushed right past the guards, jostling them in the process. Branigan's black leather gloves were probably of no use. Like all the guards, he could only have been bewildered at first by the panorama of uncontrolled youth.

At about 11 p.m. reinforcements began to arrive in significant numbers, with orders to set up cordons and drive the crowd away from the theatre, using forcible means—but not batons—to regain control of the streets. But they were allowed to *draw* their batons, which had a strong visual effect on the crowd. As verified by the *Evening Herald*, "guards drew their batons and dispersed about a thousand demonstrators from Poolbeg Street . . . as bottles and other missiles" were thrown at them.[37] Late into the night and early next morning groups of teenagers were still roaming the city centre, hooting and shouting, singing, throwing objects, and keeping the guards on alert.

The next day's newspapers covered the whole unpleasant story, the lawlessness that many adults cited as the worst aspect of the rock-and-roll "rebellion." Citizens wrote to newspapers calling it "disgraceful," "uncivilised," "intolerable." By contrast, "Tempo," who had observed the event largely from inside the Theatre Royal, told her readers that the teenagers she saw were "certainly better behaved . . . more civil than rugby crowds." Summing up the evening, she called it "jolly fun."

When Bill Haley and his Comets left Dublin the next morning for Belfast he graciously expressed appreciation to his devoted Irish fans for their "enthusiasm."

———

Haley's electrifying two-day visit to Dublin prompted a resurgence of interest in his film in local cinemas, forcing Branigan back on duty to cope with the youngsters' enthusiasm. On 12 August 1957 the Lyric Cinema experienced a disturbance when teenagers became unruly and "there were blows on all sides," with glass smashed outside the cinema. Branigan was called to halt the trouble and disperse the crowd.

Appearing in court a few days later he confirmed to Judge Nunan that he had now seen the film some *sixty times,* adding that it "did not excite him." When this revelation made the front page of the *Evening Herald,* under the heading "He Has Seen 'Rock' Film 60 Times," all the readers knew who "he" was. And his assignment was far from over.

Shortly afterwards Garda Branigan was given yet another special duty. It was a brief detail but one he knew would impress Alick, Declan, and Helen. He was about to meet the face of rock and roll close up, as minder for the British singing idol Cliff Richard.

Richard was coming to Dublin and needed protection during his visit. Because of Branigan's rapport with rock-and-rollers, and his success in handling unruly groups, he was the logical choice for the job. Before Richard's arrival Branigan was briefed on his role and told that the singer had "just been subjected to a series of mobbings in England and other countries by fanatical, screaming teenagers." He had had some close calls, which frightened him. Swarms of uncontrolled fans could be a real threat to the safety of rock-and-roll stars, as some had found out. Without constant, close protection, over-exuberant teenagers could get at their heartthrobs, mobbing them, ripping clothes, knocking them down, bruising and nearly suffocating them. Cliff Richard had recently had a frightening experience in England when the car in which he was travelling was surrounded by a sea of crazed fans, who rocked the vehicle and pounded on the windows with a force that could have smashed them. He was terrified. Branigan was informed of all this.

In Dublin, Cliff Richard was to perform at the National Stadium in Harold's Cross and then be taken directly, and safely, to the Gresham Hotel. Branigan's orders were to remain at his side at all times—even in his hotel room.

Branigan liked him straight off. He was not the type of egotistical, demanding teenage idol one might have expected. Quite the opposite: he was a modest and appreciative young man, polite to everyone around him. Branigan was very protective, explaining that "he was very timid and nervous . . . He was scared that a mob would appear from nowhere and over-turn his car."[38] As his minder, the most challenging job was to keep screaming, adoring girls at bay. This was not something taught to recruits at the Garda Depot. "My most difficult task was escorting Cliff to and from his dressing-room," through a throng of near-hysterical girls, pushing and clawing to get near him and touch him. "I did so without incident . . . Cliff was amazed at my control of the crowd." With one hand on Richard's shoulder, and his black gloves in the other, Lugs would bark at fans to back away when they came too close.

Once he was safely inside his hotel room, everyone heaved a sigh of relief. Then Branigan posted two other guards, McCarney and Mulderrig, directly outside the door. Within the room he checked with Richard to make sure everything was to his satisfaction. He then had the opportunity to relax and get to know him personally. Unspoiled and courteous, the teenage sensation was as nice as his own children. "What impressed me the most," Branigan would later say, was that Cliff "phoned his mother every night to say he was all right," first thing after every performance.[39] After which Lugs and the rock-and-roll star sat back, shared tea and talk, and plenty of laughing.

On leaving Dublin, Richard profusely thanked Branigan as the best bodyguard he had ever had.

————

The count continued . . . 61, 62, 63. Would the furore over Haley's film ever subside? The Garda Síochána was now regularly receiving requests from cinema managers in distant places around the country to "borrow" the services of Garda Branigan, just for a weekend or so. They had read in the Dublin papers that he worked miracles in the capital's cinemas, quelling teenage uprisings. The Garda brass had to explain to them that it was, unfortunately, an impossible request.

On 4 July 1958 Jim Branigan received a much-deserved (and belated, swore his Garda mates) upgrading to Detective-Garda James Branigan, after twenty-eight years' service. In this there would later be a story to be told—after retirement.

Congratulations poured in from friends, judges, solicitors, Government members, and the press, but none more sincere and warmly expressed than those of people on the street who stopped him to offer their congratulations. He was met with hearty handshakes and pats on the back every few steps. Even some former gang members and gougers thrust their hand out for a shake and a kind word, many telling him he was not only the best and toughest but the *fairest* policeman they had ever known.

The *Evening Herald* published a congratulatory article, christening him the "Rock-and-Roll Cop," as he had already become known to many, crediting him with "almost single-handedly" quelling the Teddy-Boy lawlessness in Dublin and noting that by now he had seen *Rock Around the Clock* an estimated *ninety times*.[40] Later in life Branigan would good-naturedly confess that "seeing him [Haley] that many times, I got cheesed off."

By the time the "Fabulous Fifties" ended, Detective-Garda Branigan had accumulated quite an array of titles: Leinster heavyweight boxing champion, "Battling Branigan," "Breaker of the Animal Gangs," "Terror of the Teddy Boys," "Ireland's toughest, most fearless garda." And now, the "Rock-and-Roll Cop."

More would be added over the remaining years of his career, some of which would never be mentioned by the press or become widely known. Yet to Branigan, a few would be the most meaningful, especially those names bestowed on him by the downtrodden and abused women of the often-cruel inner city.

Chapter 9

"GUARDIAN" GARDA

"Oh, men used to give *shocking* treatment to women—
banging them. You'd get a few punches, getting kicked,
falling to the ground . . . and you *had* to stay with him!"

(MARY WALDRON, 82)

"Their husbands coming home drunk and beating the
daylights out of them—that was *always* the thing with
him, that they should *not ever* abuse women. He *hated*
that."

(DECLAN BRANIGAN)

"He was a tough cop when he *had* to be—and yet so
humane, so gentle behind it all, to people who needed it."

(UNA SHAW, 80)

"I cannot *stand* any man assaulting a woman. I would give
him the clatter."

(GARDA JIM BRANIGAN)

"Women—oh, he was a *god* to them!"

(GARDA JOHN COLLINS)

One thing enraged Jim Branigan, made him "see red," as his Garda
colleagues vouch.

Reared in the relatively sheltered environs of the South Dublin Union,
he was largely spared exposure to the appalling brutality of men towards
women that was endemic in the tenements, where savage husbands often beat
their wives and children mercilessly, especially when drunk. There existed a
culture then of male dominance, in which wife-battering was accepted.

Only when he began walking his daily beat in the Liberties did he begin to witness the abuse inflicted on women. As a young guard in his twenties he heard the advice of older, more experienced colleagues to stay out of "domestic disputes," which were regarded as "a personal matter." Such was the prevailing Garda policy at the time. Most guards would rather step into a pub brawl or street riot than become embroiled in an ugly domestic battle. Those could at least be settled, brought to an end, whereas a domestic row could be like a quagmire, beyond all hope.

As Senan Finucane found when he began his duty in the Liberties, the husband might come in drunk and give his wife a few clouts, but guards "wouldn't interfere in nine cases out of ten." They saw embattled tenement rooms as "no-go" areas.

Lugs Branigan became the notable exception. Feeling free to use his discretion, he assumed a "guardianship" role in the lives of oppressed and abused women, not merely as a police duty but as a humanitarian act of compassion and protection. His was an instinctive sympathy for the poor and downtrodden.

Over his long career, Branigan's role of active guardianship in the lives of countless women was one for which he was most appreciated yet was little known or acclaimed by the press or public. Which is the way he wanted it. Nor did the Garda authorities want his exploits in domestic conflict made public, because they often involved his dispensing his most severe forms of "summary justice" to brutal men.

As a consequence, there is no written record of this aspect of Jim Branigan's career, and we must rely on the oral testimony of witnesses who possess first-hand knowledge of his guardianship role. These include his sons, the guards who accompanied him and saw him in action, and citizens who personally observed his handling of abusive men. Their accounts of his dedication to battered women are remarkably consistent.

————

In those days the commonly used term "hard husband" was a euphemism for men who were often cruel and vicious. Abusive husbands were the bane of a poor woman's life. Drink usually fuelled the violent outbursts, which could be triggered also by an inherent domineering and bullying character, frustration over a job (or lack of one), the boredom and frustration of unemployment, debt, gambling, jealousy, or a wife's failure to satisfy sexually, or to be subservient enough. Perhaps his dinner was not on the table at exactly the right minute. Or babies were crying. Perhaps it was anger with himself. Frustration with the whole world.

Branigan's mate Séamus Quinn explains: "Family rows between husband and wife could flare up for a great number of reasons, even trivial reasons, and then get blown out of proportion." Tenement life was a life of endless stress and hardship, and often conflict.

In my book *Dublin Tenement Life: An Oral History* (1994) the pathetic plight of poor women is graphically recorded.[1] There were all degrees of physical abuse, from being slapped to being beaten bloody, with broken bones or left unconscious on the floor. "It was *shocking* treatment," says Mary Waldron, who saw too much of it during the 1930s and 40s. Nancy Cullen grew up in Cook Street, where she also saw such treatment. As her mother used to tell her about one neighbour, "he's no use—he's an *animal!*"

Maggie Murray had to experience it at first hand in her own tenement room in Queen's Terrace, off Pearse Street. Her father was a docker, a boxer, and a terrible bully. He drank and gambled away his wages, leaving his wife and seven children in dire poverty. Then he took his fury out on *them*:

> He'd come in *locked* drunk, and she'd be beaten. *Brutally* beaten! All her life, beaten. She had black eyes every day. Ah, we got a boot in the face when we were small. We were all terrified of him . . . We had a terrible life.

To May Hanaphy, now aged ninety, who lived in the most wretched tenements of Golden Lane, seeing injuries inflicted on women was a natural sight. "Ah, you'd see black eyes nearly every day of the week." The saddest sight was the Sunday-morning parade of battered women traipsing slowly to Mass, having survived another Saturday night of terror, slipping silently into their seats, hoping others wouldn't stare at their cuts, bruises, missing teeth, or patches of hair torn out.

John Dwyer, a publican in York Street, a tough tenement district, asserts: "The women were *slaves!* It was part of the culture at the time." Men felt they had a right to dominate them. Tony Gregory TD agreed that back in his mother's generation "the inner-city mother accepted her lot" in life.[2]

Trapped in marriage, they could not escape their plight. Bad marriages didn't justify "broken homes," despite broken bones: both religion and the prevailing culture forbade liberation. Seeking sympathy from priests was useless. "*So many* women beaten," recalls Máirín Johnston, "and if you went to the priest and said your husband had beaten you he'd tell you it was your *duty* to stay—it was his *right!*"

Mary Doolen of Francis Street knew scores of women burdened with ten, twelve or fifteen children (she herself was one of thirteen children) who couldn't properly feed or clothe them. When they would plead with the priest for help in stopping their husband's bullying, or forced sex leading to more babies, "the priest would say, 'You're married: you *have to suit* your husband. That's it!'"

Nor could desperate women turn to the law or the police for help. Around Máirín Johnston's part of the Liberties, "most women beaten by their husband felt there was no point in calling the police, because they wouldn't interfere in a domestic quarrel. Husbands attacking their wives was ignored." Mary Waldron remembered: "The police might be called—but the husbands were *never* charged with anything." In fact that might well prompt some men to retaliate by giving their wives even worse treatment.

Battered women were thus both helpless and hopeless. According to Máirín Johnston, the "attitude of the law and the Church to battering made it culturally acceptable—and so the victims had no support." Many such women straggled into Patrick O'Leary's pharmacy in Thomas Street, where, for nearly forty years, he would dispense a few "nerve tablets" along with consoling words. "It was appalling, with black eyes and bruised face . . . They just didn't know *who to talk to*." In those days there were no social workers, no counsellors or women's support groups, nor women's shelters to which they could flee in fear and desperation.

––––

Branigan would come to learn about all this suffering. He knew by the mid-1930s that other guards would walk beneath an open tenement window, hear a wife screaming or crying out in fear as her husband lashed out, and walk on. It was a "domestic" problem, not a legal one, though the next day they might see the physical injury resulting from their non-intervention.

Branigan could never tolerate this. It infuriated him. Declan remembers that his father could never abide what he considered inhumane behaviour: "He *hated* that." He would instantly intervene and halt it. However, as he would learn along his beat, the worst abuse was that committed behind closed doors. "He *knew* what they were going through," says John Collins, "being abused by their husbands," and was determined that they should not get away with it simply because it was taking place in their own homes.

After the demise of the "animal gangs" in the early 1940s he was able to devote more time to dealing with the problem of the abuse of women. Gradually it became a regular part of his routine to check on battered women and their husbands, especially on Saturday night, when such men went on their worst rampages. He could learn of a case on his own or be informed by others. When Gerald Byrne began serving alongside him he saw Branigan's reaction. "If he ever saw a man abusing a woman he was in there *right away*," even if this meant breaking through a door.

By the 1950s, when he was permanently based in Kevin Street station, Branigan had become the man to see in such cases. His partner, Senan Finucane, marvelled at the number of women who regularly sought his help: in the open street, in shops, outside churches, and at the Garda station. He also received tip-offs on behalf of women who were being mistreated in various ways, from family members, friends, a local shopkeeper or chemist. Sometimes on the street a girl or lad would timidly approach him to plead, "Me ma needs your help . . . Will you stop by?" Garda Val Lynn relates that "I often saw him on the street with five or six women around him, thanking him for what he had done for them. And maybe one might say, 'Will you call to me?'"

During the fifties his desk at Kevin Street became his "confessional," as his mates often joked. Troubled women made a pilgrimage there to confide, seek his help. For many it was a journey of last resort, as they were at their wits' end with a life of torture from a brutal husband. Sometimes there would be a queue of distressed women waiting at the station when he arrived. He began arriving early before going on duty to devote his own time to them.

He had a remarkable knack for knowing just how to deal with women in all sorts of distress. Everyone acknowledged this. Says Lisa Lee, a Liberties resident: "Women around here were beaten by their husbands, *battered,* and they went to see him—they wouldn't tell *anybody else.* He was the man they'd go to. And he would sort it out." He assumed a multiple role of counsellor, adviser, social worker, psychologist—and *friend.*

Priests, predictably, were judgemental, critical, even damning of women seeking help. By contrast, Branigan was a husband and father, sensitive to problems of married life. He *understood* them. They *trusted* him. Séamus Quinn came to know his confessional manner well:

> There could be a queue knocking down his office door in Kevin Street, to see Jim. And he'd *listen.* And be taking notes. Oh, he got their history first, take down their problem. And *then* he would reply. He devoted the *time* to these women.

To John Murphy, he just had a natural gift for relating to the women. "He was good at getting their information. He'd listen to them, and he'd get an earful . . . and they trusted him. And then he'd try to make peace if it could be done." He never wanted to resort to using force against a husband, unless it was absolutely necessary. This meant the women had to follow his suggestions. "People *took* his advice," confirms Gerald Byrne, "and it was *good* advice— 'cause he was the guy to see."

By the time Michael Reid had become a chief superintendent he had known a multitude of capable guards, but never one with Jim Branigan's ability to help mistreated women:

If *ever* there was a section of the community that had respect and admiration for him it was those women in rows and fights with their husbands. They would come to him seeking his advice, to *talk,* to try and find out what to *do.* Their perception of him was that he could help them, more so than their priest. His function was one that he himself created. Those women . . . he *loved* them.

Some of the women called him a "godsend." To others, he was their "guardian."

––––

He was especially adept at dealing with the proverbial "street angel and house devil," the clandestine bully and batterer who hid his real character, a wife-beater behind the door and a cordial chap out in public. Though such men might be clever in the concealment of their cruel, cowardly acts, neighbours could hardly miss their wives' black eyes and split lips. They often fooled their pub mates, postman, greengrocer, all the while a "bloody bastard" behind their cloak of gentility. Therese Murphy knew quite a few of them. "There *are* house devils, you know, and street angels. Molesting his wife and torturing the children . . . a life of misery. Women cry bitter tears . . . [over] the depth of suffering."

This deception never fooled Branigan. And he dealt with such men harshly. Their scarred wives might come to him for help, or family members or neighbours might report his true character to Branigan. "*Many* are the stories of Branigan finding out about men beating their wives," says Joe Kirwan, "and he'd *go after them.*" He had methods for dealing with every sort of abuser. The most fortunate got off with a warning. His warnings were often delivered as direct threats, so that there would be no misunderstanding. As there was no purpose in trying to talk sense to a drunken fool, Branigan preferred a strategy of catching such men cold sober out in the bright light of day. Matthew Fagan observed this a number of times. "He would stop him in the street and say to him, 'I *know* what you're doing. Don't do it any more! Or I'll be coming *after you!* I I'm giving you *fair warning*.'"

Una Shaw, who lived in Rutland Street, near the tenements of Summer Hill, tells of a battered woman she knew who asked for Branigan's help. Her husband got drunk and beat her up, "*every* Friday night regularly." Finally she asked him, "Is there *anything* that can be done about it, Mr Branigan?"

"Just leave it to me," he told her.

Rather than going to her tenement room to confront the husband, he waited for his street opportunity. "Now, this man was a *tough nut.* But Branigan accosted him on his way home—and *whatever* happened, he didn't ever do it again. It stopped."

Senan Finucane, who served beside him for twenty years, saw him in action and realised his impact as well as anyone. It became quite common, he says, that all an abused wife had to do was to issue a warning herself to her husband: "I'll *get Branigan* for you! And he'll *chastise* you!" Countless times Finucane saw those few words work miracles. And, he adds, "of course he was available day and night." To such men, the mere spectre of Lugs Branigan being called to their door to deal with them was sufficient motivation to change their ways.

When Branigan actually had to confront a batterer in his home, quite a different scenario was played out. Ostensibly his intention was to have "a bit of a chat," as he might ominously phrase it. On Branigan's first visit, body language was an important part of his delivery. He liked to place the man in a chair, then draw up a chair for himself, placing it directly facing him, their knees almost touching—and one set of knees probably knocking. He would lean closer, eye to eye, just to get the man's full attention.

Gerald Byrne often accompanied Branigan on such missions and always enjoyed his performance. With his steely gaze and perfect diction, Branigan would speak slowly and with unnerving deliberation:

> He'd *lay it on the line! Straighten him out.* "If you *continue* this way, I'll be *back!*" He'd certainly threaten them. "This is it, sunshine. If you don't toe the line, I'll be *back!*" Oh, they'd listen . . . That straightened out a *lot* of men.

According to Tony Ruane, most men receiving such a warning swore to abide by it. "Branno would say to the husband, 'If I hear *one more word* about you . . .' And it was 'Yes, Mr Branigan. It won't happen again, Mr Branigan.'" He always knew that the critical part of his deterrent role was to follow up on his warnings to make sure the man was behaving.

Mary Barnwell, a market dealer, saw that Lugs's methods of "putting manners into them" almost always worked. Nonetheless there were those who failed to heed his warnings and his direct threats to "be back." Drink can cloud a man's memory and impair his judgement, and this might necessitate a return visit by Branigan. He could never allow any doubt that he was a man of his word. On second visits he didn't rely upon warning lectures. He had no hesitation in using his gloves, or his fists, when there was justification for doing so. When he resorted to force, word of the incident would spread around the area like wildfire. All part of his larger deterrent scheme.

Fifty years or so ago, cases of domestic violence were seldom mentioned in newspapers. When they did appear, such as one on 27 February 1962 in the *Evening Herald,* most readers found it shocking:

He used abusive language, caught the seven-year-old child by the hair and dragged her into the hallway where he punched her in the face . . . Took off his belt, beat the child and his mother-in-law with it, and, after striking his wife, tried to choke her.[3]

To Branigan, the most heinous acts were those of a man against a pregnant wife. As Máirín Johnston personally witnessed, "women were beat something terrible—*even* when they were pregnant. And many miscarried as a result of men's brutality." There were cases of women seven and eight months pregnant being kicked down the stairs of tenement houses by drunken husbands. Billy Byrne describes what he witnessed as a young lad in Dolphin's Barn, where a pregnant woman living in his house was beaten regularly by her husband. One time the violence spilled out into the street:

And he was chasing her, in such a temper, this guy. But *who* came to the scene but Jim Branigan! Oh, he took no *mercy—straight in!* 'Cause she was pregnant! And he was never abusive to her after that.

Lisa Lee knew of a similar incident, in which a pregnant woman was being "beaten up by her husband," until someone informed Branigan:

He came and took that man out of the house and brought him up to the top of the road—and *gave him a hiding!* And he *never* raised his hand to his wife after that again.

————

Branigan understood the mentality of "hard" husbands, that they felt it their right to beat their wives about, confident that they were beyond the reach of the law. After all, most guards did ignore what were termed "domestic disturbances." Branigan, however, dealt with reality. He knew that such men understood only a forceful fist used against themselves. And that most of them were, in fact, cowards.

When a case of battering called for the use of force against force, he didn't like pussyfooting around: he was decisive and swift. As Val Lynn simply puts it, "if a husband needed a bit of shaking up, he'd *shake* him up!" Guards who served beside him saw his methods as both necessary and justified, best judged by their extraordinary success rate. Far better than the courts. John Collins fully endorsed Branigan's strong-arm method of dealing with violent men. "He'd read the Riot Act—and *then* [when necessary] give them a few clips." Noel Hughes was thankful that Branigan single-handedly halted many violent men in their tracks:

[There were] some terrible bowsies of husbands in the tenements, and their wives would get a dig. If he was called he would just *go in*—and that was it! I've seen it myself. It was the right thing to do, to stop a vicious husband.

Jeanette Cashin, a resident of the Liberties, had a neighbour tell her how Branigan stopped her husband's beatings:

He walked in the door, pulled me outside, and locked the door after me. And he dealt with him *there* and *then*. Then he opened the door and dragged him outside. And told me if I *ever* had a mark on me again he would be *back*.

He then made a note in his book and promised her that he would check back with her periodically. It worked.

———

It may be argued that Branigan's harsh method of doling out "summary justice" to abusive husbands was more justified than in any other cases, the rationale being that the courts consistently failed to punish violent husbands or protect defenceless women. In the great majority of abuse cases the men got away with it. Even when they were brought to court they were usually out again a day or two later. Having learnt no lesson.

What too often happened, to Branigan's frustration, was that he would be called to an abused woman's rescue, when she would plead with him to arrest her husband and drag him away—in other words, follow the legal procedure. At the time of the arrest the beaten wife would be shouting that she never wanted to see the brute again. A day or two later, all had changed. "You'd take him into court and charge him," explains John Murphy, "then in court the wife *wouldn't* give evidence!" After reflecting on it overnight she might realise that if her husband got a sentence of weeks or months he would be out of work, and no money would be coming in. Furthermore, "she would often think, 'Then I'll *still* have to live with him'—so sometimes she'd even say *good* things about her husband," just to keep him out of prison. "You couldn't win!"

Even in cases of serious assault, adds Paddy Casey, women habitually had a change of heart when their husband, now sober, was hauled before the judge. Typically the wife would say, "He was drunk last night, your honour. He's all right today."

This revolving-door routine exasperated Branigan. Though he was sympathetic to their plight, he implored abused women not to have a change of heart when in court. Justice *must* be served. Yet time and again he was let down.

Tommy Lowry used to enjoy going into court to watch the proceedings when Branigan was on and often saw this scenario played out, much to the guard's chagrin:

> Women always threatened their husbands, "I'll get Branigan!" And she'd bring up Jim and cry on his shoulders. So he'd *give it* to your man, and then bring him in. But she'd go to court the next day, and she *changed* her story ... that now "he was sorry and wouldn't do it again." *Then* Jim would say to her, "*Listen,* the *next* time he knocks you about, don't send for me, please. Because I won't be coming." He was very fair in that way.

As it turned out, far too few of the wife-beaters served terms behind bars. For the most part, wife-beating remained a culturally accepted offence. Much to Branigan's frustration.

On Saturday nights superintendents could have despatched battalions of guards throughout the city to protect women who were regularly beaten by their husbands. As a sort of lone crusader against domestic violence, Branigan and his methods might have seemed inconsequential; but as a *deterrent*, his role was widely effective. He knew how news spread far and fast by word of mouth. When he bolted up the stairs of a tenement to thrash a savage husband, news of the incident was known throughout the area, and beyond, by the next day. Word of his forceful intervention spread like wildfire, affirms Val Lynn; "then the *whole* place would be hushing ... 'Oh, Branigan is around!'" It may as well have been broadcast by loudspeakers. Every "hard" husband got the word.

This, of course, was part of Branigan's strategy. Giving a violent husband a hiding was a proven deterrent. "I cannot stand any man assaulting a woman," he said. "I would give him the clatter."[4] In Branigan's vocabulary a "clatter" was his most severe form of punishment, reserved for the most grievous offences, far beyond his more common single-punch "clip." His purpose was twofold: teach the man a painful lesson so that he would halt his abuse, and send the same message to like-minded men.

One such man was a Mr Humphrey who lived in Matthew Fagan's flats, "a terrible man for drink, and he'd *murder* his wife in the house. A *very big* guy, a strong man." No-one dared cross him. But when he was in one of his violent rages against his wife, "*up* would come Branigan!" There was no-one else to protect the woman.

Incidents such as this, says Una Shaw, in which a bully got a good hiding from Lugs, were disseminated around the tenements to keep many violent men in line. "'Cause the story *then* went around—and *other* men became scared that *they* might be *next.* Oh, they were *afraid* of him, no question about that. Such a big, commanding man!" Men feared not only the physical clattering but all the following gossip about how they had been cut down to size.

———

Nothing so infuriated Branigan as the sight of a woman bloodied by a man's fists. His response was instantaneous, as if he had heard a battle cry. To such men he showed no mercy. Séamus Quinn gives an illustration of his ire being ignited by the sight of a woman bleeding:

> If there was a physical row with wife-beaters and there was blood drawn— *blood drawn*—oh, Jim *saw red!*
>
> We got a call one night, and this guy was quite drunk, and he had drawn *blood* from the wife. And he wouldn't answer the door. So Jim put his foot to it, and in went the door. And he immediately grabbed the husband and with his *fists hit* him. He fell on the kitchen floor.
>
> Jim was not normally one to use his fists on the spur of the moment, but ... Then I picked him up and put him onto the settee. And immediately he started crying and apologising. Yeah!

To Branigan, one of the most compelling justifications for using force to halt a man's violence was that battered women could become despairing and hopeless, desperate to end their suffering somehow, even if it meant eventually taking their own life. From all his dealings with women, this he knew for a fact. And it wasn't a rarity.

Half a century ago, suicide was still a taboo subject in society and the press. It carried such a stigma for both the victim and their family that it was simply not spoken of in public. Una Shaw speaks candidly of those days:

> Some women, God love them, they just couldn't cope any more, trying to feed their families—and *then* to have to put up with the *brutality!* Sure what other way out did they see? All they wanted was peace ... and that's what they did.

In her ninety years of life in the old Liberties, May Hanaphy saw too many cases of women beaten into despondency, and desperation. "Oh, *many* took their own life, out of despair ... Many were lost." They simply no longer had the willpower or strength to endure their life of misery.

Drowning oneself in the Liffey was a common method. Because of the tragic nature of the death, newspapers typically treated it as an accident. "With suicides, the newspapers back then would say, 'She *fell* into the river'—not '*jumped* in'," says May Hanaphy. "Or just 'a death.' Oh, a dreadful stigma was attached to suicide." A good many found gassing the easiest way out of a life of being endlessly battered. Many times Branigan confided that encountering suicides, especially of women whom he knew, was the most traumatic experience in his work.

Suicide was treated as a secret yet was well known to those who were aware of the woman's suffering at the hands of her husband. By intervening with force and rescuing a woman from further beatings, Branigan doubtless saved some once-hopeless lives over his long career.

——

A domestic violence problem that increased markedly in the 1950s and 60s was that of sons, usually drunk, assaulting their own mothers, often in a frenzied effort to get money for drink or gambling. It was part of the changing culture in which many children, including adult children, no longer showed any respect for their parents.

A few cases made the newspapers, including one in the *Evening Herald* on 1 January 1965. On the evening before, New Year's Eve, Mrs Mulvey of Ash Street opened her door at a quarter past seven to see her son standing before her in a drunken, agitated state. Knowing what harsh treatment awaited her, she told him he was not welcome in that condition and should go home to his own place:

> He kicked the door and broke the glass . . . and struck her in the face. Both fell and when she was getting up she narrowly missed a kick from him.[5]

It was not the first time she had received such treatment from him. After a neighbour reported the incident, one of Branigan's colleagues from Kevin Street, Garda William Dwyer, arrived and saw the marks on her eye and face. In court Judge Molony told Mulvey, "A man who strikes his mother must not expect any leniency in this court," and sentenced him to six months' imprisonment.[6]

Val Lynn recalls a particularly atrocious case in which *three* sons ganged up on their mother and beat her badly. He was on duty that night with Branigan when they were called to the scene. Climbing the stairs together, he could detect Branigan's readiness for battle:

> Now, he was afraid of *nobody*. So we were going into Marrowbone Lane, where there were *three* fellas that had been beating their mother. Three *brothers!* And he knew these fellas, because he had refereed them in boxing in the Stadium. They were in their twenties. And he said to me—and I'd *never* heard him say this before—"Val, make sure you have your timber [baton]: they're as *mean* as they can be! Make *sure* you have your timber."
>
> So we went in . . . And he went in first. And they were after beating their mother. And one of them, when he saw him, said, "Oh, Mr Branigan, *please*

don't hit me!" and he put his hands in front of his face. And he was a man of about sixteen stone, with very strong arms. But Jim *hit* him with a swing across the solar plexus and laid him out. *Down* he went!

And the other two fellas were saying, "Oh, Mr Branigan, *please* don't, *please* don't . . ." Well, he had the three of them *laid in a lump* in seconds. Without ever throwing his straight punch at any of them.

They were the cowardliest three I ever saw, *begging* for mercy—and *boxers!* . . .

As the three of them were shaking with fear, in case Branigan was not finished with them yet, Lynn heard their mother say, "You're great bullies—but you're not great bullies when Mr Branigan is around."

Many more times Lynn would see Branigan in his role of guardian garda. "He was loved by all of them, traders on the streets and old ladies in shawls. He was a kind, gentle man . . . *Great* respect for him." It was a role that never made the headlines or gained him promotion, or even formal accolades within the force. Which was fine with him. But at his funeral, mothers and grannies would pack the church, spill outside, and flood the streets with their tears.

Chapter 10

THE EARLY SIXTIES: BOWSIES, HOOLIGANS, AND BEATLES

"The tempo of crime here has accelerated . . . The Government should seriously consider arming the police force . . . for handling nests of impossible 'Bowsies'."

(LETTER TO *Evening Herald*, 13 FEBRUARY 1962)

"It wouldn't happen in the jungle, and I'm going to stop it happening in Dublin . . . I'm putting an end to hooliganism, where packs of youths take the law into their own hands."

(JUDGE O'HAGAN, 1964)

"A belt on the mouth was often the best medicine for a tough kid."

(GARDA JIM BRANIGAN)

"Beatlemania gripped Dublin last night . . . Gardaí battled against a crowd 3,000 strong in a night they will long remember."

(*Evening Herald*, 8 NOVEMBER 1963)

Jim Branigan was fifty years old at the dawn of the 1960s, a decade of schism in Dublin: a period of prosperity and poverty, progress and stagnation, hope and despair. The juxtaposition of decrepit tenements and prison-like flats with gleaming office buildings and attractive, comfortable new houses was startling. Dublin was conspicuously a city of haves and have-nots.

In his book *The Best of Decades: Ireland in the 1960s*, Fergal Tobin writes that the 1960s were a time of "success, a sense of buoyancy and achievement, the possibility of some sort of decent life in Ireland."[1] Living standards rose by half during the decade in an "unprecedented surge of affluence . . . Prosperity was the key to everything."

Not for all, however.

Dublin had long been a city of economic and social division. In the 1960s, when the middle classes expanded and prospered, the poor were more alienated than ever. As Ronan Sheehan and Brendan Walsh explain in their book *The Heart of the City* (1988):

> If material well-being or affluence became the norm for most people, for large numbers development meant poverty and marginalisation. The city-centre communities went in the opposite direction to the national trend as their economic base deteriorated.[2]

Antiquated factories and shops closed, and old trades and crafts were made obsolete. Work at the docks dried up when containers and air freight took over. People in the heart of the city were left unemployed, uneducated, and unfit for the new Dublin emerging, left out of the "good life" they saw blooming around them. The new affluent classes bought houses in the suburbs and new cars, frequented expensive pubs and restaurants, took holidays abroad, sent their children to university.

But if you lived in Benburb Street, Sheriff Street, Engine Alley, the Coombe, Francis Street, Seán MacDermott Street, or North King Street, your life was stagnant.

To exacerbate the problem, old districts were demolished to make space for new, gentrified developments. Residents who proudly traced their roots back generations in their street were insensitively uprooted and transplanted to sterile blocks of flats, soulless and dehumanising. Young people trapped in the process were unemployed, idle, bored, and without hope; some turned to vandalism and crime. It was little wonder that they fought back, lashed out. Branigan witnessed the dynamics of Dublin's dramatic transformation in the early sixties, and saw that it meant trouble ahead.

The "animal gangs" were now history. The Teddy Boys, though past their heyday, could still be a troublesome street presence at times. On the rise were new types of gangs of youths and young men, bonded together not by their music or rock-and-roll culture but by their shared affiliation with their block of flats and feelings of alienation and frustration. The worst areas were breeding-grounds for violent youths who roamed at night in packs. In contrast to the colourful attire of the Teddys, they mostly wore jeans, T-shirts, leather jackets, and heavy boots: they found that the Brando and Dean image suited their own "rebel" behaviour.

Some groups, such as those at St Teresa's Gardens, off Donore Avenue, became notorious for their nightly crime sprees and clashes with gardaí, in which Branigan was regularly involved. News of their "reign of terror" often appeared in the newspapers, and in the courts. There were also assorted bands of hooligans and seasoned bowsies who would drink, become disorderly on the streets, and cause havoc in the city's ballrooms, cinemas, arcades, and chippers, even attacking bus crews and passengers.

Dublin gardaí had their hands full; and fifty-year-old Lugs Branigan had better reason than ever for maintaining his rigorous physical regimen. At least three times a week he exercised strenuously at the National Stadium, doing calisthenics, skipping, weight-lifting, punching the light and heavy bags, and engaging in spirited sparring sessions with young Garda boxers. He claimed to be as fit and strong as those lads thirty years his junior. He was bigger than ever—a solid seventeen stone—and his punch carried a more powerful wallop. However, he knew realistically that his reflexes and stamina were not what they had been in his days in the Garda Boxing Club. But he was ready to take on any new cast of "villains" who might challenge him.

———

Funnily enough, however, there was one man he plainly didn't know how to handle. He wasn't exactly a bowsie or a hooligan—but he was certainly a "street nuisance." He first appeared in Branigan's life in the summer of 1959 as a sort of amusing annoyance, whose bizarre shenanigans were a source of considerable entertainment to all the gardaí in Kevin Street station—at least at first.

Larry Quinn was a labourer and part-time docker from Crumlin who was a regular at Johnny Quinn's pub (no relation), just across the road from Kevin Street Garda Station. During most of the week he was a pleasant and peaceable man; but on Saturday nights, when he drank considerably more, there occurred an astonishing transformation. Bursting with bravado and delusions of greatness, he would embark upon his weekly crusade to challenge and "take down" the famous Lugs Branigan. While other men in Dublin strove to stay clear of Branigan's fists, Larry would stamp straight across the street, seeking to do battle with him.

To his pub mates and the gardaí at the station, Larry was an enigma. To the best of their knowledge, he had never had a run-in with Lugs, so his motivation couldn't have been revenge. In fact he seemed to harbour no animosity towards him; but on Saturdays he set out to destroy him—*every* week. His pub mates tried to calm him down, reason with him, keep him seated in the pub; and always it was a futile effort, as he barged out the door. Branigan's colleague Gerald Byrne watched the performance weekly:

Larry used to get tanked up, *every* Saturday night. And after Larry's blood was up, it was "I'm going to *call out* Branigan!" And people would say, "Larry, sit down, *don't* do this now." "No, I'm going to sort this out." And he'd go to the [station] gate and *shout, "Branigan, I want you! Come out, and I'll have you, Branigan!"*

During the early weeks Branigan would either ignore him altogether or, Byrne says, patiently go outside and say, "All right, Larry," and tell him to cease his little charade. When Lugs would refuse to put up his fists Larry would usually say, "What, Mr Branigan?" Then he'd salute him and walk off.

That small bit of attention seemed to pacify him. Some pub men and gardaí were convulsed with laughter over it all, a real Saturday-night show. For a while.

———

By contrast, in the early 1960s some of Dublin's ballrooms became real battle grounds, not only between rival gangs but between bouncers and troublesome patrons trying to enter. Branigan was constantly called to settle such skirmishes. Ordinarily, other guards assumed that the management was in the right and patrons in the wrong. Not so Branigan. His experience had taught him that doormen and bouncers could be over-exuberant, even bullying, and often the guilty ones. Unlike many of his of his colleagues, he always took the time to seek all the facts in an incident, on both sides.

Just such an episode occurred on 14 May 1960 at the Olympia Ballroom in Parnell Square on a Saturday night. The case was described by the *Evening Herald* in its heading as a "Savage brutal assault at ballroom." But this was misleading. The real story was that a young man and his friend had been turned away for some minor reason by an over-zealous doorman. This led to what was called a "bit of a tussle" between the two, during which the sleeve of the young man's jacket was torn off. He then peacefully departed. A little later he returned to the ballroom, simply to retrieve his sleeve. On seeing him again the doorman "dragged him into the room and struck him twice in the face, knocking him to the ground, then kicked him in the neck and arms."[3] He would end up in hospital for five days with the injuries.

When Branigan arrived he found the young man with cuts over both eyes and "a lot of blood on his face." The doorman rushed to claim that he was justified. When Branigan did his detective work, talking to witnesses, he found quite the opposite.

In Dublin District Court, before Judge O'Hagan, Branigan testified that "this was a savage, brutal assault by a man who possesses some slight authority but who does not know how to use it."[4] He had seen such bullying ballroom staff before. O'Hagan gratefully accepted Branigan's testimony and fined the doorman for unjustifiable violence. He added that if he were not married with three children he would have sentenced him to prison.

It was because of countless such cases that Branigan's reputation for fairness was earned—and why he was respected by Dublin's lawbreakers as well. They always knew that they could expect fair treatment from him, on the street and in court.

Tony Darcy can vouch for this as well as anyone. By his own admission, as a wayward youth he ran foul of the law, which led to some time in prison. Over his lifetime he saw the full spectrum of law enforcement methods, both fair and unfair. Nearing seventy now, he reflects on one particular experience involving Garda Branigan:

> I broke into a shop with another fella and robbed a lot of sunglasses . . . I was so drunk. The guards caught us and gave me an *awful* beating with their batons, on me ankles.

They also broke his watch. He and his mate were young and defenceless. Unable to walk, he was dragged to Kevin Street, where Branigan happened to recognise him as a lad whom he had refereed in the boxing ring. "When he seen me in the cell he asks, '*What* happened to you?'" After getting the details of the minor robbery, and seeing the marks of the beating, Branigan marched over to the guards and took them aside. Their baton-wielding spoke for itself. He then ordered them, Darcy recounts, to "give me station bail—and drop me home . . . Oh, he *didn't like* police brutality—honest to God!"

That was not the end of it. The next morning, a Sunday, he heard a knock on his door:

> He *made that guard* come up to our house on a police bike—and I couldn't get out of bed to stand—and *apologise!* And, he had to *pay me* for the watch he broke. And in the court on Monday he got the case cleared for me. Oh, I *had respect* for that man—he was a gentleman. *Fair!*

Joe Kirwan, now in his eighties, relates a similar incident. One night he and a few pals had been playing snooker and were walking home about midnight. When they were crossing a road to a fish-and-chip shop an unmarked Garda car pulled up. When ordered harshly to "stand over there!" he politely asked what they were being charged with. He was told "jaywalking." At midnight on an empty minor road! When he asked incredulously what "jaywalking" meant at that hour of the night, one guard swung towards him "and with that hit me in the mouth." They were hauled into the station, where a surly sergeant summarily ordered, "Get two cells ready. We'll put these gurriers in them."

"And we did *nothing*. So I was trembling, because my father was very strict.

The next thing, this door bursts open and in walked Jim Branigan." Like so many youths, Branigan also knew Kirwan from refereeing boxing. "When the other guards saw him it was, 'Oh, hello, Mr Branigan. How's things going?' They were very respectful to him." Spotting Kirwan, whom he knew as a polite young man, he asked him what had happened. After hearing the explanation he approached the station sergeant and said, "I want that man brought home." But he explained to Kirwan that he couldn't do the same for his friends: as he didn't personally know them and couldn't vouch for their character they would have to await clearance later. "*That* was Mr Branigan. Oh, he had tremendous integrity."

Rare was the garda who would openly stand up for the rights of a mistreated prisoner against his own colleagues; yet many are the stories of Jim Branigan doing just that.

———

It was about this time that Dublin gardaí faced a new, gruesome crime spree by bored, vicious youths in the inner city: extreme cruelty to animals.

No garda was more furious than Branigan. When the first incidents made the newspapers they were nearly too shocking for people to read. Some said they couldn't read beyond the headlines, such as that in the *Evening Herald*: "Youth gangs set fire to live terrier." Those who did read further were horrified:

> Gangs of youths in Seán MacDermott Street set a terrier on fire after pouring oil on it. They have strung up cats on lamp posts and riddled them with air gun pellets as they hung in the air screaming.[5]

Garda stations were besieged with pleas to stop the hideous acts. Branigan also understood that for many poorer and older inner-city people the company of their dog or cat was akin to that of a friend, crucial to their welfare. To have them tortured to death was beyond comprehension.

The papers reported that "pet owners have been terrorised by the gangs . . . and are now locking up their dogs and cats day and night." Gardaí in the areas were put on alert, and the Dublin Society for the Prevention of Cruelty to Animals offered a reward of £20 for information leading to the arrest of the culprits. The secretary of the society, Mrs M. Ardagh, cited one case in which a woman who loved her little dog "is demented at the loss . . . In her flat the woman wept beside the flame-charred body of her pet" as she waited for the vet to arrive and put it out of pain.[6]

Branigan regarded this as more than a street nuisance. He would make his presence increasingly known in areas where such cruelty took place.

———

With the arrival of spring weather in 1960, Larry Quinn was energised and became bolder in his taunting. Some Saturday nights, recalls Gerald Byrne, he would go beyond the gate and come inside, where "he danced around the station swinging his fists." Alick knew his father was by now getting fed up with the old act. "The fella was jarred . . . and *pounding* on the station door. 'I *want a go* with Branigan—*send* him out here!" Branigan's patience was wearing thin. The *Evening Herald* treated Larry's antics as a sort of comedy-drama series for readers. But to Byrne and his colleagues at Kevin Street, Larry was fast wearing out his welcome:

> *Religiously,* every Saturday night—"Branigan, *come* out!" *Ad nauseam.* See, we got used to it after a while, and someone would say, "Oh, it's only Larry." But then it was "Larry, *shut up* and go home!" 'Cause the guy was waking up the whole neighbourhood.

Saturday was the busiest night of the week for gardaí, and Larry was now interfering with their work, and straining relations with nearby residents. Furthermore, Branigan was almost always out of the station on duty on a Saturday night. For those in the station, Larry had evolved from amusing character to annoying pest.

Finally, when he became too aggressive, the irritated guards at the station arrested him and brought him before the court on charges of drunkenness and disturbing the peace. He was let off with a scolding and a warning to cease his behaviour. Judge McCourt told him that "if he did not cut out the drink he would find himself in jail the next time." Larry looked up at the judge and, in the sober sincerity of morning light, swore to him that he "intended to take the pledge."

Unfortunately, by midsummer Larry had grown even more bellicose, and to the gardaí his disruptions were more annoying than ever. One Saturday night he put a new twist in his routine by showing up at Pearse Street station, where he shouted for the toughest guard to come out and put up his fists. Before long a large garda emerged, with no smile on his face, eyed Larry, hauled him inside, and slammed him in a cell.

That Monday morning Larry again found himself in court—for his eighteenth appearance. Judge O'Hagan, himself running out of patience, told him he had picked on a guard less indulgent than Branigan—a "garda big enough to eat him alive and then look around for a really solid meal," as the *Evening Herald* described him.[7]

Then, on 14 July, Larry ended up in front of Judge O'Hagan for yet another time. Much to his surprise, the judge found that "when Larry is sober he is a *moralist.*"[8] He had begun arguing for better working conditions for the new women gardaí who had begun joining the force from 1959. Where this "cause" came from, no-one in the court could imagine, as Larry began lecturing like a reformer. He was under the impression that male and female guards were housed together in living quarters, which he felt was indecent. Judge O'Hagan was able to inform him that women guards lived outside the station.

Then the judge returned to the case at hand, telling Larry that if he did not cease his obsession with fighting and trying to "take down" Garda Branigan he was definitely going to "land up in Mountjoy for a long spell." Despite O'Hagan's admonition, a reporter in the court wrote that Larry still could "not see the light of reason." This time he was fined £2 and sentenced to seven days' imprisonment. O'Hagan's ominous parting words to him were: "You'll get yourself killed one of these times, because someone will lose his temper with you."[9]

––––

At home in Drimnagh Road, Branigan could listen to the cheerful chirruping of his budgies rather than Larry's tiresome rants. The peace and quiet of home life meant more to him now than ever before. Home offered a near-rural setting, with fresh air, gardens, pets, congenial neighbours, and the smell of baking and cooking in Elsie's kitchen. By comparison with the troublesome youths with whom he had to deal, his three teenagers were models of good behaviour and respect for parents. Alick was now eighteen, Helen sixteen, and Declan fourteen, all well mannered and well liked by others. Branigan was immensely proud of his children and wanted each to be happy and fulfilled, to find their own way in life—as he had done.

Alick, however, suspected that his father had expectations for him to follow in his footsteps, to a career in the Garda Síochána, though this was never explicitly said. It was quite common for a son to follow his father in this way—indeed both Senan Finucane's sons would become gardaí, and both would eventually rise to the rank of superintendent. Alick was certainly tall enough, nearing his father's stature; but any such hopes his father may have had were dashed in Alick's school years, when "I had trouble in class seeing the blackboard . . . and I had to get a pair of glasses." He detected a veiled disappointment:

My father, I think, had ideas that maybe I'd go into the Gardaí eventually. But you couldn't join the Guards at that time with glasses, with spectacles. So I know he was quite upset at the fact that I *had* to get the glasses. And the *only* reason I can think of was that he wanted me to join the force. Although he would have been a hard act to follow.

As it turned out, it was all for the best, as becoming a policeman did not at all fit Alick's character, by his own admission.

Nor had Alick any ambitions to follow his father into the boxing ring. Nonetheless, his father did manage to get him into the ring a few times, ostensibly as a lesson in self-defence, which he regarded as a good thing for any youth. By the age of eighteen, Alick's general physique was resembling that of his father's; but upon closer scrutiny his frame was seen to be scrawny, compared with the bulk of his father. He particularly remembers one time his famous father actually got him into the ring to spar with him:

> My father *tried* boxing with me, and we'd sort of spar. I was a rake, about eleven-and-a-half stone but nearly six foot three . . . too light for my size. But, like Muhammad Ali, I could move around well in the ring—"float like a butterfly."
>
> Now, the first time I went in with him it was "C'mon, *hit me!* C'mon . . ." And I was dancing around, trying to avoid his jabbing. So eventually he said, "*C'mon*—will you *hit me!*'" So, I whacked him! And I got him right on the cheek.
>
> Well, the *next* thing, I was *on the canvas!* Oh, yeah; because he came back with a good swing—just to *show* me . . . that he'll get you back, you know.

Exactly what his father's lesson for him was that day he was never certain. But it didn't encourage him to take up boxing. Anyway, he says, "my mother wouldn't have been keen on me going into boxing"—adding with a smile, "'cause she could picture her 'beautiful son' getting his face all mashed up."

Then there was the day his father tried to introduce Alick to yet another sport, this one even more ill-suited to his physique. Perhaps recalling how Alick as a young lad had heaved a barrel full of manure over the garden fence, his father "tried to get me to take up the hammer." Not as a carpenter. He had a friend who was an Irish hammer-throw athlete and champion. How he ever envisaged his skinny son as a hammer-thrower one cannot know. The idea fizzled out fast.

Declan, a natural athlete, had problems of a different sort with the sport of his choice: hurling. He not only loved the game but was excellent at it from an early age. He found, however, that being the son of the famous Lugs Branigan had its drawbacks:

> See, people knew how famous he was—and picked on me because of who I was when I was growing up. Some hurling teams would pick on me. I was singled out, but I just had to accept it. I mean, my father *was* who he *was*, and I couldn't get away from that.

As his father watched his matches he made no complaints over "rough play" for his son, apparently feeling that it toughened him up for life.

———

By all indications, Elsie and Jim Branigan were happy together, and he a devoted father. His hobbies remained gardening, rearing budgies, caring for Cochise and Geronimo and their goat and hens. They were "comfortable," but by no means "well off."

Financial security seemed to be his only worry in life. A guard's pay was not keeping up with the cost of living, and quite a few of his colleagues felt compelled to leave the force to seek better-paying jobs. This he could never do, for it was his vocation, his true calling in life. But even as he and Elsie "scrimped and saved," it seemed that they never had as much in life as they needed.

Never was this more evident—and painful for him—than when Alick informed him of his ambition to attend veterinary college. He had always encouraged his children to follow their own dreams, find their desired path in life—just as he had done. Now he had to tell his eldest child that his ambition was out of reach. "I *wanted* to become a vet," says Alick, "but he couldn't afford the fees to get in. He would have had to go into debt to afford it." In those days "going into debt" was a daunting prospect, one he wanted to avoid. Having to say "sorry" to his son may have been even more crushing.

Branigan spent precious little on himself. Supplies for his budgies and his garden were a modest necessity, and occasionally the acquisition of a new bird or two. His biggest indulgence was a trip to England every now and then to attend a Manchester United match, as he was a faithful follower. Sometimes he could combine this with meeting other bird-fanciers in England. By the early sixties he had become a serious, and quite expert, breeder of budgies, in which he took great pride. Alick likes to tell the story of his father once bending the law a little in his favour, when he was returning from a Manchester United match and bringing home a couple of birds as well:

> They were in his pocket, just sort of stuck in there, 'cause he wasn't *declaring* them to the customs! See, he'd just go over and bring them back that way ... But there was this *one* time when they started *chirruping!*

He can't recall what the customs officer did when the budgies "squealed" on Garda Branigan for carrying contraband into the country. Luckily, it was one story missed by the papers.

———

Towards the end of 1960 there were the usual calls about disorder and rows at ballrooms and cinemas. One Saturday night in November there was an affray at the Swiss Chalet in Merrion Row involving some unusually tough men. Garda Flanagan, who was first called, had great difficulty with four men who needed to be arrested. When Branigan was summoned he toned them down and shoved them into patrol cars. When one of the men "jumped out of the patrol car and ran away," he was quickly caught—and chastised.

A few weeks later, in December, the manager of the Tivoli Theatre, Patrick Monaghan, put in a desperate call for Garda Branigan when groups of youths began fighting and tearing his establishment apart. By the time he could arrive, the vandals had ruined nearly a hundred seats, scraping the veneer off the back and pulling out the padding. People were becoming more familiar with the term "juvenile delinquents," as they were called by sociologists and newspapers. Branigan had his own terms for them.

———

On 8 December, Larry Quinn launched a new assault against Branigan; and this time he crossed the line.

On this Saturday night, Branigan, in no mood for Larry's absurdity, marched out of the station to confront him and order him to cease. But, as the *Evening Herald* reported, the sight of Branigan "was like a rag to a bull to him . . . His language became vile and he put up his fists."[10] Still Branigan remained patient. Then, however, directly to his face, Larry began "to make threats against Branigan's family. Naturally, the Garda took a poor view of that . . . A threat to his family was a serious matter."[11] Without hesitation he acted, giving Larry a few sharp "taps," in his own terms, resulting in a black eye and bruises.

On Monday morning Larry was back in court, before Judge Reddin this time. For his twenty-third appearance. Straight away, Branigan explained to the judge why Larry finally "had to be given a few clips." Reddin understood. Then, for the first time in court, Larry "expressed real sorrow" for his behaviour, saying he "did not mean a word" of his threats. He further explained to Judge Reddin and Garda Branigan that his Saturday night escapades all stemmed from the deaths of his father and brother within a close span of time, which caused him to drink more. Reddin decided to give him one last chance to "turn over a new leaf." His sentence next time, he was warned, would *automatically* be imprisonment for many months. Branigan was in agreement with the judge's humanity. A court reporter for the *Evening Herald* summed up Larry's finale:

Larry, the truculent one, had lost all his fight. It took a black eye and badly bruised eyes to bring Larry finally to his senses. Larry was in real bad [trouble] and, for the first time since he opened his vendetta, he showed signs of real repentance. The few "clips" may have had their salutary effect.[12]

———

The year 1961 was notable for a historic rebellion in a Dublin ballroom, one involving more than a thousand participants and one in which Garda Jim Branigan was an important figure for the role he *refused* to play.

It began in the autumn of 1961 with an event that severed the cohesion of the Garda Síochána, pitting colleagues against one another. The dispute arose over a new pay agreement, which angered young gardaí, who felt they had been cheated of a fair wage increase, and put them at odds with senior gardaí. "Their anger was because of a ham-fisted pay deal that had left those with less than five years' service with a pay increase of exactly nothing."[13] Those who had negotiated the deal had "lost touch with the rank-and-file gardaí," who were paid £8 and £11 a week, depending on their service. "Not exactly a princely sum."[14]

For weeks during September and October discontented young gardaí met secretly in groups to discuss strategy for opposing the deal. Station sergeants expelled some of them from such meetings in stations. Eventually the Macushla Ballroom in Buckingham Street was selected as an ideal central meeting-place. The meeting was planned clandestinely, to take the authorities by surprise.

On Saturday 4 November, at 4 p.m., an estimated 1,000 to 1,400 "mostly young men . . . [showing] their anger," crammed into the ballroom. They had arrived, without notice, from all over the country, sharing their dissatisfaction along the way. By the time the meeting was to begin, emotions were running high and tension was palpable in what some newspapers would call the greatest revolt of its kind. Tony Ruane, a twenty-year-old garda at the time, remembers vividly the high drama of the event, how split the force was over the explosive issue, how some of the senior officers were "on the side of the lads . . . but some were not."

Commissioner Daniel Costigan and Garda Headquarters had learnt about what the press would dub the "Macushla revolt." The commissioner ruled the meeting illegal, and a number of superintendents were despatched to the ballroom to inform the guards that they were in violation of the regulations and hence "now liable for dismissal." Eleven of those present would be dismissed on the spot. The others held their ground.

Unable to crush the revolt with threats, the Garda authorities needed to gather facts and evidence about what was transpiring within the ballroom. Who was in attendance, who were the leaders, what was being said? They needed a few keen observers and note-takers, who could also elicit some inside information on the revolt. As Tony Ruane plainly puts it, "they were looking for *spies*." For such an investigative role there was no-one better than Garda Jim Branigan, no-one more trusted, no-one better at taking down meticulous notes. Some of his superiors were despatched to enlist his service.

They had approached the wrong man. He knew that "informer" is one of the most despicable terms in Irish history. He considered it so offensive even to be asked that he regarded it as an insult. A good many years later he confided to his friend Tony Ruane about his feelings at the time:

> I refused. These were decent lads, just looking for a half-decent wage and conditions. I refused point blank—and they knew I meant it. *"Sack me if you like!"* I said. But they didn't.

The dispute was eventually resolved, to the general satisfaction of most, after the intervention of Archbishop John Charles McQuaid and the Minister for Justice, Charles Haughey, who worked to have the dismissed men reinstated. Branigan emerged even more respected than before for his courage, fairness, and moral principles.

———

In the early 1960s Commissioner Costigan expressed concern over the "rise in the general incidence of crime" in the city. He noted that nearly half the indictable offences reported to the Gardaí throughout the country were in the Dublin Metropolitan Division. He was particularly dismayed that guards themselves had become targets for the city's thugs. Branigan constantly brought this problem to the attention of the Garda authorities and judges, telling them that lone guards, particularly young men, out on patrol at night had become "sitting ducks" for drunks and thugs.

One night a station mate of Branigan's, Garda John McGoldrick, was passing three Teddy Boys on the footpath when they sensed an advantage and attacked him—for no reason. Seriously injured, he was taken to hospital. Not long afterwards another of Branigan's friends was seriously assaulted and injured.

It seemed as if some ruffians were preying upon vulnerable policemen. As Branigan told one judge, "young guards are fair game for this type of youth at night." One alarmed citizen wrote to the *Evening Herald* suggesting that the "Government should seriously consider arming the police force . . . for handling nests of impossible 'bowsies.'"[15]

Shortly before midnight on Friday 2 June 1961 Garda J. F. Courtney faced a mob of nearly forty violent drunken youths. He called for help. When a sergeant arrived to assist him, stones and other objects began flying, and he quickly suffered a badly fractured nose that would require an operation. When another guard showed up he was beaten. Only when Branigan made his appearance did the men scatter in fright. In court he told Judge Lanigan-O'Keefe that such riots were well beyond the capability of a few guards to handle. He had arrested a few, but there were "still others to be arrested." He assured the judge he would track them down and have them in court.

After thirty years of experience as a garda, Branigan had devised what he considered to be his own nearly foolproof strategy for nabbing runaway hooligans and criminals. With his elaborate network of contacts throughout the tenements and flats he could extract the information he needed to track his suspect down. Then he awaited the best opportunity to "pounce," a moment when the culprit was least suspecting and most vulnerable. Which was in his own bed at about 5 or 6 a.m.

Branigan discovered the success of this method early in his career, when he was hunting down a young thief whom he called "Billy Boy." At first Billy was elusive, but after some detective work and questioning residents around Patrick Street, Branigan got the tips he needed to find out where the culprit lived. But he was a tricky fella to pin down. He decided that the element of complete surprise would work best:

> So I formed a system *on my own* for getting people off their guard. So we knew the location of our suspect, and at 6 a.m. we were at the door of his home—and Billy Boy was in bed.[16]

Rousing him rudely from his slumber, Branigan and another large guard caught him groggy and non-resistant. Within minutes, "we took Billy Boy to the station and interrogated him."

Because of the success of this early-morning surprise tactic, he used it regularly to catch suspects when they were least likely to try to escape or put up a fight. Amusingly, the toughest thugs could be as meek as lambs when caught in bed, dazed, and probably wondering if they were dreaming. The worst nightmare for a miscreant was to be awakened rudely, and often roughly, in their own bed by Lugs Branigan, towering over them. Seldom did they put up any resistance.

Over his career, it would be a strategy that never failed. And as his method became widely known throughout the city it became a powerful deterrent to trouble-makers. As Alick liked to say about his father's "bedtime manner," everyone knew "if he didn't get them *then* [out in the open], he'd get them *later*."

On 20 April 1963 he encountered a 22-year-old ruffian from Dolphin's Barn who was acting violently at a fish-and-chip shop, endangering other customers. Two guards tried to restrain him, but he struggled wildly. Branigan was summoned. Within seconds he had him as calm as a sleepy infant. As he explained in court to Judge Ó Riain, sometimes it was better to dispense with the leather gloves and make a more lasting impression. "He tried to kick me, and he was very violent and roaring and shouting . . . I had to give him a few taps to quiet him."[17] Well done, conceded the judge. Then Branigan continued, stressing that many violent resisters carry weapons: "Make no mistake about it, many of these lads would stick you with a knife or broken bottle as quick as they would look at you."[18]

Then Branigan let loose with one of his classic lines—in open court: "A belt on the mouth is often the best medicine for a tough kid." No objections were heard. When the *Evening Herald* published its article headed "Detective gave man a few taps"—one of the few times his use of physical force was documented in the press—it did not draw a single outcry or letter of protest against his brand of summary justice.

————

Reading about the increase in crime in the city, highlighted by specific cases of violence in which knives, razors and knuckledusters were used, made Dubliners fearful of intervening on the streets to assist a guard or a fellow-citizen in trouble. Stories of such non-involvement were often in the newspapers, such as that in March 1963 when 22-year-old Noreen Farrell drew £250 in wages from a bank in Grafton Street on behalf of her employer. A young man rushed up, grabbed it from her hand, and dashed down the street. One brave bank customer gave pursuit, actually caught the thief, and engaged in a scuffle. Even when it was apparent that the thief was giving his assailant a severe beating, crowds passed by without lifting a hand, despite pleas from Miss Farrell. Later a Garda spokesman stated: "It is a disgraceful commentary on the civic spirit of the people in Dublin" in this day and age.[19]

In court, Branigan regularly had to explain to the judge why he sometimes had to resort to a "clip, clout or tap" to subdue a violent man who was endangering other guards or citizens. He gave graphic descriptions of how angry men used their head, knees, elbows, or feet, as well as teeth to bite and fingers to poke eyes.

As a case in point, Branigan once brought before Judge Molony a man of small size who got the best of a large, tough boxer during their dispute in the Kosmo Bar in Bridge Street. Physically, the men were ludicrously mismatched; however, the smaller man suddenly used his head as a battering-ram to smash the other man, who was caught off guard, dropping him cold. Judge Molony told the assailant how dangerous, and disgraceful, his act was. "The three *lowest* forms of assault are striking a man with your head, attacking him with a broken bottle, and kicking him in the groin."[20] Branigan could surely have added a few more, but remained silent. The man was sentenced to two months' imprisonment.

It was during this period that judges increasingly came under criticism for being too lenient. The prevalent public attitude was that they needed to crack down harder on lawbreakers, especially the violent ones. Branigan agreed, but he understood that sometimes the judge's hands were tied by archaic laws that prevented them from handing out harsher sentences for certain offences.

In 1962–3, therefore, it was of great interest to press and public when several judges, fed up with hooliganism, made mention in their courts of a "new" type of punishment based on old laws. On 12 December 1962 Judge O'Hagan was outraged when several teenage ruffians vandalised and destroyed a shop and home owned by a Mr O'Leary and his wife. When they returned from a short trip to find their little world robbed and torn asunder they were devastated. When Garda Connolly arrived to inspect the premises he found it in appalling condition, "an utter wreck, shelves emptied, tables overturned, doors battered down."[21] Upstairs in their living quarters everything had been similarly ravaged by the intruders, who "threw furniture and clothes around . . . Nothing in the place went unharmed." O'Hagan could see how the experience had left the couple emotionally distraught. When the youths were hauled into court he declared: "The place was wrecked as if a hurricane had gone through it . . . These boys should be horsewhipped."[22] It was little wonder that so many judges openly approved of Branigan's gloves and "clips."

A year later, in December 1963, a heinous crime occurred in which a 26-year-old man assaulted an elderly woman. Judge Barra Ó Brian was so repelled by the brutality of the act that he ordered the court's legal staff to research whether "flogging is still lawful in this country."[23] They found that an act of 1861, still apparently valid, "makes the sentence of whipping lawful for various offences."[24] It had last been imposed in 1941, for armed robbery.

Several newspapers picked up the judge's proposal, knowing it would fascinate readers. The *Irish Press,* digging into the matter itself, noted that the law remained open to varying interpretations. A legal scholar, Martin Kennedy, gave his opinion that while whipping had never been formally abolished, he "was not certain of the position" of the law in the 1960s.[25] In a provocative front-page article headed "Flogging is still lawful in Ireland," the *Evening Herald* succeeded in bringing flogging into the limelight of public consciousness.[26]

The increase in crime in Dublin, the outcry for stricter laws and more severe punishment, even the demand for arming the Gardaí, along with the court's serious references to horse-whipping and flogging, could only have validated

Jim Branigan's method of doling out forceful punishment on the streets, in ballrooms and cinemas, and elsewhere.

———

Nonetheless, there were a few times when even Lugs Branigan, Ireland's undisputed toughest and most fearless garda, understood that discretion was the better part of valour. It was in the early sixties that Matthew Fagan of Meath Street witnessed one of these rare moments when he and a few friends were at a carnival in the Liberties run by Travellers, who annually visited with the show. There was often trouble between the Travellers and local people over various issues, among them gambling. Women would often report to Branigan and other guards that their husbands were losing the housekeeping money in illegal gambling operations. When complaints were made, a garda had to attend to the problem. Most gardaí dreaded this order, as Travellers could be a rough bunch, and the task usually fell to Branigan. Fagan describes the scene as he stood only feet away:

> There was a carnival used to come to this area, and there was this one *big* blondie guy with curly hair, and he ran the carnival. 'Big, bad Bob' they called him at the carnival. A *huge* guy!
>
> And Branigan came in and tried to close down the gambling, and the blackjack. And this fella came out of his caravan and he f*** didn't care *who* was there! And Branigan told him to stop the gambling, this "wheel of fortune" thing, 'cause gambling wasn't allowed. And he told Branigan, "You put that out and I'm going to put *you* out!" Yeah!
>
> So then, Branigan said he was going to go and get a court order to get it done. Now, with *anyone else* he would just have pulled it down. But, see, he *knew* that this guy was *well able* for him! And that guy didn't *care!* So Branigan, he just walked away, went off. He left it. Oh, he would have got the worst of it . . . He *would* have.

How Branigan might have handled it at the age of thirty, rather than his early fifties, one can only speculate. He may well not have known himself.

———

The year 1963 began with a spell of harsh weather, which turned into one of the worst winters of the century. Blizzards, heavy snow and arctic temperatures paralysed transport and communication, caused accidents and deaths, created great hardship for people. With the bitter cold and slicing winds, gardaí suffered while trying to make their rounds, When trouble arose it took them longer to reach the scene. On days of blizzards, Dublin seem deserted, with virtually no crime on the streets. Branigan and his Kevin Street colleagues huddled around their station fire.

On the evening of 11 March he was off duty and decided to see *The Manchurian Candidate* at the Star Cinema in Crumlin. *The Manchurian Candidate* was billed as a real "thriller," a mature film with complex dialogue. He was seated in the balcony, his leather gloves on his lap. About a third of the way through the film he was distracted by a "racket" down below. By the time he could make his way down it had erupted into what the manager, James Kelly, called "a state of chaos" in the cinema, with its 1,100 patrons. Many were "howling and carrying on something atrocious," said Kelly, and he heard shouts of "Hit him . . . hit him!"[27]

When Branigan ploughed his way through the crowd "there were about a hundred youths standing on the seats, roaring and screaming and surrounding a number of attendants. I went into the fracas . . . to stop the shoving and hitting of the attendants."[28] When the lights were turned on the riotous youths spotted the figure of Lugs, instantly calming down and moving off. But there were a defiant few who he would tell the court were "hitting, kicking and resisting violently," and he received a severe "kick on the shin." As he explained to the judge, a few glove lashes and clips were necessary to "tone them down" before he was able to arrest them.

As revealed in court, the cause of the row was plain boredom and restlessness, the youths admitted. They felt cheated at having to pay for what they regarded as a dreadful film. Surprisingly, but in keeping with his belief in fairness, Branigan told the judge, as a mitigating point, that he too thought the film was "boring in parts." Though he hardly condoned their behaviour.

Considerably more exciting for Branigan was the visit of the American singing sensation Engelbert Humperdinck. He needed a good minder to keep the crowds at bay; once again the Garda authorities asked Branigan to assume this role, which he gladly accepted. Crowds gathered early to squeeze into the Arcadia Ballroom, where he was appearing.

"When I was minding the glamour-boy singer Engelbert Humperdinck," he recalled, "girls were swooning over him, and one girl was in a semi-coma after she was knocked to the ground in a crush to see him." When he offered to have her removed to hospital, she declined; instead she asked him if she could just *see* him, adding, "I'd be all right then." Branigan took her inside, introduced her to the "good-looking pop idol," who was very nice to her, giving her not only an autograph but a "peck on the cheek." After which he watched her miraculous recovery.

———

On 11 June 1963 Dublin was struck by a violent act of nature that threw people into panic and forced the Gardaí into crisis mode. The *Evening Herald* called it "a freak thunderstorm . . . one of the most devastating electric storms of the century."[29] Striking suddenly, it "swamped out hundreds of homes, caused chaos to traffic, ripped up whole sections of roads and tumbled walls like matchwood." Families were trapped in their houses, marooned upstairs, with food brought in by small boats and lifted up in baskets through windows.

Pedestrians caught out in the typhoon-like storm were at nature's mercy. The *Irish Times* wrote that Kevin Baker was scampering along Pearse Street, seeking shelter from the storm's wrath, when a blast of lightning hit the footpath and he "was thrown high into the air."[30] One of the greatest emergencies for the Gardaí was trying to restore order in the streets, as "traffic jams were the greatest ever experienced in the capital."[31] When it was all over, the gardaí, fire brigade and ambulance services were commended for their "devotion to duty."

Only two days later several tenement houses, weakened by the drenching rain and wind, crumbled, with occupants inside. One was the "collapse of two houses in Fenian Street where two children were killed," reported the *Irish Press*, "and an elderly couple also died in a house collapse in Bolton Street."[32]

Tenement-dwellers around the city were nervous, asking gardaí and firemen if their buildings were safe. In the Liberties, which had some of the most decrepit tenements in the city, worried inhabitants would come to Kevin Street station for advice. It was difficult for Branigan and his colleagues to know what to tell them. He hoped more building inspectors would show up as soon as possible.

———

At this stage in his life Branigan was heavily involved in refereeing boxing matches. Continuing involvement in the world of boxing gave him great satisfaction, as well as the opportunity to remain in regular contact with young lads, many of whom needed a bit of guidance in their life. He was known not only as one of the best referees but perhaps the fairest of them all. He offered his services all around Ireland when he had time to do so. It was sometimes said that Dublin referees tended to favour Dublin boxers; but not Branigan, affirms Seán Horkan, who first met the famous guard when he refereed one of his fights as a young lad and who would go on to become a boxing judge himself:

> I first became aware of Jim Branigan as a great referee on my first visit to the National Stadium as a competitor at the national junior championships in 1954, and in later years with the other young boxers from the west of Ireland. We *always* felt we got an honest call from Jim . . . A *fair* referee, in

contrast to some other Dublin city referees, who appeared to favour their own competitors.

Over the years, as he grew into adulthood and got to know Branigan well, Horkan was even more impressed by his humanity outside the ring. "I was in awe of this larger-than-life garda, who could command a great presence when he walked into a room." In his capacity as referee he often felt by intuition that a lad was troubled in his life and could use some counselling. Completely on his own, he would seek out the lad and have a chat with him, give him advice and encouragement. Seán Horkan recalls:

> When a young boy would get into trouble Jim would take him aside and advise him, and often get him a job. And then invariably get him to join the local boxing club, to keep him out of trouble. And *then* Jim would keep in touch with him, until he knew the boy was on the right track. Many men today owe Jim a lot as a result of his interest in their welfare.

On 18 June 1963 Branigan was awaiting a much-anticipated boxing match, one in which he was not acting as referee—though he would certainly have loved the job. He and his Garda boxing colleagues had been speculating about the big event for weeks. It was a heavyweight bout between Cassius Clay (soon to become Muhammad Ali) and the British champion Henry Cooper, to be held at Wembley Stadium in London before 35,000 spectators. Branigan regularly engaged in spirited "fight talk" with friends in the station and was already a well-known admirer of Clay's dazzling speed and power. No-one was disappointed, as it turned out to be a real thriller, with an early surprise. As the *Irish Independent* described it, "Cooper got the contemptuous Clay with a beautiful left hook and sent Cassius crashing to the canvas."[33] Branigan knew exactly how that felt. But that was to be Cooper's moment of glory, as Clay made him pay for it in the later rounds.

Branigan would never get to meet his ring hero. But he would one day meet and chat with Ali's arch-enemy, Joe Frazier, whom Branigan always said he also admired for his sheer determination. He knew something about that as well.

———

A bigger excitement for Dublin in June 1963 was yet to come. Planning for the visit of the President of the United States, John F. Kennedy, was a huge challenge for the Garda authorities. Security would be paramount, and virtually every garda in Dublin would have some role in the operation. An estimated three thousand guards would be on duty at various posts in the city, though only a select few would be chosen to form part of Kennedy's personal security detail.

Branigan, a great admirer of Kennedy, felt sure he would get one of the coveted slots. Gardaí were receiving orders about having their uniforms clean, pressed, looking crisp, with shoes polished to a shine and brass buttons gleaming. Knowing he would be in plain clothes, he didn't give much thought to his dress. However, as the day approached he may have noticed that his attire perhaps looked a little too plain, and worn. Perhaps sensing Branigan's concern, his superintendent decided to play a bit of a joke on him, but for his own good. Branigan normally wore a sports jacket and trousers, never a suit. His friend Con Hearty recalls sixty years later with amusement:

> His superintendent, with tongue in cheek, told him that only men of outstanding physique, wearing lounge suits, would be allowed on escort protection with the president. Of course no such directive was actually issued. But Jim took the bait—and the following day he appeared in a new suit!

He showed up dressed to the nines on 26 June, when Kennedy arrived for his three-day visit. O'Connell Street alone was policed by more than three hundred gardaí. The *Irish Independent* reported that some exuberant onlookers "almost forced a break in the solid phalanx of guards" at various points.[34] In his immaculate new suit, Garda Branigan dutifully carried out his escort-protection role without mishap.

―――

On Saturday 27 July 1963 Dublin was rocking again. Chubby Checker, known as the "King of the Twist," was appearing at the National Stadium in Harold's Cross. After the Bill Haley episode a few years earlier, the Gardaí were on alert, and ample numbers were posted in and around the stadium.

No trouble erupted. Chubby's twisting was apparently too mild for *real* Dublin rockers.

But as Chubby and his fans were "twisting the night away," over at St Teresa's Gardens lawless youths were on the rampage again, drinking, vandalising, terrorising the community, and battling with gardaí. In late July, Inspector P. J. McCarthy spoke of it as a kind of war zone for police called in to try and halt the rioting:

> In the past six months the guards have received at *least* three or four calls *each* night to go to St Teresa's Gardens. The area is a constant source of trouble . . . Youths in mobs throw stones and bricks, property is damaged, doors and windows smashed.[35]

Stabbing and robbery were common. It had become a "no-go" area for outsiders, even taxi-drivers. Gardaí ordered into the area typically faced mobs of between sixty and a hundred youths, high on cider and "out of control," as described by local residents. The guards were always at high risk of injury amidst the barrage of flying missiles, including bottles, and with no protective gear in those days. When they drew their batons they were always outnumbered, and out-armed, and their foes knew it. It was a dreaded duty for guards, who were being injured all the time. The authorities did not know how to stop the uprisings.

Inspector McCarthy told Judge Carr that a guard "had been stationed there permanently, but he almost needs a shelter around him to protect him."[36] It was surely the most hazardous Garda post in the city, like a lone US cavalry soldier in hostile Indian territory.

Branigan disliked this strategy, knowing it placed the solitary guard at high risk. He was more familiar with St Teresa's Gardens than anyone, having waded into the mob scene countless times. He knew all their guerrilla-style hit-and-run tactics of confronting guards with curses and missiles, then breaking up into smaller bands and scattering into the dark nooks and crannies to hide, ready to emerge minutes later for another attack. Since the youths had broken most of the lamps in the complex, the gardaí could barely see them, or identify them in court later.

In the summer months Branigan had his hands full trying to cover the entire city's streets, ballrooms, cinemas, and chippers. When he was called, time and again, to St Teresa's Gardens his patience was thin, and he was cocked to unleash his gloves and deliver his "belt on the mouth" to those whom he grabbed.

The teenage delinquents found it a lark to take on a dozen or so gardaí in their hit-and-run game; but they all feared facing Lugs Branigan, because they were aware that he knew most of them by name, which flat they lived in, and how to catch them when he wanted to do so. He never had to run after them. Nothing intimidated them more than his strategy of showing up at their bedside early one morning and yanking them up. Without their late-night "rat pack" they were only whimpering youngsters. Being awakened by the lash of Lugs Branigan's gloves was a memory never forgotten.

On the night of 27 July 1963 Branigan was called to St Teresa's Gardens for the umpteenth time. On arrival he saw "a crowd of between forty and fifty, who shouted and jeered and threw stones at gardaí." Several guards had been assaulted, one injured seriously. Branigan bolted from his patrol car, fuming. When the cry of "Lugs!" went up they disbanded and vanished. As he would tell Judge Carr, the instant he showed up "they began running away." He nabbed a few of the leaders and made notes of others he would round up later.

On 21 August another handful of teenage troublemakers were arrested and brought into court before Judge Carr. Branigan, his exasperation growing more conspicuous, told Carr candidly that "if there was going to be respect for the law and its officers, the *courts* would have to enforce it." Carr seemed to agree.

The same week, another station colleague of Branigan's, Garda Patrick Mulqueen, was attacked by two hooligans while out on his beat, suffering cuts and bruises. They were brought before Judge O'Hagan, who seemed to be in agreement with Branigan when he declared that such attacks were savage, like something "in the jungle." He vowed that "I'm going to stop it happening in Dublin ... [I'm] putting an end to hooliganism where packs of youths take the law into their own hands."[37] *How* he was going to accomplish this he did not say.

––––

On 22 September 1963 Dublin gardaí found themselves having to control a wild crowd of some 87,000 people, which "forced thirty gardaí to draw their batons."[38] Not bowsies this time but over-zealous spectators who had just seen Dublin win the all-Ireland football final at Croke Park over the Connacht champions, Galway. Throngs of delirious supporters swarmed through the city centre, celebrating by drinking, singing, shouting, and lighting bonfires, some in dangerous places. Not wanting to go home, people hung around the streets, celebrating. And drinking. Traffic was tangled, creating chaos in the streets. People were knocked down and injured. Rows broke out. The thousands simply disregarded the efforts of gardaí to impose control.

Where Branigan was amidst the pandemonium is not documented. It is highly likely that he had attended the big match with Alick and Declan. Thereafter he was doubtless swallowed up by the carousing revellers.

The same month a far less publicised problem came to light, one that Branigan had long been familiar with but was able to do little about. A number of owners and managers of establishments in O'Connell Street complained that some Teddy Boys and other unsavoury elements were frequenting the street's gaming premises, causing trouble and sullying the once-dignified thoroughfare. Mr David Andrews, representing McDowell's Jewellers, expressed concern that the "historic place" was being "desecrated by gaming emporiums."[39] Their patrons were turning it into a "Soho" district. In support, Miss E. Bourke, for the Gresham Hotel, argued that no more such places should be allowed. Representatives of all the "respectable" businesses along O'Connell Street wanted Garda Branigan and other guards on duty there to keep a tighter watch over the unruly social elements damaging the street's ambience.

Branigan, seeking to be fair, saw both sides of the problem. Young people wanted to have fun at the entertainment parlours, while the business establishment wanted to keep the street dignified. If Teddy Boys and others were not actually breaking the law, he could not order them to leave. It was a delicate situation. But Branigan most probably was in agreement with those opposing any more gaming parlours in O'Connell Street.

Another problem along O'Connell Street, constantly brought to the attention of Branigan and other guards, was the brazen hawking of black-market cinema tickets. In 1963 complaints were flooding in not only from citizens but from visitors and tourists as well, who were boldly preyed upon. An American tourist, James Summers, wrote a letter to the *Evening Herald* in which he praised Dublin as a whole but stated that along O'Connell Street, as he was passing the GPO, he was hounded by *five* women aggressively hawking tickets. "It leaves a blot on what is one of the finest countries in the world."[40] It had become one of the most persistent street nuisances facing Branigan—a minor problem, to be sure, but a nagging one that consistently drew complaints. The Gardaí were supposed to "stamp it out." More easily said than done.

As if he didn't need any more annoying problems along the streets, in October the *Irish Independent* exposed another type of public menace: an epidemic of "drunken cyclists." The paper argued that "a cyclist guilty of drunk driving should be treated more seriously" than in the past.[41] Indeed scores of pedestrians were injured every year by speeding and wobbly cyclists, zigging and zagging in all directions. Some accidents were fatal. Only because of his agility had Branigan himself escaped their path many a time. He and his fellow-gardaí were now being asked to give this ancient street nuisance more attention. Somehow.

————

By the time November 1963 rolled around, Dublin was beset by "Beatlemania." For days before the "Fab Four" were to arrive in the city the Gardaí were preparing for what the Garda authorities were calling "Operation Beatles." Unfortunately, the operation was flawed from the outset, as the authorities had designated a total of only fifteen guards to handle the event. Though the brass had seen newsreels of the Beatles' appearances in Britain and elsewhere, where masses of hysterical teenagers had run amok in the streets, they inexplicably expected better from Irish youth. A Garda spokesman naïvely predicted that Beatles fans might "provide a headache" for the police but expressing confidence that they would "keep their enthusiasm within proper limits."[42] The *Evening Herald* predicted a rather more dramatic impact:

> Tomorrow the Liverpudlian Beatles hit Dublin and if they do not have the same effect as an exploding bomb the gardaí will be profoundly grateful.[43]

They would be appearing at the Adelphi in Middle Abbey Street for a one-night stand, giving two performances and staying overnight at the Gresham Hotel, which venue was ludicrously supposed to be secret.

As with Bill Haley and his Comets a few years earlier, the big challenge for the Gardaí was crowd control in the theatre and in the surrounding streets. With all his experience in handling excitable and rowdy teenagers, Branigan was assigned to be a central cog in Operation Beatles, so long as the higher-ups provided ample manpower. No-one knew better than he did how nearly impossible it was to control a sea of young people gone wild over their music and idols. But, as Garda Paddy Daly would recall, "when the Beatles came to the Adelphi Theatre there was more trouble than with Bill Haley, 'cause there were crowds, *crowds* . . . and for Branigan *that* was his worry."

On the evening of 7 November a crowd began amassing hours before the Beatles' first performance. It was a hodge-podge of mostly decent, excited teenagers and clusters of Teddy Boys and plain hooligans mixed in. The three thousand ticket-holders had to force their way through the packed crowd to gain entry.

When the first show began, thousands of others were milling about anxiously outside the theatre but in high spirits. Apart from some rowdies, the crowd was behaving lawfully.

When the Beatles stepped off the stage after their first performance, the "exploding bomb" was dropped. As the *Irish Times* reported it, "the trouble began when the first of the Beatles' two shows ended at 8.30, when nearly 3,000 people" leaving the theatre collided with those scrambling to get in for the second performance, made more chaotic by others without tickets who were trying to sneak or force their way in, causing anger and skirmishes.[44]

At this point the fifteen guards on duty tried frantically to form a cordon to establish some control. But the surging crowd kept easily breaching the cordon. The tiny police contingent was simply swamped by Beatles fans. An emergency call was put in for reinforcements, as mayhem reigned.

As more guards rushed to the scene, even more teenagers poured into the area, swelling the size of the crowd. Before long there were nearly a hundred guards in the street. As time for the second show neared, desperate patrons clutching their tickets feared they would not be able to get in, triggering a stampede. "I remember that *clearly* . . . the *crowds,*" says Dan Walsh. "Jim Branigan, he *had* to be there—but it was my introduction to mass hysteria . . . and girls fainting. It was the *crush* of sheer numbers."

Branigan and his fellow-gardaí quickly realised that their presence was scarcely even noticed. Hyper-excited teenagers were oblivious of everything but the Beatles. By nine it was pandemonium.

More Garda reinforcements were called in, bringing the total to almost 150—ten times the original number. And still woefully inadequate. Missiles were now flying through the air, and hooligans began breaking shop windows. In the mad stampede, young people, mostly girls, were knocked down and trampled on, some suffering serious injuries. Others fainted to the ground. Ambulance crews fought to reach the casualties. One ambulance-driver blurted out: "This is shocking—they've gone mad!"[45] An *Irish Press* reporter found himself trapped in the midst of the madness:

> Young girls, caught up in the mad rush, lay on the street injured and crying . . . Gardaí were pelted with pieces of coal . . . Victims sustained fractured ankles, gashed legs and cut faces. Said one Garda Sergeant who had his cap whipped off with a flying object, "This is really *mad* . . . I have seen everything now!"[46]

One very large guard, apparently frustrated, rushed the mob alone, only to have a dustbin full of rubbish lifted and planted on his head, to the delight of the crowd. So much for police control.

By about half past ten the force of guards had burgeoned from its original fifteen to "about 250 from all stations" in the metropolitan area, including some twenty patrol cars.[47] Doing their best to cope with the teenagers' mass hysteria, "they grappled for hours with a crowd of screaming, whistling Beatlemaniacs." By the time the night was over at least twenty girls had been removed to hospitals and more than fifty youths treated on the spot for injuries. Throughout the night and into the morning hours some rowdy youngsters roamed, as gardaí kept close surveillance.

The next day's papers captured the full story of Dublin Beatlemania:

Irish Independent: "Gardaí battle with Beatles fans"

Irish Press: "Many injured as Beatle crowds run riot in city"

Irish Times: "Many arrested as city crowds riot"

The references to "riot" and "battles" distressed law-abiding citizens. Perhaps the *Irish Press* summed it up best, at least from the viewpoint of Branigan and his colleagues: "Last night was the wildest night in Dublin in many years."[48] The papers documented what had happened: more than seventy people injured, cars overturned, windows smashed, lampposts and bollards damaged, guards assaulted. Readers vented their disgust by also criticising the Garda authorities for their mishandling of Operation Beatles.

Many letter-writers wanted to know why the fire brigade had not been called in to use their powerful water hoses to disperse the unruly crowd; but a

Garda spokesman pointed out that fire hoses could not be used against people unless "in case of dire emergency, and by direct Government order."

One citizen called it "black anarchy," while another suggested that the "hoodlums" be rounded up and carted off in lorries, to "remove the male and female thugs—riff-raff—from our streets."[49] Another concerned citizen wrote to the *Evening Herald* to express his opinion that probably reflected the sentiments of many Dubliners:

> Sir,—The ineptitude of the Gardaí in dealing with a few real trouble-makers and a large crowd of high-spirited teenagers bodes ill for the ability of the police to control any real trouble.[50]

The debacle of its mishandling of Beatlemania was a blow to the Garda Síochána, which ordinarily enjoyed high esteem for its difficult work. There was no criticism of Garda Jim Branigan, who had not been responsible for the strategy that called for fifteen guards to cover the expected "headache." It is more likely that citizens felt some sympathy for the impossible situation he had been placed in. And many doubtless believed that the disorder around the Adelphi would have been worse without his presence.

———

December was a month of mixed emotions. On the twentieth Branigan and scores of gardaí felt both sadness and nostalgia when the Garda Training Depot's last passing-out parade was held in the Phoenix Park. It was where they had done their training, met one another, made the transition from civilian to police life, where they had been moulded from lads into men. Each one had his own personal history and memories there. As the *Irish Independent* wrote:

> The Depot was a place of pageantry . . . police recruits seen wheeling and stamping about the parade ground . . . the Garda band in a practice session. It is to be no more. And the Park will be the duller for it.[51]

It was also in December 1963 that Garda Branigan was finally—after thirty-three years—promoted to sergeant. Very belatedly, in the opinion of all his friends. The reason for this belatedness was a sensitive matter, one he would only discuss years later, after his retirement. For the moment he was happy to receive the promotion, along with accolades for his sterling service, covered in the newspapers. Friends and colleagues heaped congratulations upon him, some messages coming from as far away as America, Canada, and Australia. In court the judges, solicitors and staff added their praise. Judge Molony spoke for all when he stated that it was "highly deserved."

On reading of Branigan's promotion, one citizen, J. F. Higgins, was motivated to send a unique congratulatory tribute to the *Evening Herald*. It was a jingle he had written, set to the the theme music of the popular American television series "Bat Masterson," which was a hit in Ireland as well. He clearly saw parallels between Dodge City's sheriff and Dublin's "sheriff," Jim Branigan:

Soon after Civic Guards began,
There joined a man named Branigan;
He was a boxer, sound and grim,
They called him Jim—Jim Branigan.

He wore no cane or derby hat,
But still he put them on the mat.
He kept the peace both clean and trim,
And he was Jim—Jim Branigan.

And now he is promoted up,
To cause concern to many a pup.
May more success still come to him,
Whom they called Jim—Jim Branigan.[53]

One would imagine that "Sheriff" Branigan got quite a kick out of it.

If one were to extrapolate a bit further, it could be reasoned that Branigan, befitting his new lawman's position, needed a posse of select deputies to hunt down lawless villains across Dublin's territory. Perhaps 1964 would be the year.

Chapter 11 ∿

THE RIOT SQUAD AND "BLACK MARIA"

"Juvenile crime took on a new, menacing aspect with the arrival of knife-wielding gangs. The life and limb of the ordinary citizen is thus placed in danger."

(*Evening Herald*, 17 APRIL 1967)

"It may sound rather dramatic to say that there is a reign of terror now ruling Dublin, but it is true."

(LETTER TO *Evening Herald*, 2 JUNE 1967)

"To combat the increasing gang warfare in Dublin, a new Riot Squad has been formed. In charge is Garda Sergeant Branigan, former heavyweight boxing champion."

(*Evening Herald*, 3 AUGUST 1964)

"He had his henchmen with him, other guards, and I drove for him. We'd get calls about rows . . . People got badly hurt in them—and you could get badly injured yourself."

(GARDA MATT MULHALL)

"The riot squad helped make me notorious . . . a reputation around the city for being a tough guy, a fearless cop."

(GARDA JAMES BRANIGAN)

The year 1964 began with a rash of rows and flick-knife stabbings. Disputes were now often settled not with fists but with blades. People were being assaulted on the streets in random, senseless acts. Courts were becoming backlogged as some judges continued to talk wistfully of flogging for hooligans. Newspapers wrote of a "reign of terror" as people grew more fearful of going out at night for entertainment in the city centre. Dubliners were critical of the "revolving door" system in the courts, whereby criminals were arrested, tossed in jail for a short time, then released to prey upon the public again.

Others blamed everybody in society: "If the parents, teachers, clergy and gardaí close their eyes to the crowd of young ruffians," lamented one distressed letter-writer in the *Evening Herald,* "then it is a sad day for this supposed holy land."[1] Another angry writer suggested a military solution:

> Sir,—Something has to be done at once, as Dublin is most dangerous at night . . . stabbings, assaults, robberies every night. I appeal for having streets patrolled by Army Jeeps during those dangerous hours.[2]

August was the peak holiday season, with myriad social events and sports activities. The streets, ballrooms and cinemas would be packed with people. On the evening of 3 August, when Dubliners picked up their copy of the *Evening Herald* they saw a headline big enough for announcing the end of the Second World War:

"CITY RIOT SQUAD"

The story dominated the front page. Rather than news of a war ending, it told of a battle about to be waged in Dublin against the elements of crime. A new concept, a Garda "riot squad," sounded impressive, and forceful.

Everyone wanted to know what was behind the new idea. Was it as forceful as it sounded? Whose concept was it, and exactly what was its purpose?

Essentially, it was the brainchild of Sergeant Jim Branigan, who for years had championed the idea of a special quick-strike force comprising chosen men with the mobility to cover the entire city with speed. From the outset, within the force it was regarded as "Branigan's baby," as he was designated commander of the squad. He was in control of all operations and decisions. As Branigan himself described his new squad:

> In effect, the riot squad was composed of a Bedford van, a driver, myself and other guards. We were on call to any place in the city right through the night. Our function was to break up fights and rows.[3]

The squad's function was considerably more complex than Branigan's modest description. "Fights and rows" included full-blown battles and mayhem of every imaginable sort.

The press enthusiastically hailed the formation of the riot squad as a breakthrough in Dublin policing methods. The *Evening Herald* gushed: "Sergeant Branigan has been responsible for the arrest and conviction of hundreds of people who committed crimes of violence," calling him the "fittest, toughest and fairest" garda, who still "does two hours of physical training every day." Various papers referred to him as "a former heavyweight boxing champion," famous "gang-buster," and one-man deterrent against thugs and criminals.

Branigan's first responsibility was to select an elite team. He would pick all the men himself. His superiors told him that he had the entire Garda pool from which to draw. His criteria were just the right *combination* of qualities: strength, skill in boxing, wrestling or judo, agility, courage, discipline, and loyalty. Men of good character, intelligence, judgement—and fairness. Cool under pressure. No hotheads, "tough-acting" fellas, or braggarts. They would be carefully selected and tested "under fire"; some would make it, others not. Candidates who made the squad regarded it as an honour, and a high responsibility. Though their mates respected them, they did not envy them their task.

––––

Branigan had a few prime candidates in mind right off, men he had worked with previously or knew about. At the top of his list was Tom "Sonny" Heany, who was well known and liked within the force and would become his most reliable sidekick. At six foot three, he possessed a block-solid physique and enormous strength, making him a powerful tug-of-war champion. Apart from his strength, he was agile in a tussle with bowsies and good at spotting ringleaders. Moreover, he was perfectly compatible with Branigan. The two "giants" made an imposing match. Sonny gladly signed on with Lugs. The two would become lifelong friends.

The garda selected to be his first driver was Val Lynn, who had joined the force at the age of twenty-one. In his youth, he admits, "I never wanted to be in the Guards—didn't *like* the Guards!" But his mother convinced him that it was a secure and pensionable job. When he joined up he found himself stationed at Kevin Street with Branigan. Says his friend Gerald Byrne: "Val was a *tough* guy . . . *very handy* [with his fists]." Branigan discovered this himself one night, quite convincingly. Lynn, a modest man, now seventy-five, reflects on the circumstances. One night he was called to a massive brawl on the quays in which ultimately thirty-four gardaí were involved. As a young garda, he didn't recognise a notoriously tough man, a docker nicknamed "Nobber," who was mowing down one guard after another like bowling pins. By the time Lynn arrived on the scene he found injured guards strewn all over the place, including Branigan's friend Senan Finucane. As he recounts it:

This one fella had done ten or twelve, beating up the guards. He beat up a guard from Wexford and left him with blood coming out of his ears . . . in the Adelaide Hospital for six or seven weeks. Anyway, this fella turned around and threw a swing at me, and it hit me on the cheekbone. But he had half turned around—and I hit him under the chin and knocked him out *cold*. And, as God would have it, up Bridgefoot Street in a squad car came Tommy Kelly and Mick O'Malley—and *Jim Branigan!* "So," says Jim, "what happened?"

After Lynn told him the story, Branigan walked over, yanked Nobber up and said to Lynn, "Do you know who this is?" He hadn't a clue. "It's *Nobber!*"—the bane of the guards who had suffered his blows. Even when batons bounced off him, he swung back. Branigan had seen enough. Better yet, he found out that Lynn had taken a special driving course, all making him an ideal candidate for the new squad.

Each man would have his own tale to tell of how he came to be chosen by Branigan for his squad. "It was *fit* people he wanted with him, people who could handle themselves," says Séamus Quinn. "I was recommended to him because I was a judo black belt."

Bosco Muldoon was an excellent prospect because of his superior physical condition. "I was rowing at the time—I was fit. So I went with him and Sonny Heany."

Gerald Byrne was unexpectedly approached by Branigan one day and asked to substitute as driver for Val Lynn. He was told straight out what he was getting into if he accepted:

He saw me in the mess hall one day and says, "Would you fancy taking over as driver for Val?" But he *also* wanted someone who could pitch in and do his part, do *his stuff* as well. 'Cause he said, "It might be dangerous, now; we're going to be involved in rows." And we had no helmets or shields and that sort of thing.

Dan Walsh also felt honoured to be asked. "Oh, we were in *awe* of him, really. Of his reputation. He could do no wrong."

Similarly, Paddy Daly welcomed the chance to join the elite squad. "See, he had a 'team.' He took his men from different stations, fellas who were big and tall. I used to drive for him."

The elements of camaraderie and equality were important to Branigan, recalls Matt Mulhall, who proudly became a member:

He would have his henchmen with him, two or three other guards, and we'd be patrolling . . . I drove for him, and we'd get calls about rows, and people got badly hurt in them—and you could get badly injured *yourself.* But you never had any problem with him, he never pulled rank. We were *all equal.* No airs or graces—we did the job. He wasn't a glory-hunter.

Despite the honour of invitation, it was not always an easy decision for men to join. There were several important factors to consider: it was all-night duty, demanded changing sleep patterns, involved real risk of injury. Young single men were best suited, as it didn't mean disruption for a family as well. As men like Byrne assessed it, "it was a short duty—and *then* you were finished. But *dangerous!*" On the other hand, Muldoon notes the appeal of the geographical freedom, which squad members found very liberating. "You weren't *confined* to one district: we covered the *whole* city . . . You'd feel free to roam all over Dublin, *everywhere*—even out to Bray." Far more interesting than being stuck on one turf; it offered a variety of scenery and experiences.

Branigan encouraged men to consider all the factors before making the commitment. Most accepted. Once he had his team formed, he used men on a revolving basis, with special capabilities for specific assignments. On Saturday nights—"hell night" for gardaí—he always wanted to select a top team.

———

Mobility for the crack force was provided by a rather unlikely vehicle. It was not a sleek, supercharged pursuit car capable of accelerating in seconds to top speed, spinning around corners; instead it was blocky, slow, and awkward to manoeuvre in traffic. But Branigan and his team were thrilled to have it. As Dan Walsh brags, "we had a black Bedford van that held about eight people, and there weren't many of them around." Though its maximum capacity was eight, on ordinary patrols three or four guards were aboard. Lugs always travelled in the front seat, next to the driver, with a full view of what was ahead, so as to give instant orders. He had no baton, though his men carried theirs; he had his fists and his gloves.

The purpose of the van was not to chase getaway cars through the streets but to get the squad to the scene of a row or a riot as quickly as possible, and haul away hooligans. Drivers had to be skilled in quickly squirming and squeezing their way through Dublin's clogged streets to reach their destination. Newspapers played up how the squad's van "will be a mobile patrol with two-way radio and all other necessary means of communication"[4] (leaving readers to wonder exactly what "other means of communication" meant). But for the Garda Síochána half a century ago it was indeed the latest communication system, with direct radio contact with Garda Headquarters in Dublin Castle.

Particularly impressive to squad members was the fact that their van had an official code name that would quickly be modified. As Branigan explained, rather proudly, "the riot squad was officially Bravo 5, but patrol [headquarters] always said, 'Come in, *Branno* 5'."[5] His own squad members gradually began calling him "Branno," and over the remainder of his career "Branno" would become a name used fondly by his Garda colleagues. He seemed to like it.

––––

Within the first few weeks of August, the readily identifiable black Bedford was given another name by people in the street: the "Black Maria." Usually carrying three or four tall, broad-shouldered guards, it became a comforting sight at night as it rumbled along O'Connell Street, College Green, or around St Stephen's Green. Pedestrians often cast a friendly wave to Branigan and his squad. While some may have derided its boxy, plodding image, it was clearly a welcome sight on Dublin's night scene to law-abiding citizens.

Lawless elements, who knew all about the formation of the riot squad, felt just the opposite. The newspapers emphasised that the new force was to cover all parts of the city where crime erupted, within minutes. This was a daunting prospect for bowsies and gougers out on the prowl at night. They were now aware that they were no longer beyond the quick reach of Lugs and his squad. The sight of the black van cruising the city's streets was a definite deterrent to troublemakers, by their own admission.

During its first two weeks out on patrol the black van seemed to make quite a positive impression. On 18 August the *Evening Herald* lauded the work of the riot squad in a front-page headline "Riot men check gangs." Declaring it a great success, the newspaper wrote:

> The Riot Squad which came into existence at the beginning of this month has had a wonderfully deterrent effect on gangs of youths. Since its inception there has not been one serious case of gang warfare.[6]

Quoting a Garda spokesman who stated, "It seems to be having the desired effect," the *Evening Herald* gave clear credit to its leader, Sergeant James Branigan. "It is a tribute to the respect in which he is held by the toughest elements in Dublin that the Squad's work" has been so effective.

Branigan was at the pinnacle of his fame. With all his accomplishments and the generous media praise, he was now truly achieving a legendary status among Dubliners. Yet, as Tony Ruane affirms, "no-one was envious or jealous." Friends and colleagues knew that he deserved his "notoriety," as Branno himself always liked to call it. In fact, adds Ruane about his Garda mates, most "wouldn't *want* to be him," because of the demands and the risks of his position.

––––

With all the early accolades for the riot squad, some thought it might be too good to last. Branigan included. He knew that his team had not really been tested under fire yet. They had encountered no major riots or gang wars, no all-out ballroom melees. Too much praise too fast probably made him feel uncomfortable. He didn't want public expectations to be unrealistically high.

Nightly patrols followed a schedule devised by Branigan. Rather than random cruising around the city, he always mapped out in his head their itinerary for different nights of the week. There were always designated targets and times. No-one knew the rhythms of Dublin after dark better than he did.

Monday to Thursday were normally the calmest nights. The black van usually pulled out from Kevin Street station at about half past eight or nine o'clock and, if all went well, returned by two or three. On Friday night there were greater crowds and more lawless incidents, often keeping the men out past three o'clock. Saturday was "Armageddon" night in Dublin. Gardaí could count on it. Three to five of the toughest men headed out at about eight and were typically kept busy until five or six on Sunday morning. As Gerald Byrne puts it, "the most dangerous times were when the dancehalls and the chippers closed." Some chippers could stay open virtually all night, drawing the last of the trouble-makers for the Gardaí to deal with.

The van's crew pinpointed the known trouble spots, checking in at certain dancehalls, pubs, cinemas, and chippers, asking the staff—who were always glad to see them—"How are things going tonight?"

Cruising the city at night could have its own pleasant tempo, rolling slowly through the colourful, neon-lit districts of O'Connell Street to College Green, Dame Street, Grafton Street, St Stephen's Green, past luxury hotels, restaurants, the cinema and theatre crowds. By sad contrast, scouring Benburb Street, the dark quays and docklands, the guards saw humanity at its lowest: the drunkards, dossers, depraved. And the pitiable prostitutes, or "pavement hostesses," as Branigan preferred to call them, whom he treated kindly and sought to protect from their exploitative pimps and "clients." Along the way, when Dublin's social pariahs would catch sight of the black van passing by, they often just stared.

When young Gerald Byrne joined the riot squad he had his first real exposure to the seamy side of Dublin life. He saw every sort of human degradation: bloody beatings, knife fights, murder, suicide, sickening accidents with mangled bodies. "You'd see practically *everything* at night, life in the raw ... decapitations ... go to the autopsies, and the horrible smell. You'd be well seasoned!" Branigan's partners often commented on how even the bloodiest scene didn't seem to affect him, though it forced them to grimace and turn away at times. But he still didn't like to be near a corpse.

As they trawled the city's streets for trouble at night they were always ready to respond to an emergency call of "Branno 5" from headquarters. The best drivers could adeptly whip the Bedford van around and put it on a new course quickly. The most stressful situation occurred when there were multiple alarms, and a decision had to be made about which were most urgent. Priority would always be given to a guard in danger, as happened in August 1964.

At about 1 a.m. Garda Joseph Marshall intervened to halt a fight between two men, Tutty and Finn, in Donore Avenue. However, within minutes "a crowd of about two hundred people, hostile to gardaí," had gathered threateningly around him.[7] This encouraged the two brawlers to turn on Marshall, attacking him violently, one biting him severely on the finger. When Branigan arrived he quickly restrained Finn, but Tutty ran into the flats to hide.

Then, reported the *Evening Herald*, Branigan did something that no other guard would probably have dared to do. He strode alone into the hostile flats where Tutty had taken refuge. Within minutes he dragged him out, "without any trouble."

In court, Branigan used this as another opportunity to explain to Judge McGivern what lone guards faced, telling him that "the crowd would back the wrongdoers" almost every time, placing the guard at great risk.

———

Monday and Tuesday nights could be uneventful, even dull, as the hours stretched slowly, while Friday and Saturday nights seemed constantly explosive, leaving the men fatigued by sunrise. One never knew what to expect, which was one of the "charms" of being in the riot squad.

Branigan wisely made an effort to fit in some pleasant diversions during each night's duty. No break was more anticipated by his men than a few minutes off to enjoy one of Elsie's famous tarts. She made it a tradition to bake daily for the lads at night. "He could either bring the treat with him," recalls John Collins, "or we could swing by his home in Drimnagh and collect it fresh out of the oven." And, he adds, smiling, "She *might* even have *two* apple tarts, and she'd say, 'There you are, boys.' That was *every single night* on our duty." Branigan knew that this treat was psychologically important to them, helping to keep their spirits up, despite the stress of duty that night. Elsie was becoming legendary in her own right.

While they usually ate in the van, they sometimes liked to combine their break with a short trip down to the docks to visit Branigan's brother Frank, who worked on a Guinness boat at night. This was a welcome diversion, as it allowed the men to get out, stretch their legs, inhale fresh sea air, and engage in some pleasant chat. But also, one squad member confides, "many a time we pulled up and Frank'd have a few bottles of Guinness to give us. We could have *one* . . . something to wash down the pie." Branno didn't drink but enjoyed this break as much as anyone.

Another regular stop was at certain hospitals that regularly had problems with night patients who were inebriated and troublesome. Some were bowsies who had been fighting each other and when they spotted one another again in the same hospital would try to resume their brawl, creating a terrible situation for the staff. On behalf of the poor nurses, doctors and others trying to control such unruly men, Branigan made it a practice to stop by and make his presence known.

"He went to a *lot* of hospitals, to see that there was no trouble in the Casualty Department," says Matt Mulhall. "He was *so well known* to them . . . He was particularly fond of the Meath Hospital." When necessary, he would administer his own brand of sedative to calm disorderly men. Members of the hospital staff always offered him and his men a cup of tea, and they often brought their pie in to have with it.

In accordance with Branno's wishes, night patrol always ended with the ritual of making the rounds of the newspaper offices. "He always did that, collected newspapers, every night," says Séamus Quinn. These papers were supplied free. First they would go to the *Independent* and *Press* and "take them to radio control in Dublin Castle for the lads. Jim was always thinking of other people." Then, "for his wife, we had to go to the *Irish Times,* to get *her* paper . . ."

To carry out their regular night patrol, members of the squad had to change their normal daytime life-style. Their sleeping pattern was turned topsy-turvy. Some men adjusted easily, others not. Working through the dark night and sleeping during bright daytime hours did not suit everyone. But most men could end their night tour, go home and fall into bed for a decent sleep until around midday or early afternoon. This still allowed them some daylight time for normal activities.

But not Branno. His schedule was by any standards remarkable and to many was beyond comprehension. He seemed to function on ridiculously little sleep. It was one of the real "mysteries" of the man.

Unlike most gardaí, he had to be in court *every* morning at about ten with culprits he had apprehended—a seemingly endless stream of them. As his night duty regularly ended somewhere between 3 and 6 a.m., he had to get home to Drimnagh Road, catch a few hours' sleep, and be back in the city ready to face court duty. Which he *loved.* Leaving court at about one o'clock, he headed back home for lunch and a nap.

None of his mates could ever figure out how he managed it, especially as he never looked tired or complained of sleep deprivation. He simply seemed superhuman in this regard. Year after year, Val Lynn marvelled at it, yet could never understand it—"he slept very little . . . *very* little!" It even bewildered his family, says Alick, because his father was always clear-minded and energetic:

> He might be in at three or four in the morning. Or later. And *then* in court early, at ten. My mother'd see him for breakfast. Then he'd come back at maybe half one or two, have a bit of lunch. And then I'd find him in a chair with a newspaper over his face—getting "forty winks," you know. And my mother'd always say, "Sshh, your father's having a nap! Leave him, and don't make any noise." And maybe he'd take an hour nap then. It was just his work habit, and we accepted the way it was. My mother got used to that.

It meant that Declan, who was eighteen in 1964, could not play his rock-and-roll music during his father's nap time; but he understood. "He *had* to sleep in the afternoon—his body adjusted to it. A completely different rhythm, but he got *used* to it—it just came natural to him." It meant that he typically got no more than four or five hours of *solid* sleep per night, and often only three. He somehow survived on a brief snooze in the afternoon. Most remarkable was the fact that he managed this in a house with a family, lodgers, and two huge dogs. Somehow he always emerged rested and regenerated, rising energetically from his chair to head out and care for his budgies or do a bit of gardening.

———

Throughout the late summer and autumn of 1964 the riot squad were busy, contending with gang fights, ballroom rows, and a few rumbles at circuses. As well as a murder at a hotel. Then hooligans began a long reign of terrorising buses. If any members of Branno's team had second thoughts about joining up, they never showed it. All seemed well up to the challenge, while their leader clearly thrived on the action.

He deplored the senselessness of many of the crimes. During a minor dispute at a dance club one youth was so savagely punched and kicked that he lost an eye. Soon afterwards two seventeen-year-olds were arguing when one pulled out his flick-knife and plunged it into the other's chest. Another night Branigan luckily happened along Camden Street just after David Pickett, a mapping draughtsman, had left a café and was viciously attacked by an eighteen-year-old thug for no apparent reason and was left bleeding on the pavement.

Dancehall brawls were becoming a headache for the riot squad, with injured victims strewn about the dance floor. Here the risks to guards themselves were high. Branigan's men had to burst into a dancehall to face a tornado of flying bottles, chairs, and broken table legs. Lugs was always the first through the door; he would have it no other way.

In the 1960s the most violent melees were between gangs armed with flick-knives and razors. Several dancehalls were particularly notorious. "There were some *quite violent* riots at night," recalls Séamus Quinn, "through gangs, mainly at dancehalls. The Top Hat in Dún Laoghaire was one, and the Olympic, and the Crystal Ballroom . . . and another one in Parnell Square." Mass fighting at these dancehalls had become a regular Saturday night event. Unfortunately, the riot squad could only attend to one affray at a time.

St Anthony's Hall on Merchants' Quay was one of the worst. "Branno 5" calls were constantly received about rioting there. One night in late summer a message came in to the van that all hell had broken out there again. On duty with Branigan this night were Sonny Heany, Val Lynn, and another guard. Dances at St Anthony's Hall normally went on until about 2 a.m., when the worst fights usually broke out. When the riot squad arrived, Branigan reported that he found it "chaotic, with the whole place in turmoil." Multiple skirmishes were going on everywhere, with chairs and missiles flying in every direction, causing frightened patrons to duck under tables for protection. Several local guards had arrived before Branigan and tried to quell the rioting but were quickly overpowered by "a crowd of big youths." Things were completely out of control.

Branno and his men had dealt with the same ruffians so many times before that they were in no mood for sweet talk. He knew exactly who the ringleaders were, and how to handle them. Ahead of his men, he strode in, grabbed the major culprits roughly. When one bellicose youth failed to heed his warning to halt he paid the price with a sharp clip to restrain him. When several people roared "Branigan's here!" most ceased and scrambled to get out.

In court, Branigan told Judge Molony calmly that "a mob of rowdies took over the place," and when one culprit resisted arrest "I had to give him a clip" to quieten him down and get him into the van.[8] Well done, the judge agreed. Lastly, Branigan expressed his belief that the "hall authorities were doing their best to conduct the dance properly" but simply could not cope with the hooligan bunch that invaded and took over. Perhaps the judge might want to consider closing the dancehall down if it continued.

Not long afterwards a "Branno 5" call from the Castle sent the riot squad to what was a rare crime scene: a double murder. They were summoned to the Ormond Hotel at Upper Ormond Quay, where a party crowd had spilled out onto the road when a fight broke out among some men. Instead of settling it with fists, knives were drawn. Paddy Daly was on duty with Branigan that night, and they first assumed it to be a routine call:

> We drove into this mob of people. Well, Lugs got out with his black leather gloves, 'cause he thought it was just an ordinary row. But two people were *murdered*—stabbed to death. Blood all over the place.

Branigan quickly "scattered everybody," and the bodies were taken to the old Richmond Hospital in North Brunswick Street. The murderer was caught and eventually sentenced to life imprisonment.

It was around this time in the early sixties that gardaí were experiencing many more problems with drunken and disorderly women who resisted arrest. This was explained in part by a dramatic social reform in Dublin, when pubs began to take down their "Men only" signs, allowing women in to drink, even at the bar. It was the era of the women's liberation movement, when women asserted their rightful independence in myriad ways. Going out with friends or on their own to drink was one of the more dramatic changes. During the 1960s the increase in female inebriation in public places was conspicuous—and a delicate problem for the guards who had to cope with it.

As Branigan and his colleagues were finding, an intoxicated woman could be just as verbally and physically difficult as many men. Indeed a woman could unleash as much fury as a man, fighting a garda with her fists, nails, knees, elbows, or sharp heels. Trying to restrain such a woman was very awkward for a guard, as he did not feel he could use his basic holds, such as wrapping his arms around her chest, or grabbing her legs.

One summer night in 1964 Branno and his men were called to a row in Temple Bar, only to be accosted by a 21-year-old woman who "started shouting and roaring and calling him names . . . and was very abusive," according to newspaper reports. This was behaviour he would never tolerate from a man; but with a woman he always made every effort to avoid direct confrontation and arrest. In this case, just as he was pulling away in the van, "she made several punches at the patrol car."[9] This act, along with her incessant screaming, incited more disorderly conduct from those around her. He had no choice but to make an arrest.

When he got her to the Garda station she continued the abusive behaviour and even "kicked a witness." In court, the judge fined her 40 shillings (£2) and gave her a seven-day prison sentence. Judges were now commenting that they were seeing nearly as many cases of drunken women as men. For Branigan and his squad it was a problem that would only grow worse.

―――

No "Branno 5" calls were more dreaded than those despatching them to an all-out clash at a carnival between the roustabouts and a mob of angry local men. Even for Branigan it was a nightmare trying to break them apart and reason with both sides. Local guards who were called in first were injured badly.

Many carnival crews were Travellers, who didn't always abide by local laws or social customs. The roustabouts were the strongest men, who erected the tents and put up the big structures at every site. They were muscled fellas who handled mallets, axes, iron bars, chains, and picks. And who fought bare-fisted for fun. Their hard work made them thirsty; drinking could make them contentious. Local dockers were iron men as well, wielding their shovels, chains, and large hammers. They were legendary pint-drinkers, commonly putting away ten to fifteen at a single session.

At some of Dublin's regular circus sites, the roustabouts and dockers seemed to fall into annual conflict easily and frequently. The fighting was always bloody, and Branigan didn't like exposing his men to it. But when the violence broke out, local residents called the gardaí to come and stop it so that they could enjoy the carnival. This happened in late August in Irishtown, where the two groups were smashing each other up with what the *Irish Times* called "offensive weapons," resulting in grave "bodily harm." When the black Bedford appeared, dockers were easier for the riot squad to handle. They respected Lugs and didn't want to be hauled off to a prison sentence, knowing their stevedore might give their job to another man. They were more inclined to listen and obey orders from the gardaí. Roustabouts often simply didn't seem to care about authority in any form. Fortunately, at Irishtown the riot squad quelled the brawling before serious injuries were incurred.

Not long afterwards, however, there was another carnival war, based on bad blood going back years between the roustabouts and local people. It had evolved into a fierce feud. Gerald Byrne was on duty with the riot squad when this combat broke out:

> There was a *bad* confrontation at this carnival, up in Santry . . . And the roustabouts and local gangs—the local *mafiosi*—were at loggerheads. And it erupted one night and lasted about *four* different nights. So we got a call—and we *had* to go in! People *all over* the place, and weapons being used, *all* sorts of things—even a *sword!* But the *ace* up our sleeve was always Jim Branigan.

As soon as the van skidded to a halt, the first thing the combatants saw was the hulking forms of Lugs Branigan and Sonny Heany marching towards them:

> The locals would say, "Here's Branigan!" And they'd put their hands in their pockets and walk away. It was his *reputation*—they were afraid of that . . . that he was a boxer, and had his gloves. And he'd *use* them!

The guards' real tussle was with some resistant roustabouts who hadn't got the full message of who Branigan was, and how he operated. But they could learn fast. "We had to manhandle some guys into the van. A couple of guys went into hospital, but none of our guys." For four nights the fighting flared up. By the time it was over, "Jim had an *arsenal* of weapons he took off the fellas."

There were endless problems for the squad to contend with, major and minor. Out in Inchicore the newspapers were reporting that "a new type of vandalism has broken out." The first victims were local traders, whose large and expensive windows were being smashed nightly by gangs of youths, who seemed to be making a sport of it. A grocer, Michael Corrigan, had to send for the glazier twice in three days. Next, the vandals turned to breaking windows in private houses.

When Branigan learnt that these packs of destructive youths were "roaming at night, striking fear in the heart of residents," as one newspaper described it, he decided to put Inchicore on his agenda for a while, in the hope of sending a message to the culprits.[10] If he caught them in the act they were prime candidates for his leather gloves.

———

Unknown to him at the time, Jim Branigan was about to embark on a new, unique relationship. One fine summer day he and Bosco Muldoon were walking together into Kevin Street Garda Station when they happened to notice a young lad peering fixedly through the iron gates. He was obviously fascinated with the routine comings and goings of the guards and their patrol cars, standing for hours just watching them. Along the street, other children his age—about seven—were carrying on with the usual summer games and antics; but Mickey Edmonds just stood alone, gazing. It was only natural that Branno, Muldoon and some of the other guards would eventually become curious about him.

The friendship began tentatively when Branno and Bosco casually cast a few waves and smiles Mickey's way. His expression showed pure delight. Soon afterwards a few friendly shouts to Mickey elicited no reply. He just stared. Finally, approaching him delicately one day, they discovered that he wasn't able to speak. "Mickey suffered from a rare genetic condition known as fragile X syndrome," explains Tony Ruane. His world of silence was a lonely one: he was unable to communicate normally with other children and so was left out. Watching the guards whizzing around became the joy of his life.

One day Branigan and Muldoon invited Mickey into the Garda station. It opened a door to a new life, one where he would find a second home and lifelong friendships.

———

Just after Christmas, on 28 December 1964, Branigan and his squad were cruising past the Metropole Cinema in O'Connell Street when they noticed a skirmish taking place among a large crowd gathered for a popular film. Following some altercation at the door, a twenty-year-old man decided to "jump forward and strike the doorman, Daniel Meehan, on the mouth." An off-duty garda grabbed the attacker. Branigan hopped out of the van, "went to the aid of Garda Garvey [and] caught the man by the arm," and, as the newspaper phrased it, he quickly "ceased struggling."[11] The paper didn't specify how he was so easily calmed. Such small, routine incidents within view of crowds of people, and often reported in the newspapers, were countless. And all contributed to Branigan's growing reputation.

The period 1965–6 saw the worst epidemic of stabbings in Dublin's history, many of them random and senseless. Carrying flick-knives had become the "in" thing for young thugs as well as seasoned criminals. For the slightest of reasons, drawing blades was now a natural reaction. They became the weapon of choice because they were easy to acquire, and quick to use and conceal. As one man said, "You need only *look* at a person the wrong way today to be stabbed!"

It seemed as if stabbing stories were in the newspapers nearly every day. In 1965 a man walked into a pub in Old Bride Street, got into a minor disagreement and bit of a scuffle, then pulled his knife and stuck it in the stomach and head of the other man. Branigan was called to disarm him. Two weeks later an eighteen-year-old named Fitzpatrick had words with a burly 23-year-old, who, without warning, "then flashed his knife and plunged it into his head," reported the *Evening Herald*.[12] When he was taken to Sir Patrick Dun's Hospital in Grand Canal Street, Dr Trimble horrifyingly "saw the knife sticking out of his head as he approached him, protruding from behind the left eye." Perhaps to ease people's worries, the paper followed with a front-page article on the "Control of flick knives," quoting the Minister for Justice, Brian Lenihan, that "legislation to control the sale of flick knives was forecast in the Dáil" very soon.[13]

Unfortunately, stories of riots grabbed the headlines to keep the public alarmed. The most publicised riot of 1965 was dubbed by the press the "Battle of Malahide." On the night of 16 October a "Branno 5" call came in from Garda Headquarters telling them to head out to Malahide pronto: big trouble was brewing. It was a fierce clash at the Spanish Arch Hall between rival gangs from Swords and Donnycarney, who had a deep hatred of one another. More than a hundred combatants, along with their frenzied supporters, were in savage warfare with flick-knives, bottles, sharpened steel combs, iron bars, and knuckledusters. Some had even armed themselves with swords. The guards who had first been called to quell the riot faced such a hailstorm of bottles and other objects that they could do no more than seek cover themselves beneath tables. Even when the Garda Dog Unit arrived with their alsatians they were helpless to halt the battle. Blood was being spilled everywhere, as fighting was carried outside into the streets. How could the riot squad be expected to halt the gang warring?

Branigan and his squad had now been in action for over a year, during which time, by trial and error, they had devised their strategies for such mob scenes. It began with the arrival of the black van, which was intended to be dramatic, delivering a shock to rioters. Electrifying action was meant to disorient trouble-makers and trigger their exodus. As one of Branno's favourite drivers, Gerald Byrne was in on this action many times. "We'd *pull up*, and it was *'Okay, now—all out!'*" It was his job to bring the van in speedily, then halt. All the men would then *leap* out for maximum visibility, hoping to create a sort of "stunning" effect. From then on, every man knew his role.

When need be, the van could carry up to eight hefty guards. Together they could be an imposing sight to rioters. They followed a tactical procedure, says Quinn, in which "Branigan was the leader of the group—he *always* went in first, into the crowd. With his leather gloves he *bulldozed* his way into the crowd until he got his object." This was clearly the most dangerous position, and other guards might quickly have been felled for daring to do so. But Branigan's instant recognisability usually deterred even drunken men from swinging at him. Towering over most of the combatants, he scanned the maelstrom for ringleaders. Often he knew them by sight, and name.

Over their years in action the riot squad faced hostile crowds of two or three hundred or more. Yet, Byrne vouches, "I *never, ever* saw him saying, 'There's too many!' *Never*. That would never happen." His obvious fearlessness infused in his men the confidence *they* needed. Bosco Muldoon was forever awed by his unwavering determination in the most dangerous situations: "There could be rows, *huge* crowds . . . gangs, fighting with fisticuffs, knives . . . but I *never* saw him afraid! And when you were with him you always felt safe." As Dan Walsh puts it, "It was the way he commanded a situation, took control. His appearance anywhere *commanded* that respect."

But he needed to be able to count on his men behind him. As Quinn affirms, "Jim wanted his back-up when he *needed* it." Branigan was well aware of his own vulnerability, on all sides. There was always the risk of being seriously injured, even unintentionally, by a swinging weapon. Or perhaps some boozy thug daring to surprise him with a punch, then vanish into the crowd. Therefore, explains Quinn, in violent riots such as at Malahide, Branno needed a tight, protective formation as he plunged forward. Often Quinn found himself providing this support:

> We were back-to-back with him, facing the *opposite* direction. Oh, yes. We walked backwards! Jim walked forwards. We were always touching his left

or right shoulder—he *knew* we were there. And that gave him confidence. We rarely used our batons, *rarely*. We dealt with the person through our boxing techniques, judo, or whatever.

But there were never any guarantees of safety for Branigan or his squad, and not infrequently they suffered injuries. Being struck by flying missiles and kicked were particularly common. More than being outnumbered, Branigan worried about the group psychology—the mob mentality. This factor was always unpredictable. He had to count on his own monumental reputation as a safeguard. According to Mulhall, "he might be outnumbered . . . but he didn't have any fear, because *once* he arrived at a scene, once they *saw* him, they had the respect—and the fear." Once the inevitable clarion call of "It's *Lugs!*" or "*Branigan's* here!" rang out, Mulhall never failed to see the crowd dispersing and scattering.

As Gerald Byrne likes to tell it, "everyone knew, you *don't mess* with him!" No-one wanted to confront him face to face; and no-one wanted him to show up at their bedside before dawn.

On the night of 16 October, when the riot squad showed up at the "Battle of Malahide," the usual scenario was played out as the riotous crowd began disbanding at the first sight of the van and Branigan, although additional guards did need to be called for assistance to completely clean up the disorder. A total of nineteen culprits were rounded up, to be charged with assault and disorderly conduct. The *Irish Independent* reported that there were many injuries, including "two youths taken to the Richmond Hospital suffering from head injuries from bottles."[14] Two days later it was announced that "a special report will be sent to the Department of Justice by the Gardaí" for consideration about how to handle such outrages.[15]

On 7 November, only three weeks after the Malahide debacle, there occurred what the *Sunday Press* called the "Clondalkin Battle." It was a near-replica of Malahide, when between fifty and a hundred gang members clashed at the Mayfair Ballroom around midnight. Apart from the usual flick-knives, razors, sharpened combs, and bottles, several brawlers wielded tomahawks. Even darts were used as missiles.[16] Only a few weeks before, Branigan had been called to a pub in the Richmond Hill area of Rathmines, where he found a 35-year-old man collapsed on the floor with a dart sticking out of his chest following an argument.

At the Mayfair the riot squad, a few other patrol cars and the Dog Unit halted the gang violence. Once again it was mainly the grim spectre of Branigan on the scene that sent the rioters scurrying for escape.

Two months later a new form of teenage vandalism was on the rise, making the job of the Gardaí all the more difficult. Packs of vandals called the "catapult gangs" by newspapers were roaming the city late at night, smashing the street lamps for the sport of it. The *Evening Herald* reported on 23 December that "vandals with catapults and stones have smashed *half* the street lamps in Dublin, over 12,000 were broken."[17] Night-time assaults and robberies were now easier to get away with, under the cover of darkness. It presented a real problem for guards on night patrol. For Branigan, it was another new headache.

_____

After Mickey Edmonds had been invited into the Garda station in the summer of 1964 he was quickly won over by all the smiles and warm gestures—along with generous offerings of biscuits, lemonade, and chocolate. As all the guards got to know him he counted them as new friends. But he always stuck closest to Branno and Bosco when they were around. They were slowly becoming his new family. Branigan, in his mid-fifties, was grandfatherly, while Muldoon, only twenty when they first met and fresh from his family's farm in Co. Offaly, still retained his youthful playful instincts. To Mickey he was like an older brother. The two guards were the perfect pair to come into Mickey's life. His mother, Annie, and the rest of the family lived just across the road and were grateful for all the kindness of the gardaí towards her son.

Gradually he was adopted by the Kevin Street gardaí. In the mess hall he was given tea and meals, his own plate, mug, and cutlery. He even had his own locker. He eventually became an "honorary member" of the Garda Síochána, with his own shoulder number, 300A.

Mickey idolised Branigan and Muldoon, tagging along fondly like a puppy. "Jim was *very* good with Mickey," says Muldoon. "That was his nature. Yeah, he put a lot into it." As he did himself. "I had a good way with kids, and I just befriended him and used to bring him out to my house, and we'd be playing ball."

_____

In 1965 another unexpected new friend entered Jim Branigan's life, one he welcomed with unabashed awe and enthusiasm. One day he was called into the superintendent's office and asked if he would be willing to take on a new short-term assignment. A very important one. It was felt that he was the perfect man to handle it. As it was explained to him, a Hollywood film was to be made on location in Dublin, in the Liberties in fact. It would take about a week to ten days. A guard would be needed to act as minder for one of the stars on the set. Would he be agreeable to taking on such a duty? Her name was Elizabeth Taylor.

Minding the most famous film star in Hollywood—also acclaimed at the time as the "most beautiful woman in the world"—was beyond his wildest dreams. He jumped at the offer—not only for personal reasons but because he wanted to make absolutely certain that she was safe while in Dublin.

She was not actually acting in this film, just accompanying her husband, Richard Burton, who was the principal star. The film was *The Spy Who Came In from the Cold,* based on John Le Carré's Cold War thriller. It also featured Claire Bloom, Oskar Werner, and Cyril Cusack. The segment was being shot in Malpas Street, not far from the Coombe. The cast were staying in the Gresham Hotel, and Elizabeth Taylor had brought along her four children. A caravan had been set up for her in a yard near the set for when the filming was under way. As Branigan saw his role, "I was her personal bodyguard. My job was to prevent autograph-hunters pestering Miss Taylor. I was to see that nobody caused them any trouble—I could keep them at bay."[18]

She was surprised, and possibly concerned, to see that he carried neither a firearm nor a baton. The Garda authorities assured her that he didn't need them.

They hit it off straight away. Within days they were friends. When needed, he was at her side; when inappropriate, he gave her privacy and kept his distance. He especially liked strolling around the streets with her and through St Stephen's Green. "She would frequently say, 'Come for a walk, Jimmy,' and we would go." Naturally, people were taken aback when they spotted them, and some indeed approached to greet her, or seek an autograph. Tactfully, he deterred them. "Liz was amazed that the Irish people were so obedient, because when I told people not to annoy Miss Taylor they would go away."[19] As it turned out, his biggest problem was spongers seeking money from her by trying to pass her notes or letters.

He befriended Burton as well, who, at the end of filming each day, often invited him to have a drink with him at the Gresham, and he would order a mineral. He found them both to be "extremely nice," unpretentious, and warm. As a parting memento she gave him an autographed photograph inscribed: "Jimmy, you are the greatest," which he always treasured.

Years later, on his retirement, as he was reminiscing about the experience, he commented that she was "one of the most beautiful women I ever saw." But then he added, "She was not my idea of a sex symbol." On which he did not elaborate. Clearly, to him she was a lady, not a pin-up.

———

For many readers of the *Evening Press,* the year 1966 began with something of a shock when they saw a headline on 17 January: "World's toughest cop dies."

An Irish policeman famed for his toughness, courage, fearlessness, and gang-busting. Long acclaimed by the press and public. A beloved figure. As they read a bit further they were relieved:

> Irish-born Johnny (John J.) Broderick, the "world's toughest cop," whose beat was on Broadway, and who shot it out with prohibition era gangsters died at his home in Middleton, New York at age 70.

The parallels between Broderick and Branigan were indeed striking. Both men patrolled their roughest districts at night, covered the most notorious dancehalls, bars, and hang-outs for thugs and criminals. Famously fearless, their fists were their primary weapon. Neither smoked nor drank. Both were immediately recognisable by sight and reputation, acting as a potent deterrent to crime in the streets.

Broderick, like Branigan, had become a legend in his own time. According to local lore, the New York policeman got his title "world's toughest cop" from tangling with the likes of the famous Jack "Legs" Diamond, one of New York's most dangerous gangsters. As the story goes, Broderick had been informed that Diamond was (ominously) "looking for him," which he clearly took as a threat. Like Branigan, he didn't take kindly to threats. So, he set out to catch up with Diamond instead. Finding him just off Broadway one night, he told the gangster-bootlegger straight to his face: "I understand you want to take me for a ride!" To which Legs replied somewhat sheepishly, "Listen, Johnny, can't you take a joke?" "*Not* from you!" he shot back at the gangster—then knocked him out with one punch.[20]

As did Branigan, he also served as minder-bodyguard for the most important public figures of his time, including the heavyweight boxing champion Jack Dempsey, who said of Broderick: "He's the only man I wouldn't want to meet in a fight outside the ring and its rules." In 1936 President Franklin Roosevelt requested him as his bodyguard when he attended the baseball world series in New York.

Branigan probably saw the article about Broderick's death in the newspapers; if by chance he missed it he was surely directed to it by friends. What he thought of it we can only surmise. Because of the strong connections, and even visits, between the New York and Dublin policemen over the years, the two men certainly knew of one another. The two legends may well have even met personally. If not, they *should* have.

———

In January the stabbings continued. On 16 January, in a completely unprovoked case, Peter Stafford was walking past Dollymount Park with his girl-friend when a number of youths encircled them, then stabbed him in the stomach.

Not long after, four youths attacked the occupants of a car, saying to them, "Do you want to be stabbed?" Next, an eighteen-year-old described by his mother as a "quiet boy who seldom goes out" was set upon by knife-wielding youths outside the Kingsway Ballroom in Granby Lane and stabbed in the face and back. There was no way that the Gardaí could protect people against such random crimes.

The problem of violence at dancehalls and chippers was increasing. This meant that the cruising range of the black van also had to be extended beyond the core of the city. Even when the dancehall staff barred hooligans they often hung around outside. "At dancehalls there was a *rough* element at that time," says Paddy Daly. "They'd get barred, and *then* they'd hang around outside . . . and rows would start up. Oh, a *lot* of rows at dancehalls . . ."

To remain an effective deterrent, Branigan had to take his squad to wherever trouble erupted, as John Murphy found out when he served with him:

> Jim *covered the city* in that van. So, if there was a row in Cabra, he was *out there.* Or one in Stillorgan. Or *wherever!* He had the manpower and the wherewithal. And when Branigan arrived in the van—*that's it!* They'd either break it up, or *he'd deal* with it!

"Branno 5" calls from headquarters were now routinely sending the squad out to dancehalls in Dún Laoghaire and Bray. They were running the wheels off the Bedford van, and breakdowns were becoming a problem.

In contrast to showing up at the large dancehalls, Branigan also tried to respond to calls for help from chippers, where often one man, or his family, were doing their best to run a small business and make a living. Tommy Lowry faced this problem in the mid-sixties. A lad of the Liberties himself, he had known Branigan since his childhood. Though he got off to a bad start in life by being sent to Artane for five years for mitching from school, Branigan gave him encouragement to follow a positive path in life. In the 1960s he was in his thirties and had set up a small but prosperous fish-and-chip shop at number 41 Pleasants Street, off Camden Street. He gave it the name "Romano's," because it sounded more exotic. It did brisk business at night, being close to the Olympic Ballroom. But proximity to the popular ballroom brought problems as well. "Fellas would come out of the dancehall, often 100 or 150 people outside the Olympic, and have drink, and cause me trouble." They would drift over to Romano's and begin messing and arguing, interfering with business and driving away customers. He finally resorted to asking for help from Branigan, who told him not to worry, that "he'd take care of it."

From the very next night the black van began to swing by, making its presence obvious as it paused outside the chipper, capturing everyone's attention. "Jim came around practically every night," recalls Lowry, "sometimes *twice* a night on weekends." When he caught a pack of rowdies raising a row or actually fighting, "Jim would grab a person and put them into the van." Before long the mere sight of the black van arriving had the troublemakers on the run. "And the next thing," says Lowry, "someone would say, 'Here's Branigan!' and they'd *all* scatter. That was it. Oh, they'd all be gone." Romano's became known as a chipper where hooliganism wasn't allowed, and business returned to normal. For ever after, Tommy Lowry felt indebted to Branigan.

When John Collins served beside Branno on the riot squad they were often called to a chipper late at night after crowds had been drinking. He likes to tell of one amusing incident when they were summoned to a little chipper in Parnell Street where there was a minor hassle of some sort. The guards climbed out of the van and calmly walked in to see what the problem was. Collins was standing behind Branigan as he was asking a few questions. Then, "one guy was getting a bit obstreperous, and your man was English, and he asked Jim for his identification," having no idea who the plain-clothes Branigan was. Branigan decided to have a little fun. "So he reached in his pocket and pulled out a photograph of this country-and-western singer named Slim Whitman," and held it before the man's face as his identification. "With that, John Reardon [another guard] and myself nearly fell around the place laughing." The befuddled man ran out the door and up Hill Street, where he was nabbed.

From boyhood, Branigan was known for his sense of humour and for his love of pulling pranks. As leader of the riot squad he enjoyed joking with his men. It relieved pressure and passed the night hours more lightly. It was only natural that during some of the long hours of an uneventful night, usually a Monday, Tuesday, or Wednesday, squad members fell into some conversation about their personal lives—the usual talk of family, wives, girl-friends, in-laws, money matters. Because of their close camaraderie, they tried to help each other out with problems or dilemmas. Such sharing could be therapeutic. Sergeant Branigan was about twice the average age of his squad and was clearly perceived as a strong father figure to many. He was also a patient, practised listener, who dispensed wise advice. Rumbling along in the black van in the darkest hours of night, he often provided helpful counsel to his younger colleagues. It was, in fact, one of the benefits of serving in his squad. But Branigan never pried into his men's personal affairs. Furthermore, as Séamus Quinn remembers, while he was always glad to listen to his men's problems and help them out, "I drove for Jim for almost three years, but he *never* spoke of personal problems, his family, etc." Perhaps he had no such problems.

———

One thing everybody knew about Jim Branigan was that he despised prejudice and discrimination in any form; and he wouldn't tolerate discriminatory treatment by others. In the 1960s Dublin was experiencing a trickle of foreigners coming in for purposes of work, education, or settlement. The most conspicuous group were black people from various African countries, and some from Britain. Many were seeking higher education in the universities. Unfortunately, it didn't take long for prejudice to raise its ugly head. Branigan was witnessing this more often; and he didn't like it one bit. He saw black people cursed at, spat on, physically mistreated. He knew that all foreigners were highly vulnerable.

One night in the mid-1960s Matt Mulhall was on duty with the riot squad when they were called to Jervis Street Hospital, where the staff were having trouble with a recalcitrant bowsie. Upon arrival, Mulhall went inside with Branigan to see what the problem was. Immediately they both recognised the man as a particularly despicable lout. Mulhall describes what happened next:

> When we arrived he was a casualty and needed to be stitched. He had a gash on his head. And the doctor who was going to do the sutures was coloured. So, this fella was causing *absolute mayhem!* And this lad said, "No *black bastard* is going to sew me!" That was his attitude. So Jim turns to the doctor and says, "Are you ready to sew?" And he says, "Yes." So we put your man up on the table, and Jim says, "Now, doc, we'll hold him, you sew him." And he sewed him up.
>
> Now that's only part of the story!
>
> So the doctor says to this lad, "You can go now." And so he hops down and goes up to Branigan's face, *straight up to him!* Like he was going to kill him, or whatnot. And I saw Jim turn sideways. And I said to myself, *Look out!* 'Cause that's the way he operated: he turned sideways to you, and he had a short punch. Oh, once Jim turned sideways to you, *look out!*
>
> And he *hit* him and *drove* him down on the floor. He was sliding along the floor. And *out through* these doors, 'cause *coming in* through these two swinging doors were Dublin Fire Brigade men bringing in a fella on a stretcher. And this lad went *swish!* right out the doors—*straight* out the doors.

Branigan had dealt with this thug before. "We *knew* him, a hardened criminal, in his thirties, who gets a few jars on him and takes on the world." He was hauled out to the van and driven to his block of flats, where he was told to get out. "He had quieted down and that was it—end of story."

——

One fine day in March 1966, Jim, Elsie, Alick and Alick's wife, Anne, climbed into the car for a trip to the convent orphanage in Blackrock. There was an air of excitement and anticipation among the four. It was to be a big day in their lives: for on the way back home there would be five in the car.

As they approached the large building and rang the bell, all felt a slight nervousness. A nun greeted them and escorted them into the hallway. They cast a silent smile at one another as they followed the nun down the corridor. Alick knew the moment was near:

> We were brought into this very big room with cots down both sides of it, with some babies in them, and directed down a bit further to where about a dozen beautifully dressed children were playing on the floor. One was pointed out to my mother and father, and the nun said, "There's your Denise."

The cherubic eleven-month-old child was lifted gently up and held close to her new parents. Tough Lugs Branigan beamed with delight. "Father and Mother doted on her from day one," says Alick. At the age of fifty-six, Branigan had a mature appreciation of fatherhood. The instant joy the infant brought to all the family was palpable. They all adopted her equally. Branigan's off-duty hours at home became more precious than ever.

———

Meanwhile at Kevin Street Garda Station, by 1967 young Mickey Edmonds had become "part of the furniture." After three years, Branigan was still his mentor and friend, as was Bosco Muldoon. Branigan concentrated on language with Mickey, convinced he could help him with learning to speak. And now he was making real progress. Branno had the patience to slowly teach Mickey words and their pronunciation, coaxing him to try to enunciate them. He worked regularly on his verbal skills at a sensible pace, heaping encouragement on him at every step. As he learnt to communicate on a basic level with those in the station, it was realised that Mickey possessed some astounding mental skills. As Tony Ruane explains, "he was intellectually challenged—but Mickey knew every key and combination in the complex, and phone numbers poured out of him on request, like a mobile directory." His memory astounded everyone.

His mother and family were thrilled. However, it eventually became evident that Mickey was picking up some lingo at the station that was not part of Branigan's lessons. His mother found that sometimes when Mickey was in bad humour or frustrated he would push his elbow against the wall and start saying things like "fuhin eejay!" At first she couldn't decipher it; finally she did. Though on occasion she would have to deny it, especially when a very religious neighbour would visit her and ask what it was Mickey was saying. She would nonchalantly reply, "Oh, I've no idea."

————

In the early months of 1967 there was a fresh spate of youth rioting and violence around the city. In a single night there was an outburst of hooliganism from O'Connell Street and Merrion Square to Ballyfermot. Trying to douse all the flare-ups was running the riot squad ragged. In O'Connell Street a mob of youths taunted guards with shouts of "Gestapo bastards!" and threw stones at them. A total of seventeen arrests were made.

Shortly afterwards there occurred a truly savage attack in the Metropole Ballroom in O'Connell Street, right out on the dance floor. It resulted when one patron politely asked another not to bump into him. In retaliation, "two brothers jumped on him, pushing him down the stairs, kicked him and tried to strangle him," after which one of the attackers actually "bit two fingers off his right hand." In court, Judge Molony declared: "Man is descending to the primitive. First we had kicking and now it is *biting*. These two were like wolves seeking whom they could bite."[21]

In April 1967 the riot squad was called to St Anthony's Hall for the umpteenth time. Branigan arrived with Garda Sheehan and Garda Wilcox. The three entered the hall to face a shower of bottles and other missiles as people cowered beneath tables for protection. He grabbed the usual brawlers, all aged between nineteen and twenty-one, and jammed them into the van, to be charged with riotous conduct. This time, in consultation with Branigan, Judge Molony decided to revoke the hall's dancehall licence. This was meant also as a message to other dancehalls that he was fed up with the repeated mayhem and violence at the clubs.

On the night of 14/15 April, Dublin experienced what the *Sunday Press* called a "night of terror." The violence occurred between the hours of eleven and one—but the fear lasted far longer.

It was a balmy spring night, the streets alive with entertainment-goers who had been to the city's cinemas, theatres, dancehalls, and restaurants. Out on the prowl was a pack of youths, roaming the streets in search of prey to attack. According to newspaper reports, during the night of terror the gang went on a two-hour rampage of stabbing and slashing, from Kevin Street to Harold's Cross and Rathmines.[22] They used flick-knives, sharpened steel combs, and even a "steel-tipped umbrella with which they stabbed one person in the throat."[23] By the end of their stabbing spree they had wounded a total of eight people, five of them unconscious and lying in a pool of blood on the pavement. After their string of violent acts the "teenage attackers went to ground very quickly."

The next day every paper carried the horrific story. People were fearful of going out at night. Even in well-lit O'Connell Street, filmgoers who ventured out to see the popular *Doctor Zhivago* at the Metropole quickly headed home. The term "pack of wolves" used in newspapers was especially unnerving.

Branigan immediately made the case his priority. One newspaper assured its readers that Sergeant Branigan and his men had "searched a wide area for the culprits," in his typical unrelenting manner. As a peerless street detective, he knew the right people to interrogate about such a crime, and he quickly got the information he was seeking. Tips were leading him to St Teresa's Gardens, where by now he knew every troublemaker well. While there was a general Garda search throughout the city for the slashers, people were confident that Branigan and his squad would track them down before long.

On 17 April the *Evening Herald* published an editorial headed "Crime in the streets," which contended that, because of the "new, menacing arrival of knife-wielding gangs . . . the life and limb of the ordinary citizen is thus placed in danger." The paper argued that "society must be protected and crime punished." Somehow. One letter-writer expressed his belief that there now existed a continuous "reign of terror ruling Dublin," while another wrote to say that "the police are doing a very fine job in bringing these thugs to book—but they are not getting any help from the courts."

By the end of the day, scarcely seventy-two hours after the crime spree, Branigan and his team had identified the gang and had arrested three of the youths and taken them into custody. Two were seventeen-year-olds from St Teresa's Gardens, the other an eighteen-year-old from nearby Lourdes Road. They were charged with taking part in an affray with intent to maim, disfigure and disable their victims, "having maliciously wounded and caused grievous bodily harm" to them.

Branigan told Judge Molony he needed a little more time to round up the others. He asked for the three youths to be remanded in custody, explaining that if the defendants were granted bail they could interfere with his enquiries about the others. His request was granted.

On the 20th he was back in court to inform Judge Molony that he now had all five attackers, aged between seventeen and nineteen, under arrest, with solid evidence against them. He also informed the judge that all eight of their victims were progressing well after their stabbings, and glad to be alive. One of them, he said, "got over twenty stitches in his face and will be marked for life." He thought the judge should know this. Judge Molony agreed. Branigan and his squad received commendations from the court, press and public for their superb job in ending the reign of terror so quickly.

For their part, more judges were pledging to get tough as well. Only a few weeks after the April episode a similar band of youthful miscreants was hauled into court before Judge Lanigan-O'Keefe. He said he was "horrified by the boy-gangsters" brought before him. One youth's father made a plea to the judge to give his son a chance to escape punishment by joining the British army—a ploy that sometimes worked in the courts. He informed the judge that he already had the necessary application papers; to which the judge retorted sharply: "I would not disgrace Ireland by sending a boy like that to the British army. The *French Foreign Legion* is the place for him—if they would take him!"[24]

———

During the summer of 1967 there were "Branno 5" calls for the usual skirmishes at carnivals and circuses. Ringsend was particularly notorious for serious clashes between the carnival crews and local men, especially dockers. Val Lynn recalls one night when they arrived at Ringsend to face a powder keg about to explode.

A huge circus was being held, and some of the roustabouts had been accused by local people of making improper advances towards the daughter or wife of a local man. When Branno and his men arrived they confronted a situation in which both sides were armed and in a fury. Lynn was told to position himself close to Branigan:

> It was like *Dunkirk!* Those dockers had picks and hooks, and they wanted to *get* the circus fellas that interfered [with their women]. What Branigan wanted to do was to *separate* them, to get the dockers *out* and the circus crowd back in.

The dockers were always easier to handle, as they instantly recognised Branigan, and respected him, and were prepared to follow his orders. The men running the circus could be unpredictable, especially when drinking. On this night, as the riot squad tried to drive a wedge between the two groups, one man obstinately stood his ground. He was the leader of the circus crew, and they followed his lead. Immediately he became Branigan's target, as Lynn stood close by and watched:

> This one circus fella, he was *huge*. He was the "strong man" in the circus. *Way bigger* than Branigan himself. Branigan standing in front of him looked *small*.
>
> So Branigan was *trying* to get him in, but he was moving nowhere. So, Jim was standing in front of him, *very* close, nearly breathing into his mouth—and he was making up his mind what he was going to do with him. And the *next* thing—at the *last* moment—didn't Branigan give him this *two-handed push*, this great *heave* into his chest—and knocked him

down. Because your man had his two feet *together,* and Jim caught him when his balance was off—and flattened him down. And he fell, and he shook the ground around him! *Down* on his back. And that was rough ground, with stones and all.

Now, I was right behind Jim, so if he needed anything I was in the right position. But Branigan had *absolutely* no fear in him! And any resistance that man had in him was gone when he got up. He went back where he was told. Oh, I had respect for him!

All the men who served with Branigan over his 43-year career felt exactly the same, especially members of the riot squad. He knew how to handle anyone, from a brash lad to a circus strong man, both physically and psychologically.

As Dan Walsh says of his years in the squad with Branno and Sonny Heany, "I was never in a situation with him that I was nervous . . . in any confrontation. *Never.* He was *in control!* You never had a moment with him when you felt, Is this going to get out of hand?"

To Paddy Daly it was his presence and leadership that made the riot squad what it was. "Never saw him sick. If he had been sick it would never have been the same—because, I mean, he *was* the van! He was the *man!*"

––––

That didn't make him infallible. He made mistakes: bad decisions, snap judgements, inappropriate acts of "summary justice." He acknowledged this, never claimed to be perfect, and didn't hesitate to apologise.

Nor did everyone like him. "There were people who didn't like him," vouches Matthew Fagan. "Yeah, because he lived by his own law. A lot of times he wouldn't arrest people, he'd just give them a couple of digs." Critics accused him of sometimes being "too quick on the trigger" in doling out his street justice. It could be an injustice if he got things wrong. Reacting too hastily could lead to an innocent person receiving a glove lash or sharp clip. It did happen. As Noel Hughes says, "many men he gave a hiding to, and many teenagers, were left black and blue—for perhaps no real reason." In some such cases the person may have spoken disrespectfully to Branigan, or refused to follow his orders.

It was well known that when Branigan gave an order to "move on," "go home," "stop fighting," or whatever, he expected instant compliance. No exceptions, no excuses. Which sometimes meant not allowing time for legitimate explanations. He had absolutely no tolerance for any cheekiness or hint of disrespect, in word or gesture. "He had his own tactics with his gloves," says Dan Walsh. "If a youngster might be inclined to give him a bit of cheek Jim'd give them a slap with his gloves."

Billy Byrne recounts the time as a youth when he and a pal were simply standing on the pavement next to his friend's house when Branigan came along and told them to move on. "But my best friend, he *lived there*," and he tried to tell this to Branigan. "And without another word, he got the gloves across the face—if you *answered back*, you got the gloves. And a big swelling came out of my friend's face."

One night in the mid-sixties Michael Eivers "saw him in action," as he puts it. He was standing in a queue outside a club at Burgh Quay waiting to get inside. "There was a fight between the bouncers and three or four fellas. Then a van pulls up, and he was unmistakable." Spotting Lugs, the troublemakers darted back into the queue and tried to hide. After consulting the bouncers to get descriptions, he began walking along the queue, like an executioner picking out the victims. Then he halted. "I heard one of the guys say, *'Please* don't hit me, Mr Branigan!' And with that, *boom!*—into his solar plexus. And into the back of the van he took two or three." Hopefully the right ones.

Mick Gillis likes to tell of the time his belt was confiscated by Branigan, utterly without any good reason. It occurred in the 1960s, when youth gangs were using heavy belts with huge metal buckles as weapons. One lad had recently lost an eye to such a belt. On this summer night Mick and a friend were standing on the bridge in Dolphin's Barn watching youngsters playing in the canal below. All of a sudden the riot squad pulled up and frisked them. "Then he took our belts off us. He thought it was a weapon. And took our belts away." No recourse, no reimbursement.

Las Fallon, a Dublin fireman, cites a classic case of mistaken identity and unjustified punishment. The experience happened to "a friend of mine who fell foul of him and got a thumping before he convinced Lugs of his innocence." His friend worked for a jeweller, fixing broken necklaces, bracelets, and the like. One evening he went to visit his sister, who had gathered some broken jewellery items from her friends to be repaired. As he was leaving for home he stuffed the jewellery into his pocket and began his walk across town. It was late at night. Along came the black van. "Lugs and his crew pulled him over and searched him. When they found the jewellery he got a few belts to encourage him to confess." When these interrogation tactics failed to produce a confession they took him to his sister's house to verify his story. She confirmed his account. "Then they threw him out of the van to continue his journey home—no police complaints board in those days!" Whether or not Branigan apologised in this case is not known.

Women were not immune from his summary justice. Matt Mulhall cites an occasion when he saw a woman receive a mild lesson in manners from Sergeant Branigan. Like all gardaí, he knew that women under the influence of drink could be threatening and quite violent. And he carried many lifelong scars to prove it. In a riotous situation the shrieking of a woman could incite others to action. And some women had a special talent for taunting guards right before their face. Sometimes their wild behaviour had to be defused before control could be restored, as Mulhall experienced:

> This one girl was part of the rioting. And she *really* got under his skin! She was belligerent, and she came up and remonstrated with him. So he just gave her a slap—and that was it! And he took her away. I don't know if he charged her. He probably talked to her when he got her to the station . . . His attitude would probably have changed completely.

The purpose of the slap was to startle and quiet her, to help quell the emotions of those around her. And it could sometimes be the only defence against violent kicking. Some of the worst gashes on his shins and legs were from women's pointed heels, which penetrated like daggers. Many a guard was sent to hospital for treatment from injuries caused by a woman's kicking.

Branigan was known to apologise when he erred. His riot squad all vouch that, in reality, he used his methods of "summary justice" sparingly, considering what he was up against. As Mulhall verifies, "he'd *only* hit you when you *needed* it—if you were a threat to him," or to others around him. Over his years spent with Branno he regards his use of measured force as perfectly appropriate, justified—for the times—and highly effective. As did Garda Headquarters, and the courts, for he was never reprimanded or asked to change his methods.

While there were those who alleged that Branigan had been too harsh with them, there were many more who came to appreciate in later life his stern treatment. Still around the Liberties are scores of older men who today credit Lugs with teaching them the lesson they needed at the time and putting them on the right path in life. For it kept them out of Artane, and prison, later on.

Then there were the fellas who wore a lash or clip from the famous Lugs Branigan as a badge of distinction, to be bragged about. "See, some fellas used to *love* being able to say that 'Branigan hit me'," attests Muldoon. "Oh, they'd *boast* the next day . . . go around telling their mates, 'Last night I got a *belt* from Branigan!'"

As the author found in 2012, there were still a good few old-timers around the inner city who relished telling their tale of how the legendary Lugs Branigan once gave them a good whack, for their own good. How it helped them to "grow up" fast. Without a hint of recrimination. It's fascinating to listen to them today, sixty or seventy years later, speaking of him as friend, mentor, father figure. Some even with tears during the telling.

———

In January 1970 Garda Jim Branigan turned sixty, an "older man" by the standards of the time. Still the leader of the riot squad, he remained fit, energetic, and enthusiastic—yet, inevitably, showing his age in subtle ways.

For a man born in 1910 it was an altogether new age, a different society—new types of crime and criminals. He had dealt with the "animal gangs," Teddy Boys, flick-knife gangs and other "villains" over the decades. But in the 1970s gardaí were facing dangerous new criminal elements: drug-dealers, professional thieves, criminal families. And with guns. Special units were being trained and assigned to cope with the new crimes. Including murder, which was becoming shockingly more common in Dublin. Some guards were now themselves armed. Branno still declined to carry even a baton.

His job essentially remained the same, cruising nightly with the riot squad to combat thuggery and violence in the street, in dancehalls and other public places. He had recently heard on the news about some problems in Britain caused by new subcultures called "mods," "rockers," and "greasers." From what he saw of them on television they appeared to be simply a new form of the generic hooligans and thugs he had known. They merely had different names, looks, dress, lingo.

Some of the articles about them in the newspapers were worrisome. According to one story a planeload of police had to be flown from London to Hastings in Sussex to deal with a wild battle between mods and rockers. Mods were scooter-riders, wearing suits and clean-cut outfits, while rockers wore leather jackets and rode large motorcycles, like Brando. The two groups fought mostly with flick-knives and chains.

Branigan didn't like their sort, didn't want them on the streets of Dublin. Or anywhere else in Ireland. But he knew that some were sure to show up somewhere. Sure enough, in the summer of 1970 a scattering of English mods and rockers appeared in Bray, fighting and distressing local people and visitors. Paddy Daly recalls "Branno 5" calls despatching the riot squad to the seaside resort:

> Now, out in Bray with the mods and rockers, rows broke out—and Branigan would be called out there and was very much involved. See, they'd come over in the summer, and that'd hurt Bray as a holiday resort.

To Branno they were more like "pups" than real toughs. The young English youths learnt very quickly about Lugs Branigan, Sonny Heany and the black van and created no major problems. And they spread the word back home.

Skinheads and greasers posed a more serious threat. The two cultures originated in working-class London society and were prone to very violent fighting. Skinheads were quite menacing-looking, with shaved heads, jeans, braces, and heavy army or work boots. When the Irish versions first appeared in some Dublin streets they looked "battle-ready" as they marched along with hostile expressions. They always seemed to be looking for trouble.

Greasers, also called "long-hairs," had their hair long and greased back, with a pompadour or "duck's arse" style. They too liked motorcycles and boots, denim jackets and "rockabilly" music and carried stiletto flick-knives. When the rival groups began appearing in some Dublin streets Branigan kept a close eye on them. They all acted tough, but he knew they were phonies. A swat with his gloves could bring tears to some.

There were, however, some newsworthy clashes between the skinheads and greasers that drew the public's attention. On 28 March 1970 a bloody battle broke out between two groups, with thirty to forty combatants, about evenly divided, at a camping ground just outside Dublin. Using the usual knives, belts, steel combs, and a car jack, they fought furiously. One of them remarked when he was hauled into a Garda station: "We should have carved them up!" In court, Judge Lanigan-O'Keefe was disturbed by the primitiveness of their violence, commenting that "something must have influenced them to behave as they did . . . They went berserk, some were frothing at the mouth. Drugs may have been involved."[25]

Branigan was now seeing evidence of drug use in Dublin. It greatly distressed him. While he felt great sympathy for those afflicted by addiction, as well as their families, he was at a loss to know how best to handle them. And he hated the drug-dealers. He wasn't an expert on drugs; it was best that he was finishing his career as drugs were becoming more prevalent.

Skinheads gave him more trouble than any other group. They were vicious and aggressive, always ready to brawl. The riot squad was now getting regular calls from the Castle to rush over to Club-a-Go-Go in Abbey Street, which was a favourite hangout of the skinheads and greasers. These fights then often spilled over during the night to chippers, where they met again. One night, reported the *Irish Press*, "a gang of Skinheads went on a rampage in the city centre breaking shop windows, doing other damage and generally running wild."[26]

For the most part, these new trouble-making youths presented a minor problem for Branigan and his riot squad. A far more serious and pervasive problem during the late sixties and into the seventies was that of violence and vandalism on buses, upon which the Dublin public critically depended. It had persisted for years, finally reaching the point where busmen pleaded for Branigan's help to quash it once and for all. His role in personally confronting this crisis would constitute a memorable chapter in his legendary career.

Chapter 12 ↪

BRANNO AND THE "BUS WARS"

"On the Ballyfermot bus war front, the last bus was shadowed to the terminus by police under Garda James C. Branigan."

(*Sunday Independent*, 1 MARCH 1970)

"It is disgraceful that people cannot travel on the late night buses because of these rowdies . . . They might pull knives, it is dangerous."

(Letter to *Evening Press*, 6 JANUARY 1973)

"Hatchets in Howth bus riot: Five held."

(Headline, *Sunday Independent*, 24 OCTOBER 1965)

"The drivers and conductors, they'd call for Branigan. And he'd sort it out on the bus—he commanded it!"

(GARDA DAN WALSH)

In the halcyon days of bus and tram transport, drivers and conductors, in their immaculate uniforms with peaked caps and brass buttons, enjoyed a status of respect akin to that of a ship's captain.

William Condon, born in 1898, can vouch for it. Having served in the British army during the First World War, he got a job as a tram-driver with the old Dublin United Tramways Company. Reflecting back at the age of ninety-five, he asserts they were "all respectable men—and you had to have a clear character." This had to be verified by a letter from his parish priest and a policeman in his district. It was a coveted job, with great responsibility and much satisfaction.

29. Crowd sprinkled with Teddy Boys outside the Gaiety Cinema in Manchester, waiting to see *Rock Around the Clock*. When the film hit Dublin, "all hell broke loose." (© *REX/Associated Newspapers*)

30. Teddy Boys in their Edwardian attire proudly strutted the streets like peacocks. (© *Popperfoto/ Getty Images*)

31. Gangs of tough Teddy Boys began carrying flick-knives and other weapons, a menace to the public. (© *Trinity Mirror/Mirrorpix/Alamy*)

32. Garda Jim Branigan was assigned as minder for the British rock-and-roll idol Cliff Richard. (*Courtesy of Garda Paul Maher*)

33. The notorious Teddy Boys of the 1950s and early 60s with their flick-knives and other weapons caused fear among citizens.

34. In his forties and fifties Branigan weighed nearly 17 stone, worked out rigorously at the National Stadium, and was as fit and strong as gardaí twenty years younger.
(*Courtesy of Paddy Daly*)

35. A wave of savage knife attacks during the 1960s terrified Dubliners.

36. In August 1964 "Branno's" famous riot squad was established to fight crime around the city. (*Courtesy of Garda Paul Maher*)

37. The riot squad had to contend with the most violent rows and riots in the streets, dancehalls, cinemas, and pubs, taking on the toughest hoodlums and thugs in Dublin.

38. Daughter Helen's ordination, 1965. *Front row:* Branigan, Helen, and Father Clarence (Garda chaplain). *Back row:* Declan, Elsie, and Alick. (*Courtesy of Alick Branigan*)

39. With Cochise, one of his two alsatians, c. mid-1960s. The other was Geronimo—both named after famous American Indian chiefs. (*Courtesy of Alick Branigan*)

40. By the 1960s, Garda Jim Branigan was regularly capturing newspaper headlines, as his reputation grew.

41. Alick's wedding, 1970. *Front to back*: Denise, Declan (*left*), Anne, Alick, Helen, Elsie, Jim. (*Courtesy of Alick Branigan*)

42. Jim and daughter Helen at Alick's wedding, 1970. (*Courtesy of Alick Branigan*)

43. During the late 1960s and early 70s, Dublin's buses were under siege by violent teenage gangs. Branigan led the attack against them in what newspapers called the "bus wars."

44. Branigan (*left*) and two members of the riot squad in a patrol car trailing a bus troubled by young hoodlums, 1970. (*Courtesy of Garda Paul Maher*)

45. Branigan as bodyguard for the Manchester United football star George Best, c. 1970s. (*Courtesy of Alick Branigan*)

46. At home in his aviary with beloved budgies, a favourite hobby. (*Courtesy of Alick Branigan*)

47. Branigan served as a boxing referee for nearly forty years, earning a reputation for his fairness. (*Courtesy of Dave Whittaker*)

48. Displaying some of the weapons confiscated from gangs and thugs, from his massive collection. (*Courtesy of Alick Branigan*)

49. Leaving the courts on his final day as a garda, January 1973. Newspapers described him as "sullen." (*Courtesy of Garda Paul Maher*)

50. Retirement party, October 1973. *Left to right:* Helen, Garda official, Elsie, Declan, Branigan, Alick, Denise. (*Courtesy of Alick Branigan*)

51. Showing off his retirement gifts and farewell card from his "pavement hostesses," 1973. (*Courtesy of Garda Paul Maher*)

52. In retirement, 1982, enjoying fun with Alick's children. (*Courtesy of Alick Branigan*)

53. Reminiscing with a scrapbook covering his life from the early 1930s. (*Courtesy of Garda Paul Maher*)

Tough cop 'Lugs' dies at 76

Det. Sgt. Branrigan direct tactics

DUBLIN's toughest cop, Jim 'Lugs' Brannigan, died last night at the Adelaide Hospital.

The 76-year-old former garda sergeant became famous for his unique method of dealing with the tougher elements of Dublin's criminal underground.

Rough and instant justice sorted out many a young man who would otherwise have gone further astray.

By
ANNETTE BLACKWELL

Sgt. Brannigan made his name in the 1930s when he tackled the Teddyboy gangs in the city.

He joined the force in 1933 and in 1936 he was assigned to Kevin Street, where he later became head of the riot squad.

It wasn't just on the streets that Jim Brannigan earned his nick name Battler Brannigan. He was associated with the successful Garda boxing teams in the 30s and 40s, and continued his boxing career as a referee.

The funeral to Mount Argus Church takes place tomorrow at 5.30 and on Saturday he will be buried after 11 a.m. Mass in the cemetery at Summerhill, Co. Meath.

54. Newspaper obituaries for the first time referred to "Lugs" Branigan in print.

55. Mickey Edmonds at Branigan's grave site, 1985. (*Courtesy of Tony Ruane*)

56. Photograph and plaque of Garda Jim Branigan in the lobby of Whitefriars' Street Church, Dublin.

About 1930 he made the switch to bus-driving. At first he drove a Leyland single-deck bus but soon took the controls of a double-decker. Drivers and conductors had a close relationship, because, as he puts it, "you pulled together . . . and you could work together for your lifetime." They were a team. "Conductors were very popular with the passengers, and they'd have their little chat and joke." It was an age of formal politeness and civility. "Oh, the *politeness!* People were different in those days." Children and adolescents were respectful and obedient; if not they could expect a sharp yank on their ear or smack on the head from a disapproving adult.

Hugh Maguire also loved his job. Starting out in the 1930s as a ticket-taker on trams at Nelson's Pillar, he graduated to bus conductor in the early 1940s. His job was important back then, he explains, as very few people owned a car, and "buses were *essential.*" There was a dignity attached to his work that made him proud of his position, and he enjoyed *"great* respect" from passengers, many of whom he saw every day. When he was working on the Clontarf bus on Sunday mornings a woman would "come out for the bus crew with tea in a can and some sausages and bread." For William Condon and Hugh Maguire and their brethren there was no better job. Maguire enthuses: "I'm *delighted* that I was alive at that time and a bus conductor."

Jim Branigan of James's Street grew up in the same early era of buses and trams. As he didn't drive a car, he was as dependent on such transport as most other Dubliners. As a consequence, he had an especially high respect for the drivers and conductors. When the age of good manners on public transport began to decline, and drivers and conductors began to be mistreated, he took the offence personally.

During the 1940s, Hugh Maguire recalls, politeness on his bus still prevailed. It was during the 1950s—the "youth rebellion"—that the rot set in. It was a decade of economic hardship, unemployment, heavy drinking, discontent. Old inner-city communities were being destroyed as tenement houses were bulldozed, their residents uprooted and transplanted to sterile, soulless housing estates outside the city. Traditional society was in flux, and people felt unsettled and estranged. Many old customs and traditions were vanishing, among them courtesy and simple politeness in public.

Hugh Maguire and his fellow-busmen first noticed it in the creeping rudeness, even aggressiveness, of some passengers, and in a selfish attitude and lack of respect for others around them. Coarse language began to be heard in public. While Condon, Maguire and their peers may not have comprehended the larger social ramifications of the changes they witnessed, it certainly made their daily job less pleasant. A new disrespect was most evident among youths. In earlier years the most a conductor had to worry about was a snowball thrown while he was standing on the platform, or reckless lads trying to "scut" the bus. Innocent pranks. But times were changing.

Inner-city families uprooted from the city felt stranded out in their barrack-like estates. Planners had provided for few, if any, amenities for residents, whether shops, pubs, cinemas, recreation centres, sports facilities, banks, post offices, or meeting halls. Young people especially felt isolated, bored, and frustrated. Their only escape was to cram into the buses taking them back to the bright lights and amenities of Dublin, particularly at weekends.

And thus began the trouble. Restless teenagers with pent-up energy and frustration boarded weekend buses in mobs, bent on fun and often hell-raising. Part of their "youth rebellion," inspired in part by rock-and-roll music, was to establish their own identity and behave in an uninhibited manner. They were most rebellious when fuelled by drink. Before long it was common for throngs of teenagers, many having been drinking, to barge onto a bus, shoving, shouting, cursing, rude and threatening to anyone in their way. It was the beginning of the busmen's nightmare. Their late-night journeys home on Saturdays became "hell night" for bus crews.

The aggressive youths had been out to dancehalls, pubs, cinemas, entertainment arcades. Many were drunk and prone to trouble-making and fighting. Some travelled in actual gangs. They always bolted for the top of the double-decker bus and took over as if they were an invasion force. Decent passengers shuddered. It would grow worse year by year.

————

Buses and busmen were not very newsworthy, except for the occasional bus strike or traffic accident. Every now and then a guard would be called to remove an obstreperous passenger, usually under the influence of alcohol. Or a row between two ruffians.

One of Garda Branigan's first publicised bus cases actually made the front page of the *Evening Herald,* under the curious heading "Man sank teeth into brother's arm." It occurred on a Saturday night in April 1956 on a crammed late-night bus travelling along Cork Street when the conductor, Michael Connolly, approached two brothers, both drunk, to ask for their fare. At first both brothers feigned sleep. When Connolly persisted, one brother paid up; the other, however, a strong 29-year-old labourer, grabbed the conductor by his jacket and threatened to beat him up. Connolly then "ran upstairs and rang the emergency bell, and a guard had to be summoned."[1]

Garda Branigan and Garda Culloty from Kevin Street station arrived shortly and found the two brothers sitting stubbornly in the long seat of the stationary bus. When Branigan ordered them to get out of the bus and into the patrol car, one obeyed without demur, but his belligerent brother "gripped the rail of the stairs and the boarding rail." Because of his vice-lock on the rails and the awkwardness of the position, it took considerable force by Branigan to pry him loose and haul him off the bus. Dragged to the patrol car, he again gripped the door and the roof, and only Branigan could finally "drag him inside the car." Once inside "he became more violent and tried to butt Garda Culloty with his head." On the way to the station, bodies became entangled as the two guards struggled to restrain the writhing, kicking man. Branigan described what happened next:

> While in the car, J. Maguire saw an arm which he took to be *mine*—and sank his teeth in it! He continued to hold the arm in his teeth until we arrived at the Garda station, where he *then* discovered that it was the arm of *his brother* that he had in his teeth![2]

When the newspaper reporter got wind of the bizarre incident, he knew he had another colourful "Branigan episode" for readers.

During the rock-and-roll craze of the later fifties and the appearance of the troublesome Teddy Boys, teenage passengers grew more cheeky and disrespectful towards bus crews. Sometimes they mocked and jeered the men in uniform, and even verbally abused them. They treated the passengers with similar disdain.

Gradually, CIE and the crews realised they were losing control of the situation. People began dreading late-night travel on buses, with Saturday by far the most frightening.

In January 1963 a serious incident of a different sort occurred on a number 35 bus as it was travelling through Glasnevin. Passengers were startled when shots rang out and windows on the bus were suddenly shattered. A few days later a bus travelling along Harcourt Street was struck by what appeared to have been .22 calibre bullets, as several windows were smashed.

A more alarming incident happened on the night of 22 January when two schoolgirls, Maureen Larkin and Susan Carr, missed serious, possibly fatal injury "by about two inches," estimated the *Evening Herald*, as they travelled on a number 19 bus through Glasnevin.[3] They were sitting in the front of the bus when the window just in front of them was splintered by bullets, again of .22 calibre. Then, "almost instantly," the window just behind them was also shattered. Of the eleven people upstairs on the bus, all luckily escaped injury. The conductor, 29-year-old Leo Eustace, was shaken by the attack, immediately calling the Gardaí and showing them the evidence.

Newspapers wrote about the "mystery gunman" preying on buses, creating widespread public fear. From reading the stories it seemed that passengers were sitting ducks for some madman. Drivers and conductors who *had* to go to work knew they were easy targets. Gardaí were put on full alert.

In July a bus strike paralysed the city's transport for weeks. Hordes of citizens resorted to bicycles or thumbing lifts. It created what the *Irish Independent* called "an outsize problem for Garda pointmen . . . as every available Garda was on duty."[4] Eighty army lorries were called out to help haul citizens around Dublin. Branigan suffered the inconvenience like everyone else, though he didn't mind walking into town from Drimnagh Road when necessary. Fortunately, he often got a lift from a patrol car.

To exacerbate matters, in September the newspapers reported that a "maniac stabber" was preying on passengers waiting at bus stops. One young woman, Olive Woolmington, was standing at a bus stop near the junction of O'Connell Street and Cathal Brugha Street when she was stabbed by a man. Shortly afterwards another young woman was similarly stabbed. The papers called the unknown attacker "mentally unbalanced . . . dangerous," making citizens all the more wary of bus travel.

––––––

In the period 1963–4 the problem of troublesome teenagers on late-night buses increased to a more serious, violent level, placing crews and passengers at physical risk. Bedraggled bus crews began returning to their garages after the Saturday-night shift reporting to their supervisors that bedlam had broken out, with fighting, stabbing, bloodshed. Groups of teenagers, sometimes gangs, were making the top deck of buses their battleground. And the crew had better not interfere.

In August 1964 two blockbuster films, *How the West Was Won* and the Beatles' *A Hard Day's Night,* drew aggressive youths into the city centre on buses in droves. The Beatles film put them in the mood for partying, singing, jiving— along with some drinking and hell-raising on the way home. On the top decks some began vandalising: damaging seats, breaking windows, smearing graffiti on surfaces. Conductors feared trying to stop them. On 12 August the *Evening Press* reported that a driver got into a dispute with a passenger who resorted to seriously biting him on the arm.[5] It was one of the first cases in which bus crews would be physically attacked by uncontrollable passengers.

On one Saturday night in August 1964 a mob of unruly teenagers began rioting on a bus in St Stephen's Green before it even departed on its late run. The conductor put in a call to Garda Headquarters, saying that things were already out of control. Branigan got the order to respond. Boarding the bus with giant strides, he instantly identified the three ringleaders, aged between seventeen and nineteen, grabbed them, and arrested them, without a whimper of protest, as the others quickly settled into their seats peaceably and quiet.

When Branigan brought them into court before Judge Farrell on charges of "riotous and disorderly behaviour on a bus," they meekly pleaded guilty, promising their best behaviour in the future. The *Evening Press* covered the incident, illustrating once again how easily Branigan handled hooligans and restored law and order, how his reputation and mere presence served as a potent deterrent to street—and now bus—crime.

Sergeant Jim Branigan suddenly seemed the logical solution to the problem. CIE, the Garda authorities, citizens and, most of all, bus drivers and conductors perceived him as the man to wage battle against what newspapers were now calling Dublin's "bus wars." He would have to take it on as a special assignment, in conjunction with his role as leader of the riot squad. As the bus violence took place at night, during his patrol hours, his superiors considered it a viable plan. The seriousness of the problem demanded at least the effort.

Branigan himself was confident he could tame the bus bullies. He knew enough about youthful misbehaviour to be certain of one thing: if their disorderly actions were left unchecked, the teenagers would take it as *carte blanche* to commandeer buses and hold crews and passengers hostage to their bellowing and brawling. They had to be *challenged*.

After consultation with both the Gardaí and CIE, he was given discretion regarding strategies to employ in the "bus wars." As he would tell abused women who sought his help, he assured CIE: "Just leave it to me."

At the outset, he and several members of his riot squad, foremost among them Sonny Heany, talked to drivers and conductors to determine the routes on which there was most trouble. Could they identify the most troublesome groups, and their ringleaders? What weapons did they carry?

At first the Ballyfermot buses had the reputation for the worst trouble. But Paddy Daly, who Branigan selected to be part of his special bus team, considered several others just as bad. "The worst buses were the Ballyfermot bus and Cabra West and O'Devaney Gardens" (off the North Circular Road). The Crumlin buses were also experiencing violence. Different conductors and drivers had their own selections.

After establishing a priority list, Branno devised his strategy for taking some control. It began with periodic surveillance of specific buses at certain points along their route during the late hours. This was not carried out in the conspicuous black van but in an unmarked car, usually carrying Branigan, the driver, and one or two other guards. They could well handle a busload of teenagers who thought they were tough. As usual, he occupied the front passenger seat, for the best view and quick decision-making.

Gerry Creighton, a teenager at the time, remembers often seeing Branigan's bus squad out on patrol. "He *always* rode shotgun on the Ballyer [Ballyfermot] and Finglas route, to deter troublemakers." He was able to discreetly stalk a select few buses on Saturday night, especially the 78 bus to Ballyfermot. This placed responsibility on the Garda driver to skilfully stay close enough for observation without being detected and not to fall too far behind in the traffic—no easy task on Dublin's streets. Talented drivers were some of Branigan's most valued men. They had the knack of manoeuvring into position and trailing buses at just the right distance.

But as time passed, it would become more difficult to avoid being seen. Once the public, and disorderly youths, learnt of the riot squad's bus patrols from the newspapers they were on the watch for them. It was said that they were easy to identify beneath street lamps at night: huge men stuffed into a small car, their heads nearly touching the roof, easily setting them apart from other motorists. When not trailing behind buses, the guards would sometimes cruise ahead to investigate bus stops where the rowdies gathered waiting to board, to get a sense of their behaviour or drunken state.

Though Branigan didn't want to be spotted during his clandestine bus patrols, he did want aggressive youths to know that he was now out "on the prowl" for troublemakers. Therefore the more newspaper coverage the better. His message was "beware!" Widespread knowledge of his shadowing strategy would be the greatest deterrent to rowdies, as they could never be sure if he was behind them. When the *Evening Herald* printed a photograph on the front page, taken from behind, clearly showing Branigan and two other large guards in their car just behind the Ballyfermot bus, it sent a graphic warning. He hoped that every teenager in Dublin saw the photograph.

Shadowing doubtless gave a good fright to many misbehaving youths, as some decline in disorder was noticed by bus crews. But he knew that this alone would not eliminate the problem. When called for, it would have to be supported by action. And youths weren't stupid: they knew that Lugs could only trail one bus at a time. The "bus wars" therefore became a double spying game, as teenage mobs on the top deck of buses began posting look-outs to see if they were being shadowed. At the beginning of the power struggle, many may have assumed that if caught causing trouble on a bus they would simply be ejected. Branigan had in mind a more impressionable penalty.

Branigan and the guards who patrolled with him understood the causes that motivated disenchanted youths to swarm aboard buses bound for the excitement of Dublin. They could even sympathise with their plight in having been stuck out in a barren environment, devoid of social and recreational facilities. They got a "bad deal"—no doubt about it. But it hardly justified their threatening behaviour and violence.

When serving with Branno on the bus patrol, Matt Mulhall was sensitive to both sides:

> Ballyfermot was new, and they had been put out there with *no* facilities—and *any* kind of diversion was good. But I remember following the buses, and there'd be trouble with a crowd of lads, after dark, after drink, going home—and there'd be *mayhem!* But the conductors, oh, they'd *know* we were behind them going out to Ballyfermot and Finglas and places like that.

The predictable problem was that when the riot squad would select a few buses there would be eruptions of trouble on other routes. And Branigan had to keep in mind that the bus crisis was extra night duty for him and his men. They still had to contend with the larger battles in streets, dancehalls, pubs, and cinemas. Though he was making every effort to balance his various duties, there was no doubt that his services were being strained at this point. But there were no complaints.

———

At 11:40 p.m. on 19 January 1965 the "bus war" turned uglier. So far it had mostly been youths fighting among themselves, disrespecting bus crews, pushing people around, frightening passengers. Not actually *attacking* passengers. On this night a mob of mostly drunk, aggressive youths barged aboard the number 79 bus to Ballyfermot, and within minutes "a row started on the top." As reported by the *Evening Herald*, a "wild panic" ensued in which weapons were drawn. Apparently, several adult passengers tried to intervene and halt the violence. One of them, Dominick O'Flanagan, was stabbed. A girl sitting nearby fainted from fear when "blood was splashed on seats" around her. It may as well have been an all-out street fight—except that it was all happening on a bus, with passengers trapped in the fray.

When he was able to do so, the driver pulled over, allowed the passengers to escape, and put in an emergency call for the Gardaí. Branigan was not shadowing that bus at the time, but he and his squad received a "Branno 5" call to rush to the scene. On arrival he charged up the stairs, barked out the command to halt, and confiscated the weapons. He immediately recognised the stabber as an incorrigible hooligan with three previous convictions for assault. In fact he boasted to Branigan that "this knife went into somebody tonight," information that Branigan passed on to the judge. He was sentenced to six months' detention in St Patrick's Institution.[6]

Up to now, Branigan had welcomed newspaper coverage of his shadowing operation, convinced that it acted as a deterrent. But on 20 January, when people read about bloody violence breaking out on the bus and a passenger being stabbed, a new level of fear set in. To Branigan as well it elevated the level of danger now facing passengers. This meant he would need to intensify his "bus war" strategy.

He instituted two new schemes. Firstly, he and his men would cruise around the notorious bus stops, halt, step out, and interrogate groups of suspicious-looking teenagers waiting for the late buses. Secondly, he would selectively board some dangerous buses in the role of passenger and implant himself on the upper deck in the back seat—dead centre. Then sit silently and wait—like a hawk.

No other garda would dare do this. Or be *allowed* to do so. It would mean facing mobs of as many as twenty drunken, possibly dangerous young hooligans, with the one exit, the stairs, being easy to block. Whether or not this risky plan was formally approved by his superiors we don't know, or whether any of his squad members sought to talk him out of it. After all, he was in his mid-fifties, unarmed, with no radio, and not even a baton. But he had thirty-five years of experience as a garda on his side. He had no hesitation.

Often, as rowdy youths clambered aboard the bus, there was a competition to push and shove going up the stairs to see who got the favourite seats. Along the way they were commonly rude or mocking towards the conductor. Or threatening. From his perch, Branigan could hear below as the poor man struggled to do his job. He could hear their shouting and profanities as they mounted the steps. They regarded the top deck as their playground, a "no-go" area for decent people on the late-night buses. What followed next could be described as either high drama or high comedy. A few youths in front of the pack glanced back to suddenly see Lugs Branigan sitting dead straight, stony-faced, staring directly at them, black leather gloves in hand. Not a word spoken.

Their pals ascending behind them were still whooping it up. One by one, as they reached the top and spotted the apparition on the rear seat, a hush would fall over them. They would politely take their seats, instead of climbing or jumping over them, and sit mute or whispering quietly. Down below, the driver, conductor and passengers could hardly believe the miraculous transformation they were witnessing. As one retired driver told Tony Ruane, whenever he saw Branigan on his bus "I was *delighted* he was there."

To catch trouble-makers off guard, Branno used a different ploy at times. He arranged with a bus crew to allow a mob of rowdies to get on the bus first, happy to see that Lugs was nowhere in sight. Before long they would fall into their riotous routine and perhaps start fighting or vandalising. Then, several stops later, the driver would pull over and Branigan would board. Very often the wild teenagers failed to notice this in the dark. Joe Kirwan regularly travelled on the Crumlin bus when it was plagued with trouble and often saw the remarkable scene when Branno secretly boarded:

On the bus to Crumlin, the number 81 or 83, fellas got drunk, and upstairs they'd be shouting and roaring. And the bus conductor, Jimmy, he'd wait for Branigan at this bus stop. And Branigan would walk up the steps to the upper floor—and there would be *complete silence!* Just the *look* of Branigan! . . . I was on that bus when it happened, *many* a time.

The spectre of Lugs Branigan suddenly appearing at the top of the stairs, blocking their escape, gloves conspicuously in hands, had an almost paralysing effect. Most sat not only silently but motionless. Joe Kirwan smiles when recalling it.

———

When Branigan successfully quelled disorder on one bus route it often sprouted on other buses. Sometimes on a completely unexpected route. On the night of Saturday 23 October 1965 the last bus departed from Lower Abbey Street for Howth. As always, it was packed. Shortly before midnight there was heard a "noisy, rowdy group on the top deck." With each mile the situation deteriorated. Passengers downstairs felt rumblings above them as if a volcano were about to erupt. Before long it became a drunken free-for-all, with angry shouting and fighting. After several brave attempts, the *Sunday Independent* wrote, the "conductor was unable to stop the rowdyism," reporting to the driver that the brawling was completely out of control and that weapons were being used.[7] Sounds of struggle and screaming were heard. Passengers became terrified as fighting broke out; as well as two hatchets, "a wood chisel, screwdrivers and steel combs with backs sharpened like razor blades were used." Boxed in as they were, the combatants fought viciously at close range. Then passengers saw blood-soaked victims stumbling down the stairs. One newspaper wrote:

> The whole top of the bus was then in a mass of fighting, screaming, struggling youths. Passengers in the lower deck panicked.[8]

As one visibly shaken passenger would later tell a reporter, "it was rough. We were all *terrified* and didn't know when the fighting would be carried downstairs."

The driver contacted his despatcher, who put in an emergency call to the Gardaí. This was immediately passed by headquarters to Branno 5. Within minutes the black van was speeding on the road towards Howth. The driver had pulled the bus off the road to let the frantic passengers disembark as quickly as they could, consoled by the conductor as they waited for the gardaí. Some were in emotional tatters. Meanwhile, on the top deck the pandemonium continued.

When the van pulled up, Branigan was the first out, charging up the stairs.

His resounding command to drop all weapons was met with unhesitating compliance. Next he ordered the youths to file down the stairs peacefully and submit to the waiting guards. By now there were two more patrol cars on the scene, with a total of about ten guards. The most seriously injured were taken away by ambulance to hospital. Others were questioned and taken to the Garda station. Meanwhile several of the passengers, completely unnerved by the incident, declared that they had no intention of boarding the blood-splattered bus again. "Following the incident," a newspaper confirmed, "a large group of passengers had to continue their journey home on foot," in the middle of the black October night.[9]

The following day the *Sunday Independent* splashed the blood-letting on its front page:

Hatchets in Howth bus riot: Five held

The next day the Garda authorities declared it "one of the most serious Saturday night rows Dublin has experienced this year." As the newspapers continued to cover the "bus wars," it no longer seemed like hyperbole.

———

In the wake of the Howth bus riot, Branigan began using another pre-emptive tactic. He and his squad would select bus stops and late-night buses at random and sternly interrogate crowds of youths, even though they had not caused any trouble. Inevitably, many innocent teenagers were caught in his net and frightened. It was carried out as a sort of commando sweep, to defuse any trouble that *might* be contemplated. To Branno any group of teenage bus passengers were now suspect. It was a time of widespread gangs, armed with weapons, and CIE welcomed the strategy.

Bernard Warfield, one of the youths innocently caught in one of Branigan's sweeps one night and terrified when ordered up against a wall, tells his side of the story:

This was about 1965, and I was a teenager. And it was all gang warfare at that time, around Ballyfermot and all. A *lot* of gang warfare between Ballyfermot and Bluebell . . . but I was one of the *good* guys. I never took part.

Anyway, I'd *heard* so much about Lugs Branigan, he was *so* well known and respected. Now the night I met him I was coming home after leaving my girl-friend in Clondalkin after going to the pictures. And the last bus home left about twelve, and most of us lived in Bluebell and Inchicore. And there were about thirty fellas—but we didn't *know* each other. So anyway, a *whole bunch* of us were on this bus together. And two squad cars pull up with about eight policemen. And *himself*—Lugs Branigan!

I'd never met the man before—but his name *did* put a bit of fear into you. So you didn't say anything to him. It was a summer evening, and he was in plain clothes, and all the rest were in uniform. So he lined us *all* up against the wall and asked everybody their names, where they'd been, the whole lot. And most of us had been with our girl-friends.

And there's a little fella standing beside me and he's asked, "Where were you?" And he says [in a loud, annoyed tone], "With my girl-friend. Why do you want to know?" And you don't say that! The fella was cheeky with him. And Branigan gives him a clatter across the face . . . and he made a bit of a moan.

———

Interspersed with his efforts to halt trouble on the buses, Branigan occasionally encountered other odd cases to be dealt with. On 26 December 1965, the day after Christmas, when Dublin was usually calm, he received a "Branno 5" message about a "runaway bus," whatever that meant. His orders were to head the van towards the junction of Dorset Street and the North Circular Road. All he knew from headquarters was that "somebody had taken over the conductor's job." Drunken youths again?

When he reached the stationary bus he had the passengers disembark and stand outside so that he could confront the culprit. The driver hurriedly explained to him what had happened. It was one of the last buses of the night, jam-packed, when at one bus stop the conductor hopped off for a minute to enter a shop. An intoxicated passenger saw this as his opportunity to act as conductor by striking the bell for the driver to pull away. The driver, not realising at first what had taken place, drove off. When worried passengers informed him, the impostor became belligerent.

As Branigan stepped aboard to meet the "new conductor," Sergeant Prendergast and other guards waited outside. Sitting obstinately alone on the bus was 35-year-old T. Keogh, still too plied with Christmas cheer to heed Branigan's order to step off the bus. In fact he stood up and issued a challenge to the guard towering over him.

In court, Branigan would tell Judge O'Grady how he handled the situation: "The defendant refused to leave and started to give trouble . . . He put up his chin for me to hit him."[10] Declining the offer, Branigan again tried to talk sense to the man, asking him to step out peaceably. When the fellow grew even more resistant, Branigan simply told the judge that he "toned him down" a bit, by necessity, without going into detail. After which the man gladly left the bus. The judge told the defendant that Sergeant Branigan had "used great discretion," for which he should be grateful. Then he slapped a £3 fine on the defendant for disorderly conduct.

Branigan had an assortment of ways for handling common drunks and louts who made a bus conductor's job difficult. He liked to teach them a lasting lesson. Alick remembers one such instance:

> One night my father got on the bus to Ballyfermot, and the driver says, "There's a fella and he won't pay his fare." So my father went up to him and said, "All right, give me the money for the fare." And your man handed over the bob [shilling]—'cause obviously when he saw my father he didn't want any hassle. And then, to cap it all, my father says, *"Now—get off the bus!"* So he had to *walk* home. It was a kind of rough justice . . . a double whammy!

———

The year 1967 was one of the worst in Dublin's "bus wars," as conductors were increasingly abused, cursed at, spat on. Apart from vandalising buses by damaging seats, windows, and walls, some youths were now using the rear of the top deck as a toilet, urinating freely and causing a stench that wafted downstairs. Along with torrents of vile language.

In the spring the bus war advanced to a new front when conductors were openly threatened and shoved about. Then the beatings began.

On Saturday 29 April a conductor, 35-year-old Patrick Feely, was first shoved and then "beaten severely and kicked in the head" by four attackers.[11] Somehow he managed to ring the bell, and the driver heard him calling, "Help, Joe, help!" He later collapsed in hospital. When hearing the testimony of the brutal beating, Judge Ó Donnchadha said: "The court must take a serious view of this. Public servants, like members of the Gardaí, bus drivers and conductors, are entitled to protection."[12]

Nine days later, on 8 May, a young conductor, James MacArdle, was off duty and heading home late at night on top of a 15A bus, still in uniform. Though weary from his shift, he couldn't help but notice three youths who were "barracking a single passenger" further up the bus. Ever dutiful, he remonstrated with the youths, who continued their bullying. When they "kept roaring," he ordered them to quieten down. To no avail. Shortly afterwards he reached his destination and stepped off the bus. Within seconds, he noticed that he was being followed by the three youths, who immediately set upon him. He later described to a reporter from the *Evening Herald* how he had been "savagely beaten by the three youths at Kimmage Crossroads. Two held him on the ground while the other kicked him in the face, then ran away."[13] Luckily, a passing motorist spotted him lying in the road with his nose badly damaged, black eyes, and other injuries, "bleeding and with his shirt full of blood." Garda

Ryan and Garda Shaughnessy were called to the scene to take him to the Meath Hospital. Details of the vicious crime were reported in the next day's papers.

Ten days later, on the night of 18 May, a conductor, 34-year-old Thomas O'Brien, was stabbed by a youth on the 15A bus at Terenure Road West. When he boarded the bus but refused to pay, O'Brien ordered him off the bus. The youth drew what appeared to be the sharpened handle of a steel comb and thrust it into the conductor. The driver, Christopher O'Brien (no relation), chased the attacker but was unable to catch him—a brave, if perhaps foolish, act on behalf of his friend.

The spate of beatings and stabbings of conductors sent shock waves through CIE. The next morning, 19 May, it was announced that "Dublin busmen will meet within the next few days to consider what action they will take following the injuries to conductors." CIE worried that busmen might begin refusing to show up for duty on some late-night buses; indeed a few men had already done so. Such an action could paralyse late-night travel and leave people abandoned when trying to get home after having been in the city for entertainment or work. Buses were their indispensable lifeline.

One could hardly blame the defenceless drivers and conductors for wanting to refuse duty on the high-risk routes late at night. Already the health, both physical and mental, of late-night crews was suffering. They suffered from bad nerves, hypertension, insomnia. Pure fear. Those on the bad routes were clearly working on "hazardous duty," but they were not receiving extra pay. Their families also bore the worry and fear that they might be beaten or stabbed on any night, merely doing their duty. Added to the physical threat was the emotional distress. Busmen who had begun their career in the days of respect and civility felt a sense of personal degradation amid the violence, vandalism, and urination—on *their* bus.

Many citizens were no less outraged. Letters flowed in to newspapers expressing anger and offering ideas on how to handle the miscreants. Almost all championed sterner "get-tough" policies. Many writers had themselves been victims of, or witnesses to, late-night bus violence. One citizen, signing himself "Act Now," wrote to the *Evening Herald*:

> Sir,—A reason for the shocking beatings and stabbings . . . young people "high" on drinking, on their homeward journey at night assume a "pack" mentality, looking for victims, armed with knives.[14]

Letter-writers commonly made reference to "wolf packs" and "predators." In his letter of 25 May 1967 one man said that the principal topic of conversation at his local was the recent attacks on bus conductors. The consensus, he stated, was that the police, especially Sergeant Branigan and his riot squad, were doing their very best, but the courts were so lenient that the hooligans were not made to pay sufficiently for their lawlessness. Many of his pub mates argued for the return of flogging with a "birch" or rod, or with the "cat o' nine tails." When he asked his mates for their opinion, "everyone was wholeheartedly in agreement." His message to readers was clear:

> The scoundrels . . . the young blackguards . . . always given "another last chance"! The justices have been doing this for years now. The gardaí must be sick and tired of bringing them to book and exposing themselves to violence in doing so. What a disheartening job![15]

Such letters brought to mind again the musings of some judges about reintroducing flogging, if only it were legally allowed. All of which implicitly validated Branigan's tough methods of summary street justice.

Quite a few letter-writers suggested stationing guards on all late-night buses—a quixotic notion, not only because of limited manpower but because of the personal risk. There was only one man who could pull it off. Surely no superintendent could have been so foolish as to allow it. Other letter-writers hastened to agree that the idea of placing ordinary guards on hooligan-loaded buses was irrational and would prove futile. One impassioned writer, identifying himself as "A Victorian," deplored the "brutal attacks on busmen" but stated that "I don't believe that the presence of policemen on buses is going to deter the attackers." His opinion was based on personal observation:

> I have come to the sorrowful conclusion that the hooligans no longer have any respect for the guardians of the law . . . The young pups stand up to them—which I have *seen* happen. And lenient justices let them off with a caution and small fine.
>
> Experience has shown that a few weeks in jail is no deterrent to them. I beg them to cut out the namby-pamby treatment and give the police some authority when dealing with hoodlums. There is nothing better than corporal punishment to make an impression on them.[16]

A few letter-writers offered other unconventional solutions, such as that submitted on 2 June 1967 by "Fight Fire with Fire":

> To stop blackguardism on our buses I suggest sentences of one year—but not in Mountjoy. Put them to *work* at eight o'clock in the morning and bring them back at six o'clock in the evening, the same on weekends—deprive them of their free time.[17]

In response to the outbreak of violence against conductors, Branno stepped up surveillance and interrogations, identifying several new routes. He also increased his communication with drivers and conductors. This led to the initiation of a new alert system between the bus-driver and patrol car trailing behind. Branigan suggested a simple sos signal that drivers could use to alert his shadowing squad when they first detected any trouble on the upper deck. Gerald Byrne, who was serving with him at the time, found it effective:

> We'd just trail the buses in an unmarked car, or we'd use the van. And if there was trouble we had an agreement with the driver that he'd put the lights *on and off* when there was trouble aboard.

This simple means of communication allowed the guards to jump aboard the bus quickly, Branigan in the lead, to quell trouble before it became more serious. His men always blocked the stairwell to prevent any hooligans from escaping. With Byrne and his mates looking on, Branno would double-step his way to the top in seconds:

> So we got the fellas who were having rows with the conductors—Branigan would just get *on* the bus, and get them *off*. And they'd *go!* I don't *ever* remember anyone saying, "I won't go, Mr Branigan."

Throughout the late 1960s, Ballyfermot buses remained the most explosive. At one point a number of busmen felt obliged to refuse duty on the late-night runs, unless Branigan and his squad were protecting them from behind, or if other guards could be posted at bus stops along the route. Impossible demands. As a compromise, on 28 February 1970 CIE and the Garda authorities agreed on a trial plan. While it was not possible to post Garda "minders" on all buses, they could at least station them at some of the strategic late-night bus stops. This was intended as a highly visible show of force, and to be published in the newspapers, in the hope that it would intimidate trouble-makers and calm public fears.

But the main responsibility in the battle to win the "bus wars" still fell on the shoulders of Sergeant Branigan and his riot squad. However, the myriad demands upon them to deal with problems in the city's streets, dancehalls, pubs, and chippers, as well as the extended bus network, were taking a toll on all the men. It was not only wearying but exasperating—the impossibility of covering so many "hot spots" around the city. Though too much was expected of them, they never complained. This would have been unseemly for "Branno's men."

It helped their spirits that Dublin's newspapers were generous in their praise of the riot squad's successes. For instance, on the last day of February 1970 the black van shadowed one of the most dangerous Ballyfermot buses, prompting the conductor to say to a reporter that "things had never been so quiet on a Saturday night before."[18] It was like a transformation. To credit Branno and his squad, on 1 March the *Sunday Independent* wrote of this most unusual night of tranquillity:

> All was quiet on the Ballyfermot bus war front last night . . . The last bus was shadowed to the terminus by gardaí under Garda James C. Branigan. The protection was there last night. Apart from a sing-song on the last bus from the city by youths who gave a melodious rendering of "I wanna go home" on the 78 Bus, all was bliss on this route.[19]

––––––

Unfortunately, successes were too often followed by violent outbreaks, especially on the Crumlin and Finglas routes. On 10 March 1970 Gerald Brennan, a conductor on the Howth bus, was attacked without provocation. The ruffian caught him around the neck and beat him, shouting, "Your lot will be scraped into little bits."[20] The driver quickly halted the bus, and the attacker fled.

In mid-March 1970 the manager of Dublin city bus services called for a meeting with the Association of Combined Residents' Associations to discuss the crisis. One CIE official seemed to express the view of the majority when he stated: "It is disgraceful that people cannot travel on the late buses because of these rowdies—the *only* way to stop them is to prosecute."[21] With which most guards surely agreed as well.

On 30 April 1970 a meeting of the CIE authorities and various residents' associations was held to candidly discuss the increasingly serious problem of "attacks on bus crews." The room was packed with irate, frustrated and visibly fearful citizens. A reporter from the *Evening Herald* was in attendance to cover the evening's discussion and elicit some newsworthy quotations from citizens fed up with the violence. Almost everyone, it seemed, had a story to tell or an idea to suggest. Emotions ran high, as a number of audience members had been victims of bus abuse in one form or another.

A delegate from Little Bray Residents' Association told how the plague of bus bullies and violence had spread to his area. When the "big bands" played in Bray, he said, the last buses were always full and trouble a certainty when young hooligans simply took over and held decent passengers hostage. Heads nodded in agreement. People stood to share personal experiences of being treated disrespectfully, pushed, cursed at. Some had been physically struck. On buses there now existed an atmosphere of general intimidation. Everyone concurred that when rioting erupted on the top deck they immediately feared that it could spill below at any time and engulf them. And all in the room knew of people who had grown so fearful of late-night bus travel that they no longer dared step aboard and take the risk, thereby being deprived of the simple freedom to travel safely to evening events.

Predictably, once again the idea was proposed that the Garda Síochána should post guards on all high-risk buses; and, just as quickly, it was batted down by those who cited the practical constraints of the suggestion. There was no such simple, "quick-fix" solution, unfortunately. Mr A. Conlon of Kilmore-Coolock Residents' Association chimed in with a cogent counter-point. If guards were placed on buses for protection, he reasoned, they should "just as well be assigned for the protection of taxi-drivers and petrol pump attendants," who were also vulnerable to assault.[22] His solution was to install two-way radios on buses, which would at least help if it did not solve the problem.

As the evening wore on, some controversial ideas were expressed. One man suggested that "bus inspectors should board the last buses and ask the people for their co-operation." In other words, make an appeal to the passengers to forcibly protect themselves on their bus—against gangs of drunken, armed young hooligans, to act as a sort of on-board vigilante committee. This idea immediately roused opposition among the crowd. Ordinary citizens, men and women, were being asked to wage battle in the "bus wars." A brave few dared to oppose the majority by saying that the idea might have some merit.

A delegate from Cabinteely shot to his feet to speak with fervour about an incident he had recently witnessed. Noting that in his area "all attacks were in buses that were full," he told of being on the bus when rowdies assaulted the conductor. As if amazed, he told the crowd that he "deplored the fact that with fifty or sixty people on the bus *no-one* came to the aid of the conductor."[23] In his judgement, this "showed a lack of civic spirit." He failed to mention whether *he* had ever assumed such a courageous role. A flurry of hands shot up to remind everyone of some of the weapons the gangs carried: knives, razors, sharpened combs, knuckledusters. What chance had unarmed citizens against them? The consensus was that to act as a good samaritan was plain foolhardy.

At the conclusion of the meeting, everything focused once again on the Gardaí and the courts and on the need for them to act on behalf of defenceless citizens. In particular, judges who had been too lenient in the past needed to crack down hard on offenders.

On their way home, it may have struck some of those in attendance how appalling it was to even need such a meeting about how to defend themselves against violent youths who had invaded their buses, threatening and beating busmen and passengers. Only a few years earlier it would have been inconceivable.

By late 1972 and early 1973 things would erupt again.

Probably no front-page newspaper article more distressed CIE than that of the *Evening Press* that was headed: "Terror on late night buses." It was now being reported that drivers and conductors on the Bray to Dún Laoghaire run "are seeking police protection against gangs of rowdy youths."[24] Some of the rowdies only sang "bawdy songs" and leaped around like lizards, shouting and partying; others threatened crews and passengers, wrecked the bus, and engaged in beatings and stabbings. One conductor, at his wits' end, confided to a reporter about his torment:

> In all the years I have been on this run I have never seen such rowdyism. Gangs of youths . . . their conduct can only be described as shocking. They kick up dreadful rows, and it is dangerous to try and stop them, for they might pull knives. Some use the back of the buses as toilets. Several passengers have left buses and taken taxis home.[25]

––––

During the early 1970s the bus wars continued like a roller-coaster, an alternating pattern of calm and crisis. A disorderly spree might be followed by weeks of perfect order. Branigan, now in his early sixties, continued as leader of his riot squad, giving as much attention as possible to the bus wars.

There was no way to win a decisive victory in the bus wars, to bring things to a complete halt. Nor was there any way to reach a formal "truce." Instead, several positive developments combined to gradually reduce the problem, easing public fears. Judges indeed began handing out harsher sentences to bus rioters hauled into court; and two-way radio communication on buses was introduced from the mid-1960s. Coincidentally, the formerly isolated outer housing estates from which the teenagers fled began to develop their own amenities for residents—adults and youths alike—with some recreation facilities, shopping centres, pubs, and cafés. Gradually, they were no longer compelled to need escape from the barren "wilds" to the bright lights of the city. Though many youths still took the bus into town for weekend events, they became more civilised in their behaviour.

Branigan's role in the "bus wars" of the 1960s and early 70s was immense, considered critical by both CIE and Garda Headquarters. For it was he who imposed a measure of control over the spreading problem, acted as a crucial deterrent in preventing it from worsening. On the most notorious routes, his singular presence intimidated bus hooligans and significantly curbed their lawless behaviour. The shadow of Branigan hovering over them—knowing that he could identify them and "get them" sooner or later—instilled a healthy fear in their ringleaders. As the press and public came to realise, this is what kept them in check. As they admitted themselves later.

It would not be hyperbole to say that in the minds and hearts of Dublin's busmen Lugs Branigan became a heroic figure. When needed, he came to their rescue, provided safety and sometimes sanity. Old-time bus drivers and conductors swore they would never forget his help.

———

In October 1972, three months before Branno's retirement, Senan Finucane Jr, son of Branigan's old sidekick from the 1940s and 50s, was waiting to be called to the Garda College in Templemore, having already passed his interview and medical exam for admission to the Garda Síochána. He was proud to be following in the footsteps of his father, as was his brother Eddie. Not knowing how long his wait might be, he decided to spend the interim productively. He accepted work as a bus conductor, "to get used to the shift work and dealing with members of the public." New on the job, he was kept busy trying to take fares and give change correctly, hardly able to notice the faces of all the passengers boarding and finding their seats. Though he had met Branigan a few times before, through his father, he had not seen him for quite a while:

> One morning while I was conducting on the Drimnagh route, the driver called my attention to a passenger who had got on the bus. I had not seen the man enter, as I was upstairs at the time. He asked me not to charge this man the bus fare. I asked him, Was this man someone special? And he told me he was "Lugs" Branigan, who was coming home from the courts.
>
> He also informed me that Lugs had helped out CIE busmen on many occasions when they had trouble with gurriers on the bus routes—that he was held in the *highest* esteem with CIE personnel.

Chapter 13 ∾

| IN COURT: "CENTRE STAGE"

"He *loved* going to court. That's when he could project himself, to the justice and the people in court. He was on *centre stage!*"

(DECLAN BRANIGAN)

"In court he had the reputation of being tough, honest. *Fair.* And he wasn't afraid of judge or jury! He'd say, 'Your honour, I *clipped* him"—gave him a punch. Oh, the judges had *great* respect for him."

(SUPERINTENDENT JOHN MURPHY)

"To Jim, in court everybody was the *same*—a judge, a prosecutor, a beggar, a prostitute. He treated them *all* the same!"

(GARDA PADDY DALY)

"I gained notoriety for 'speaking out my mind' in court."

(GARDA JIM BRANIGAN)

He relished the theatrics of the courtroom: the challenges, the fight for justice. To those who witnessed it, his performance in the decorous courtrooms matched that in Dublin's tough begrimed streets.

It was one of Lugs Branigan's greatest contradictions that he was as comfortable and capable in the solemn legal world of the courts as he was in confronting thugs and criminals along Benburb Street. In striking contrast to his famed steely character, he also possessed what some called his "soft side," often manifested in the courtroom.

No-one loved being in court more than Jim Branigan. Or appeared more often. Or assumed so many diverse roles. Apart from his duty as a guard in court, he variously acted as social worker, counsellor, sociologist, psychologist. Sometimes philosopher. And often a mentor to young gardaí intimidated by the formality of court proceedings. On occasion even court jester—to either the dismay or the delight of those in court, always to the appreciation of newspaper reporters on hand.

———

His most memorable early court appearances were those related to the famous "Battle of Baldoyle" in 1940. As a thirty-year-old guard he earned respect for courageously, and capably, giving critical testimony against gang members and racketeers responsible for the debacle at the racecourse. Despite receiving threatening letters and phone calls and even being offered bribes to keep him from testifying, he resolutely rejected them and took the stand. It was here that his court reputation—and, one day, legend—began.

Over the following decades he honed his courtroom skill to a degree hardly paralleled within the Garda Síochána. His number of court appearances became staggering. Retired Chief Superintendent Michael Reid marvelled at Branigan's court capabilities:

> He was in court every day—*five* days a week! Going to court daily took tremendous discipline and intelligence . . . with so many cases. And he was doing it all himself.

Not only did he enthusiastically march into court every day, adds John Collins, but "if there was a court on Sunday he'd *be* there! Ah, he was part and parcel of the courts."

He had a natural gift for "performing" in court, which was quite evident to judges, solicitors, court staff, and reporters. Even defendants had to admire it. Visitors commonly came to court just to watch him perform. His knack in appearing before a court audience depended on a flare for language, drama, gesticulation. No-one could match his talent in presenting evidence and giving demonstrations when appropriate, whether it was lugging in barbaric weapons to show the savagery of brawlers or hiking up his trousers to exhibit some of his "battle scars," as he called them. In court, when Lugs was "on," everyone perked up. One never knew what the unpredictable Garda Branigan might say or do in court. It certainly kept judges on their toes.

———

It was this bold unpredictability and spontaneity that made him so captivating to watch in court. As Alick says of his father, "he wasn't afraid to *speak out!* He'd say what he was *thinking.* That's why journalists loved him." They never knew when they might catch a new Branigan story, or at least quip, and sometimes a wonderfully quotable line. These were unique "Braniganisms" for newspaper reporters, all of whom had a genuine fondness for Lugs. Even *Garda Review* wrote that he was "by his nature a man who spoke his mind and was not the type to blindly follow the official line."[1]

Garda John Murphy was often in court at the same time as Branno and observed how the journalists were always hoping for some nuggets for the next day's paper: "The journalists were always looking for headlines. They'd take no notice of another guard, but with *him!* Once he got the *name,* that was it." As Tony Ruane tells it, Branigan had gained a court celebrity status by his fifties:

> When he was in court it was like the theatre. It was better than any show in town! When Branigan went to court and had a few prisoners it was like a floor show, you know. The court would be *full.* 'Cause they didn't know *what* he was going to say next—or *do* next.

He let loose at any moment with colourful descriptions of various characters or scenes in the streets or dancehalls relating to the case at hand— all impromptu. Presenting lively portrayals that were directly pertinent to the proceedings, making testimony from other participants seem frightfully dull. It just came naturally, he always said—"speaking my mind."

But his mastery of court procedure began with thorough preparation. His success in court did not come as easily at it appeared. No-one in the Garda Síochána was known to prepare so diligently or meticulously as Jim Branigan. This involved the entire process of preliminary detective work: note-taking, interrogation, organisation, and presentation of evidence. As well as coping with a defending solicitor's sharp queries. Superior preparation became his forte, especially when pitted against the most egregious criminals and aggressive solicitors. What always puzzled his Garda colleagues was how he found time to accomplish this, with all his other duties—and on little sleep.

He even typed all his court materials. Today this may seem unimpressive, but half a century or so ago it was highly unusual for a guard. As Michael Reid affirms, "back in the fifties and sixties there weren't many guards who could actually type—but *he* did. Now, he was a two-finger man, but very good, and *fast.*" The sound of Branno's rhythmic clacking away was a natural part of the scene at Kevin Street Garda Station. At top speed, it meant "do not disturb." It was a rather amusing sight to see the heavyweight boxing champion, with his huge hands, hunched over the typewriter, pecking away furiously with two fingers. But, says Val Lynn, he always got the job done in time, "and he came in *prepared,* with all his statements—and they were very well done, very *precise.*" The time pressure never seemed to bother him. It was a wonder for others to watch. "Oh, he loved it," says Bosco Muldoon, "to type out his own charges with an old typewriter."

There was also a psychological purpose in typing his court documents. Other guards were happy to show up for court with a handful of papers and scribbled notes; but Branigan was determined to enter the courtroom as a *professional,* in his mind placing himself on the same level as his "competition." And in court he was as competitive as he had ever been in the boxing ring.

As another tactic, he would stride into the courtroom with his own leather attaché case—unheard of for gardaí. "He was the first man in the Garda Síochána ever to go into the courts with all his statements in one of those leather bags he got," verified Lynn. "Only justices and solicitors had them."

He was not going to give his court opponents an edge. To his mind, typed documents and a leather case were tangible and psychological "equalisers" in court. He was not to be outdone by pin-striped solicitors with university degrees. John Murphy vouches: "He wasn't afraid of judge or jury!" His reputation for fearlessness was as strongly established in the courtroom as in a riotous pub or dancehall.

———

That he didn't fear lordly judges, pompous solicitors or political potentates was due to his egalitarian nature. He didn't distinguish between people according to status or value. As Paddy Daly simply puts it, "to Jim, in court everybody was the same . . . There was no such thing as 'bigwigs' to him." All in his presence were deserving of the same respect and treatment. He honestly saw every individual as having their equal human worth and dignity. In his eyes, a dosser deserved the same respect in court as a doctor.

"The hallmark of his evidence was fairness," contends Michael Reid. "He was *extremely fair.* He just told it like it was. And for that reason he was very well accepted by the judiciary." His truthfulness could be disarming. He didn't mince words or distort facts to mould the evidence in his favour.

Branigan became known for speaking directly from his heart with candour, for which he was occasionally reprimanded for an innocent slip of the tongue. This sometimes occurred as a result of his unvarnished vocabulary in describing defendants he brought before the judge. When he knew a man and his background well, he knew into which category he best fitted, whether "gentleman" or "gurrier." Other guards dared not use street lingo in court in describing a defendant or a scenario; by contrast, Branno was not a bit afraid to call a man by his deserved name. But he did so without a hint of prejudice or unfairness—because he always had the evidence to support his case.

He chose his terms as accurately as possible from his rich lexicon. Judges came to know the differences between "rowdies," "ruffians," "hooligans," "blackguards," "criminals," "common thugs." They also became familiar with phrases he favoured and found useful for placing a defendant in an accurate perspective for the courts, such as "a good man gone wrong," "a decent lad just gone astray," "a troublesome fella when he's on the drink," "a mean bully," "a cute fella" known for cunning and conniving—all terms reflecting Branigan's experience with the person. And he would call a man out straight a "vicious wife-beater," a "gouger" or a "bowsie" when he believed the court needed to know. Says Paddy Daly, "Jim had his own way of speaking to the judge in court." If his vocabulary became a bit too earthy or colourful to be appropriate, judges had their tactful ways of letting him know to ease up, sometimes with a mere expression that Branigan understood immediately. However, a solicitor hearing his client called a "gouger" in court was sure to hop to his feet in protest.

Branigan admitted that his descriptive language sometimes got him into a bit of trouble in court—"notoriety for speaking my mind," as he put it. Nonetheless he stood by his principles. "I would not call a thug a 'gentleman': I called him a 'gouger', or a 'skinhead.' I was booked for this."[2] Being "booked" by a judge who unashamedly admired him usually equated to a light "slap on the wrist," often just to appease the defendant and his solicitor. "The judges, they *all* liked him, knew that he was a *fair, decent* man," says Paddy Daly. Because of his unfailing truthfulness and sense of fair play—as well as integrity— Jim Branigan earned a reputation in Dublin courts as a man utterly beyond dishonesty or corruption in any form.

Because of the high respect in which he was held, judges allowed him extraordinary freedom in court, in expression, in cross-examination privileges, and in demonstrations, often asking openly for his opinion on cases, even sentences—quite a concession for proud judges. Sometimes a judge would specifically ask him for a recommended sentence for a miscreant, and then follow his recommendation. As Michael Reid explains, these were judges who had worked with and observed Branigan in court for years, saw that he was *"highly proficient* in giving evidence . . . well spoken," versed in every aspect of court proceedings. They perceived him therefore as a valuable source of expertise on which to draw. Judges, and solicitors, found that Branigan could answer without hesitation nearly any question they put to him in court, in a clear and comprehensive manner.

———

In court he was also forthright about his own behaviour, his "unconventional" methods of dispensing summary justice on the streets. With which all the judges were quite familiar. In cases where he had needed to apply physical force of some kind, he always brought up the facts himself at the outset. Judges learnt the difference between his terms "clip," "tap," "clout," "toning down," and "clattering." These covered every level of force, from a wispy glove lash to a solid, disabling punch reserved for a brutal battering husband or wild man endangering those around him. As John Murphy witnessed many a time, Branno had no compunction in stepping before a judge and saying in a loud, clear voice, "Your honour, I clipped him"—meaning a good smack. Judges became accustomed to hearing it. It was accepted in court as Branigan's unique brand of policing. Moreover, judges knew that Garda Branigan had tacit approval from the Garda Síochána to carry out his methods of punishment and deterrence on the spot. For it was indisputably effective.

When a court case began with the admission of a "clip," judges were inclined to assume that it was justified. They came to regard Branigan's "summary justice" as a means of "forceful persuasion" that accomplished several things. It restrained a disorderly or violent person, served as punishment, taught them an instant and often lasting lesson—*and* usually kept them out of court, making their job easier. Keeping the courts clear of common bowsies and hooligans saved both time and money—no small consideration to overworked judges. As Alick explains it, judges like Ó hUadhaigh, Reddin and Molony saw his father realistically as a potent force in maintaining law and order on Dublin's streets:

> It was the fact that he was keeping things *under control!* Able to deal with the bad guys . . . The judges loved that, you know. They had a *very high* regard for him.

There was no doubt that his tough methods on the streets and in dancehalls served the judges well. Matt Mulhall observes: "See, the courts didn't seem to be able to stem the violence then . . . they were so lenient." Consequently, Lugs was given the benefit of the doubt. Paddy Daly agrees:

> I was in court with Branigan, and the judges there, they were *totally* in favour of his ways. They *were!*

On one occasion Branigan brought before Judge Molony a bully who had viciously beaten his own sister, explaining: "I had to give him a clip to tone him down—then he came quietly to the station." Perfectly reasonable, agreed the judge. Another time the *Evening Herald* headed an article "Detective gave man a few taps" after Branigan told Judge Ó Riain that the "few taps" were necessary to restrain him.[3] The court fully approved.

Very seldom did defendants protest in court that they had been mistreated by Branigan. When this occurred, Lugs calmly expanded his explanation of the circumstances requiring physical force so that the judge had a better picture of what happened and why, prompting many judges to tell the defendant that they "got off easily" and were lucky Branigan had not exerted a stronger hand. Paddy Daly recalls judges turning to a defendant, wagging their finger at them, scolding them, saying, "Why didn't you go home when Mr Branigan ordered you?"

"Oh, Jim could do *no wrong*," swears Daly.

Even Branigan's well-known policy that "a belt in the mouth was the best medicine" for a thug made sense to most judges. "And the judge would *never* challenge him," John Murphy vouches. "They *accepted* what he said." In court, his word seemed inviolable. Daly can't recall a single time in court when Branno was seriously reprimanded, or even criticised, by even the strictest judges. "In court, Judge Ó hUadhaigh was a rough-and-ready justice, but *whatever* Jim would say he'd go by it." Other guards could only watch with wonder what Lugs got away with, knowing they would be slapped down fast if they tried to use his tactics. Paddy Daly dared not try it:

> See, Jim'd get up in the box and say, "Justice, last night I met these two gurriers . . ." Now, if I had said that I'd be chastised for being very bold. But *he* got away with that. And then he'd say, "These guys were messing, and I had to give this guy a slap, or a tap of his gloves, because he was being unruly." He'd *say* that—but I'd be *destroyed* in court!

Judges had no intention of pruning back Branigan's successful methods. In the early 1960s Garda Eddie Finucane, Senan senior's son, happened to be in court when a mild complaint was lodged against Branigan by a defendant:

> The defendant complained in court about being ill-treated by Jim. It would appear that Jim used a bit of his "summary justice" to sort out the unruly character he arrested. Jim explained to the judge that he *had* to chastise him a little. The judge then exclaimed, "That's all right, Sergeant Branigan." The District Court justices *realised* that Jim Branigan was necessary for public order.

———

On one memorable occasion Judge Ó hUadhaigh and the others in court that day got a dramatic demonstration of the validity of Branigan's famous "clout," how it could instantly restore order on the spot and spare injury to innocent persons. Branigan had hauled into court a notoriously abusive pimp whose women were ordinarily too frightened to give evidence against him. But one young woman had the courage to do so. Branno knew her well as a kind and gentle soul trapped in sad circumstances. He detested pimps, placing them with battering husbands at the bottom of the human species. He admired the "pavement hostesses," as he always called them, who took the risk of testifying.

What happened in court during her testimony was so unexpected and swift that everyone was startled. Fortunately, John Murphy was on hand to mentally record the scene:

> This pimp was using this prostitute, he had her out on the town. And this girl was giving evidence against him. And he was *watching* her give the evidence from where the prisoners sat. And *suddenly* he made a *dive* for the witness box where she was. *Oh,* he made a dive *for this girl!* He tried to *get* her. In *court*—in *front* of the judge! *So fast* that almost nobody saw it.
>
> But Jim was as *fast as lightning,* he leapt over and clipped him on the jaw—and *down* he went. *Flat out!* And Jim wasn't a young man at this stage. So he was lifted up and put on the bench and his head was hanging over. Oh, he was knocked out. And the judge says, "Put him back [in the cell] till two o'clock."

As John Murphy was walking out of the court building a short time later he said to him, "Jim, that was a mighty one. Are you going back at two to finish the case?" He knew that he always headed home after court to catch lunch and a nap, as he had riot squad duty that night at about eight o'clock. *"I certainly am!"* he said.

———

His primary objective in court was to get at the bare truth so that justice could be rendered. With often conflicting testimony from both sides, the truth could be murky. Branno was masterful at cutting through legal rhetoric and twisted reasoning to unearth the simple facts of the case. And he was unruffled when the cleverest solicitors grilled him: in fact he seemed to enjoy the challenge of a spirited legal tussle with the best of Dublin's solicitors. As Bernard Neary reveals, one of Branigan's main opponents in court was the well-known solicitor L. Trant McCarthy, something of a court legend himself, who defended many of those arrested by Branigan.[4] Even when he lost a case to McCarthy he had great respect for him. The feeling was mutual.

When allowed the opportunity he excelled at questioning witnesses; and some judges gave him *carte blanche* to unravel complex cases. By the mid-1950s he was exhibiting his sharp interrogation skill, often to the dismay of opposing counsel. In September 1954 a case made the *Evening Herald* when Judge Mangan permitted Garda Branigan to take over some cross-examination in a convoluted case. With the precision of a scalpel, he began to lay bare the facts. Before long Mangan was satisfied that he had heard enough of the truth, declaring pithily that he found the "charge of assault proved."[5]

A year later, in June 1955, Judge Mangan again allowed Branigan to carry out cross-examination in the case of the "Battle of Dolphin's Barn." Some of the arrested youths alleged that several gardaí had used excessive force with their batons. Each side disputed the other. Branigan sought to find the *truth*, be it on the side of the youths or his own colleagues. He was in a delicate position. Ultimately he was credited with proving that the defendants were in fact "tapped with a baton," as he discreetly phrased it. However, the charge of *unnecessary* force was questionable. As a consequence, Judge Mangan, while not declaring that the guards had "acted wrongly," intimated that the case was mishandled, and he dismissed the charges.[6] Once again Branigan showed that he did not automatically assume youthful defendants to be in the wrong and the authorities right.

He treated conflicts at ballrooms and cinemas the same way, with an open mind from the outset. He never showed up assuming that the doormen or bouncers were right in their actions and patrons were the offenders. He looked carefully at both sides of such disputes. The chips didn't always fall where expected—or where wanted.

———

By the mid-sixties Branigan had an astounding "average of 400 cases being brought to court each year," according to *Garda Review*[7]—a figure beyond the imagination of other guards. His court experience accumulated over the previous thirty-five years was unparalleled. Judges regarded it as a reservoir of knowledge to be drawn upon in court. Thus he became a valuable liaison officer between the streets and underworld of Dublin and the courts of justice. In this role he could act as both interpreter and interlocutor between uneducated defendants and erudite judges and solicitors. Says Dan Walsh: "In court he'd have judges that *understood* what he was about, and gave him that certain respect" to proceed on his own. He came to be sometimes referred to in court as an "unofficial social worker," representing the best interests of needy defendants.[8] Essentially, he assumed whatever role was necessary to see that justice was achieved. As Declan recalls, "he was always up before one judge, Judge Ó hUadhaigh, a very tough judge, and he would come down on people very hard. But he *always* took my father's word." Whether Branno recommended a harsh penalty or a light sentence, judges took it to be the right one.

Behind the scenes, his compassion for battered wives and abused prostitutes was largely known only to his closest colleagues, but in the courtroom his kindness and sympathy were on full display. No-one admired this facet of his character more than John Collins. "In court he was *very humane* in his own way. He could see the difference between an out-and-out blackguard and others"—those who had a deprived background and deserved a chance in life. As Michael Reid saw it, "Jim was very intuitive: he was able to assess people extremely well. If he felt a person was a reasonably decent, upright person, then he would *help* him." His "humanity," as many friends came to call it, was seen consistently in his efforts to redeem those in whom he saw some innate goodness and future promise. In this regard his insight into human nature and human failings was uncanny. Declan understood his father's rationale for wanting to help those less fortunate and misguided:

> In court, one thing that always stood out was his thinking that there's *always some good* in everybody, that nobody was *completely* bad. Now, some of these were "no-hopers," like rats, used to a life of causing trouble. But he had this knack for seeing that there was a *chance* for some people . . . and then this *soft side* of him came out. He was very good for standing up for [decent] people . . . and he was unique there.

In sharp contrast to his public image as the garda who toppled the most feared thugs and criminals, in court he could be an "old softy" at times. As unpredictable as ever, he sometimes surprised everyone in court by switching his role from accuser to defender. After arresting a person, perhaps even dishing out a bit of "summary justice" on the street, he dragged him into court before the judge; then, doing what was unthinkable to some, he switched positions and spoke up forcefully on behalf of the arrested person. No-one would be more surprised than the defendant, who might stand dumbfounded.

John Collins remembers many times seeing the astonishment on the face of one of Branigan's own prisoners when, during the hearing or the sentencing stage, the mighty Lugs began saying positive things on their behalf:

> A lot of fellas were brought into court thinking they were going down [going to prison]. But Jim, at the end of the case, he'd put in a soft word for them . . . very humane. If you were a bowsie he treated you like a bowsie, but if he thought there was a bit of good in you he took care of you.

Branno knew a great deal about life in a reformatory, such as Artane or Letterfrack, and about prisons, such as Mountjoy—how they hardened and worsened many men who ultimately came out more of a menace to society than when they went in. Yet he had also seen the other side, how it had taught some inmates a hard lesson and put them on the right track in life thereafter. It was always unknown exactly how a man might turn out if he was sent there.

Better or worse? It was always a gamble. So, when a judge might ask him for his recommendation for sentencing it was a difficult decision. He could only follow his best intuition. Over his long career, his judgement in "betting" on a defendant's future was remarkably successful. For when Branigan "went out on a limb" for a defendant, the man was not only grateful for his support but felt an obligation to live up to his good faith in him—knowing also that if he failed to make a good effort Branigan would come down hard on him the next time. So it was chancy on both sides.

One thing that always troubled Branigan was seeing young lads, little more than children, sent out to Artane for five years merely for stealing an apple, mitching from school, or throwing snowballs at a bus. That was not his type of justice. Perhaps he knew even then what took place in such institutions.

He knew that his words counted for a lot in court, in their influence on judges. And that this carried a lot of responsibility—perhaps too much. There was no doubt about it, confirms Tony Ruane, "he had *great clout* with *all* the judges." And some solicitors didn't like it one bit.

Noel Hughes often wandered over to the court to watch Branno exert his unique influence. "Justice Ó hUadhaigh allowed Lugs to cross-examine as much as he liked—and he could *convince* the judge! He knew something about psychology, I'd say." Many a time, only a few words from Garda Branigan seemed to work miracles. And many are the stories around Dublin even today from people whose lives were changed by his intercession on their behalf. When Séamus Quinn began to work with him in court he saw him as a champion of the oppressed and disadvantaged, dispensing "welfare for people that went wrong, went on the wrong path."

From the standpoint of the judges, it might have seemed that Branigan simply had a gift for picking out the "bad apples" from the good—most of the time. But it could place them in an awkward position as well at times, as they didn't want to appear too chummy with Branigan. Some judges in particular had a close relationship with him, far beyond what they had with any other guards. But in their minds it served the best interests of the court and justice. "When my father would speak up on behalf of people he had arrested," declares Declan, rarely would the judge fail to follow his recommendation for a second chance.

Sometimes, almost amusingly—except to opposing solicitors—the judge and Garda Branigan could seem to drift off into a personal conversation while everyone else in the court sat merely listening in. "He would engage in conversation with the judge," says Tony Ruane, "and the judge would then ask him for his *opinion* as to what he should do." As if they were in the judge's private chambers. Séamus Quinn believes that many judges came to defer to

Branigan's expertise, accepting that he honestly knew best what punishment fitted the offence:

> Jim had great influence in the courts, influence over the judge in the sentence the person got, be it a fine or a custodial sentence. The judge would *actually ask* him, "Sergeant Branigan, what do *you* think I should do with this person?" And Jim would say to him, "Well, judge, maybe if he got a day or two in jail it might put him on the right path, show him what that life was like."

Tommy Lowry regularly attended court as an observer and saw judges defer to Branno's judgement as a common practice. He cites one day when the judge casually asked him for his recommendation. "'Oh, Jim said to the judge, 'I think fourteen days in Mountjoy would do him no harm,' and the judge said, 'Okay'. Oh, the courts had great respect for him."

Very seldom did Branigan's humanity, or "soft side," make the newspapers for the public to see, as reporters would be looking for more lively incidents about Lugs. However, on 11 May 1962 the *Evening Herald* published a front-page article headed "Man gets another chance," featuring his softer side and redemption policy. In this case a nineteen-year-old from Inchicore had been found guilty of maliciously wounding a man on the street and faced a tough sentence from Judge Conroy. Normally, Branigan showed no mercy for those who carried out malicious assaults; but he knew the lad, and his parents, and found some mitigating factors. Over his three decades as a garda he had seen many young fellas about the same age in similar trouble, tottering between taking the right road and the wrong road in life. In this case he believed a prison sentence would nudge him in the wrong direction.

Judge Conroy's inclination was to put him behind bars, with miscreants of all sorts. Branigan stood before the judge to present some positive testimony on the lad's behalf. Conroy listened intently to his reasoning, asked a few questions. In summation, reported the paper, "Detective-Garda J. Branigan said he had not been in trouble before and he was 'worth a chance.'"[9] Considering Branigan's testimony, and on his recommendation, Judge Conroy decided to follow his advice, giving the lad a six-month suspended sentence.

In such cases Branigan always corralled the young defendant after court to have a talk with him about his future. Sometimes with his pointed finger touching the man's chest, he spelt out his expectations: his good behaviour, getting a job, being respectful to his parents. If he let Branigan down after he stood up to the judge on his behalf he could expect no mercy the next time. He had better make the best of his second chance—or else.

This aspect of Branigan's humanity, going the "extra mile" for those he helped in court, was often not known even to the judge, as it all took place outside the court. But his close Garda friends saw this caring side of him all the time. Séamus Quinn, who would come to regard him as a father figure, admired him immensely for giving so much of his time and effort to helping wayward youths, and adults as well. Time and again "I saw him going back *after* court cases, to families whose son or daughter had got on the wrong path, speaking to them. And *advising* them. Not in a way which depicted his rank but more as a friendly father. On his *own time!* Jim felt they needed guidance. I really admired that." He wanted to see their misguided son or daughter get a job, be respectful. And he would take the time to make follow-up visits to check on their progress.

Not all second-chancers chose the right path. In such cases Branigan would often recommend to the judge that they try a dose of bitter medicine in a reformatory or behind bars. And indeed for some this proved to be a cure. Many years after Branigan's death Tony Ruane continued to hear the endless tales from those crediting Lugs with saving them in life. "I've heard reformed young criminals state that the *best thing* that ever happened to them was Branigan getting them a stretch in a juvenile institution."

Mary Barnwell, now seventy-three, knew countless young lads and girls who ran foul of the law, only to be helped by the compassionate Lugs Branigan— giving them the opportunity to mend their ways. And most of those she knew made the best of their second chance and kept their promise to him:

> He *always* gave them a chance if they were in any way good but unfortunately fell into trouble. He'd speak up for them. And many of them when they got older looked back and said to themselves, "If it weren't for him . . . I'm lucky I took his advice."

James Quinn, writing in *History Ireland,* concedes that some of Dublin's most notable criminals had a grudging respect for him, and he was often on good terms with their families.[10]

————

To be sure, Branigan's court appearances had their lighter side. He unabashedly liked to "show off" in court, so long as it was pertinent to the case. He would display his astonishing arsenal of weapons collected from gangs, Teddy Boys, skinheads, common hooligans. And he was always ready to show off his most recent "battle scars," on his arms, legs, or face. He was a natural showman in court. "Jim could be very dramatic in court—a *performer,*" Dan Walsh laughs. "Yes, he was *on stage.* But it produced the goods. It *worked!*" Declan knew how his father loved "to project himself, to the judge and the people in court."

He had a natural wit and a gift for amusing, colourful phraseology that was appropriate to the decorum of the court and conspicuously pleased those in attendance. When Branno was "on" in court, he could elicit smiles and chuckles without even trying—though he often *did* try. And even hearty guffaws heard from the back seats. For the most part, judges didn't mind a bit.

Of course he had a fascinating cast of colourful and quirky characters in supporting roles. From time to time some of the galaxy of Liberties characters would show up in court for some minor infraction or a warning: Mad Mary, Johnny Forty-Coats, Hairy Lemon, Bang-Bang, Damn-the-Weather, Jembo No-Toes, Shell-Shock Joe, and others. In most cases the judge just wanted to give them a little talk, or a bit of scolding, about their behaviour, to keep them out of more serious trouble. Most of them were afraid of the court and were highly nervous. Only Branno could calm them by appearing by their side. They were there mostly for some harmless disorderly conduct or mischief. Many, Branigan well knew, had mental and emotional problems or suffered from alcoholism. While some people saw them as "head cases" or "loonies," most residents of the Liberties were understanding and sympathetic. Jim Branigan, who was their minder out on the streets, assumed a similar role for them in court.

In some cases, such as that of Shell-Shock Joe and other men suffering from shell shock or the effects of mustard gas contracted during the First World War, it was a sorry sight for the court, for there was no satisfactory solution to the problem. Branno's comforting hand on their shoulder was a mercy in itself. He saw to it that the judge understood all the mitigating circumstances of their unfortunate life. Whatever was going on in court, Branigan was happy to attend that day.

In January 1965 judges, solicitors and court staff were all uncharacteristically grumpy. The entire heating system in the building broke down, and frigid temperatures permeated the courts. As the *Evening Herald* reported, "justices, officials, gardaí and prisoners shivered in 'arctic' conditions in the District Courts to-day. There was no heating of any kind."[11] People wore heavy overcoats all day and fumbled with frozen hands. Judges were further annoyed when "at times the proceedings were interrupted by the sound of hammering on pipes," as maintenance men worked frantically to fix the heating apparatus. For weeks the Office of Public Works banged away installing a new heating system. Many people found reason not to show up on some days. So far as we know, Branigan was not among them.

————

It would not be hyperbole to say that, apart from the immense respect he commanded in the courtroom, Branigan enjoyed a certain "celebrity status."

He was so often genuinely entertaining that it was deserved. There was simply no-one quite like him appearing before the judges. He actually drew a following of regular observers, who traipsed over to the court solely to see what he was up to. "When Lugs was up," exclaims Noel Hughes, "*anything* could happen!" His mate Séamus Quinn, who enjoyed the entertainment as much as anyone, adds: "Oh, you wouldn't know *what* he'd come out with!"

He was often annoyed with what he felt was the leniency of some judges in cases of brutal wife-batterers. On one occasion he had brought before the judge a beast of a husband who regularly bashed his wife with his fists and kicked her when she was on the ground. Even Branigan's "clatterings" had failed to reform the bully. Lugs wanted him put behind bars for a long spell, to give his family some safety and sanity. However, the judge decided to give the habitual assaulter another light or suspended sentence. This left Branigan openly fuming about what he would like to do to the culprit:

> I told the judge I would like to *wring his neck!* I knew the man should have been jailed and taught a lesson—he had beaten the hell out of his wife on three consecutive occasions. And I *stormed* out of the court at the decision.[12]

He never had any regrets about this outburst over the judge's decision. Nor did the judge take any action against Branigan; he was probably wise enough to realise that if he made an issue of the matter, and all the facts of the case came out in the newspapers, it would be *he* who would come off badly in the public's judgement.

But his most publicised case was an unusual one in which, for once, he actually got into serious trouble. The story's origins can be traced to the faraway Congo. In 1961 Irish UN peacekeeping troops were serving there under dangerous conditions in Katanga province, and in November nine were killed in an ambush by Baluba tribesmen, sometimes even referred to as "savages" and "cannibals." For many years afterwards in the Irish lexicon the term "Baluba" was used as a social slur, meaning an unruly or primitive person.

The affair began with a routine arrest over a row at the Olympic Ballroom in Pleasants Street. Branigan apprehended an unusually violent man, who resisted with all his means. When struggling to cram the man into the patrol car, Branigan was viciously kicked, receiving a painful injury. Once in the car the man continued thrashing about wildly in an attempt to kick the windows out, forcing Branigan to concentrate on pinning down his dangerous legs. Unfortunately, this left him in the vulnerable position of having to face away from him. Taking advantage of this opportunity, the arrested man decided to bite him in the buttocks, clamping tight in a vice-grip. Branno, in acute pain, nonetheless kept his grasp on the man's legs to restrain him—all the way to the station. It left a wound serious enough to require medical treatment.

On the day of the court case a few reporters from the *Evening Herald* and *Irish Press* were on hand in the hope of picking up some juicy tidbits when Lugs was "on." They were not to be disappointed. After covering the essential facts of the incident, Judge Reddin asked Sergeant Branigan to describe the severity of the assault upon him—and to show the court the injuries. Branigan hoisted up his trouser leg to expose an ugly gash. And now could he also show his bite wound? Well, hesitated Branigan, unfortunately not. And why? asked the judge. Because, replied Branigan, "the defendant bit me on a place I could not produce in court. I'm *sitting* on it, justice." Reddin asked him to expand:

> The defendant kept his teeth sunk in my posterior. . . [while] we drove for ten minutes to the Garda station, in the back of the patrol car. I had to count to ten to myself or I would have destroyed him.[13]

Chuckling rippled through the court. Judge Reddin, barely concealing his amusement, shook his head and exclaimed with disgust, "Savages!"

Branigan's testimony could—and should—have ended there. But, feeling the frivolity of the moment, he launched his famous addendum:

> *Worse than the Balubas*—at least they would *cook* you first!

Reporters scribbled down their juicy story. The next day this "Braniganism" appeared in the newspapers. The Garda authorities and the Department of Foreign Affairs were *not* amused. Branigan was put on the carpet and given a sharp reprimand for his remark. Years later he would confess that for a few days he had been worried about losing his job:

> A priest had to speak to the commissioner on my behalf, for fear I would be sacked over the incident. I was told by my superior several years later that I had created an international situation for commenting that the defendant was "worse than the Balubas."[14]

Interestingly—some would say hypocritically—following this episode several judges and solicitors took to occasionally calling hooligans "jungle boys," "savages," even "Balubas." Retired Superintendent John Murphy, now eighty-one, recalls the episode with both amusement and admiration for his friend's brashness:

> Oh, if he said that *today*—the commissioner would be answering, and everybody. And the minister would be up in the Dáil! But he really just said it as it is . . . Isn't that the way it should be?

Branno loved to tell the tale till his last days.

Of all Branigan's roles and contributions in court, none was more important than that of mentor to scores of younger gardaí over several decades. Standing for the highest standards of integrity and fairness, he was a model for men who drew upon his experience and talents. "He was a great man as a tutor for the younger men who had just come out of the Depot," says Tony Ruane. "He was an educator, in a general way." Guards of any age could seek his advice, and it was freely dispensed. Younger guards especially could learn more from observing Branigan in the courtroom than from reading any textbook when it came to giving evidence and interacting with shrewd solicitors. And these were lessons imprinted on their minds. Superintendents would encourage other guards to observe Branigan in action whenever they had the opportunity. It was always well worth it.

Taking this advice, young guards such as Eddie Finucane made it a practice to hang around in court for a few minutes when possible after their own cases to watch the master perform:

> Jim was respected by young gardaí. He was exceptionally good at giving evidence in court and had the respect and listening ear of the judiciary. Young gardaí in attendance in court for their various cases benefited from this. They often waited on after their court cases had ended—to hear Jim's presentation.

It was a tutorial they valued above all others, a combination of knowledge, tactics, and style. All agreed that Branno was as peerless in court as he was in the street.

For many other gardaí the most important thing he taught them was *confidence* in the courtroom. Shaky guards with limited experience could be quite intimidated by the entire courtroom procedure, from its magisterial setting to the legal formalities. Countless times, Branigan personally interceded on behalf of an insecure guard with the jitters. As the most formidable adversary against the premier solicitors, Branigan knew all the tactics to teach unseasoned colleagues. When he saw a younger guard fumbling with his presentation or being bullied by an aggressive solicitor, Branno could come to his rescue, as Tony Ruane puts it. Very often, Michael Reid vouches, Branigan would actually step in, with the judge's approval, and take over in assisting a young guard:

> One thing that endeared him to younger members of the Garda Síochána was that if a young guard was in any way troubled in the box, Branigan would step forward to ask the judge if he could help on behalf of the guard. And the judge, of course, would say, "Oh, yes, go ahead." And he would *assist* him . . . he'd be *restructuring* the questions, to produce the case the

way it *should* be produced. It was his *experience!* It was second nature to him, because he was there *every* day. He was the most competent I've *ever seen.*

It was in this helpful manner that Branigan came to the assistance of Val Lynn when he was young and faltering somewhat in court:

> In court he would *take over,* as if he were your solicitor. Like in my *own* case, or in the cases of an awful lot of young guards. He would say, "Guard Lynn, you were on duty at such a place at such a time . . . Will you tell the justice what happened?" And if the young guard was having difficulty he would turn to the justice and say, "This man is only a short time in the service." And the justice would say, "That's all right." He was the *kindest* man!

Branno's ire was aroused, however, when he saw a solicitor deliberately bullying a young, insecure guard. According to Lynn, it happened with considerable frequency, as nervous neophytes were easy targets for hostile solicitors. Lugs never failed to leap forth on their behalf and swat away their sharp queries like annoying bees. The moment Branigan came upon the scene the most arrogant solicitors adopted a more moderate, even timid, approach. Lynn recalls how the tide suddenly shifted when Branigan stepped in to assist a guard being bullied:

> If Branigan wasn't there, solicitors, they'd *tear lumps* out of a young guard if he was getting into trouble with the evidence. But the solicitors were *afraid* to bully me, or anybody else, when Branigan was helping you out.

There is no way to calculate how many of his fellow-gardaí benefited from Jim Branigan's tutorial role in Dublin's courts over his 43-year career. It is perhaps best to say that it is difficult to find guards who *don't* credit him with teaching them valuable lessons. Tony Ruane is typical. "He came to my rescue about 1970. I was glad of Branigan's intervention, because I felt rather foolish at the time." Lugs tactfully and discreetly guided him through the process, like his counsel, not making Ruane appear incapable or dependent. As always, he was sensitive to the other guard's pride. Ruane's case turned out well, as "the culprit was eventually sentenced to three months in the slammer." Thereafter Ruane's confidence grew and his performance improved. Years later, in reflection, Branigan simply said with modesty:

> I am proud that I have, in fact, helped hundreds of raw young gardaí give evidence at their first court cases, and supplied them with the formula for presenting the case for the prosecution.[15]

Beyond his practical mentoring role in the courtroom, Jim Branigan came to be seen as a "moral force" for fairness and justice. On the day of his retirement, in a courtroom packed with well-wishers bidding him farewell, Judge Ó hUadhaigh expressed to him a personal and heartfelt sentiment: "I consider you to be one of the pillars of the law, who saw that justice was done."[16]

Chapter 14 ～

PATERFAMILIAS OF THE "PAVEMENT HOSTESSES"

"The prostitutes, he was looking out for them. If some fella was beating them up he'd do his *damnedest* to get the fella who did it."

(ALICK BRANIGAN)

"Jim had a great love of the street ladies, knew them all by their first name—but he *hated* and *detested* their pimps."

(GARDA SÉAMUS QUINN)

"I call them 'pavement hostesses'—I think the term 'prostitute' is vulgar. I came to know the girls, their backgrounds . . . They're vulnerable. I suppose the girls saw me as a sort of father figure."

(GARDA JIM BRANIGAN)

"Mr Branigan, he'd pull up and inquire about our welfare . . . so soft hearted and nice and considerate . . . a protector. Many of the girls regarded him as a father figure."

(A DUBLIN "PAVEMENT HOSTESS," *Evening Herald,* 1973)

It was as if he were catapulted from one planet to another. At eleven in the morning Garda Jim Branigan could be before the judicial bench, facing a distinguished judge and esteemed solicitors in the lofty, ceremonious courtroom. That night at eleven he might be standing out in the rain beneath a street lamp in sordid, wicked Benburb Street, the pit of Dublin's underworld elements, compassionately consoling a vulnerable young woman who had been beaten by her pimp. Acting now in a paternal and protective role well beyond his defined Garda duties. The social chasm between the two settings and experiences symbolised the range of Branigan's extraordinary life.

George Bernard Shaw called prostitution the "blackest misery," the most piteous life a woman could lead, one born of hopelessness and despair. In the 1930s, when Branigan was a young garda on the beat, prostitution was common in several parts of Dublin. Around the notorious Monto (Montgomery Street) district and Benburb Street to respectable St Stephen's Green and Merrion Square, "ladies of the night" dallied along streets and stood forlornly waiting beneath lampposts.

They were a mixture of Dublin women who had fallen on hard times and country girls forced for various reasons to flee to the city. Some had been disowned by their families for the grievous crime of unmarried pregnancy and the shame it brought; others were escaping cruel husbands or fathers. Quite a few were abandoned single mothers, left on their own to provide for themselves and their child. In an age without social workers, women's shelters or government aid they turned to the merciless streets to earn money for food and rent. Condemned and castigated by society, they lived a life of loneliness, vulnerability, and abuse by men. Even insensitive guards sometimes poked them with their batons when ordering them to "move on." They were surely the sorriest sight in Dublin.

Most found shelter in the poor tenement districts. Tenement mothers living around them, usually with their huge brood of children, were typically understanding and kind towards them, showing compassion for their plight. The local dealers and stallholders were especially maternal in helping them. In harsh contrast, "Mother Church" and her priests showed no pity, only condemnation.

Mary Corbally grew up in Monto in the 1930s and 40s and knew many of the women well:

> They were called "unfortunate girls," never "prostitutes." The girls hung around the streets for money just to keep themselves going. The girls were good . . . oh, *very* kind-hearted.

She saw that they attended Mass regularly and would even buy shoes for the poorest urchins in the bitter winter months.

Billy Dunleavy, born about 1900, always felt compassion for them:

> It was a *hard* life! Girls got into trouble with a baby . . . Oh, they got a *hell* of a time of it—that's why they *had* to go "on the town." But very kind the girls were. *Respectable* girls. That's just where they finished up.

Quite a few lived around the Liberties in tenement rooms or lodging-houses, where they were accepted as unfortunate souls struggling to survive in an age when there was no helping hand. Many unmarried pregnant women, of course, ended up in the Magdalene laundries, where the abuses they suffered have now been exposed. Others turned to the streets to earn a few pounds.

While those in "refined" society may have perceived them as "low" or "immoral" women, the people who lived among them and knew them felt quite the opposite. One of these was Bridie Chambers, who lived in Meath Street in the 1940s and 50s:

> There was a red-lamp lodging-house there, Lynch's, and all unfortunate girls there. All *nice* girls, very decent—they had to do what they *had* to do. They never hurt nobody, and they'd go to Mass on Sunday. You never heard anything against them.

May Hanaphy always had great pity as well as a fondness for the women around her home in Golden Lane in the first half of the century. She understood their plight:

> Oh, once you became pregnant, the girls were *put out* of their houses . . . onto the streets. They had *nowhere* to go. They were caught! God love them.

———

Although "unfortunate girls" were a part of Liberties life when he was young, Jim Branigan knew little of them, as he had grown up largely within the confines of the South Dublin Union. Even as a lad growing up he wasn't much exposed to night life in Dublin's rougher districts. Only when he joined the Garda Síochána would he slowly learn of this sad aspect of Dublin life. However, from his first years as a garda, his sons Alick and Declan reveal, he possessed a natural sympathy for the vulnerable young women.

It was during the early war years of the 1940s that he had regular first-hand contact with prostitutes, when he and his mate Senan Finucane had patrol duty requiring them to inspect the concrete air-raid shelters to make certain they were not being used for any illicit purposes. Here they would often find a woman and "client" engaged in sexual acts. Here too they would come across an "unfortunate girl" who had been left beaten and bloody by a man who had used her.

In those days, prostitution in Dublin was almost exclusively an outdoor activity: down an alley, in a park, behind a building—or, with wealthier customers, in a parked car. They were left completely unprotected against any man's whims or cruelties. With every encounter they were at risk.

Bridie Chambers recalls how distressing it was to look on the poor women after they had been beaten up by a customer, or their pimp, the night before.

> They'd go out on Grafton Street and around the Green [St Stephen's Green] and go off with a gentleman. And some of the men used to *murder* them [beat them]! Oh, yes, girls used to come in dirty and with black eyes.

And, as Branigan found, often with far worse: bruises, facial abrasions, swollen lips, missing teeth or patches of hair. Their pimps and husbands, using them in the same way, often gave them the worst beatings.

From the early 1940s onwards Branigan took a personal interest in trying to look after the pathetically abused women, regarded as outcasts by so many others. In his mind they deserved protection, just as did the battered mothers he helped. *Someone* had to look after them.

His evolving role as paterfamilias of Dublin's prostitutes would be kept as confidential as possible by his Garda superiors. They were understandably concerned that Branigan's compassionate role might be misconstrued in the public's mind, resulting in an adverse moral judgement on the Garda Síochána itself. Gardaí and the press honoured this confidentiality. City-dwellers who saw Branigan's helping hand knew the story, of course. Admiring his kindness, they were discreet in keeping it hushed. Not until 1973, on his retirement, would the full story come out, when he granted a lengthy and candid interview to two *Evening Herald* reporters.

––––

Branigan had no training for this role. At the Depot, recruits did not receive any lessons in how to protect the city's prostitutes from abusive customers, pimps or husbands who forced them out onto the street for profit. Young guards were merely told to "move them along," keep them "out of sight" of respectable society. They were considered both immoral and scandalous by the Catholic values of the day; from the pulpit and the Dáil they were condemned. If prostitution could not be eradicated, at least it should be covered up. Guards were explicitly instructed not to have any social interaction with prostitutes. Indeed Branigan confided that "there is a superstition in the Gardaí that it is unlucky to have anything to do with them. Many a garda has had his face slashed by a girl or by a pimp." He dismissed the superstition, and was undeterred by anyone wielding a knife. He determined to defy tradition and act on his own moral principles. Using his discretion.

He even created his own vocabulary. He not only detested such crude words as "whore" and "harlot" but disliked "prostitute" as well. As he expressed it, "I call them 'pavement hostesses'—I think the term 'prostitute' is vulgar."[1] Once he adopted this name, he stuck to it. Nor would he tolerate others around him using degrading words when referring to the women. He would not hesitate to give another guard a sharp reprimand for denigrating the "unfortunate girls" in any way. They had to suffer enough physical and verbal abuse from others; at least they could be addressed respectfully by Dublin's gardaí when upholding the law.

During his earlier years, when he served mostly on daytime duty, he could not assume a major role in the lives of the "women of the night." In the later 1950s and early 60s he began a great deal of night patrol as he and his driver roamed a wide range of the city. This marked the beginning of his real commitment to looking after the prostitutes along the quays, in Benburb Street, Leeson Street, Merrion Square, and other common nightly haunts.

It was a gradual process, establishing contact through slow, cautious approaches. The reality he was faced with was that most of Dublin's prostitutes feared or hated—for good reason—the majority of policemen. Consequently, he began by periodically pulling up in the patrol car or van, disembarking on his own, and enquiring respectfully about the woman's welfare that night. Was she all right? Any abuse by her pimp or customer? Ending with a few cheery words and caution to "be careful, now." That was all. No interrogation or effort to extract information.

At first the women admitted to being highly suspicious of his motivations. As many bluntly expressed it, "cops were the enemy." To their mind, the police were always trying to get something *out* of them or to pin something *on* them. Therefore, when approached by a garda they were as reticent as possible. Most had had unpleasant dealings of one sort or another with gardaí before. Furthermore, they knew that being spotted talking to a garda did not help their business. And their watchful pimps might give them a wallop for doing so.

Branno's first effort to get to know them personally was simply asking them their first name, which he would later jot down and then memorise, thereafter always greeting them with a smile and "Good evening, Rosie." To most, it was the only kind word they would hear all night. Then, as always, he would ask if they were all right. After a few more friendly words he would pull away, as their image faded into the darkness.

As time passed, his brief check-ins became a familiar nightly routine, part of his general cruising circuit of the city. Women became less wary, more friendly. There would be some light joking. From his viewpoint, the more he learnt about the women as individuals, understood their background and lives, the better he could care for them.

To his son Alick it was a natural instinct for his father to feel protective towards women who were oppressed on threatened in any way. "*Invariably* he was looking out for them. It was like they were weaker and he was stronger—

and therefore he would try and help them." As Paddy Casey concurs, they were disadvantaged and very vulnerable: "The girls, they were generally uneducated, exploited ... [so] they'd go 'on the game.' They had an awful, sad experience— Oh, it was *very sad.*"

Before long, Branigan began to notice that some of the women felt comforted by his brief presence, even trying to prolong the chat.

Over the years he would find that many of the young women came from quite respectable, happy families, either in Dublin or down the country. For one reason or another, forces beyond their control, they had fallen into a downward spiral and ended up on the grim and unforgiving streets of Dublin. If there was one thing they needed at that point in their lives it was a genuine friend.

Most of the women were between eighteen and thirty-five, which meant that by the time Branigan was in his late forties he was old enough to be the father of most. Matt Mulhall began serving with Branigan around the time his "paterfamilias" role was evolving, seeing it as his natural predisposition towards protecting them:

> He always kept a very close eye on the street ladies. He had a certain affinity for them . . . He *understood why* they were there, that it was a *necessity*— none of them were there for the love of the game. They were there by circumstances. And if you treated them properly, dealt with them as *human beings,* they'd reciprocate. If you looked after them properly they could be your best friends.

In the late 1950s and early 60s there were more young women on the streets to befriend, forced into prostitution by two factors. Firstly, the "youth rebellion" and its sexual freedoms meant that unmarried girls became pregnant more often, and might be put out of the house and ostracised by their family. There was still little access to counsellors, women's shelters or medical or financial aid for such young women; so some turned to the streets to try to earn a living.

A second force driving women into prostitution during the 1960s was addiction, or at least dependence, on drink or drugs. When pubs began removing their "Men only" signs and admitting women to the sacred ground to drink beside men, even at the bar, too many indulged excessively. At the same time the use of drugs was insidiously creeping into many areas of Dublin, ensnaring young lads and girls. Addiction to drink or drugs began driving women into the streets at night to pay for their habit, which greatly distressed Jim Branigan, who knew that many were just young people caught in the drink-drug culture.

————

In August 1964, when he took command of the riot squad, his role as paterfamilias expanded considerably in scope. He was now solely on night duty, and with full authority to establish his patrol routine and contact points. So, along with checking in at certain troubled ballrooms, chippers, and pubs, he included in his nightly itinerary a cruising of sites where he knew that prostitutes plied their trade—meaning that they could now count on his regular visits to enquire about their welfare. This pattern of protection was not officially authorised by the Garda hierarchy: it was entirely a Branigan scheme. But a blind eye was turned.

All the men who served in his riot squad would become familiar with his protective, fatherly role in the lives of the women. Though dictionaries generally defined a prostitute in such words as "an unprincipled or immoral woman," those he befriended did not fit such a description, by any means.

Country men who joined the force tended to be more conservative, often having a more morally negative perception of prostitutes. If they seemed in any way judgemental or condemning when on duty, Branno would take them aside and give them a quick sociology lesson.

Matt Mulhall recalls that there were always a few moralistic new guards from chaste families who were put out on the impoverished tenement streets, often amid squalor, and might make a demeaning or mocking comment about one of the women. "Sometimes it was very difficult to get across to other guards that they were more to be pitied than laughed at." When Branigan got wind of this he set them straight. He hastened to educate them about the women's personal history and present plight, always stressing that they were not out on the dark, dangerous streets by choice but by dire necessity. Sometimes in desperation and as a last resort, to make his point regarding the misfortune in the women's lives, he was known to exclaim: "It could be your sister!"

Dealing with the pimps, customers and exploitative husbands was quite another matter. They could be abusive in different ways: physically, emotionally, psychologically. Many were guilty on all counts, treating the women like dirt. Branigan and his men halted it on the spot when they encountered it. Even if he found out about it after the fact, which was most common, the abuser was in trouble, because Branno would make every effort to track him down. Says Alick: "If some fella was beating them up he'd do his *damnedest* to get the fella who did it." And his "damnedest" was usually good enough. Once he caught the cowards he would teach them a memorable lesson.

There was also the powerful deterrent effect of the black van as it was seen nightly cruising the notorious pick-up spots around the city, always a welcome sight to the women and a daunting one to lawbreakers. The black Bedford van would roll along at a snail's pace in certain areas, to be as conspicuous as possible. When he halted to say "Good evening" and check on a woman he got out of the van and walked over alone. The van would be parked a bit away, and his men could get out and stretch their legs if they wished; but it was a solo act, in respect for the woman's privacy. Every word between them was confidential. *Trust* was the basis of their relationship. Often his squad members could hear them laughing. It was a good sound, one in which they could all take some pride. After a bit of chat and perhaps a laugh he'd bid the woman goodbye for the moment and return to the van. She knew he might swing by again later that night.

By the time Paddy Daly joined the riot squad Branno "knew *all* those prostitutes by name . . . 'Rosie' and 'Betty' . . . And *very* kind to them." Straight away he saw the paternal character. There was a real bond between them—no mistaking it. In every case it was the result of trust, only built up over time.

But some women were hard nuts to crack for quite a while, resisting his gentle overtures. No chatting—full stop. Most resistant were those who had had bad experiences with guards, who perhaps had pushed them around or arrested them for soliciting. Their distrust was understandable.

But Branno believed that even the hardest nut could be cracked in time. A case in point was a prostitute who had come over from England in the 1960s, a few years before Branigan met her. She was a bit older, more seasoned and wiser than most of the other women, having endured some rough treatment by the British police. To her, no policeman was to be trusted. As she put it, they were all "fishing" for something, usually information that could do them no good. Many of the younger Dublin women looked up to her and sought her advice from time to time. They had a loose organisation among themselves and met from time to time for a feeling of solidarity and security, and she emerged as a sort of leader.

After Branigan's retirement she would come forward to speak on behalf of her sisters about their relationship with Jim Branigan. Reminiscing in later years about her first impressions of this policeman named Lugs Branigan, about whom she knew nothing when she first arrived on Irish soil, she summed up her basic policy: "Let us get one thing clear: policemen and girls on the street are enemies." She proceeded to share with a reporter from the *Evening Herald* how he changed her feelings in time:

> To be frank, when I came from England years ago I thought Mr Branigan was a fruit-and-nut case. I mean, it's highly unusual for a policeman to stop a prostitute and ask how she is. In England I had never seen anything like this. Other Dublin cops would land us in Donnybrook or Harcourt Terrace station if they caught us soliciting.
>
> My suspicions of him vanished after I realised he was genuine, and not

fishing for information. My respect for him began to grow as I heard more and more stories of his acts of kindness.[2]

In speaking to a reporter, identifying herself simply as "a spokeswoman for the street girls," she emphasised that she was speaking for them collectively, representing their shared feelings. Each woman, she made it clear, had her own personal story of how "Mr Branigan" had personally helped her out in life. Once the trust was established they became comfortable in sharing not only "professional" matters but personal problems. A good many of them poured their hearts out to Branigan beneath a street lamp far more freely than they would to a priest in the confession box. He didn't judge or condemn them.

_____

Most of the women had pimps, or husbands addicted to drink or gambling, who forced them onto the streets and quickly grabbed the money from their hands. But they also had a wide range of family, health and emotional problems. To varying degrees, they became comfortable sharing their worries and woes with Branigan. He first listened attentively, asked questions, and gently dispensed some advice—not empty platitudes but specific ideas about how to better their condition. For the women, having a strong, caring man to turn to was a godsend in their lives. He was well aware that many came to depend upon him for support—"I suppose the girls saw me as a sort of father figure"—though there were a few who remained guarded and could not bring themselves to speak openly to him. Possibly this was explained by their fear of being caught by their pimp or husband getting too friendly with a policeman.

When he gave the women sound advice, he expected them to follow it and report back to him on the results; if not he might apply a bit of leverage, for their own good. Séamus Quinn was on riot squad duty with him during one notable case in which a prostitute shared with Branigan a serious medical problem:

> She was complaining for weeks that she had a lump in one of her breasts. And so every night he'd call to her and ask, "Well, did you get that looked after?" And she would say, "No." "Well, I'm giving you one more week!" he said to her. "But, Mr Branigan, I haven't the money."
>
> A week went by and he saw her another night. "Well," he said, "did you get that fixed?" She said, "No." "Okay, I'm arresting you." He put her in the back of the van and took her over to the Meath Hospital, where he was friendly with the night sister. They were introduced . . . and [later] she had her operation. And Jim took care of *all that*—the hospital stay and operation—*himself*. I know that for a fact. He was a great man.

As they increasingly came to see him in a paternal light, it was natural that he came to refer to them as his "girls." The bond was unmistakable.

From his long experience in assisting battered women he advised some of the prostitutes about their marital problems, especially those who told him they were beaten by their husband if they returned home with too little money for their night's work. He sometimes intervened in such abuse cases. According to the woman from England who often acted as spokeswoman, one of the women approached Branigan on behalf of one of her friends "forced to go on the town" because her husband "refused to give her money to support herself and the kids, and beat her up regularly."[3] Would he help her out?

Late one night he arrived to find her perched up on a wall outside her home, being threatened by her husband "to come down or he'd kill her." When he saw Branigan, the "tough husband was not long 'doing a moonlight'!" He informed the woman about the process of seeking a legal separation from her husband, and promised to help her find other accommodation for herself and her children. She took his advice and acted; as a result "she was separated and now better off." He had turned her life around.

He also had immediate and short-term strategies for helping women who, for one reason or another, were having a bad night. His immediate concern was to remove them from harm's way. When he came upon one of them who was obviously inebriated and not in full control of her faculties, or who was suffering emotional distress that impaired her, he had to act on the spot. Gently escorting her into the van, he would talk to her to assess the condition, then drive her to Kevin Street station, where he would give her security in a cell overnight.

With more and more pubs open to women, this was an increasing problem. But he understood that prostitutes often relied on alcohol to dull their senses:

> The girls realise they are dabbling in dangerous waters by practising their profession. They fortify themselves with alcohol so they will be able for the work sometimes. Often I took in some of them for their own safety after I found them lying on the street drunk. The following morning they would thank me.[4]

Apart from creeping alcoholism and drug use, some of the women suffered from psychological and emotional problems stemming from the miserable and stressful life they led. It was small wonder. It was an age in which social workers and professional counsellors were not abundant; nor were the myriad tranquillisers, sedatives and "wonder drugs" of later years. Branigan often found himself trying to assume the role of social worker or psychologist. However, he was not interested in abstract ideas but insight into the human condition on an empirical level. As he once told an *Evening Herald* reporter, his method of helping the women was not by detached "analysis" but by getting to know them well enough to feel their pain:

> I came to *know* them, and their backgrounds. Many were from respectable families—they were not out for sex, but to earn a living. And this was the best way they knew. And husbands and pimps would terrorise them and make them hand over as much as two-thirds of their earnings. I have come to see it as a "necessary evil."

Though he didn't philosophise with his fellow-gardaí about the perils of prostitution, he did share his knowledge and certain specific experiences from time to time. This was to sensitise them better to the plight of the women. "The way he looked at it," says Paddy Daly, "was they *had* to do it. And that was *it* . . . They were down and out." Those women with young children to support had the most compelling reasons for suffering the indignities of their trade, willing to do anything to be able to care for and feed their children. During the bitter winter months their life was made even more painful by the cruel weather. He would often stop the van, let his men out for some fresh air, and take a cold, shivering woman inside to sit down for a few minutes for warmth and a chat. Some of the simplest conversations were later his most memorable:

> I stopped and took them into the van and had a chat with them. To really *know* the girls. One of them told me, "Ah, Mr Branigan, I still have to make £7.50." I asked her why that precise sum. She said, "My young one is making her First Communion next week, and I want her to get a nice dress." You have no comeback for that sort of frankness.[5]

————

Taking the women under his wing as he did, it was no surprise to his riot squad colleagues to see him explode with anger when a man hurt them, something that commonly occurred. The women could face physical punishment by three sets of abusers: customers, pimps, and husbands. Branno had a policy of no tolerance when it came to any man laying a hand upon them, as Gerald Byrne saw:

> He looked after the ladies *very* well, that they were *not* going to be abused or kicked about or assaulted—or paid no money. If he *ever* saw a man abusing them he was in there *right away*. I've seen that happen quite a few times, when he had to use physical force.

He saw pimps as the scum of the earth, and showed them no mercy when they mistreated a woman. But they were shrewd devils and cleverly tried to keep out of Branigan's reach, operating in the background. When he saw one of his women with fresh bruises or abrasions he always enquired about the cause. When it turned out to be their pimp, he began keeping his eye out for the wretch. Rarely would a pimp be so foolish as to mistreat one of his women out on the open street; when it did happen he risked Branigan happening on the scene in the black van. On pimps he didn't use his leather gloves: they deserved a more lasting impression. One of these is remembered by Séamus Quinn, who was in action with Branigan one frigid December night:

> Jim had a great love for the street ladies, but he *hated* and *detested* their pimps, taking money off the girls, maybe *all* their money. Now, I recall one night in one of the red-light districts, in Baggot Street, when we spoke with one of the prostitutes. A very nice girl. And then she went off. Now later we came upon her again. But *this* time there was a row going on between herself and her pimp. A physical row—and there was blood drawn. *Blood drawn!* Oh, yes. And Jim *saw red!* This was a man as low as you can get.
>
> Now, unfortunately for him, he was on one of the canal bridges. And Jim literally *jumped* out, *grabbed* him, *hit* him, and *over* the bridge and into the water! Tumbled backwards over the bridge and into the water. And then he told me to go and fetch him—and I *had* to. I didn't know was he unconscious, would he drown, or whatever. So I pulled him out, and it was a cold early December night, and I was wet to the shoulders.

The cowardly mongrel was shoved into the van and taken to a hospital, where both he and Garda Quinn had their clothing dried. "My uniform was dried, and later he was discharged." Informed that he was now on Branigan's radar screen, the pimp was warned that a repeat would bring worse punishment.

The more widely known it became among the underworld of Dublin's villains that Branigan delivered clatterings to such as they, the better was the protection for the women. All the malefactors feared him—not only the pimps but other dregs of society that might prey upon the vulnerable women alone at night by robbing or beating them. Their abusive husbands were equally fearful of the mere threat of Branigan being called. And a good few of the women used this threat as a standard line of defence: "I'll get Mr Branigan now!" And he'd come.

One prostitute vouched: "There are stories among the girls how he put in the boot and scared the daylights out of the pimps and husbands" who beat them and took their earnings.[6] One woman in particular if she was molested in any way would cry out, *"I'll get Mr Branigan on you!"* It was a successful deterrent.

Among the dregs of society often mentioned by members of Branigan's old riot squad was a nefarious fellow by the name of Henchico. He hung around Benburb Street with his cronies like a fly circling a rubbish heap. Back in the 1960s, Paddy Daly recalls, "prostitution was rife in Benburb Street," drawing a conglomeration of the lowliest pimps, perverts, drunkards, and dangerous predators. Beatings and stabbings occurred nearly every night. Only the most desperate women plied the streets in this area. To hear members of the riot squad tell it, Henchico was a runty, small-time kingpin among the rotten elements of Benburb Street society. But he was gifted. Involved in all sorts of illicit dealings, he was cunning and conniving enough to be rarely caught. Time and again, when Branno and the riot squad would be called to Benburb Street on a "Branno 5" call, they would arrive to deal with some ugly situation only to find Henchico's name lurking behind it.

It was a world of users, conmen, and cheap criminals, a contaminated turf beyond the notice of decent society. Which meant it was fertile night territory for Branigan and his colleagues. To them, Henchico was a despicable character, yet a curious, enigmatic fellow as well. Always involved in trouble, but crafty enough to be just beyond the fingertips of the law. To Branigan, therefore, he posed a challenge: to catch him red-handed, and make him pay.

All the guards had to admit that Henchico was unique—an impressively "shadowy" figure. Val Lynn saw him as a notoriously sleazy and slippery culprit, always in their sights. "This fella Henchico, he was a pimp. And he'd *also* commit a crime himself," then cleverly place the blame on someone else. Furthermore, Lynn attests, he was a "squealer" on his own mates, yet somehow got away with it—at least so far. "He'd give the names of *other* fellas involved in crime"—a grievous sin in the underworld. He probably had more enemies than friends, but apparently they feared him.

Branigan disliked everything about the verminous character, and made no secret of it. He knew that the women on the street feared him terribly. He therefore tried to make several circuits of the district at night in the black van to keep his presence visible. What particularly irked John Collins was travelling with Branno in the van on a Saturday night and seeing how this rat, as he regarded him, had the gall to try to play up to Branigan. He would act in a friendly way, playing cute with him. Although Collins and the other guards found his act revolting, it was nonetheless fascinating to watch:

> This particular guy—and what his correct name was I don't know, he was known as "Henchico"—a small little guy, in his thirties or forties. And we'd drive up Benburb Street, and he was always hanging around there and always had a couple of young fellas with him. But he'd come over to the

van and say, "Oh, Mr Bran, Mr Bran . . ." Smiling and, you know, *playing up* to him.

He was hard to pin down . . . very cute, you know. He was an "under the table" sort of fella. And if he was up to *anything* it was *no good!* And he knew *everyone,* all the *scumbags* in Dublin—and spent his life dealing with them.

He was a target for Branigan, because he was a known pimp, terrified the women out on the streets, and was adept at having others do his dirty work for him. And pimping was only one of his lucrative illicit enterprises. If one of Branno's women got punched or kicked around, it wouldn't be directly at Henchico's hands. He'd see to that. And the assaulter dared not mention his name and implicate him.

And then suddenly he was gone. One night in 1970, Branigan and his riot squad found him dead, apparently of natural causes. As Val Lynn describes it, he had apparently been up to no good to the very end. "He was found in Benburb Street with £180 in his pocket—when other people wouldn't have a penny! 'Cause he had ladies on the town . . . in charge of prostitution." He had a long practice of robbing them of their earnings. His body was taken to Jervis Street Hospital and the money was confiscated and turned over to the proper authorities. The "pavement hostesses" could breathe a bit more easily without fear of him.

———

Dealing with troublesome customers and "messers" on the street was yet another problem for the women, sometimes requiring Branigan's intervention. At nightfall the messers came out, usually drunk, and began interfering with the prostitutes, taunting and tormenting them, cursing at them, swearing that God would punish them for their sin, trying to rob them, sometimes even trying to bargain for free favours. Not uncommonly one of them would slap or strike a woman, grab at her, or spit on her. Some were habitual molesters. If the black van happened to swing by, Branigan would hop off and chase them away, at least for the moment. Putting up with verbal abuse and threats was a continual part of the women's life. It was demeaning, and took a toll on some emotionally.

Customers came in a wide variety, native and foreign. Dubliners usually knew the scene and were familiar with Branigan. Men from distant places, however, who were in the city for business or a match at Croke Park, could be very disrespectful of prostitutes, starting rows with them in the street. When Branigan approached them in plain clothes and gave them a warning, or a direct order, some had no idea who he was and might fling a curse at him. At which point Dan Walsh and his mates in the riot squad knew the man was in for a lesson in manners:

> If there was a row with a client, Jim would just send the guy on his way. But *some* guys wouldn't know Jim, because they were "imports." And he would soon let them *know* who he was!

For such an introductory greeting his leather gloves were the perfect ice-breaker. Other temporary visitors came from Britain, the Continent, or further afield, usually for business or tourism. Most had no clue about some cop named Lugs. If they were not behaving properly they usually got his message and moved off without incident. But not all.

Customers who laid a hand on any of "his girls" fell into the category of battering husbands and pimps—and could expect the same treatment. Unfortunately, most of them got away with it. Following such an incident there was usually no way to track them down when they left the scene, unless they were regulars and he could be on the look-out for them. Many men saw the women as no more than objects, to be used or abused and then discarded. Perhaps not even paid. "You can *imagine* the *treatment* they were getting from their clients," says Matt Mulhall. "Sometimes a client wouldn't pay . . . and then he'd *belt* her!" Branno would find some of the women left in tatters by a cruel man, bruised and bloodied. He would make certain that the victim was taken to hospital, examined, and treated if necessary. It could leave him in a storm of internal anger, not expressed but discernible to his fellow-gardaí.

Occasionally Branigan came into face-to-face contact with the most unexpected—and unexpecting—customers. To their dismay. They covered the gamut: esteemed and famous figures from high society, business, government, entertainment, sports, journalism, education, religion. Branigan was never impressed by their position or credentials. Out on the street in the dark of night, men seeking the services of unfortunate women were all the same, be they barrister, minister, or docker.

Sometimes, however, potentates and luminaries could see it differently and would try to "pull rank" on a lowly Garda sergeant, even if it was Lugs Branigan. Which was always the most foolish attitude they could adopt when facing Branno. He had lessons for them as well. In keeping with his standard practice, he politely but firmly ordered them to cease whatever trouble they might have been causing and promptly depart the scene. If they resisted, either verbally or physically, they were informed of their liability to arrest.

Often such men trawling the streets for a sexual encounter were at least mildly, if not heavily, under the influence of alcohol, and their judgement was likely to be impaired. Branigan recognised this fact—after all, was it not he who, as a young man, had a few drinks too many and decided to climb atop a tram and traverse the city of Dublin?—and he would allow them some latitude for being "difficult" at first. But this did not permit them to be disrespectful or to try to get away with anything unlawful. And it certainly did not allow even a judge or a bishop to mistreat the women in any way.

Men of such exalted status, upon being caught in such embarrassing and incriminating circumstances, were all too happy to abide by Branigan's orders and beat a path home as quickly as possible—especially knowing that the following week or month they might be facing him again, only this time in a professional or social setting. Simply being caught by him, and identified, was punishment enough.

But there were those few who, with an air of confidence and arrogance, would announce *who* they were, how *important* they were, and the *influence* they wielded. Perhaps to tell him of the lofty Garda officers or judges they knew, and that Garda Branigan wasn't going to tell *them* what to do! For Branigan's mates this was always the beginning of an amusing performance. But it instantly became more serious if he was threatened in any way—not threatened physically but with a reprimand or dismissal, that they intended to use their influence in high places against him, make him pay for his indiscretion in ordering them around. Branigan usually gave them one more chance to follow his orders; if not they were unceremoniously ushered into the van, taken to the station, and charged. Along the way some were physically resistant and verbally abusive, meaning they would have to appear in court.

As Branigan found early in his career, this sometimes did not end the story with some men of such importance. For they might still pursue means to get the charges against them altered or dropped, as some of them did indeed know senior Garda officers or judges personally. On a number of occasions during his long career it turned out that such influence was actually used by some prominent figures to have charges against their friend dropped, possibly with veiled threats that to refuse the request might affect his career. At the time, this was all hushed. But after his retirement he intended to bring it into the light.

———

One particularly amusing case involving a big shot always stuck in Gerald Byrne's memory. It was an episode involving what he calls a big-name comedian from the Dublin stage, a celebrity widely known and admired by everyone. Garda Byrne was on duty this night with the riot squad, making their usual rounds, stopping here and there to check on the street women. Along the way a call came in for Branno 5 to go to a spot on the quays where apparently some man had put in a complaint against a prostitute. A curious reversal, to be sure. Gerald Byrne likes to tell the story in detail:

> There was a certain Dublin comedian—I won't say his name—but this comedian was with this lady one night, and when the whole arrangement was over he wouldn't pay her *any* money at all. So they were near Kingsbridge [Heuston Station], and he had her in his car, and she took the keys *out* of the car and *threw* the keys into the Liffey! And she says, "Now, *there* you are. You'll walk home now!"
>
> So this comedian calls *us* [through headquarters] to the scene and says, "I want you to charge her with the loss of my keys." And so Jim had a chat with the girl, and she told Jim, "Look, Mr Branigan, you know who I am, and I'm not getting paid here." And Jim told her, "I'll sort this out." He took the *lady's* side.

The man, immediately recognised by Branno and his squad, had called the Gardaí in the confident belief that his status placed him in a position of power relative to a lowly prostitute. As he awaited Branigan's consultation with the woman, he clearly expected that she would be charged. Instead, when Branigan returned to inform him that it was *he* who might be charged, the man assumed a haughty *"do you know who I am?"* attitude—rubbing Branno just the wrong way, and hardly helping his case:

> So Branigan then said to the man, "You leave the car and we'll look after it some way—and if I *ever see* you here again I'm going to *charge* you with being with this lady." And *then* Jim says, "By the way, if this appears in the newspapers you're going to be a very sad and chastened man, because all the facts of this will be in the paper."
>
> And your man suddenly copped on. "What? In the *paper!* Oh, God, hold on—!"
>
> And Jim says, "'Cause if you go to court your name will be mentioned in the paper. So I strongly suggest that you go home now."
>
> "Well, will you give me a lift home?"
>
> *"No. Go!"* And he just walked away. Oh, it *frightened the life* out of your man.

Branigan had long ago learnt that one of the surest ways to sober up a man and bring him to his senses was to merely mention newspaper coverage of an incident. It was fascinating to see how quickly pomposity could be reduced to humility.

———

Apart from protecting the women from physical harm, Branigan also cared for them in a more subtle yet very important way. In his own manner he looked after their mental and emotional health. Because of their dismal life, with all its stresses and anxieties, many of them suffered from depression and could topple into despair, even to considering suicide. Some carried it out. As Séamus Quinn saw when he served with Branno, some of the women could plummet "into the depths of despair," wanting only to end their miserable life.

Branigan knew all about their emotional and psychological fragility, because they expressed to him their fears and hopelessness. Some didn't have to verbalise their unstable condition, because he saw it in their faces the moment he checked with them at night. He could tell when one of the women was tottering on the brink. They immediately became his priority.

By 1964, when the riot squad was created and he began checking on the welfare of the prostitutes every night, he had many years of experience in counselling distressed and battered mothers suffering from levels of depression and despair similar to what he saw in these women. He knew that his role was to be a listener first. He would take a shaky woman aside, or into the van, and give her as much time as she needed to pour out what was tormenting her to such a desperate degree that night. Only after he had heard her full story did he gently begin to talk to her, always reminding her of her child or family she needed to think of, how she was not seeing things clearly at the moment, how he would be there when needed and see that she got medical help if she required it. She could count on him. No father could have done better.

Most of the women never reached such a desperate point, but all became depressed from time to time. It was Branigan's regular visits that kept many of them from despair, by their own admission. Branno knew that a simple dose of good cheer, delivered with a smile, a dash of humour, and perhaps an amusing quip or story could lift their spirits at the lowest moments. One of the women confided: "If we were depressed or browned off he would cheer us up, or give us a pep talk. He was *always* in good humour." It was one thing they could count on.

As time went on, his nightly visits were intended not only to enquire about personal safety but to provide a positive social exchange for a few minutes, to brighten their mood, draw out a few smiles. It felt respectful, and *humanising*. And for some of the women it made all the difference in breaking, or warding off, their bouts of depression. One of them, telling how he always had the knack of bringing a smile to even the most dejected faces, sums it up simply: "Mr Branigan always managed to snap us out of depression. He was *always* smiling, and told us clean yarns. We liked seeing him coming."[7]

The women often expressed regret that there was no way to thank him for assuming this comforting role in their lives. On occasion, however, they passed on to him tips about things they heard or saw that might interest him. In Dublin's underworld, men sometimes talked too much. Prostitutes overhearing things could share them with Branigan, voluntarily or inadvertently. And sometimes it was of real value to the Gardaí. "He got *a lot* of information from the prostitutes around the quays," John Murphy attests, "just from talking to them. The women, all knowing and *trusting* him, he'd get an earful." If it was relevant to a case and could prove valuable, Branigan might casually ask a woman to expand on or clarify what she knew. He never grilled them or used pressure of any type. As he explains it, during a friendly chat a woman might turn out to be "a source of information, and unwittingly the girls divulged maybe the number of a car, or information on a customer that might lead to the cracking of some crime." Confidentiality was inviolate, the women knew. To them, helping Mr Branigan out was an honourable act.

————

Acting as paterfamilias and protector of Dublin's "pavement hostesses" was surely one of his most humane roles, yet one unknown to the press, and kept relatively quiet within the Garda Síochána. Newspaper articles about Lugs Branigan dealing socially with "ladies of the night" would have appeared unseemly and surely would have raised many eyebrows. To moralists it would have constituted a breach of Garda propriety—"going beyond the bounds!" Local residents who knew about his role and understood the women's plight admired him for it. But even here, it remained largely a well-kept secret for most of his career.

About ten years after his retirement, Jim Branigan liked visiting his chiropodist and friend Genevieve Kearins-Creagh, often reminiscing about his Garda days. One favourite topic, she says, was his fatherly role in the lives of his "pavement hostesses." "He told me how sad it was to hear the stories of the 'ladies of the night' . . . trying to get money for their child's First Communion or Confirmation. Jim had *great* respect for women in general." He was especially proud to tell her that "I never arrested any of them for soliciting."

And over all those years of helping "his girls," as he still called them, she asked him what his superiors thought of it. He simply confided: "The head of the Gardaí didn't like that to be known."

Chapter 15 ～

THE "OLD GUNFIGHTER" YEARS

"I don't care how long it goes, I'm still the fella that's there to be taken—because I'm the 'old gunfighter'."

(SPIKE MCCORMACK, BOXING CHAMPION
AND STREET FIGHTER)

"The greatest glory for many a thug was to be able to say, 'I hit Branigan'."

(Evening Herald, 24 JANUARY 1973)

"Belted, bruised and battered . . . he has suffered more injuries outside the ring in street brawls than he did in his entire boxing career. Sgt. Branigan has now lost count of the number of times he has been assaulted."

(Evening Press, 13 MARCH 1972)

"I am always a scapegoat for the good old fella who, when he gets the smell of a cork, wants to prove 'I beat Branigan'."

(SERGEANT JIM BRANIGAN, 1973)

By the late 1960s Jim Branigan was approaching the age of sixty, at a time when a person of that age was regarded as an "older man," well past his prime. Yet he continued his rigorous exercise sessions in the gym, and faced the same high-risk duties he had carried out for decades. Even into his sixties he would tell an *Evening Herald* reporter, with confidence rather than boastfulness, how he saw his physical fitness:

> Thanks to my training I have a lethal punch. My arms and muscles are as tough as a crocodile's hide. And if I land a punch even now a knock-out is likely.[1]

He took pride in the distinction of being the oldest garda still assigned to dangerous street patrol. Clearly he continued to see himself as essentially ageless, and invincible. To those close to him, however, there were now some signs to the contrary. He had learnt from his western books and films how "young blood" gunslingers often caught up with ageing sheriffs and marshals. The fear, and ultimate fate, of many gunfighters was to live long enough to have the tables turned on them. Even six-gun duellists of the stature of Wyatt Earp and Bat Masterson found that their mantle of fame made them a target for bold young bloods when age slowed their reflexes. They might be challenged out in the open, or bushwhacked. Younger former enemies could insult, bully and goad them into a fight to gain revenge. For most of the famous gunfighters it became a real threat in later life. Both Earp and Masterson, much admired by Branigan, carried the burden. And so would he one day in the streets of Dublin.

Branno often spoke, without boasting, of the "notoriety" gained from being known as the toughest and most fearless street fighter, who took on all "villains"—the term of his choice—referring to it sometimes as if it were becoming a burden. Dublin's legendary boxer and street pugilist "Spike" McCormack learnt all too well about the curse of notoriety when he grew older. And his friend Jim Branigan had to witness it.

In his heyday, from the late 1930s to the early 50s, no-one in Dublin was more feared in a bare-knuckle fight than Spike. As his son John (himself a light-heavyweight boxing champion) put it, his father fought like a ferocious pit bull terrier, and no-one could withstand his steam-hammer hook. Yet he was admired and regarded as an essentially good man who fought mostly bowsies deserving of being laid out on the pavement, while in the ring he became Irish middleweight champion. By all accounts, he was a folk hero.

Then he grew older. By his late fifties he was content to sit on his stool in Killane's pub in Gardiner Street and sip his pint, chatting to his friends. But his reputation hung above his head like a neon sign. While it drew admirers, it also made him a tempting target for wasters and messers intent on making a quick name for themselves. As Bill Cullen observed, he became a sitting duck for men feeling tough enough to take him on, often men half his age:

> He was one of Dublin's great heroes . . . But he'd be drinking in the pub and there was always someone who'd push into him, or spill his drink, to provoke a fight. Always some hardchaw who wanted to take on Spike.[2]

But many a thug found he had made a miscalculation, as Spike would suddenly get up and strike him a single blow that would snap his head back and drop him like a sack of potatoes. He still packed a powerful punch; but with each year he became less formidable, and more conspicuously vulnerable to assault. John, always protective of his ageing father, tells of a time when Spike was again being openly tormented in Killane's pub by a complete stranger:

> I said to him, in the pub where this fella was calling him names, "How come this young guy, thirty-five years of age, and you're sixty-four, and he's here annoying you?" And he said it was because he was the "old gunfighter"— this is the way he phrased it himself. My father *was* like an old gunfighter.

It was always sad to see an old champion demeaned and diminished. Even the greatest boxing champions, like Joe Louis and Sugar Ray Robinson, got battered around the ring in their twilight years by boxers of mediocre talent. Muhammad Ali experienced the same thing. Though they all remained hugely admired after their career was over, they too on occasion had to cope with some drunken fool challenging them.

Even Lugs Branigan, like all ageing sheriffs and gunfighters, would one day have to begin glancing back over his shoulder.

———

Between 1967 and 1973, his last six years as a garda, Branigan was still indisputably in very good physical condition for a man between fifty-seven and sixty-three years of age. Not only did he continue his gruelling physical exercise at the National Stadium three times a week but he refused to reduce his usual weight-lifting, bag-punching and sparring in the ring with men thirty to forty years younger than himself. To him it was a matter of practicality—and pride:

> Even though I am sixty-three years old, I can still take on young Irish heavyweights for sparring sessions. I suffer nose bleeds and black eyes, but I can hardly feel the punches.[3]

His Garda sparring mates, without a hint of condescension, attested to his prevailing toughness in the ring. And, as in days of old, "Battling Branigan" refused to retreat in a spirited exchange. There was no doubt about it, he was still not a man to be trifled with.

Nonetheless, in his early sixties it was only to be expected that his stamina, reflexes and eyesight would be diminishing. His vision was not as sharp, nor his reactions as quick. And after a long Saturday night of wrestling with hooligans and rioters he could now feel weary by dawn. What sixty-year-old man wouldn't? But his enthusiasm and spirit never sagged, which always astonished his men. And indeed he retained a powerful punch, like his friend Spike McCormack, but still to be used sparingly.

His face looked older, more etched. He moved more slowly. His once-ramrod posture was now slightly stooped. His stride was not as quick, nor his eyes as piercing. His voice when barking orders did not carry quite the same commanding tone. If he was not exactly "slipping," he was unmistakably ageing. Some old foes were beginning to pick up tell-tale signs that he was not quite the herculean Lugs Branigan of yesteryear.

In Branigan's world, perceptions were important: how he saw himself, and how others saw him. There was no evidence that he saw himself as in any degree less tough or less capable than in earlier years; but there was some evidence that others were beginning to perceive him as less formidable an authority. And this mattered.

There were signs that his mere presence at a scene of disorder was no longer as intimidating as before. Sometimes his orders were not followed as promptly. Every now and then his word might be questioned, if not actually challenged. Lugs Branigan no longer swept in among rioters and brawling gangs like a storm that sent everyone scattering in fright. But as he was still backed up by his imposing riot squad, the impact of his arrival at a scene of trouble still quelled the turmoil effectively.

However, there were times when he was *not* accompanied by his riot squad colleagues.

In earlier years the mere notion of "standing up" to Lugs Branigan was unthinkable. Deliberately taking a punch at him or assaulting him in any way was certain to invite fast and severe punishment. It was almost always under the influence of drink that a man showed such impaired judgement. But as Branigan approached his sixties, various sorts of physical encounters did begin to occur. Most were minor and brief, a looping poke or flashing skirmish—no real harm done. It was what they *represented* that was worrisome to his friends, that anyone would dare to violate him in any way. What did it portend for the years ahead?

Of course he had the "battle scars" pockmarking his body from the early clashes with the gangs of the 1930s and 40s, when he deliberately waded into the melees. And from later riots. But these did not result from intentional, one-on-one confrontations with lawbreakers standing up to him. As the *Evening Press* would report, he had been "belted, bruised and battered," by the end of his career suffering more injuries from "street brawls" than from boxing contests.[4] They came from fists, hammers, knuckledusters, flick-knives, butchers' knives, hatchets, chains, boots. And women's sharp nails and shoes. As he conceded, "I have 'war scars' . . . My lower lip is numb where it was slashed by a knife, and my chest, legs and shins are scarred. Don't forget, the street gangs gave me as good as they got." And a deep gash in his leg from a woman's shoe became infected and he was laid up in hospital for days. At one point, the doctors even considered amputation.[5]

As the *Evening Press* confirmed, by the early 1970s he had "lost count of the number of times he has been assaulted."[6] But most were not deliberate, daring *personal* attacks. They were battle injuries.

————

During his latter years on the force things changed. A man might brazenly take him on by catching him off guard, sometimes knocking him flat on his back. Such men always sought the cowardly advantage of surprise. It was a shocking sight for those who witnessed it. Even a wild, arching swing from a drunken lout could do damage if it was unexpected and happened to land. Usually he was able to deflect these "telegraphed" blows coming his way; but every now and then he could be "blind-sided" and put down by a burly brawler. Ordinarily, these incidents happened when he and the riot squad were breaking up a disorderly crowd at a ballroom, street disturbance, or chipper.

There were also now old foes and young bloods awaiting an opportunity to deliberately strike out at an older Lugs. "Branigan lived by his *own law*," says Matthew Fagan, "because he went after you . . . And he'd give them a couple of digs or a beating—so *he had his enemies!*" These ranged from local ruffians to hardened criminals who he had put behind bars. Some were sworn to vengeance when the right time finally came. Branigan was well aware of this. In his later years he told an RTE interviewer, "I met a lot of fellas that I put away," and some clearly still held ill intentions towards him.[7]

In his later years as a garda he also had to contend with boyos full of bravado, false courage, and too many pints—the type of "young bloods" who hassled Spike McCormack and took a poke at him. Simply landing a blow on one of these street legends carried bragging rights in pubs. Alick knew that his father had become a target for such types. "I think some people, when they have drink taken, the *legend* was something to be knocked down—and they'd take a chance." Branigan's riot squad mate John Collins witnessed it:

> You had the younger bloods coming through, and some thought, "I'll take him on . . . Oh, Lugs, *I'll* take him on!" You know? Now, there *was* the time when, if they might try to take him on, he'd take them *out!* But as he got older his reflexes . . . and he hadn't the punch. And you know the way younger fellas are . . . They'd like to get their *names*—you know, "Oh, I hit Lugs, *I* knocked Lugs down!" And then they'd go swaggering, like the "hard man," to get the name of being the hard man who took Lugs out. Even though he was an old man.

Branno was savvy enough to see what was happening, telling others about his encounters with fellas who would "get the smell of a cork and want to prove

'I beat Branigan.'" Therefore he had to be constantly vigilant. As the *Evening Herald* summed it up, "the greatest glory for many a thug was to be able to say, 'I hit Branigan.'"[8]

Meeting these challenges from men half his age sometimes required following the old adage that discretion is the better part of valour, though it was a bitter pill for "fearless" Lugs Branigan to swallow—a matter of intellect and reasoning overruling instinct and emotion. He did not want his image and reputation, built over a lifetime, to be tarnished by suffering a humiliating beating that would make all the newspapers. Therefore, while he continued to stand his ground as he had always done, there did occur the rare time when Branigan, out on his own, wisely avoided a physical clash. One day while in the Liberties, Noel Hughes happened upon such a scene, when Branigan was about sixty:

> I've seen Lugs getting challenged a few times. One time was in Francis Street. And around that area there are some real fighting men. Some had been notorious members of the old animal gangs. He'd tell them to move on. But this *one* man *wouldn't*. He was in his thirties. And he circled him, and I heard your man say to Branigan, "Just *you and me!*" And he [Branigan] walked away. See, Lugs *knew* what he would be up against.

———

If he was challenged, or even took a punch, when he was without his mates, Branigan kept the incident to himself. But occasionally there were slight telltale signs, which he shrugged off. But his mates knew. However, about 1967 or 68 there began some personal assaults on him that were witnessed, a few of which even made the newspapers. In April 1967 he was attacked by a youth with a knife, and his mouth was slashed and left numb. Three months later, on the night of 27 July, two men aged about thirty saw their chance to "jump him," as he explained to Judge McGivern.[9] Fighting off the men half his age, he was "hit on the head and also got an injury to his lip," which required hospital treatment and left his lip temporarily paralysed. The judge sentenced one of the men to six months' imprisonment. The incident made the *Evening Herald* under the heading "Jailed for assault on sergeant."

Some months later he was again attacked without warning. This incident in fact occurred inside a Garda station, much to the shock of those who saw it, including Matt Mulhall, who was on duty with him that night:

> He arrested two lads around Grafton Street one night. Two *hardy bucks*. And it took a lot of manpower to bring them to Pearse Street station. They were really acting the bowsie. And while in the station a guard let go of

one of them, and he turned around and he absolutely *floored* Branigan. *Floored* him! I don't know whether he actually knocked him out or not. The punch—he wasn't expecting it. Because whoever was holding him shouldn't have let go of him . . . And he was completely taken by surprise.

When he was assisted to his feet and his head cleared, he showed no anger. It's more likely that he felt embarrassment at having been "sucker-punched" in front of his mates.

The next morning, when Mulhall accompanied Branigan to take the now sobered men to court, another surprise awaited them in the station:

The following morning Jim and I came to collect them. And *now* these were two different individuals altogether from the previous night. And they saw Jim, and one of them *got down on his knees* and apologised to Branigan. Oh, Jim accepted the apology, and we went off to court with them. There was no vengeance.

Attacks took different forms. On 18 August 1969, a Saturday night, there was a riot at a carnival in Ballyfermot. Garda Noonan, who was on duty in the area, reported a mob of about sixty youths, roaming and rioting. Out of control, they began stoning his patrol car. He called for Branigan and the riot squad. Before the van arrived, several other gardaí showed up and were also injured. One of the ringleaders was a 21-year-old hooligan armed with a knife and with a huge alsatian on his lead. As Branigan pulled up, Garda Eddie Finucane arrived from Rathmines station with several other guards—just in time to see that "Jim was there wading in to sort out the trouble and defuse the situation."

Branno quickly spotted the tough-acting youth with the big dog, approached him, and ordered him to leave the scene at once. In defiance, the youth stood his ground. Then, unexpectedly, he released his dog and gave it the command to attack Branigan. Having his own two alsatians at home, he was not frightened, as most others would be: he knew how to handle them. In fact he went on the offensive and confronted the beast. "When the alsatian dog was set upon him, this didn't deter him," Eddie Finucane says with surprise. "He feared neither man nor animal!" Indeed in court he told the judge that the dog got the worst of it, as the *Irish Independent* reported: "I took the bull by the horns and I attacked the dog. Then the dog ran away, and I ran after the defendant."

To which the judge replied, "Did the dog do you any injury?"

"Oh, no. I got there first."[10]

Newspaper stories of this sort further polished Branigan's reputation of fearlessness and physical prowess. Dubliners did not think of Lugs now as a sixty-year-old man.

It was the perfect opportunity for him to put in for a three-year extension of service, as his mandatory retirement date was quickly approaching. Such requests were unusual, and few were granted; but Branigan knew that he was in superb physical condition and still performing his duty in a superior manner. To him, retirement was not a thing to be desired but to be dreaded. He was completely confident that his request would be granted.

When his request was approved he was elated. As the *Irish Times* reported, it was granted "in recognition of his unique service record"—an honour earned.[11] The Garda Síochána recognised his exceptional performance over the previous thirty-nine years and rewarded him accordingly. Best of all, he was allowed to continue his high-risk duty with the riot squad. Other gardaí who were anxiously counting the days till their retirement found Branno an amazing anomaly—admittedly an admirable one.

In the 1970s Branno did get taken by surprise every now and then. One night he was in a Garda station with Gerald Byrne when a man who had been arrested by another guard for housebreaking was escorted past them. When he spotted Branigan it apparently triggered a revenge mechanism. "Nothing was said," recalls Byrne. "Your man just *lashed out* and hit Jim, and put him on his back. He put Jim down! Then he got up and he was okay." Once again, he had been an easy target.

On 5 June 1972 another attack made the *Irish Independent*. A man coming along Hatch Street took a mighty swing at him, which surely would have done damage had it struck him solidly, but his reflexes were still quick enough for him to avoid the worst of it. As he told Judge Good, "I saw the blow coming and I went with it, so it didn't hurt me."[12] The judge, after stating that he regarded "assaults on members of the Garda as a most serious matter," added: "It is amazing what Sergeant Branigan can take."[13] Especially at sixty-two years of age.

Though he had not suffered serious injury from the assaults on him when they were reported in the papers, they exposed the dents now being made in his perceived shield of invincibility. For the first time in the public eye, Lugs appeared vulnerable.

This was worrying to his family as well as to his colleagues in the riot squad. Fortunately, mighty Sonny Heany was now an almost constant companion, as was Séamus Quinn, who relied on his judo expertise in untangling riots. Quinn knew that the revenge motive was a serious threat:

> There were these people who got a clip and were *still* seeking revenge. And they were *not* going to *take it* [any more]. Because now that he was older he was *not*—and there was no *doubt about it*—not the man he was twenty years previous! And *that's* why we took such good care of him . . . why we watched his back.

A 23-year-old man that Branigan may have "clipped" when he was forty-five might now be thirty-eight, while he himself was sixty. Which completely changed the equation, and the dynamics, between the two men. Even after twenty years or more a man could carry a grudge over the insult of a Branigan glove-lash or punch. Séamus Quinn cites a case at a dancehall one night when Branno was about sixty-one:

> We met a guy one night at a dancehall, and he was so agitated! And he was kicking the bouncers and kicking the doors to get in. Then we arrived, and Jim told him, *"Go home,* and everything will be okay—stay *here* and you're going in the back of the van."
>
> Then he says, "And who's f*** going to *put* me in the van?" So Jim says, "I am." And he said, "Look, you clipped me sixteen years ago—you won't do it tonight!" This was a big guy: he was six foot three and I suppose seventeen stone weight.
>
> And then this fella went for him! But I dropped him with a judo throw. See, he came with his right arm for him, and I grabbed the arm, and he went over my back and onto the ground. And then in one move he went from the ground into the back of the van. So he didn't hit Jim, but technically he was charged with assault. And that guy got a month in prison.

One of the last events of Branno's career reported in the newspapers showed that he could still handle young toughs a third of his age. It happened in September 1972 after Garda Patrick Collins had arrested a 21-year-old in Fownes Street for breaking into a parked car. When he began resisting violently, Branigan was summoned to the scene. It was settled within seconds. In court Branigan told Judge Ó hUadhaigh that he was forced to "clip him, and he was subdued . . . That finished it." The defendant then testified that after Branigan hit him he "did not remember any more." The *Evening Herald,* aware that Branigan's career was coming to an end in a few months, published an article headed "Knew no more after detective clipped him."

> The boxing prowess of Detective-Sergeant Jim Branigan has been testified to on numerous occasions in Dublin District Court. Today it is the turn of a 21-year-old Ballyfermot man to tell what it is like to be on the receiving end of a blow from the detective.[14]

The article upheld Branno's image nicely.

———

Ironically, one of the clips most memorable to some of his colleagues occurred not in Ireland but in the United States; and it was one he certainly didn't want reported in any newspapers.

In his later years on the force he made several trips to the United States as a member of a Garda contingent on behalf of the International Police Association. He delighted in the visits to New York, Boston, Chicago, Philadelphia, Newark, and Cleveland. It was an eye-opener for him to see how the heavily armed American police handled thugs and criminals. These cities had police forces that included many Irish-American policemen who knew of the Lugs Branigan legend by the late sixties and early seventies. Paddy Daly accompanied him on several of these trips, witnessing his fame in America. *"Everybody* knew Lugs: he was a big celebrity." He especially liked visiting members of the New York and Boston police forces, where nearly everyone greeted him personally. "Oh, he loved America," says Daly. "And the police in America, they *all* knew about him—everybody knew that he was *the* Lugs Branigan." When reporters got wind of his visit they often showed up for a story. He could not conceal his thrill at being so esteemed. His travelling mates derived nearly as much pleasure from seeing all the attention he drew.

Because of his reputation, some police forces accorded him special privileges, one of which was the opportunity to travel along with several policemen in their patrol car at night in some of America's toughest districts. Looking out the window, he got an eyeful, and an education. American ghettos could be a shocking sight for a Dubliner, even a garda. He always enjoyed this perk, asking his fellow-policemen lots of questions along the way. He was even allowed to get out of the car and accompany them during confrontations and arrests.

One thing that particularly impressed him was that American bowsies were a whole lot bigger and more aggressive than those in Ireland, and demonstrably more difficult, and dangerous, to handle, commonly requiring the use of a baton or pepper spray and helmets and shields for the police—all of whom carried a gun, and knew how to use it. It was a different game altogether.

As one story goes—which would add to his legend—there was a night in Cleveland when he was granted permission to accompany two policemen on their night patrol. A city with pockets of appalling poverty where race riots had occurred, Cleveland had one of the highest crime rates in America. Relations between the police and residents were strained, to put it mildly.

In the middle of the night Branno and his hosts were despatched to a brawl in a black ghetto. On arrival he got out of the patrol car and walked with the two policemen towards the melee. As the two men attempted to quell the fighting they were attacked by a large man intent upon harming them. Instinctively, Lugs sprang into action. According to the account at the time, the sixty-year-old Irish policeman let fly a blow, "clocked the Negro and knocked him flat."[15] To Branigan it seemed the natural thing to do. After all, as his old sidekick Senan Finucane used to say of him, "he was always on duty, day and night." The incident was verified, but not publicised.

His trip to Washington in 1971 was even more memorable. The White House and memories of President Kennedy were all sacred to him, and his visit to the city was like a religious pilgrimage. At that time Washington was embroiled in protests against the Viet Nam war, as well as civil disobedience and violence in the streets. Travelling with his group of Garda colleagues, Branigan was shocked at his first sight of the scale of opposition and the demonstrations. Especially shocking to him was the sight of anti-war protesters with long hair and "scruffy" dress, shouting chants right outside the White House.

The more he stood and watched, the more he fumed. To him, the crowd of protesters were no more than disrespectful law-breakers. Paddy Daly observed Branno's growing annoyance with the demonstrators, knowing he regarded them as riff-raff that should be swept from the streets. Daly and a few mates tried to calm Branno down before he exploded:

> Now all this protesting, all this Viet Nam stuff outside the White House . . . and Jim said, "Oh, that *wouldn't happen* if I was in Dublin—*I'd get them out of there!* They shouldn't be doing this now." But we said, "But this is Washington, Jim, this is *not* Dublin . . . Over here you can't just go over . . ." He *couldn't understand* how they could do this—outside the White House! And Jim wanted to go over and clear them out of there! Teach them a lesson! "Oh, that wouldn't happen in Dublin!" he said.

He finally reached boiling point and was drawn into verbal combat with some of the protesters, telling them that they should be ashamed of themselves, that they were lucky they were not in Dublin, where he would properly take care of them. What the protesters thought of the "mad" Irishman angrily lecturing them one can only imagine. Wanting to avoid a minor international incident, Branno's friends managed to tactfully usher him away from the scene. Days later, however, he was still simmering over it.

————

By the autumn of 1972 the clock was again ticking towards his retirement date. His extension was to expire in the first week of 1973. How those extra three years had flown by! In a few months he would reach the age of sixty-three. It was time to request another three-year extension.

To his mind it was a simple matter. As he would later express it, "There is no other garda of my years on the beat on Dublin's streets at night. They are either retired or doing nine-to-five desk work. I was deemed fit for the street because of my physical fitness."[16] So long as he remained in top physical condition he considered himself perfectly capable of carrying on. He clearly saw his three-year extension as *renewable,* so long as nothing changed. And, to his thinking, nothing had changed. Therefore, he submitted his request with full confidence.

One can only surmise what Elsie's feelings about the matter were. One thing was certain: his "pavement hostesses" wanted him to remain on duty as long as possible. But, curiously, some of his closest friends were not saying much on the matter this time around.

By the late autumn of 1972 he had still not heard any word about his request, making him slightly uneasy. As his official retirement crept closer each day it would become unnerving.

We don't know the exact date when the hammer fell; but he had never been struck such a devastating blow. It was probably late November or early December, only weeks before the date of doom. Nor do we know how he was first informed. Was it by official written correspondence, or personal notification?

He first gave his family the grim news, then a few close Garda friends. But the verdict showed unmistakably in his face. Branno was retiring.

Word spread fast among the force. Forty-three years! As far as he let on, no reason had been stated for the denial of his request for a further extension, which left the door open for much speculation within the Garda Síochána.

He was genuinely flummoxed, unable to understand the reason behind the decision. At first the consensus seemed to be that it was "unfortunate" news for Branno, that he had been "let down," even "treated unfairly." But on reflection others came to the conclusion that it was a "blessing," as some put it, that it was intended "for his own good," to "protect him." As the weeks passed, this belief gained credence.

From his viewpoint, Branigan felt that he had been treated unjustly by the powers that be. For the first time in his forty-three years on the force he appeared visibly dispirited and gloomy to those around him. No doubt, says his son Declan, "his spirits were down." Nine times he had been put down on the canvas by the German boxer Pietsch's punches, and nine times he recovered and arose. But there would be no resurrection this time.

His friends found it awkward, not knowing what was best to say to him— whether to extend congratulations on his retirement or to offer condolences.

On 29 December, only days before Branigan was to be forced back into civilian life, Lorna Reid of the *Irish Independent* requested an interview. He agreed. He admitted to her that he had "applied for an extension of his service" but that it was "turned down."[17] He further confided that yes, he "was disappointed," even stating openly that he "doesn't want to go." She didn't probe into details of why his request might have been denied (or if she did she didn't print them). Instead she sensitively concentrated on what she called a well-deserved and hopefully happy retirement: "He will retire to a life of comparative ease and quiet—coaching youngsters [in boxing] and breeding budgies," without realising that to Lugs Branigan a life of "ease and quiet" was antithetical to his very nature. He must have winced when seeing the words in print, while those who knew him best could only have read the article with a feeling of heartbreak. They knew that to him it was like receiving a "sentence."

In retrospect, his best friends and Garda mates say that they had a difficult time getting the words "Happy retirement" out. To say they "felt badly for him" was an understatement. It was painful, some would say, to see him looking not only downhearted but strangely "defeated," for the first time in his life.

Understandably, most of the speculation within the Garda Síochána over the decision was hushed. But over time it would seep out. It was obvious that Branno had taken it as an intense personal rejection. After such a long career of being acclaimed and honoured, the blow felt all the worse. Though there was great sympathy for him, few wanted to discuss the issue with him—for his sake. But only a short time after receiving the news he opened up to Bosco Muldoon one day about his feelings:

> I remember when he asked for the extension and then he didn't get it. And it was *terrible*, because he *thought* he was going to get it. I was with him, and he was telling me that he was very disappointed. Gutted . . . *gutted!* See, he was *very sure* they were going to keep him. I'd say he would have kept going [for ever] . . . it was his *life!*

To be sure, he had his supporters who had favoured an extension of his service. "With his experience," Gerald Byrne says, "he could have gone on for a couple of more years—he really could." No-one doubted that he remained physically up to the task. Many agreed with Bosco Muldoon that what seemed to shock and hurt Branigan was the insensitive manner in which the affair was handled. He felt as if he had been "blind-sided" by his own superiors. "They *should* definitely have given him that extension," Muldoon contends. "I thought it was an injustice. I thought it was—and he just went out—bang!—you know." Had the Garda authorities held off the decision until the last minute so there would be no adequate time for an appeal? Some wondered.

The majority of his Garda colleagues seemed eventually to accept that the decision was the correct one, undoubtedly in Branno's best interests. They knew that he saw the issue purely in terms of his physical condition and past work performance—which were excellent, beyond dispute. To Branigan's way of thinking, as he had not changed over the past three years, why would his request for another extension be denied?

The answer was patently clear to others. It was not that Lugs had perceptibly changed: the *times* had changed.

Most of his mates saw the decision as one of compassion and protection for Branno. It was now 1973, not the 1930s, 40s, or 50s. Almost *everything*, it seemed, had changed. Young gardaí were entering the force with university degrees, scientific training, knowledge of new technology. Police forces were now using new techniques based on forensic science, laboratories, statistical analysis. Computers were on the horizon. And there were stricter rules governing the use of force, which had to be explained to old-time guards. The Commissioner and senior officers were now subject to acute public and press inquiry. And guns, drugs and organised crime were coming in.

Branigan didn't quite comprehend the greater legal-political-social significance of such sweeping changes, nor the ramifications for his traditional role as a guard on the streets. And those around him were not about to try to enlighten him. As Tony Ruane puts it, "no-one would *ever* say, 'Now, Jim, listen, you're getting past it . . .'"

His friend Dan Walsh was one of those who clearly saw that the changing times did not favour the continuance of Branno's old-fashioned methods of summary justice:

> In his later years our hierarchy may not have approved of his system. *His* system was of "yesterday." And Jim was *stuck* in his ways! The people at the top thought his ways were not *their* ways—that's my own idea. Some people were by then saying, "We're not standing for your kind of justice any more—it doesn't work any more." The laws were not in his favour.

Without realising the new legal and political risks that came with such actions, he continued into the early 1970s to use his leather gloves and to deliver "clips" and even an occasional solid clout to deserving recipients. His close pal Matt Mulhall, who felt protective towards him in his last years, believes that the decision to deny an extension was a wise one:

> His time was up. Yes, times had changed. He would have got himself into serious trouble—*no doubt* about that. Legally and physically. *Both.* See, he was a man of his time—but that time was now *past.* He was part of the sociology of the time in which he lived. But everything changed from the forties and fifties. There would have been complaints of police brutality . . . His era had gone.

In truth, many Garda colleagues felt relief on hearing that Lugs was being taken off his riot squad, where he had become conspicuously more vulnerable to assault and serious injury. "I'd say they were doing him a *favour,* to *protect* him, because he couldn't see it himself," confides Tony Ruane, because "he was getting old and might have been seriously assaulted and injured in the twilight of his years . . . And it'd spoil everything." In a retirement interview with the *Irish Independent,* Branigan did admit that "people are becoming more violent," because of guns, drugs, and crime syndicates.[18]

Tony Ruane speaks for most men and women in the force when he concludes: "I'd say that when he did retire, it was time."

———

Once the die was cast, he cheered up a bit and faced his last days on the force with a more positive resignation, which made those around him feel more comfortable. Each day would have its touches of nostalgia and emotion. His last Christmas week was especially meaningful. Unfortunately, he had to suffer one last painful injury, as "three days before Christmas I was badly kicked on the shin while on the beat." This caused him to limp through his final days.

Duty on New Year's Eve had always been special, beneath the great bells of Christ Church, amidst the throng of happy revellers singing and dancing, linking arms and shouting. And, of course, always on the look-out for his trophy of the "first arrest of the year." Which this year he apparently dismissed. As he milled about in the crowd on his farewell patrol he exchanged smiles and pleasantries with well-wishers. One would imagine that he must have felt a rush of nostalgia for all those New Year's Eves past.

He had a lifetime of New Year's Eves to reminisce about. They dated from the 1930s and 40s, when on that night ladies in jewelled gowns and gentlemen in top hats tripped over from the Shelbourne and Gresham and their elegant parties to stand shoulder to shoulder with dockers and draymen, all in exuberant celebration. Bottles of champagne popped as horns and sirens from ships, trains and cars erupted in a clamorous wave throughout the city.

On New Year's Eve 1972, his last as a garda, it somewhat sadly lacked the splendour—or was it the soul?—of years past. Even the *Irish Times* noted a different ambience as midnight approached: "The bells pealed as the New Year was borne in with traditional high spirits," yet the "crowd seemed smaller than previous years . . . and although there was plenty of gaiety there was little real carnival spirit."[19] Contrasting this New Year's Eve with those in earlier times, the paper cited some conspicuous differences, which doubtless disappointed Branigan and other "old-timers" gathered in Christ Church Place:

> There were six-packs of beer, but no champagne, a few sparklers but no fireworks, some paper bags on heads, but no fancy dresses . . . and, strangest of all, no cacophony of car horns near the Cathedral. The 'hokey-pokey' was sung and danced but the crowds were composed almost entirely of the young . . .[20]

Times had changed, all right.

It was a birthday he surely wished would never arrive. For on 5 January 1973, the day before he turned sixty-three, he finally faced retirement—more dreaded than any opponent he had faced in the boxing ring or on the streets of Dublin.

His last night on duty with the riot squad was Thursday 4 January. Everyone was nervous. No-one knew quite what to say, so very little was said at first. That's the way Séamus Quinn remembers it, who was assigned as driver of the black van for Branno's last night on patrol. And, of course, Sonny Heany.

When the evening started off out of kilter it made his mates wonder. "He was *late*," says Séamus Quinn. "He didn't turn up until twenty minutes to ten; he was *always* in by half eight, because he would meet people." It was not taken as a good sign. When he finally showed up, "all he said was, 'Sorry, lads. I got caught up.' Now, we didn't ask more."

As they were preparing to depart, Quinn and the squad, as well as other guards in the station, tried to engage in small talk, to ease the obvious tension. At least it was a good try:

> One of the guys said to him, "Well, let's go. Last night!" And the *next thing*, the handkerchief came out—and you would *never* see Jim take out a handkerchief. And he dabbed both his eyes. Yes, he was very emotional that night . . . he was definitely tearful. Well, it *was* the end of an era . . .

Their patrol that night was expected to be uneventful. It began routinely, with only one minor incident and no prisoners taken. "Everything was quiet," recalls Séamus Quinn. "And the next thing, radio control in Dublin Castle called his sign, Branno 5, about an incident around Fitzwilliam Square." As Branigan remembered it, "I was patrolling with Sonny and the riot squad boys, and just after midnight we got a call from patrol to go to Upper Mount Street, where there is something wrong. A 999 call has been received."

This puzzled him, because normally such calls would have been dealt with by Donnybrook Garda Station. In any case, they drove over around the Peppercanister Church, got out, and "prowled around" the area, finding not a soul in sight, according to Branno. No-one in the van could imagine what it was all about.

Just then, from behind cover, out popped a few women. Then a few more, followed by others—all happy and excited as they rushed towards "Mr Branigan." Garda Quinn was as flabbergasted as the others:

> The prostitutes came out from *everywhere!* Even those that weren't out that night came out. And they had this banner: "Happy retirement, Jim." Well, they were skipping and jumping and shouting and whatever. Young girls between, say, seventeen and mid-thirties.

Branigan was plainly dumbfounded, caught off guard and speechless for one of the few times in his life. He recognised the "girls whom I knew to be 'street girls,' in good spirits," but couldn't make out what they were up to.[21] Soon they were joined by more women. As they joyfully encircled him and his mates, all the hubbub was still a mystery to him. As their numbers grew, so did the guard's amazement at the scene. Still confused, he managed to remind them, half-jokingly, that it was illegal for them to be "congregating in twos and threes" or more, that they were "liable to be taken in." To which they teased, "Mr Branigan, you wouldn't arrest us on your last day, would you?"[22] They found him charmingly befuddled at this point.

As he recalled it years later, only when they openly confessed the truth did he finally realise what was going on. "I was amazed that the girls said they had made the bogus 999 call so they could wish me 'God speed' on my retirement." When he saw some of the women in tears he had to control his own emotions. Then one of the women, acting as spokesperson for the group, surprised him further: "We have a little something for you to remember us by." First they handed him a large hand-made card with all their names on it; then they presented to him what he calls "this very nice and expensive present . . . Most of the regular girls on the beat must have contributed towards it." His mates gathered around to watch him open the presents: a set of Waterford glass and a canteen of cutlery.

However, it was the outpouring of pure affection that emotionally moved him, as the women, themselves growing more tearful, crowded close around him. "I was moved . . . I had to keep up a brittle, tough exterior." One after another they approached to bid him "Farewell and God speed, Mr Branigan," as he thanked each one. Until finally they had dispersed and disappeared into the night they knew so well.

Some weeks later an enterprising reporter from the *Evening Herald* tracked down a few of the women who had arranged Branigan's farewell surprise to get their views on the event. In an article headed "Why we girls held Jim in such high esteem" they told of his role in their lives as a friend, father figure, and protector, a role in his long career that had never been publicised before, as Garda Headquarters "did not want it known." Now there was little they could do about it.

One "pavement hostess" told the reporter that the women had met to discuss whether or not they should go through with their plan and the presents. Would it embarrass him? One woman, named Dolores, was chosen to hand him their card, saying, "Here is something to remember us by . . . There is nobody to take your place, and you will be missed very much."[23] All the women said they "could see that he was moved . . . and we were all very glad we decided to say 'thank you' in this way."[24]

Shortly after his retirement, Jim Branigan, citizen, sat down with two reporters from the *Evening Herald*, James Cantwell and Jim Farrelly, to relive that extraordinary farewell by "his girls." However, as a matter of discretion and respect for the Garda authorities, he pruned a few details. In the article he gave the impression of a smaller number of women springing forth. To set the record straight, Séamus Quinn, who was present, estimates the number at not less than fifty or sixty.

Furthermore, one fact was omitted completely, for the obvious reason that it could have been misconstrued. In 2012, nearly forty years after the event, Séamus Quinn adds a historical footnote not previously revealed: that the women gave Branigan something in addition to the Waterford glass and cutlery:

> *Cash.* In old pounds. *That's a fact.* What he did, he took it and gave it to a place on the quays that takes in down-and-outs, a hostel for the homeless. The next day he handed the money in—*anonymously.* Yes. And he made sure that they believed it didn't come from him. He said that he got this donation anonymously.

Their card he kept. Treasuring it for the rest of his life, he proudly showed it off, time and again.

———

On 5 January 1973, his last day as a garda, no events were held in his honour. His official retirement party would inexplicably be held off for nearly ten months, until October. He spent the day signing some final official documents, clearing out his desk, and, of course, showing up for court duty. But most of the day was taken up with graciously accepting the cascade of congratulations pouring in from colleagues, friends, even strangers. Wishes for a happy retirement came in from Britain, the United States, Canada, and Australia.

In court that day Judge Ó Donnchadha joined his colleagues on the bench in lauding his outstanding, "competent and fair" treatment of people over the years, adding that he would be terribly missed for his peerless "detection and prevention of crime" in Dublin. As well as missing him personally. Through it all, Branigan masked the emotions he was feeling.

All Dublin's newspapers reported his retirement after forty-three years. Most readers had "known" him all their life; his presence was an integral part of Dublin. The *Evening Herald*, which had long been his chief chronicler, provided the longest and most detailed coverage of his life. By contrast, the *Irish Times* gave him a polite nod of appreciation. However, "An Irishman's Diary" accorded him due recognition:

Jim Branigan who has policed the streets of Dublin for over forty years is certainly Dublin's best-known policeman. Wherever there was trouble, the standard Garda response was to send for Branigan. For a man in his position, Jim Branigan has made remarkably few enemies and quite a few friends.[25]

The writer even made mention of his "soft side," the compassionate and humanitarian role far less known to the public than his tough persona:

There is another side of Jim Branigan. Many a young man convicted in District Court on his evidence has found himself taken aside quietly by the burly detective afterwards with an offer of a job, or a place to stay, or sometimes both.

It was time that the public knew this.

As the accolades faded after a few days, reality set in. And some glumness showed. His family saw how the awful suddenness of retirement hit him like a sledgehammer. Declan, twenty-seven years old at the time, saw all the signs of his father's dejection:

His spirits were down. There was no sort of "gradual let-down": it was just *"That's it!* Your time is over!" No, he missed the hustle and bustle of the job ... meeting people. It was the *human* contact that he missed.

Surprisingly, he then made a decision that would seemingly increase his feeling of isolation and loneliness. He and Elsie moved from their home in Drimnagh Road, all the way out to Summerhill, Co. Meath. Like most of his friends, Bosco Muldoon was puzzled. "His moving out to Summerhill—that surprised me ... that he would get away from Dublin city." The rationale for the decision was apparently never made clear. Was it Elsie's wish?

He was restless from the first day. He now had plenty of time for gardening, tending to his beloved budgies and other animals, reading westerns and daily newspapers. But this still left too much time to somehow be filled in every day. For more than forty years he had led a life of constant activity, and action. The sudden disconnection from that stimulating life left him emotionally disoriented.

The logical remedy for his forlornness was to make regular sojourns back into the city. *His* city. By bus, he had a good connection for visiting all his old haunts, particularly Kevin Street Garda Station and several other stations where he had pals, as well as spending pleasant times ambling around the Liberties, chatting to the dealers, picking up all the current gossip and news. It immediately brought him back to life. He flashed the old Branno smile, laughed heartily. On the footpath, friends greeted him, sometimes gathered around. Though he was now retired, many people still wanted to tell him their troubles and seek his advice. And he always had plenty of advice to dispense. It was all a great tonic.

Most important was his happy routine of stopping by Kevin Street first thing to visit "the lads." Mornings around the station always crackled with lively chatter and activity, as men and women bustled about for their day's duty. To everyone, the familiar sight of Branno's broad frame striding through the door was warmly welcomed. "Oh, he was missed when he left—because who'd take his place?" says Gerald Byrne. "And so he would still go down to the station and say, 'How's it going, lads? Any bit of advice you want?'" He was always greeted by a chorus of "How'ya, Jim!" He was always eager to be of help, mix in again. And every day there were new things for him to catch up on, good news and bad. For those few minutes at least, it seemed like old times. But when he departed there were still a lot of daylight hours to be filled.

One of his favourite treks was along the Coombe, Meath Street, Thomas Street, into the Iveagh Market, and over to Moore Street. Along the way, dealers flocked around him. Over the years he had helped nearly every one of them out in some way. Their banter and earthy wit had his spirits soaring. He also enjoyed halting at some of the city's ubiquitous newspaper stalls, where men hung around to talk sports and politics. His rounds of socialising were highly interactive and always rewarding. It was, in a sense, a reward for having helped so many people and made so many friends over the decades. *Everyone* was delighted to see Branigan. Now they were giving back to him.

———

But he was not a man to fill the rest of his life with socialising. He needed a sense of purpose. He needed to be productive, to contribute meaningfully—at *something*.

He continued his regular physical exercises at the gym, pushing himself as hard as ever. Without question he was in remarkably fit and strong condition for a man in his mid-sixties. One activity that helped him make the transition from Garda to civilian life was refereeing and judging boxing matches for the Irish Amateur Boxing Association. He had been acting in this capacity since the 1950s, but now he was able to expand his role. In retirement it became even more important to him, because it kept him at the centre of the boxing world that he so loved. He would eventually be credited with refereeing more than fifteen thousand bouts.

But it still wasn't enough to make a full, meaningful life. Unlike so many other retired people, he had no interest in golfing, fishing, boating, darts, bingo; no pub drinking and no television addiction. He was a man of action. "He was the type of man who *had* to keep *doing* something. You couldn't stop him!" says Chief Superintendent Michael Reid. "So when he left he probably said to himself, 'I *must* keep going.'" He needed some sort of mission, duty— *job.*

————

Then came a godsend. Soon after his retirement he was approached by the manager of the Zhivago night club, who made him an intriguing offer. The Zhivago was a "high-class" and booming discothèque in Lower Baggot Street, and it was in need of a "security superintendent" for three nights a week. Would Branigan be interested?

The two men sat down as the manager, Mr Hickey, explained the whole operation. It was a very respectable club, with two floors of entertainment, a wine bar, and a restaurant in which fine meals were served. As Lynn Geldof wrote in *In Dublin,* patrons were required to have a membership card and to wear "respectable" attire—no denims or runners. And, as Paddy Daly recalls, not only a strict code of dress but also a "strict code of ethics" was demanded. The verification of membership cards was taken seriously.

As the club drew not only respectable but "elite" members of society, security was paramount. However, there were always those who were bent on breaking formal codes of conduct—even breaking the door down to get in when drink so compelled them. Visitors had to be scrutinised first through a peep-hole in the door before presenting their membership card. Oh, yes, said Hickey, and it's open till half past three in the morning on Saturdays.

After listening to Hickey describe the duties required, which called for experience in handling troublemakers and for physical prowess, it sounded custom-made for Branigan. Hickey encouraged him to discuss it with his family, mull it over, and make his decision.

He didn't need much time. "Needless to say, I accepted the job," he recalled. After Mr Hickey offered him the position of "security superintendent," with appealing pay, a deal was quickly struck.

It perfectly suited Branigan in several ways. It was night work, to which he was accustomed; it required a strong man with a commanding presence; it presented a stimulating social scene; it offered good pay, nicely padding out his pension; and the club even drew some of his younger Garda colleagues when they were off duty.

But one feature of the job that clearly had a special appeal for him was the title: "security superintendent." It had an unmistakable authority to it (and the irony that superintendent was a position he well deserved within the Garda

Síochána but had never achieved). The job placed him in command again of several other men, who would work under him. It was action-oriented and exciting. As he put it, "I enjoyed the work because I can keep my hand in my old job and also be near the young people and the world of entertainment." He clearly saw it, at least in some ways, as a natural extension of his Garda career. And, importantly for him, it carried respect as well as authority.

Mr Hickey was an astute businessman, and perhaps a bit of a psychologist as well. In making the offer to Branigan he did not so much as utter the words "bouncer" or "doorman" but repeated the term "security superintendent" with emphasis. Once Branigan accepted his new position he eagerly told his friends, also stressing his title of security superintendent, especially to Garda friends. If some people talked of Branigan now being "a bouncer at the Zhivago" it was probably not done in any intentionally demeaning way—nor within earshot.

There was only one problem with his Zhivago job, that of transport home in the middle of the night, when no buses were running out to Summerhill. His resourceful solution was to make the deal contingent upon hiring his son Alick, then twenty-nine, as one of his assistants. That would provide him with a lift home. Perfect. Except for the minor point that Alick was definitely not cut out to act as a combination doorman and bouncer's assistant. Nonetheless, being the dutiful son, he agreed to work beside his father. At first it seemed like it might be a viable arrangement.

Discos were the "in thing" in Dublin at the time, and the beat was pulsating in the Zhivago from the moment one stepped in the door. But Hickey promised patrons something more with the sign he hung above the door: "Where love stories begin." Understandably, it became wildly popular. Branno found himself in the midst of Dublin's most swanky, swirling night life. And it was his responsibility to keep the club's reputation for respectability intact.

For the most part, patrons behaved well. Inevitably there were those who imbibed too heavily and became disorderly. They were discreetly ushered out before any serious trouble could arise. But every now and then a row could erupt, and Branigan and his assistants had to use force to quell it, quickly. He had several burly bouncers beside him who did their job efficiently.

A factor in Branigan's favour was that on weekends the Zhivago had become a favourite night spot for younger gardaí enjoying their off-duty time. Branno, of course, knew most of them. In the event of any real trouble he could call on them. It was always handy for Hickey to have a group of young gardaí in the club as an unofficial law-keeping presence.

Among them was Senan Finucane Jr, who went to the disco quite often at the time. "This club was very popular with younger members of the Garda Síochána," he recalls, "and, needless to say, Lugs always looked after his own, and Garda members usually didn't have to pay in." This was probably with the approval of the manager, who benefited from the free security of having gardaí on the dance floor. Finucane observes: "Patrons at the club had great respect for Lugs, who had legendary status at this time . . . and very few rows occurred at the club." Hickey was getting his money's worth.

———

In late January 1973, only about two weeks after retiring, Jim Branigan again made news. Controversial news. In a lengthy and surprisingly candid interview with Cantwell and Farrelly in the *Evening Herald* he brought up a sensitive and long-suppressed issue: promotions denied.

Everyone knew that after forty-three years of distinguished service, reaching the pinnacle of acclaim as "Ireland's most famous policeman" and "Dublin's toughest and most fearless garda," he retired as a sergeant. Already his great friend Senan Finucane, nearly ten years younger, had raced past him on the promotional ladder. As did many other guards. But no-one knew why. Branno himself never protested, never questioned the fairness of the system at the time. He silently soldiered on.

But his days of silence ended with his retirement. Now he had a few words to say on the subject. Not so much for himself—because his career was over— but for others coming up the promotional ladder behind him. As he had always done in court, he "spoke his mind." Without a hint of recrimination, he told the reporters he wanted to set the record straight:

> Now that I am retired I can say that members of the force came up from the country and were promoted over the heads of men like me who were doing all the work. Some of them got senior positions though they had no great ability and could not present a case in court.
>
> They got their promotions by "pulling the strings" and knowing the right people. I do not believe in this.[26]

Even his family probably didn't expect such candour. But few in the Garda Síochána could deny the truth of his words, for it was no secret. He was certainly not speaking of such fine men as Senan Finucane, who diligently worked their way up and were highly deserving of their promotion: he was referring to those who benefited from their "connections" from the outset. Unnamed. It was the system itself that was flawed—inherent in many police and military forces. In their article the reporters did not mince words, revealing that "he makes the charge that string pulling and red tape have jumped men with little ability into senior positions," over the heads of those more deserving.

His allegation stirred talk and controversy. Those still in the force were, of course, bound to a discreet silence for the most part. In private, however, many praised Branno for continuing to be fearless and faithful to his principle of fairness. All gardaí had their own opinion on the promotion system, which ostensibly was one based on merit, not favouritism.

———

It is only through oral history some forty years later that we can learn what his colleagues really thought about the issue, all now retired and in their seventies and eighties, men with opinions every bit as strong as Branno's, men eager now to have their say in the matter. Not gripes about their own treatment but about the raw deal their friend Jim Branigan got.

Even his promotion to sergeant took thirty-three years, to the disbelief of many colleagues. Though Branigan's service record was far superior, other guards shot past him. Some colleagues attributed it to his apparent lack of interest in proceeding through the application process for promotion. "You had to do a sergeant's exam and an interview to be promoted," says Paddy Daly, "and Jim had *no interest* in that—in doing exams." True enough. He always said he didn't want to take time away from his demanding duties to prepare for exams. He had *practical* work to take care of every day.

Michael Reid understood his friend Branno's mentality when it came to taking exams and seeking promotion:

> He never looked for a promotion—and that's what often *drives* people, the promotion. Never showed any enthusiasm to become a high-ranking officer in the Guards. *His* love was to get out and do the practical work. He revelled in it! Jim never had time to do the examination for promotion. He was quite happy and content doing what he had to do.

Nonetheless, he had been more than deserving of the promotion to sergeant for many years, and would surely have appreciated promotion, if not for the title at least for the better pay it would bring. He was tired of seeing Elsie still having to "scrimp and save" for the family.

Within the force there was what was called a "special promotion," granted to men of outstanding achievement. It meant that the recipient did not have to go through the standard procedure of examinations and interviews. Branigan had indisputably achieved this status from his "animal gang" days. With the passing of each year his colleagues waited for Branno to receive his "special promotion." Paddy Daly recalls: "I used to hear people say, 'Jim, you're not getting much recognition . . . for all you're doing.' But he *never* complained." If he wasn't frustrated and angry over not being promoted, *they* were. Some said he should have been a superintendent by then. In truth, no-one knew at the time what feelings Branigan held inside about the issue; but he was not a man who would *ask* for a special promotion.

Val Lynn, one of his closest friends from the 1950s onwards, testifies that among Branigan's colleagues, ill feelings were rising towards the authorities who, for some reason, continued to deny him promotion. On his behalf—and apparently without his knowledge—they began to express their displeasure with what they saw as an injustice. *Finally*, vouches Val Lynn, "there was an *outcry*, an *outrage*, to promote him—and *then* he was *specially* promoted to sergeant."

Yet the question remained: why had he been denied promotion for so many years? Declan confides that his father never even received any encouragement from his superiors to apply for promotion in any form. He has his explanation for this, and at sixty-eight (in 2012) his feelings on the subject remain strong:

> He was *so good* at what he was doing, so successful in controlling crime, that they wouldn't give it to him. They wanted to keep him *where he was*— and to know that *they* could go home at night and sleep, knowing that the streets would be safe. So, everybody was happy. I suppose he got used to it . . . that he got as far as detective-sergeant, and that he wasn't going to get any more promotions.

In retrospect, half a century later, many of his old Garda colleagues are in full agreement. At the time, it was expedient for his superiors to keep Branno in the front line so that those at the rear would feel secure. He was simply too competent and irreplaceable with his lower rank and street duty to be moved up.

Others, including Branigan himself, had an equally rational explanation. As Val Lynn forthrightly puts it, Branno was "an *honourable* man who *should* have gone further in the Garda Síochána. But his *big* mistake was that he was *very honest*, and dealt with everybody the *same*." In treating everyone equally, he refused to "play the game" and show favouritism or bow to privilege in any form. Even if requested—or *ordered*—by his superiors to do so. He steadfastly remained his *own man*.

This was no secret to his family and close colleagues. In those days (and perhaps still) it was common for a lower-ranking garda to receive either a request or pressure from a senior officer to dismiss or simply "not see" a particular case. Subordinates complied by tearing up the paperwork and forgetting about it. Greg Dalton in his book *My Own Backyard: Dublin in the Fifties* writes that "paperwork always seemed to be the problem for the police . . . when they found out that so-and-so was related to so-and-so who knew so-and-so. More confetti came from summonses than court cases."[27] Senior officers held the power to look after friends and make their violations vaporise.

Branigan, however, flatly refused to go along with it. He felt it was morally and legally wrong. Even if ordered, he refused to dismiss a charge against a person because he was a bigwig or friend of some senior officer. To him, a TD was as guilty as a dosser for committing the same violation. As he said many a time, if he gave in to a request or pressure to let off a prisoner because he was "important," how could he, in good conscience, ever again arrest an ordinary citizen on the same charge? It ran completely counter to his basic principles.

In his interview for the *Evening Herald* in January 1973 he exposed the problems he had experienced, without naming names. He revealed that it was his firm belief that it was indeed in large part his "unwillingness to 'shelve' cases against defendants upon the request of superiors that 'cost him promotion.'"[28]

Alick can verify it at first hand. For years he saw the Garda brass try to pressure his father into getting their important friends off the hook. And when he refused to give in they took it personally, sometimes holding a grudge against him for not bowing to their authority and "playing the game." Says Alick: "When the pressure came down from the top to drop it—from *above*— he *wouldn't!* And he always felt that *that* was the reason he never got above sergeant—that that was held against him." Even superintendents couldn't bend Branno. His own principles of fairness and equality, by which he lived as a garda, ultimately blocked his way up the promotion scale. He *knew* this—but still wouldn't yield.[29]

After retirement he told of one piece of hypocrisy that he found galling. "Several superintendents asked me why I had not been recommended for promotion—but they *themselves* failed to recommend me to the Commissioner." He attributed much credit for his eventual promotion to sergeant to one decent man. "Finally, Commissioner Costigan realised my devotion to duty and the work I was doing . . . and my slow haul to official recognition began." But no further promotions.

––––

At the Zhivago Club things were off to a promising start, and his spirits were lifted again. As he unashamedly admitted, "I was regarded as a sort of celebrity at the club." He liked all the admiring attention, which was a good tonic after the feeling of rejection over the denial of his request for an extension. The management made sure that patrons knew he held the title of security superintendent, and was to be called "Mr Branigan"—*never* "Lugs."

Then, one evening, only a few weeks following his retirement, on the way to work he picked up a copy of the *Evening Herald* and felt a body blow as he read the headline: "Branno's riot squad now disbanded."[30]

How *could* they? he thought. It was emotionally jarring to see *his* creation, his select team of men, so summarily discarded—and the black Bedford condemned to retirement like himself. He read further that "Dublin's famous Riot Squad set up nine years earlier to rid the city streets of late-night gangs, warfare, dance hall rows, thuggery and cowardly assaults, has been disbanded."

The newspaper rushed a reporter out to seek Branigan's opinion on the news. With his usual candour, he criticised the decision to disband the squad as a big mistake, explaining that "it was very useful and always first on the scene to assist in assaults, big rows, and even attempted murders."

Though Branno seemed stunned by the elimination of his riot squad, it came as no surprise to others in the Gardaí. In fact, unknown to him, it had been disbanded only about a week after he retired. No-one had dared break the news to him. He failed to understand what everyone else saw so clearly: that the riot squad was not really the Bedford van and its team of guards, it was *Branno himself.*

Shortly after the demise of the riot squad came more news from Garda Headquarters. It was announced that twenty additional detective-sergeants were to be appointed to help combat crime in Dublin, equipped with new patrol cars. To which some of Branno's mates might well have responded: "See, Jim, it took twenty men to replace you!"

Meanwhile he was holding his own at the Zhivago, with the assistance of Alick and his team of bouncers. But if Branigan was adjusting well to his new position, Alick was fast realising that he was not suited for the work. Most nights were peaceful, but as Zhivago's reputation as the place for dancing and night life grew, it occasionally drew some unsavoury characters with the rowdy dancehall mentality who were determined to gain entry whether or not they were members. If refused, their standard tactic was to try to bash the door down. When this happened at the Zhivago Club, Branigan took it very seriously. They had to be quelled quickly. Alick remembers a scene in which he had a role:

> I did bouncing with my father at Zhivago—security work. And there'd be fellas *kicking* the door, trying to get in. And my father'd say, "All right, fellas, *pull* the door open!" And we'd all *charge out,* and somebody'd get a few belts for creating a ruckus.

Alick pitched in when it came to the pushing, pulling, dragging and holding of troublemakers to restrain them. But as for Lugs's son using his *fists,* it was another matter. "I couldn't bring myself to actually *hit* them. The other fellas were giving the clips. I *just couldn't* do that . . . It just wasn't in me." Though not a fighter, he loyally stood beside his father and did his best.

During his post-retirement period, Branigan's family and friends worried about his new vulnerability. After all his years in the Gardaí he no longer had back-up if he was assaulted. As Declan saw his father, "he was now isolated. And more vulnerable. He hadn't got the security of knowing that he had comrades with him." Being out at night once again, he was wary. But true to form, from all accounts he remained "fearless."

His reputation continued to follow him everywhere, for good and ill. Overwhelmingly, people liked him and respected him; but there was always the occasional bowsie looking for trouble. The main threats were not those within the Zhivago Club but out on the nighttime streets before and after work. And here the record is largely undocumented.

It is known, however, that when he had to manhandle a disorderly patron in the Zhivago Club, the bowsie would sometimes threaten to "take care" of him later, knowing he would have no protection; and reliable sources attest to at least a few such assaults against him out on the streets. These incidents were not reported in the newspapers; nor do we know who got the best of such encounters. The best evidence would have been fresh marks of injury on his face or hands. Despite his advanced age, he would have benefited from being cold sober and able still to use his old defensive boxing technique of a crisp jab, while retaining a powerful punch. The odds were quite different, however, if he was attacked by more than one man at a time. According to some friends and witnesses, this did happen. Paddy Daly cites one particular case:

> In the late 1970s, when Jim was working in Zhivago Night Club, he was assaulted at a bus stop at Doyle's Corner, North Circular Road, Phibsborough, by two youths, who were arrested and charged with the offence. In the court both were found guilty, and the judge remarked that these two culprits would have taken their life in their hands if this would have happened thirty years before this.

The cowards doubtless realised this. It would have been unimaginable that two youths would have been so idiotic.

In retirement, he did not relinquish the ban on people calling him "Lugs." Within the Zhivago Club this did happen from time to time. Usually a scolding was sufficient; but if the name was lobbed at him in a disrespectful tone, a lesson was in order, as discovered one night by one of Gerry Creighton's pals. "A friend of mine was going into the club and said, "How'ya, Lugs!" He was a younger patron, and Branigan didn't like his attitude. "And Lugs hit him with a smack. He could do what he liked!"

———

A few years after his retirement Branigan faced a dangerous experience of his own making. It began when he popped a surprise announcement on his family: that after all his years as a non-driver, at the age of about sixty-five he decided to get behind the wheel of a car. "Oh, my!" Elsie must have thought. But once he made up his mind about something he always forged ahead. Since Alick had to act as his chauffeur three nights a week for Zhivago duty, he may have intended to assume this responsibility himself. If it worked out he would enjoy a new mobility and independence. It seemed worth the try. To his family it was admirable, if unnerving.

Unfortunately—or perhaps fortunately—the grand experiment marked an unusual defeat in his life, as Alick tells it:

> He actually *bought a car*. But his co-ordination . . . He just "pointed" the car! He really hadn't got the *feel* for it that most people have. Then he had a "little argument" with a bridge, about five miles from Summerhill . . . didn't make it around the bend and hit the side of the bridge.

Though he wasn't hurt, the car was damaged. It convinced him that this was an endeavour he would never master. He never took the wheel again, doubtless much to the relief of local residents. At least no-one encouraged him to "try again." A rare defeat for "Battling Branigan."

———

For some reason no longer remembered, his "last hurrah" was not finally held until Saturday 7 October 1973, when an official retirement party took place at the Garda Club in Harrington Street. The long delay may have had to do with his candid comments in the *Evening Herald* about promotions and the requests from superiors to drop cases against friends. But there is no evidence of this. It is just as likely that it was due to his lingering, and vocal, disappointment over the rejection of his request for another three-year extension in service. Logically, his Garda friends may have wanted time for his spirits to be revived before they held the party for him.

Whatever the reason for the postponement, by the first Saturday in October everyone seemed in high spirits for the affair. In addition to his family, Garda mates and other friends there were reporters on hand to cover the historic event. And it was a historic event. Garda Jim Branigan had joined the force back in 1931, before many of those in the room were born. On the day he joined, silent films were still on the screen. At the Metropole, Bela Lugosi was terrifying patrons in *Dracula*, while Gary Cooper was starring in *The Spoilers*, a thrilling new "talkie." By contrast, on the night of his retirement party the Capitol was showing *2001—A Space Odyssey*, and at the Savoy, Roger Moore was the suave British agent James Bond in *Live and Let Die.*

How many guests present that night perceived the historic significance of the event we don't know. But Branno's friend Dan Walsh certainly did, calling it "the end of an era." In fighting crime, Branigan was the past.

The Garda Club was packed to capacity with those anxious to honour Jim Branigan and wish him well in the future. Many were saying a sort of goodbye to him, knowing their paths in life were now likely to diverge. The mood was a mixture of merriment and nostalgia. Guests represented all the chapters of his life: his early training days in the Phoenix Park, boxing mates from the 1930s, including some who had gone with him to Germany just before the war, old guards who fought the "animal gangs" beside him, tamed the Teddy Boys, joined his riot squad. A lot of history packed in that room, Branno must have thought.

As everyone manoeuvred their way towards him to offer their congratulations, rarefied "Lugs stories" flew through the air. There should have been tape recorders around the room to pick up the rich oral history being shared by those who knew him so well. Some drew uproarious laughter; then there were the serious, often poignant moments, as when one of his old boxing pals described seeing him rise again and again off the canvas after being battered unmercifully by the German gladiator Pietsch. Listeners could sometimes only fall silent and shake their heads, perhaps glancing over at Branno across the room.

Then began the formal proceedings, as accolades began tumbling forth. Terms such as "legend," "unique," "an original," "great friend," "great man" and "last of his breed" were heard. Toasts were cheerful, sentimental, bitter-sweet. It was implicitly acknowledged that Jim Branigan had been the "face" of the Garda Síochána for decades.

Toasts and congratulations were followed by the presentation of a set of Waterford glass. Had the organising committee not been aware by this time that his "pavement hostesses" had also given him Waterford crystal?

Liam Ryan, a reporter for the *Irish Independent,* was jotting down notes for his next day's article, in an effort to merge all the sentiments being expressed. As he summed it up:

> It was a final and nostalgic farewell for the six-footer who has the scars to show he earned the undisputed reputation as the country's toughest and bravest Garda. A year ago the burly Sergt. Branigan ("Branno" to the tough guys) would have been doing his Saturday night rounds as head of the crack Garda Riot Squad, dreaded by thugs, "skinheads" and thieves. But instead, he was the toast of the party.[31]

But no speaker was better able to place Sergeant James Branigan in proper historical perspective than Chief Superintendent Edmund Doherty, who told the audience: "He is one of those people who become a legend in their own time."[32]

Chapter 16 ~

| A FAREWELL TO LUGS

"He would prefer for people to think he was invincible, and admitting to an illness could be seen as a sign of weakness."

(ALICK BRANIGAN)

"There were tumours in his head. He was starting to stagger, become very confused . . . It just jumbled up his mind."

(DECLAN BRANIGAN)

"He wasted away. He was only a shell. Oh, God, he was only about ten or eleven stone. Only a shadow."

(GARDA VAL LYNN)

"It was a huge funeral . . . There were judges there, and prostitutes. *Everybody* knew him."

(GARDA PADDY DALY)

"Whether we like it or not, we'll just have to go when the man above decides."

(SERGEANT JAMES BRANIGAN)

He liked to think of himself as invincible. And to project that image to the public. Over his lifetime he had met so many challenges and survived so many battles that he indeed seemed unconquerable. Approaching seventy, "Battling Branigan" appeared undaunted by advancing years, as fearless as ever.

His role of "security superintendent" at the Zhivago Club was carried into his early seventies, surely setting a record for Dublin's oldest bouncer. At the gym, his physical regimen remained unchanged, though his strength and reflexes were conspicuously diminishing. If he contracted a cold or sickness he would try to conceal it, even from his children, seeing it as a sign of weakness. In fact it was only after his father died, says Alick, that "my mother told me that he had pneumonia *seven times.*" Giving in to illness was a defeat, in his mind; which is why so many of his Garda colleagues say that they cannot recall him ever taking sick leave. Similarly, if he suffered an injury, either from an accident or in a row, he resisted hospital treatment. His early reputation as a "glutton for punishment," earned in the boxing ring, carried over throughout his life. He was plain stubborn. And a master of denial.

A convincing performer as well. As age began catching up on him and health problems arose from time to time, he would always put on his act to convince doctors that there was nothing wrong with him, despite diagnosis and evidence to the contrary. Alick was usually the one who had to drive him to his medical appointments, where he was sure to go through his usual routine of denial and pure fakery. Doctors and nurses saw that he was as obstinate as a child getting an inoculation, throwing his familiar tantrum. His act could be quite clever. Every time Alick thought he had seen it all, his father would come up with a new performance. It was sometimes hard for doctors and nurses not to be amused, and even admiring, for his sheer creativity:

> I remember once I took him to the Adelaide Hospital, and they were going to check him out. And he was saying, "I'm *not sick!* There's *nothing* wrong with me!" And so he actually got a wooden chair and put his hands on the seat, with the back of the chair facing away from him. So the seat was open in front of him, with his hands on the seat, so he was actually behind the chair. And he balanced himself straight across the seat—went *off his feet*— and put his *whole weight* across the top of the chair, *stretched out* across the top of it, balancing his weight on his hands, to *prove* to the doctor that there was nothing wrong with him. Oh, he was in *denial!* He just *wouldn't accept* that there was *anything* wrong with him.

It was another Branno performance worthy of the stage. To him it made perfect sense as a rebuttal of any claim by a doctor that he had a medical problem. Alick had at least to give his father credit for being resourceful.

There was one medical problem that he could not deny, as it was so prominently visible on his face. It was a large patch of melanoma, a malignant tumour containing dark pigment over his left eye. It had grown more aggressively in recent years, to about the size of a postage stamp. In previous years, because of its slow growth, he had paid it little heed; now the doctor told him that its darkened colour and raised surface meant it would have to be removed.

For many years it had simply appeared to be one more scar on his forehead. The popular belief was that it was a "bash from a bottle" incurred during one of his street battles. He never either confirmed or denied this; the myth suited him fine. He certainly didn't want people perceiving it as a "medical problem."

The day finally came, however, when the doctor told him he had to have it removed—"or else." There was also a smaller, less visible one on one of his ears to be likewise removed. Reluctantly, he agreed to the surgery. It involved removing the tumour and covering the place with a skin graft from his thigh. "It was just something to be dealt with," says Alick. "But it wasn't a good match for his face, because it left a light mark; you could see it stand out." Branigan did not seem to be bothered by the aesthetic outcome but did confide to Alick after the surgery that the "graft from where they had taken the skin from his thigh was sorer than where they had put it."

Even when he was presented with a positive diagnosis of a medical condition, he was not very faithful in following his doctor's orders about treating it. By his later sixties he also had diabetes but was lax about following instructions. His chiropodist and friend Genevieve Kearins-Creagh, who enjoyed going to the Zhivago Club, saw him popping chocolate biscuits into his mouth all evening.

———

Alick believes that his father had always hoped to enjoy the gift of longevity enjoyed by his namesake uncle, who "lived to be 103 years old and lived a very active life." He was quite unprepared, therefore, when in his late sixties the combination of ageing and illness conspired to become the most insidious foe he had ever faced.

The first signs were subtle. He had a heart condition and some nerve problem that, according to Declan, resulted in "his balance being affected." Only slightly at first, but progressive. The only signs of decline noticeable to others were his slowing gait and reflexes. Mary Barnwell and the other traders along Thomas Street noticed his slightly stooped posture, which had always been as "straight as a poker." His voice remained strong, but his hands might quiver slightly at times. Noel Hughes remembers that "at the end he was getting very nervous . . . I observed that his nerves were gone." Walking behind him along the street, people sometimes noticed that his step seemed a bit uncertain, and that he could meander a bit from his straight course. It became worrisome to his doctors and family when his equilibrium began to show small signs of abnormality.

How aware he may have been of his slight slipping we don't know, because he certainly never made an issue of it. It was simply not discussed. He probably dismissed it as a minor annoyance. His Zhivago job, gym exercises and regular socialising remained unchanged. His mind seemed lucid and his speech strong.

Eventually, Declan relates, "he was starting to stagger." It was a definable moment in his decline, for it was unmistakable, even to him. If you didn't know better you might have thought he had been tippling. Nonetheless, Alick saw that his father would *still* try to get the upper hand with doctors, insisting that he was really "fine . . . nothing *wrong*" with him. With a bemused smile, he adds, "you've got to admire his ingenuity and determination . . . to get out of trouble." Doctors, aware of his shenanigans, politely listened to his excuses— then proceeded to carry out the necessary examinations anyway. Branno seemed satisfied that he had made his point—though it had done him no good.

As his equilibrium became more unstable he began to stumble now and then. It was when "he fell a couple of times in his last years," confides Declan, that his family began to seriously worry about his welfare out on the street. One day Tommy Lowry witnessed such an incident:

> Outside Whitefriars' Street Church, in Aungier Street, he collapsed one day. *Strain.* And somebody saw him on the ground, and they got a police car from Kevin Street and took him to the Adelaide Hospital.

He was always embarrassed when such incidents occurred, and wanted to be removed from public view as quickly as possible. He didn't want people to see his vulnerability. It was hard enough when someone might notice his nervousness or shakiness and kindly say something like "Now, you take good care of yourself, Mr Branigan," but to be seen on the ground was a humiliation.

Yet, ever true to form, even when he staggered or fell and needed help he still insisted on being in charge of those helping him, whether it was local residents, fellow-gardaí, or ambulance crews. Genevieve Kearins-Creagh remembers him telling her one time the terms he always demanded:

> If he needed an ambulance Jim would *insist* that he wouldn't go to *any* hospital but the Adelaide. He would say, "If you can't bring me *there* you can leave me on the side of the road." But he always got his wish.

At the Adelaide Hospital he knew all the staff, felt like part of the family. They had all known him for years. They understood.

The saddest phase of decline for his family and friends, as Declan tells it, was when his father's mental and verbal capacities began to be affected— only slightly perceptible at first, perhaps merely forgetting, slurring a word, becoming confused, or seemingly disoriented. It was a painful realisation.

———

In 1983, after nearly ten years, he gave up his position at the Zhivago Club, whether of his own volition or at the management's request is not known. But it was inevitable. He had had a "good run" at the disco, socially and financially. And he was appreciative. His fading health now made it impossible for him to continue. Because of his growing instability in walking, and fear of a fall, he began spending more of his time at home, gardening and caring for his budgies. Old friends would come out to Summerhill to visit him. But he would still make periodic sojourns into Dublin to visit the lads at Kevin Street, then rambling around the Liberties, where he knew every stone.

Elsie saw that he was happy poking around in the soil on a sunny day, doting on his budgies, actually relaxing for once in his life. No pressures, no schedules. For the first time, he seemed content without a need for action. He enjoyed reading and rereading his collection of books on the American west. Long gone, however, were the days of great "cowboy and Indian" films; the age of portraying the historic sheriffs as heroes was just about over.

One day—Alick can't recall the date, but it was in the last year or eighteen months of his father's life—he was working in his garden, seemingly oblivious of the troubles of the world. Elsie was inside, engaged in her household chores. After what seemed like a longer spell than usual for him to be gardening without a break, she decided to go out and check on him:

> My mother realised she hadn't seen him for a while . . . And she went out, and he had collapsed in the garden picking blackcurrants. And she couldn't get him up. He'd had a heart attack, basically, but he was conscious. Then they got him into the kitchen and then to hospital.

It wasn't a crippling heart attack, and he survived well, returning to what had been his normal life. It didn't seem to have made a major change in his thinking about his general condition. He may have confided his real feelings to Elsie but didn't feel the need to discuss it with others. As well as he could, he continued to project an image of being in top form. His close friends, of course, knew about his diabetes, heart attack, falls, and mental lapses; but they were not about to broach the subject, knowing his feelings about illness being a weakness. He'd bring up the topic if he wished.

———

In the early part of 1986 there occurred a dramatic manifestation of decline. "He was starting to *really* stagger," Declan recalls, "and he became *very confused* in the last couple of months. The problem was taking over. It just jumbled his mind." He was taken to the Adelaide Hospital for a barrage of examinations, this time without a whimper of disagreement. It was now sometimes difficult to decipher what he meant when he spoke; yet at other times he was quite clear in expressing himself. Medication also probably took its toll on his thought processes and verbal capacity.

Determining that he was seriously ill, his doctors called for a brain scan. The result came back quickly—and conclusively. Alick understood the diagnosis clearly:

> It was a brain tumour that got him. His brain tumour was located in a very inaccessible, or difficult, area to treat. They did a biopsy, and decided that they couldn't do anything about it. And they just said, "Sorry, but you have a brain tumour, and it's going to get bigger, and so on . . . and there's nothing we can do about it."

Branno took the news unflinchingly. The rest of his family did their best to follow his example, to honour his obvious wishes, but they found the news devastating. They too had come to regard him as invincible. With a shocking suddenness, the doctor's blunt, definitive diagnosis was difficult to accept, intellectually and emotionally. Declan remembers how overwhelming the medical evidence was that there was no hope:

> I remember them doing the biopsy—and there was a football field of tumours in his head! And they just closed it up. They told my mother that it was just a matter of time . . . I'd say he knew.

Wholly consistent with his core principles in life—courage and determination—Alick says that his father quietly, stoically decided that he would "see the thing through to the end." On his own terms.

———

Elsie and the children didn't know how long he might have to live. The doctors simply said, "Not long." No-one wanted him to suffer pain in his last days, and he was medicated accordingly. There were no futile attempts at prolonging the inevitable, says Alick; "with the tumour, I don't think he had any chemo or radiation . . . just [allowing] a progression of the tumour." And, says Alick, "he never complained of pain to me." He was taken into the Adelaide Hospital and made as comfortable as possible. Some of the nurses there had known him for years, from when he would stop by at night to assist them with drunken bowsies threatening the staff. They could always count on him. Now here he was, the one in need of their care.

Days passed. Word spread about Branno's terminal illness. Friends began a pilgrimage to visit him, and the staff had to limit the number allowed to reach his bedside. Some moments he was fully conscious, chatty, even smiling; the next he was in a haze of confusion. But with each day he faded a bit more. Visitors who arrived to bid him farewell who had not been informed of his deteriorated condition were often visibly shaken by the sight. This was not the Lugs Branigan they knew.

In a short space of time he had withered from 17 stone to about 11 stone. Some friends would admit to being so stunned when entering his room that they could barely get a few words out. One visitor, leaving his hospital room, said, "I'm afraid this is one fight that Branno won't win."

Yet there were spells when he was alert and wanted to chat. With old pals his favourite topics were, naturally, old times. He could still manage a weak chuckle. Then he might ask, to their surprise, how Manchester United were doing. And who was attending to his budgies? He especially responded to seeing family members and old friends like Val Lynn, who had been the driver of the black van that first night back in August 1964. With mates like Val there was plenty to reminisce about. When Branno was up to it they'd chat; other times he could just sit quietly beside his bed.

With each visit it seemed as if his friend had grown a bit smaller. When sometimes asked to arrange Branno in a more comfortable position, he would steel himself emotionally, realising how much he had shrivelled. "He was only a *shell* . . ." He tried to prepare others before their visits so they wouldn't be taken aback so much.

Though it was always painful, Val stayed with him longer than most others:

I often spent a half hour or more with him. And he'd say, "Val, can you lift me up?" And I would *think* of this sixteen, seventeen-stone man . . . *wasted away.* Oh, God, he was only about ten or twelve stone! He was only a shadow . . . barely able to speak.

The Garda chaplain, Father Clarence, made regular visits to his bedside. Branno, the former altar boy, found his presence comforting. He had been a devout Catholic, and his faith had been an anchor in his life. When Father Clarence administered the last rites it must have sent him the clearest message of impending death. Yet when his strength was up to it he could still erect a fortress of denial and even put on a good act. He told some visitors that he would be up and out of hospital before long. He even gave a brave final performance for Val Lynn on his last visit, telling him in a feeble voice that he hoped to be out of hospital within a week. "Ah, that's good news, Jim," Lynn replied. Then he said what would be his last goodbye.

———

Outside his window, life went on. May is always one of the most cheerful months, a time of rebirth and fresh hopes, bright colours of nature and people's clothes, streets bustling with life and laughter.

By the third week of May, Branno was slipping away. "He was incoherent in the last couple of weeks—very confused," remembers Declan, "but he didn't suffer."

Joe Kirwan was one of the last to see him alive. He was a long-time friend of Branigan's, having known him since the 1940s through an interest in boxing. He had heard that he was in the Adelaide Hospital and quite ill but had no idea that he was facing death. When he entered the room and saw his shrunken form he was stilled. He thought, "Such a big man . . ." During the visit Branigan enjoyed a few moments of mental clarity when his words sounded perfectly convincing to Kirwan:

> I was with Jim Branigan the night before he died. Myself and a pal went up to see him—and we didn't *know* he was *dying*. And I said, "Hello, Jim. How are you?" And he says, "How are you, Joe?" And he said, "I expect to be getting out of here next week." Oh, yes. Oh, he *expected* to come home! And I was delighted that I went up to see him. But he was dead the next day! If I had *known* he was dying I don't know *what* I would have said to him . . . I was glad that I didn't know he was dying.

No-one knew what Branigan really believed at that moment, whether he was delusional, still in denial, or putting on a classic last act. But Declan saw that his father was fearless up to the last round.

> He was *not* afraid of death. He was resigned finally, only at the very end. He said, "Whether we like it or not, we'll just have to go when the man above decides."

––––

"'Lugs Branigan is dead!'" Word swept around the city like wildfire. The news reached every part of Dublin well before the newspapers could announce in their "late news" that the famous Jim "Lugs" Branigan had died on 21 May 1986 in the Adelaide Hospital.

Declan was out of Dublin at the time and had to be notified. "He died during the day, and I was away, down the country, and I got a call to come back home." The immediate family, including Branigan's brother, Frank, soon arrived. A general notice was put out by the Garda Síochána to all members. The news fell especially hard on the men and women in Kevin Street station who had continued to see him regularly. Around his Liberties, people could talk of nothing else but the loss of Lugs. In great sorrow they traipsed to churches and chapels to say prayers, light candles. It was like a loss in everyone's family. Women market traders wept openly. The normal gaiety of the streets was missing as local people talked to one another about what he had meant to them, how he had helped them. In pubs, the staff and regulars were uncharacteristically solemn and reflective. There were few who had not been touched by him in some positive way in their lifetime.

Newspapers rushed to get out the news of Sergeant Jim Branigan's death, accompanied by tributes. Fuller obituaries would follow. On its front page the *Evening Herald* headed its announcement: "Tough cop 'Lugs' dies at 76." It told readers how "he became famous for his unique method of dealing with the toughest elements of Dublin's criminal underworld," especially noting that "rough and instant justice sorted out many a youngster who would otherwise have gone further astray."[1]

Stephen Dixon in the *Irish Independent* wrote a portrait of the beloved Lugs Branigan, comparing him to some of the characters played by John Wayne, evoking once again the analogy of a western sheriff and old gunfighter. He called Branno a unique copper who "quelled the 'rock 'n' roll' riots," a garda for whom the city's "gougers had a healthy respect . . . and Dublin's prostitutes."[2] He reminded readers that Branigan had acted as a minder for Elizabeth Taylor, Cliff Richard, and other celebrities.

By contrast with the sentimental coverage in the *Herald* and *Independent,* the *Irish Times* published a brief factual notice, hardly doing justice to such an extraordinary man. At least his picture was placed on the front page.

By ironic coincidence, on the day of his death the *Evening Herald* published a prepared article about the Garda Síochána's new "elite 38-man crime task force,"[3] with its code name X-ray, a "quick-action response group" and a "high-powered fleet" of cars. A superintendent was quoted as saying that "crime busting is a young man's game," noting that all the guards on the new task force were in their twenties—prompting the journalist who wrote the article to comment, "It seems to have taken a small army to replace Garda Jim Branigan."

Because of its unintended timing, the article turned out to be a fitting final tribute to Jim Branigan and his riot squad.

———

The funeral Mass was held at eleven o'clock on Saturday 24 May in Mount Argus. Well before the Mass began, people were arriving and filling the church. Among the early arrivals were reporters, photographers, and television crews. Though Elsie and the children had expected a large turn-out, they were awed by the massive outpouring of affection for Lugs. When the church reached capacity, people congregated outside to pay their respects. The overflow crowd grew and grew, as Declan describes it:

The funeral was *massive!* I suppose it was a smaller version of a state funeral. People from *all* walks of life—politicians there, and chiefs of the Gardaí ... *hundreds* of guards. And *lots* of people from the Liberties ... and *all* the surrounding areas. There was a genuine feeling of grief from people ... a *lot* of people there just because they wanted to say goodbye.

It was doubly difficult for members of the riot squad, who had served so closely with him in his last decade, among them Paddy Daly, who remembers the funeral Mass not for its astonishing size but also for the conspicuous diversity of mourners and their span of ages:

There were judges there, there were prostitutes ... a *huge* crowd ... People went because it was Jim Branigan. How many *generations* knew Jim Branigan!—one of the biggest funerals that was ever seen.

On 24 May the *Evening Herald* published an article headed "A final honour for 'Lugs'," which included a long list of eminent mourners who attended the Mass, among them Commissioner Éamonn Doherty, joined by the former commissioners Edmund Garvey and Patrick McLaughlin. Also there were old former boxing champions: eighty-year-old Mattie Rogers, Maxie McCullagh, Ollie Byrne, John Ingle, and others. But what most distinguished the funeral Mass for Jim Branigan was its diverse and egalitarian character— the extraordinary social mixture of those who came to honour him and to bid him farewell. For among the multitude was an amazing cross-section of humanity: gardaí, politicians, priests, journalists, judges, solicitors, writers, publicans, shopkeepers, businessmen, "pavement hostesses," dancehall staff, cinema ushers, market dealers, coalmen, boxing champions, street pugilists, dockers, dossers, former gang members, criminals, old thugs and hooligans, ageing Teddy Boys, milkmen, street-cleaners. Saints and sinners, the meek and the mighty. All packed shoulder to shoulder in the stuffy church. All equal friends of "Lugs" Branigan. A perfect composite of who the man was in his life.

When the Mass was over, Elsie and the children greeted people outside, thanking them for their sympathy and condolences. *"Everybody* was offering their sympathy," remembers Alick. "He was known *all over* the country. But they weren't things I hadn't heard about him a million times before."

Most expressed simple sentiments, such as "he was a great man," "we won't see his likes again," "oh, he was good to women," "we'll all miss him now." But many wanted to linger and tell their "Branno stories" one more time. Judging by their comments, it was apparently all right now to call him "Lugs."

As Declan and the rest of the family were preparing to leave the church grounds, he heard some surprising words. As the last mourners were drifting off, two men whom he did not recognise approached him respectfully, as if they had been waiting for the right moment:

> Funny enough—and this always brings a smile to my face—I remember standing outside the church, and these two men came up to me and introduced themselves, and said, "We were members of the 'animal gang'— and we just came to pay our last respects." I thought that was a lovely touch.

———

The death of Jim Branigan affected many of the younger guards with whom he had worked and had influenced profoundly. Their most poignant feelings about him were not expressed to his family on the day of his funeral, for it took some time for most of them to fully realise what he had meant to them. Only years later would men like Bosco Muldoon and Séamus Quinn come to grasp its deeper meaning.

Twenty-five years after his death they wanted to share some feelings with the author. As Bosco Muldoon simply expressed it, "he was like a father to me . . . looking after me . . . telling me what to do." Séamus Quinn echoes the sentiment: "Oh, I loved knowing him . . . I was proud. The big heart that man had . . . his generosity in showing me a new side of life . . . like a father figure. I missed him . . . *a lot.*" Many other guards said the same.

———

The burial took place in Dangan cemetery, near Summerhill. From Mount Argus all the way to Summerhill the cortege was accompanied by a Garda motorcycle escort. Father Clarence officiated, and television, newspapers and radio covered the event. Alick and the family regarded it as a great honour that such importance was attached to his funeral:

> When we headed for Summerhill to the graveyard there were police outriders at all the crossings on the way—at all the crossroads and junctions. So we had a clear run all the way down . . . The traffic was *all* stopped for him. That was a privilege given to him. The funeral was on television that night, and on the radio.

As the cortege wended its way through the streets of Dublin and then out on the main roads, many people along its course who saw the motorcycle escort and media vehicles probably mistook it for the funeral of a person of exalted rank—hardly a mere Garda sergeant.

Later that Saturday night, a mild spring night in Dublin, pubs in the city were packed, and men took their pints outside onto the pavement. The dominant topic of conversation throughout the inner city was the death of Lugs Branigan. Everyone, it seemed, knew him. Branno tales flowed as niagarously as the Guinness taps. Perhaps Stephen Dixon of the *Irish Independent* best captured this tribute:

> One thing is certain tonight—in any of the Dublin pubs where older villains gather, Lugs Branigan stories will be told. Most of them will be told with affection, and perhaps that is his finest epitaph.[4]

Chapter 17

POSTSCRIPT: LEGEND AND LORE

"When they made Jim Branigan they threw away the mould. Oh, he's a legend!"

(JOE KIRWAN, 81)

"His reputation was international. He achieved a legendary status."

(*Irish Independent*, 23 MAY 1986)

The place of James "Lugs" Branigan in Ireland's pantheon of legendary figures is as yet undetermined. Bernard Neary affirms his status not only as a "legend" but as "part of Dublin mythology and folklore," deeply embedded in the city's oral history.[1] However, "living legends" do not always survive long after their passing: they endure only as long as their stories are passed down to later generations through books, poems, songs, films, and oral history. As Noel Hughes puts it, back in Branigan's day "his reputation, it was higher than Nelson's Pillar!" But Irish history dealt Nelson an unexpected blow. History can be fickle.

A century after his birth, Lugs Branigan's legend remains enshrined in both personal reminiscences and oral testimony. Scores of older Dubliners still have personal recollections of him, and their tales are legion. Parents and grandparents pass down some great Lugs stories to their descendants. Among his surviving friends and fellow-gardaí he is commonly spoken of as "legendary"—more so today than ever. "Oh, *he's a legend!*" verifies retired Superintendent John Murphy. Paddy Daly contends that "Jim Branigan is a legend—like a sheriff in the Old West." How his legend will endure is less certain. As his friend Bosco Muldoon mused in 2011, "I wonder, in forty or fifty years will he still be a legend?"

Those who knew him best, and loved him the most, who are now in their seventies, eighties and more, express the hope that his reputation will not be tarnished by "revisionist" historians and others who might find fault with Branno's unique brand of "summary justice." As with all legends, he must be fairly appraised through the prism of the age in which he lived. When he first put on his Garda uniform, Ireland was a newly independent state, and the Second World War was still a decade away. Wild gangs were a terror in the city. Branigan became Dublin's toughest and most fearless garda, and paid a price for it with his patchwork of "battle scars"—to be acclaimed as the most effective deterrent to crime in the city.

The stuff of legend, to be sure. But in retrospect, future chroniclers could distort the truth of the times in which he lived. As Paddy Daly concedes, "he wouldn't have existed today! But he was the *right man* for that era—a man of his time." Accurately and fairly defining his historical role is challenging, as stated in *Garda Review*:

> The legacy of Jim "Lugs" Branigan is difficult to distinguish in modern Garda history. In the era of the Garda Ombudsman, Branigan's "belt on the mouth" method seems completely out of place.
>
> However, his ways and means of policing his patch were of his own virtue.
>
> Before the term "anti-social behaviour" was ever coined, Branigan declared war on Dublin's street thugs, making a name for himself as a legendary policeman from a bygone era.[2]

The *Evening Herald* prophesied that Branigan would be remembered as "a fearless cop and terror to weapon-wielding thugs in the city."[3] But retired Chief Superintendent Michael Reid contends that if Jim Branigan were remembered solely for quelling riots and belting hooligans it would be a travesty, a distorted, one-dimensional portrayal of a great man. Like so many others, he wants Branigan to be remembered as well for his immense humanity and compassion for the downtrodden souls of Dublin. He was, Reid says, a very complex and paradoxical man—and should be treated as such:

> He was *contradictory*. There was this public perception of him . . . a boxer with strength. But this distorted the *real* man. His strength was the way he *understood* people as human beings, how he dealt with them. Ultimately . . . he'll *never* be *thanked enough* for the work he did. *Never!* He was an amazing man.

In other words, the "soft side" of Lugs Branigan should be a centrepiece of his enduring legend. A wish shared by family and friends.

———

No-one has been more protective of Branigan's reputation and legend than his family. Over the years they have declined requests for interviews from the media, out of concern that their words might be misquoted or twisted. They did not want any writers or film-makers misrepresenting or showing disrespect for his life. In the 1980s, his friend Genevieve Kearins-Creagh recounts, not long before his death, he confided to her that a film-maker had expressed an interest in making a film about his life. However, his family apparently opposed the proposition, on the grounds that some aspects of his career—such as acting as paterfamilias for the "pavement hostesses"—might not be handled accurately and sensitively.

However, in September 1985 RTE obtained permission to make a short five or six-minute documentary segment. Though this was only about nine months before his death, his health was good enough for him to be able to actively participate. Essentially, he strolled around the Liberties with the interviewer and camera crew, reminiscing about his life. He seemed to enjoy it. Unfortunately, when it was edited and shown on television it emphasised his tough character, the interviewer gushing about his "iron fists," "famous black gloves," "discoloured shins from steel-capped hobnail boots," and how he "faced platoons" of thugs and Teddy Boys on the streets. And of course the camera showed his "fighting array of weapons" confiscated from street gangs over forty-three years. It could only have disappointed his family and friends.

In the last few years of his life his attitude towards fame, or "notoriety," as he always called it, changed. While he still immensely enjoyed rambling around and visiting friends, he came to dislike public attention:

> Everybody *knows* me, even on the bus, or in a shop. I see people nudging each other and whispering, "There's Branigan!" But I like to be by myself and have my own life.[4]

———

After his death, around the Liberties he became more than merely a legend: by some he was viewed as a sort of "patron saint" of ordinary people. To this day people in the area confide that they continue to pray for him, remembering how he had helped so many oppressed women. Tangible evidence of the reverence in which he is held is the conspicuous tribute inside the entrance of Whitefriars' Street Church. Here hangs a large plaque with a photograph of Garda Branigan in uniform, looking strikingly proud. Among all the other sacred photos and memorials on the church's wall, Branigan's was purposely placed in the close company of Mother Teresa and Éamon de Valera. Below his photograph the text reads:

Jim Branigan, the tough cop and terror of Dublin lawbreakers, slipped quietly away on Wednesday, May 21 1986 . . . In his prime a warning about "Lugs" or "Branno" was enough to clear a Dublin street of those bent on mischief. He got a big kick out of being a Garda. To him it was a vocation to which he brought a sense of duty.

A last irony is that, while a memorial plaque hangs in Whitefriars' Street Church, not even the smallest testament to Jim Branigan can be found in Kevin Street Garda Station. In 2011, when conducting research for this book, the author walked into the station one fine spring morning and was met by an amiable young garda in his twenties. After proper introductions with other guards in the station I decided to hit them flat-out with the question: "Do you know who Jim 'Lugs' Branigan was?" After a pause, one garda politely volunteered: "Branigan . . . em . . . Wasn't he supposed to be some kind of a legend or something?"

"Yes, quite right. Can you tell me anything specific about him?"

"No, sir, I'm sorry, I can't." Blank, sheepish expressions all round. But hardly their fault.

————

Alick, now seventy-two, has his own personal memorials to his father. "One of my sons is actually called 'Lugs'; and 'Little Lugs' is my grandson." He is also a master propagator of dahlias and has created his own varieties. The most splendorous one he named after his father, officially registering it in the National Dahlia Society's classified directory as a "red cultivar of exhibition standard." It has a brilliant, non-fading red bloom reaching ten inches in diameter. "I bred that and called it the Jim Branigan. Oh, he'd think it was fantastic."

Over the more than twenty-five years since his father's death he has travelled widely around Ireland for business and holiday, meeting many people. When he would introduce himself there has often been an immediate name recognition. "Somebody might say, 'Branigan . . . Oh, *Lugs* Branigan?'" He's always proud. Up to the present day one statement is heard more than any other—over and over again:

People say—and this is what I hear *all* the time—"Oh, God, if *only* Lugs was around *today!*'" So, the legend endures.

* * * * * *

NOTES

Prologue (p. 1–8)
1. Liam Ryan, "'Branno' Says a Last Good-Bye," *Irish Independent*, 8 October 1973, p. 24.
2. "The Battle of Baldoyle," *Evening Herald*, 22 January 1973, p. 9.

Chapter 1 (p. 9–26)
1. *Irish Times*, 6 January 1910, p. 9.
2. "German War Scare," *Irish Independent*, 6 January 1910, p. 9.
3. Kearns, *Dublin Tenement Life*, p. 12.
4. "I Am No Bullyboy," *Evening Herald*, 23 January 1973, p. 6.
5. Neary, *Lugs*, p. 114.
6. "I Am No Bullyboy," *Evening Herald*, 23 January 1973, p. 6.
7. "I Am No Bullyboy," *Evening Herald*, 23 January 1973, p. 6.
8. "Boxing Celebrity," *Evening Herald*, 24 January 1973, p. 7.
9. "Boxing Celebrity," *Evening Herald*, 24 January 1973, p. 7.
10. "I Am No Bullyboy," *Evening Herald*, 23 January 1973, p. 6.
11. Breathnach, *The Irish Police*, p. 119.
12. "I Am No Bullyboy," *Evening Herald*, 23 January 1973, p. 6.
13. "I Am No Bullyboy," *Evening Herald*, 23 January 1973, p. 6.

Chapter 2 (p. 27–39)
1. "I Am No Bullyboy," *Evening Herald*, 23 January 1973, p. 6.
2. "I Am No Bullyboy," *Evening Herald*, 23 January 1973, p. 6.
3. Breathnach, *The Irish Police*, p. 181.
4. *Webster's Collegiate Dictionary*, 1973, p. 326.
5. "Scene at Mountjoy Jail," *Evening Herald*, 19 June 1931, p. 1.
6. "Scene at Mountjoy Jail," *Evening Herald*, 19 June 1931, p. 1.
7. "Collision with Guards," *Irish Independent*, 20 June 1931, p. 6.
8. "Story of Baton Charges in Dublin Last Night," *Evening Herald*, 19 June 1931, p. 1.
9. "Boxing Celebrity," *Evening Herald*, 24 January 1973, p. 7.
10. "Boxing Celebrity," *Evening Herald*, 24 January 1973, p. 7.
11. "Boxing Celebrity," *Evening Herald*, 24 January 1973, p. 7.

Chapter 3 (p. 40–52)
1. Gillespie, *The Liberties of Dublin*, p. 9.
2. Fitzpatrick, *Dublin*, p. 156.
3. Lorcán Ó Diolúin, "Growing Up in the Liberties," in Gillespie, *The Liberties of Dublin*, p. 94.
4. Lar Redmond, Show Us the Moon (Dingle: Brandon Books, 1988), p.16.
5. Redmond, *Show Us the Moon*, p. 16.
6. Éamonn Mac Thomáis, "Ladies and Gents of Dub," in Gillespie, *The Liberties of Dublin*, p. 84.
7. "I Am No Bullyboy," *Evening Herald*, 23 January 1973, p. 6.
8. "I Am No Bullyboy," *Evening Herald*, 23 January 1973, p. 6.
9. "I Am No Bullyboy," *Evening Herald*, 23 January 1973, p. 6.
10. Kelly, *Me Darlin' Dublin's Dead and Gone*, p. 19.
11. Éamonn Mac Thomáis, "Ladies and Gents of Dub," in Gillespie, *The Liberties of Dublin*, p. 86.

12. Redmond, *Emerald Square*, p. 42.
13. Johnston, *Around the Banks of Pimlico*, p. 79.
14. Johnston, *Around the Banks of Pimlico*, p. 76.
15. Johnston, *Around the Banks of Pimlico*, p. 82.
16. Dunne, *Streets Broad and Narrow*, p. 27.
17. Dunne, *Streets Broad and Narrow*, p.27.
18. "Boxing Celebrity," *Evening Herald*, 24 January 1973, p. 7.

Chapter 4 (p. 53–72)
1. "Hooligan Activities in Dublin," *Saturday Herald*, 7 November 1936, p. 2.
2. "Hooligan Activities in Dublin," *Saturday Herald*, 7 November 1936, p. 2.
3. "Dublin Charges: We Are the Animal Gang," *Irish Times*, 24 September 1934, p. 1.
4. Donal Fallon, "Taming the Violent Animal Gang," *Sunday Independent*, 9 October 2011, p. 9.
5. Donal Fallon, "Taming the Violent Animal Gang," *Sunday Independent*, 9 October 2011, p. 9.
6. Donal Fallon, "Taming the Violent Animal Gang," *Sunday Independent*, 9 October 2011, p. 9.
7. Breathnach, *The Irish Police*, p. 120.
8. Lee Horsley, "Crimeculture: Introduction to the Gangster Films of the 1930s," at www.filmsite.orgcrime films.
9. Eric Larson, *In the Garden of Beasts* (New York: Crown Publishers, 2011), p. 134.
10. Redmond, *Show Us the Moon*, p. 42.
11. "Tough Lugs Branigan, A Fair Cop," *Irish Independent*, 23 May 1986, p. 1.
12. "I Am No Bullyboy," *Evening Herald*, 23 January 1973, p. 6.
13. "I Am No Bullyboy," *Evening Herald*, 23 January 1973, p. 6.
14. Neary, *Lugs*, p. 92.
15. "Boxing Celebrity," *Evening Herald*, 24 January 1973, p. 7.
16. "Germany under Adolph Hitler: Some Attractive Features of the New Regime," *Irish Times*, 6 November 1936, p. 4.
17. "Irishmen in Berlin," *Irish Times*, 8 January 1938, p. 18.
18. "Irishmen in Berlin," *Irish Times*, 8 January 1938, p. 18.
19. "Irishmen in Berlin," *Irish Times*, 8 January 1938, p. 18.
20. "Boxing Celebrity," *Evening Herald*, 24 January 19 73, p. 7.
21. "Boxing Celebrity," *Evening Herald*, 24 January 1973, p. 7.
22. "The Battle of Baldoyle," *Evening Herald*, 22 January 1973, p. 9.

Chapter 5 (p. 73–101)
1. "Hitler Leading His Army," *Evening Herald*, 10 May 1940, p. 1.
2. "Germans Continue Fierce Onslaught: Allies Retire," *Irish Independent*, 14 May 1940, p. 1.
3. "Dublin Football Venue Onslaught," *Irish Times*, 24 March 1940, p. 1.
4. "Batons Drawn at Dublin Football Match," *Irish Press*, 25 March 1940, p. 1.
5. "Rival Gangs Have Fight in Dublin Suburbs," *Irish Press*, 29 March 1940, p. 1.
6. "Men Jailed for Assault on Guard," *Evening Herald*, 13 May 1940, p. 2.
7. Breathnach, *The Irish Police*, p. 134.
8. "Battle in Dublin Street," *Evening Herald*, 7 May 1940, p. 1.
9. Neary, *Lugs*, p. 29.
10. "Many Bank Holiday Attractions," *Evening Herald*, 13 May 1940, p. 2.
11. "'Fair Ina' Unbeaten Filly," *Irish Independent*, 14 May 1940, p. 10.
12. "Baldoyle Selections," *Irish Independent*, 14 May 1940, p. 10.
13. "Baldoyle Selections," *Irish Independent*, 14 May 1940, p. 10.
14. "The Battle of Baldoyle," *Evening Herald*, 22 January 1973, p. 9.

15. "The Battle of Baldoyle," *Evening Herald,* 22 January 1973, p. 9.
16. "The Battle of Baldoyle," *Evening Herald,* 22 January 1973, p. 9.
17. "The Battle of Baldoyle," *Evening Herald,* 22 January 1973, p. 9.
18. "The Battle of Baldoyle," *Evening Herald,* 22 January 1973, p. 9.
19. "Fashions at the Baldoyle Races," *Irish Independent,* 15 May 1940, p. 10.
20. "The Battle of Baldoyle," *Irish Times,* 20 November 1940, p. 1.
21. "The Battle of Baldoyle," *Evening Herald,* 22 January 1973, p. 9.
22. "The Battle of Baldoyle," *Irish Times,* 20 November 1940, p. 1.
23. "Jockey Injured: Horse Killed," *Irish Independent,* 15 May 1940, p. 10.
24. "Gardiner Street Gang Used Bottles on Us," *Evening Mail,* 22 1940, p. 6.
25. "The Battle of Baldoyle," *Evening Herald,* 22 January 1973, p. 9.
26. "Fracas at Race Meeting," *Irish Independent,* 15 May 1940, p. 11.
27. "Stabbed Man Cross-Examined," *Irish Press,* 22 November 1940, p. 2.
28. "'Battle of Baldoyle' Witness Hostile," *Evening Mail,* 21 November 1940, p. 6.
29. Stabbed Man Cross-Examined," *Irish Press,* 22 November 1940, p. 2.
30. "'Battle of Baldoyle' Witness Hostile," *Evening Mail,* 21 November 1940, p. 6.
31. "Many Hurt in Irish Racecourse Clash," *Irish Press,* 15 May 1940, p. 7.
32. "Excitement at Dublin Greyhound Meeting," *Irish Independent,* 15 May 1940, p. 11.
33. "Many Hurt in Irish Racecourse Clash," *Irish Press,* 15 May 1940, p. 7.
34. "The Battle of Baldoyle," *Evening Herald,* 22 January 1973, p. 9.
35. "The Battle of Baldoyle," *Evening Herald,* 22 January 1973, p. 9.
36. "The Battle of Baldoyle," *Evening Herald,* 22 January, 1973, p. 9.
37. "The Battle of Baldoyle," *Evening Herald,* 22 January 1973, p. 9.
38. "Shop Early for Christmas," *Irish Times,* 22 November 1940, p. 6.
39. "Dublin Bookmaker Led Gang Story," *Evening Mail,* 19 November 1940, p. 8.
40. "Dublin Bookmaker Led Gang Story," *Evening Mail,* 19 November 1940, p. 8.
41. "Dublin Bookmaker Led Gang Story," *Evening Mail,* 19 November 1940, p. 8.
42. "Dublin 'Bookie' and Henchmen Get Penal Servitude," *Evening Mail,* 2 December 1940, p. 6.
43. "Fracas at Race Meeting," *Irish Independent,* 15 May 1940, p. 11.
44. "The Battle of Baldoyle," *Evening Herald,* 22 January 1973, p. 9.
45. "Rival Gang Clash Described," *Irish Press,* 23 November 1940, p. 2.
46. "Baldoyle Riot Charges," *Irish Times,* 23 November 1940, p .6.
47. "Dublin Bookmaker Led Gang Story," *Evening Mail,* 19 November 1940, p. 8.
48. "Dublin 'Bookie' and Henchmen Get Penal Servitude," *Evening Mail,* 2 December 1940, p. 6.
49. "Baldoyle Races Riot," *Irish Times,* 3 December 1940, p. 6.
50. "Baldoyle Races Riot," *Irish Times,* 3 December 1940, p. 6.
51. "The Battle of Baldoyle," *Evening Herald,* 22 January 1973, p. 9.

Chapter 6 (p. 102–17)
1. "Waves of Planes Rain Bombs on Belfast," *Irish Press,* 17 April 1941, p. 1.
2. "Hold What We Have," *Irish Independent,* 26 April 1941, p. 5.
3. "Hold What We Have," *Irish Independent,* 26 April 1941, p. 5.
4. "Boxing Celebrity," *Evening Herald,* 24 January 1973, p. 7.
5. "Bombs in Dublin This Morning—Many Killed," *Irish Times,* 31 May 1941, p. 1.
6. Pádraic O'Farrell, "The North Strand Bombing," *An Cosantóir,* September 1981, p. 283,
7. "The Dublin Bombing," *Irish Press,* 2 June 1941, p. 2.
8. "Éire Pledged to Defend," *Sunday Independent,* 29 June 1941, p. 1.
9. Johnston, *Around the Banks of Pimlico,* p. 74.
10. "'Commando' Raid on 'Toss Schools'," *Evening Herald,* 25 June 1942, p. 4.

11. "'Commando' Raid on 'Toss Schools'," *Evening Herald*, 25 June 1942, p. 4.

12. "Raids on Toss Schools," *Irish Times*, 27 June 1942, p. 3.

13. Mac Thomáis, *Me Jewel and Darlin' Dublin*, p. 16.

14. Johnston, *Around the Banks of Pimlico*, p. 74.

15. "Ireland—Suburb of a City on Fire," *Irish Press*, 7 February 1941, p. 3.

16. "Time of Greatest Danger to Our Nation," *Sunday Independent*, 26 January 1941, p. 1.

17. "Irish Citizens in US May Be Called Up," *Irish Times*, 23 March 1942, p. 1.

18. "Japan's Communication," *Irish Press*, 23 March 1942, p. 2.

19. "N.B.B.I. Suggests Potato Bread," *Irish Times*, 23 March 1942, p. 1.

20. "Fewer Horse Shoes for Éire," *Irish Times*, 21 March 1942, p. 1.

21. "'Battle' at Tolka Park Followed 'Invasion' in Commandeered Boats," *Evening Herald*, 23 March 1942, p. 1.

22. "Fight at Football Match," *Irish Times*, 23 March 1942, p. 1

23. "Fight at Football Match," *Irish Times*, 23 March 1942, p. 1.

24. "'Battle' at Tolka Park Followed 'Invasion' in Commandeered Boats," *Evening Herald*, 23 March 1942, p. 1.

25. "Man Thought Dead after Park Riot," *Evening Herald*, 23 June 1942, p. 3.

26. "'Battle' at Tolka Park Followed 'Invasion' in Commandeered Boats," *Evening Herald*, 23 March 1942, p. 3.

27. "Man Thought Dead after Park Riot," *Evening Herald*, 23 June 1942, p. 3.

28. "'Battle' at Tolka Park Followed 'Invasion' in Commandeered Boats," *Evening Herald*, 23 March 1942, p. 3.

29. "Tolka Park Case 'a Very Serious One'," *Evening Herald*, 1 April 1942, p. 1.

30. "Accused Men Do Not Give Evidence," *Evening Herald*, 23 June 1942, p. 4.

31. "Five Men Sentenced for Tolka Park," *Evening Herald*, 23 June 1942, p. 3.

32. "Accused Men Do Not Give Evidence," *Evening Herald*, 23 June 1942, p. 4.

Chapter 7 (p. 118–40)

1. Tobin, *The Best of Decades*, p. 3–4.

2. John D. Sheridan, "The Passing of the Tramcar," *Irish Independent*, 1 March 1947, p. 6.

3. Family Tells of Attacks," *Evening Herald*, 17 November 1952, p. 1.

4. "Commando Tactics by Guards," *Evening Herald*, 13 September 1954, p. 1.

5. "Commando Tactics by Guards," *Evening Herald*, 13 September 1954, p. 1.

6. "Kevin Street Families Tell of Hardships," *Evening Herald*, 1 September 1954, p. 4.

7. "Crowd Fought in Street," *Evening Herald*, 1 December 1950, p. 2.

8. "Disorderly Scenes in Patrick Street," *Evening Herald*, 5 June 1952, p. 7.

9. "Disorderly Scenes in Patrick Street," *Evening Herald*, 5 June 1952, p. 7.

10. "Disorderly Scenes in Patrick Street," *Evening Herald*, 5 June 1952, p. 7.

11. "Disorderly Scenes in Patrick Street," *Evening Herald*, 5 June 1952, p. 7.

12. "Disorderly Scenes in Patrick Street," *Evening Herald*, 5 June 1952, p. 7.

13. "I Am No Bullyboy," *Evening Herald*, 23 January 1973, p. 6.

14. "I Am No Bullyboy," *Evening Herald*, 23 January 1973, p. 6.

15. "I Am No Bullyboy," *Evening Herald*, 23 January 1973, p. 6.

16. "I Am No Bullyboy," *Evening Herald*, 23 January 1973, p. 6.

17. Neary, *Lugs*, p. 96

18. Neary, *Lugs*, p. 96.

19. "Life with the Stars," *Evening Herald*, 26 January 1973, p. 6.

20. "Guards Sought Piece of Man's Ear," *Evening Herald*, 18 December 1952, p. 1.

21. "Guards Sought Piece of Man's Ear," *Evening Herald*, 18 December 1952, p. 1.

22. "Three Card Trick," *Evening Herald*, 11 September 1954, p. 7.

23. "Man Who Loves to Hear Crash of Glass," *Evening Herald*, 12 August 1954, p. 1.

24. Cullen, *It's a Long Way from Penny Apples*, p. 91.

25. "I Am No Bullyboy," *Evening Herald*, 23 January 1973, p. 6.

Chapter 8 (p. 141–68)

1.   Blain, *Stealing Sunlight*, p. 218.

2.   "'It's Trash,' Says Bing," *Irish Press*, 24 June 1957, p. 1.

3.   Blain, *Stealing Sunlight*, p. 219–20.

4.   Blain, *Stealing Sunlight*, p. 219–20.

5.   "Teenagerism," *Evening Herald*, 13 November 1963, p. 6.

6.   "Bishop Says Teenagers Are Wrongly Blamed," *Irish Press*, 18 April 1967, p. 1.

7.   "Throwback to Tribal Rhythms," *Evening Herald*, 1 March 1957, p. 1.

8.   "Roaming the Streets," *Evening Herald*, 8 October 1955, p. 2.

9.   "Outraged Youth," *Evening Herald*, 22 August 1964, p. 4.

10. "The Story of the Teddy Boy Movement," at www.hectic-hillbilly.co.uk.

11. "Gangs of Youths at Dolphin's Barn," *Evening Herald*, 23 October 1956, p. 1.

12. "Vicious Assault in Teddy Boy Style," *Evening Herald*, 13 October 1955, p. 13.

13. "Vicious Assault in Teddy Boy Style," *Evening Herald*, 13 October 1955, p. 13.

14. "Teddy Boy Tactics," *Evening Herald*, 6 August 1964, p. 6.

15. "He Shouted 'The Russians Will Be Here in 2 Years'," *Evening Press*, 6 June 1955, p. 1.

16. "I Am No Bullyboy," *Evening Herald*, 23 January 1973, p. 6.

17. "He Shouted "The Russians Will Be Here in 2 Years'," *Evening Press*, 6 June 1955, p. 1.

18. "Trousers Width Led to Row," *Evening Herald*, 12 October 1955, p. 1.

19. "Trousers Width Led to Row," *Evening Herald*, 12 October 1955, p. 1.

20. "Theatre to Bar 'Teddy Boys' From Entering," *Evening Herald*, 6 October 1955, p. 1.

21. "Theatre to Bar 'Teddy Boys' From Entering," *Evening Herald*, 6 October 1955, p. 1.

22. "Scene Outside City Ballroom," *Evening Herald*, 3 October 1955, p. 2.

23. "Boxing Celebrity," *Evening Herald*, 24 January 1973, p. 7.

24. "Teddy Boy and Girl Gangs," *Evening Herald*, 15 May 1957, p. 2

25. "Pontiff's Pity for Teddy Boys," *Irish Independent*, 18 August 1964, p. 1.

26. "Be Courteous, Guards Are Told," *Evening Herald*, 4 April 1956, p. 1.

27. "Dig This, You Cats!" *Evening Herald*, 6 June 1955, p. 4.

28. "Life with the Stars," *Evening Herald*, 26 January 1973, p. 9

29. "Dig This, You Cats!" *Evening Herald*, 6 June 1955, p. 4.

30. "Youth Jived in Crumlin Cinema," *Evening Herald*, 24 October 1956, p. 1.

31. "Squib Thrown During 'Rock' Film Showing," *Evening Herald*, 24 October 1956, p. 3.

32. "Tempo Goes to the Bill Haley Show," *Evening Herald*, 28 February 1957, p. 5.

33. "A Big Night for the City 'Cats'," *Irish Press*, 28 February 1957, p. 5.

34. "A Big Night for the City 'Cats'," *Irish Press*, 28 February 1957, p. 5.

35. "Dublin 'Rock' Fans in Street Scuffles," *Irish Press*, 1 March 1957, p. 3.

36. "Dublin 'Rock' Fans in Street Scuffles," *Irish Press*, 1 March 1957, p. 3.

37. "Bill Haley & Co. Well Pleased with Dublin Reception," *Evening Herald*, 1 March 1957, p. 1.

38. "Life with the Stars," *Evening Herald*, 26 January 1973, p. 9.

39. "Life with the Stars," *Evening Herald*, 26 January 1973, p. 9.

40. "Terror of the Teddy Boys Promoted," *Evening Press*, 4 July 1958, p. 6.

Chapter 9 (p. 169–81)

1. Kearns, *Dublin Tenement Life.*
2. Kearns, *Dublin's Lost Heroines*, p. xiv.
3. "Beat Up Child, Wife and Mother-in-Law," *Evening Herald*, 27 February 1962, p. 9.
4. "The Pavement Hostesses," *Evening Herald*, 25 January 1973, p. 7.
5. "Assaulted Mother: Gets Six Months," *Evening Herald*, 1 January 1965, p. 5.
6. "Assaulted Mother: Gets Six Months," *Evening Herald*, 1 January 1965, p. 5.

Chapter 10 (p. 182–209)

1. Tobin, *The Best of Decades*, p. xi.
2. Sheehan and Walsh, *The Heart of the City*, p. 96.
3. "Savage Brutal Assault at Ballroom," *Evening Herald*, 8 July 1960, p. 18.
4. "Savage Brutal Assault at Ballroom," *Evening Herald*, 8 July 1960, p. 18.
5. "Youth Gangs Set Fire to Live Terrier," *Evening Herald*, 29 March 1962, p. 1.
6. "Youth Gangs Set Fire to Live Terrier," *Evening Herald*, 29 March 1962, p. 1.
7. "Larry Changed His Course of Action," *Evening Herald*, 14 July 1960, p. 4.
8. "Larry Changed His Course of Action," *Evening Herald*, 14 July 1960, p. 4.
9. "Larry Changed His Course of Action," *Evening Herald*, 14 July 1960, p. 4.
10. "Larry Has Lost All His Fight," *Evening Herald*, 8 December 1960, p. 5.
11. "Larry Has Lost All His Fight," *Evening Herald*, 8 December 1960, p. 5.
12. "Larry Has Lost All His Fight," *Evening Herald*, 8 December 1960, p. 5.
13. Kenny, "The Day Rank-and-File Gardaí Rose Up."
14. Kenny, "The Day Rank-and-File Gardaí Rose Up."
15. "Arm the Gardaí, He Says," *Evening Herald*, 13 February 1962, p. 6.
16. "The Cigarette Lighter Case," *Evening Herald*, 27 January 1973, p. 7.
17. "Detective Gave Man a Few Taps," *Evening Herald*, 20 April 1963, p. 3.
18. "I Am No Bullyboy," *Evening Herald*, 23 January 1973, p. 6.
19. "Fight with Bank Thief," *Evening Herald*, 15 March 1963, p. 1.
20. "Former Boxer Was Assaulted in City Bar," *Evening Herald*, 23 April 1963, p. 3.
21. "Shop Was Wrecked by Two Boys," *Evening Herald*, 4 January 1963, p. 1.
22. "Shop Was Wrecked by Two Boys," *Evening Herald*, 4 January 1963, p. 1.
23. "Flogging Is Still Lawful in Ireland," *Evening Herald*, 5 December 1963, p. 1.
24. "Flogging Is Still Lawful in Ireland," *Evening Herald*, 5 December 1963, p. 1.
25. "Sentence May Be Flogging," *Irish Press*, 5 December 1963, p. 1.
26. "Flogging Is Still Lawful in Ireland, *Evening Herald*, 5 December 1963, p. 1.
27. "Cinema in State of Chaos," *Evening Herald*, 12 March 1963, p. 6.
28. "Cinema in State of Chaos," *Evening Herald*, 12 March 1963, p. 6.
29. "Mopping-Up Operation Widespread," *Evening Herald*, 12 June 1963, p. 1.
30. "Flood Havoc Hits Dublin Suburbs," *Irish Times*, 12 June 1963, p. 1.
31. "Flood Havoc Hits Dublin Suburbs," *Irish Times*, 12 June 1963, p. 1.
32. "Drama before Houses Crashed," *Irish Press*, 2 July 1963, p. 4.
33. "Clay Floored, But Keeps His 'Promise'," *Irish Independent*, 19 June 1963, p. 15.
34. "Ticker Tape Tribute in O'Connell Street," *Irish Independent*, 27 June 1963, p. 14.
35. "They Jeered and Threw Stones at Gardaí," *Evening Herald*, 21 August 1963, p. 3.
36. "They Jeered and Threw Stones at Gardaí," *Evening Herald*, 21 August 1963, p. 3.
37. "Justice Aims to Stop Jungle Boys in Dublin," *Evening Herald*, 19 August 1964, p. 3
38. "Disorderly Scenes in Dublin," *Irish Independent*, 23 September 1963, p. 9.
39. "O'Connell Street Gaming Licence is Refused," *Irish Independent*, 5 September 1963, p. 5.
40. "Black Market in Tickets," *Evening Herald*, 7 November 1963, p.12.

41. "Drunken Cyclists and Pedestrians," *Irish Independent*, 4 October 1963, p. 10.
42. "Gardaí Prepare for 'Operation Beatles'," *Evening Herald*, 6 November 1963, p. 1.
43. "Gardaí Prepare for 'Operation Beatles'," *Evening Herald*, 6 November 1963, p. 1.
44. "Many Arrested as City Crowds Riot," *Irish Times*, 8 November 1963, p. 1.
45. "Many Injured as Beatle Crowds Run Riot," *Irish Press*, 8 November 1963, p. 1.
46. "Many Injured as Beatle Crowds Run Riot," *Irish Press*, 8 November 1963, p. 1.
47. "Many Injured as Beatle Crowds Run Riot," *Irish Press*, 8 November 1963, p. 1.
48. "Many Injured as Beatle Crowds Run Riot," *Irish Press*, 8 November 1963, p. 1.
49. "Irish Hoodlums on the Loose," *Evening Herald*, 12 November 1963, p. 6.
50. "The Scene in Abbey Street," *Evening Herald*, 14 November 1963, p. 8.
51. "The Depot," *Irish Independent*, 20 December 1963, p. 12.
52. "Jim Branigan," *Evening Herald*, 5 December 1963, p. 4.

Chapter 11 (p. 210–41)

1. "Combat Crime in Dublin," *Evening Herald*, 28 November 1963, p. 8 .
2. "Something Must Be Done to Halt Crime Wave," *Evening Herald*, 24 May 1967, p. 1.
3. "I Am No Bullyboy," *Evening Herald*, 23 January 1973, p. 6.
4. "City Riot Squad," *Evening Herald*, 3 August 1964, p. 1.
5. "I Am No Bullyboy," *Evening Herald*, 23 January 1973, p. 6.
6. "Riot Squad Men Check Gangs," *Evening Herald*, 18 August 1964, p. 1.
7. "Crowd Would Side Against Young Garda," *Evening Herald*, 13 August 1964, p. 9.
8. "Youth Banned After Dancehall Row," *Evening Herald*, 29 August 1964, p. 3.
9. "She Made Punches at Patrol Car," *Evening Press*, 3 August 1964, p. 1.
10. "New Type of Vandalism in Inchicore," *Evening Herald*, 29 August 1964, p. 1.
11. "Assaulted Cinema Attendant," *Evening Herald*, 5 January 1965, p. 4.
12. "Had Knife Stuck in His Head," *Evening Herald*, 20 October 1965, p. 1.
13. "Control of Flick Knives," *Evening Herald*, 9 November 1965, p. 1.
14. "Nineteen Held After Youth Gang Clash," *Irish Independent*, 19 October 1965, p. 7.
15. "Bars and Bottles in Battle," *Evening Herald*, 18 October 1965, p. 1.
16. "Clondalkin Battle," *Sunday Press*, 7 November 1965, p. 1.
17. "12,000 City Lamps Were Smashed," *Evening Herald*, 23 December 1965, p. 3.
18. "Life with the Stars," *Evening Herald*, 26 January 1973, p. 9.
19. "Life with the Stars," *Evening Herald*, 26 January 1973, p. 9.
20. "World's Toughest Cop Dies," *Evening Press*, 17 January 1966, p. 5.
21. "Bit Man in Dance Hall," *Evening Herald*, 23 April 1970, p. 5.
22. "Gardaí Hunt Knife Gang," *Evening Herald*, 15 April 1967, p. 3.
23. "Gardaí Hunt Knife Gang," *Evening Herald*, 15 April 196 7, p. 3.
24. "Horrified by Boy Gangsters," *Evening Herald*, 10 June 1967, p. 3.
25. "Camp Youths Hurt in Gang Fight," *Evening Herald*, 11 April 1970, p. 4.
26. "Skinheads Rampage in City," *Irish Press*, 26 December 1972, p. 1.

Chapter 12 (p. 242–61)

1. "Sank His Teeth into Brother's Arm," *Evening Herald*, 25 April 1956, p. 1
2. "Sank His Teeth into Brother's Arm," *Evening Herald*, 25 April 1956, p. 1.
3. "Mystery Shots at City Buses," *Evening Herald*, 23 January 1963, p. 1.
4. "Eighty Army Lorries Operate in Dublin," *Irish Independent*, 10 April 1963, p. 1.
5. "Bus Driver Bitten in Arm," *Evening Press*, 13 August 1964, p. 7.
6. "Boasted He Used Knife," *Evening Herald*, 20 January 1965, p. 4.
7. "Hatchets in Howth Bus Riot: Five Held," *Sunday Independent*, 24 October 1965, p. 1.

8.   "Hatchets in Howth Bus Riot: Five Held," *Sunday Independent*, 24 October 1965, p. 1.

9.   "Hatchets in Howth Bus Riot: Five Held," *Sunday Independent*, 24 October 1965, p. 1.

10. "Bus Had No Conductor," *Evening Herald*, 27 December 1965, p. 1.

11. "Bus Conductor Was Kicked in the Head," *Evening Herald*, 22 May 1967, p. 3.

12. "Bus Conductor Was Kicked in the Head," *Evening Herald*, 22 May 1967, p. 3.

13. "Saw Busman 'Being Kicked in the Face'," *Evening Herald*, 13 June 1967, p. 5.

14. "Dublin 'a Dangerous City at Night'," *Evening Herald*, 12 May 1967, p. 14.

15. "This Blackguardism Should Be Put Down—Now," *Evening Herald*, 25 May 1967, p. 10.

16. "Corporal Punishment the Answer," *Evening Herald*, 2 June 1967, p. 12.

17. "One Way to Deal with Blackguardism," *Evening Herald*, 2 June 1967, p. 12.

18. "Garda Escort for Buses to Ballyfermot," *Sunday Independent*, 1 March 1970, p. 1.

19. "Garda Escort for Buses to Ballyfermot," *Sunday Independent*, 1 March 1970, p. 1.

20. "Busmen Attacks: Action Call," *Evening Herald*, 11 March 1970, p. 1.

21. "Terror on Late Night Buses," *Evening Press*, 6 January 1973, p. 1.

22. "Attacks of Bus Crews Deplored," *Evening Herald*, 30 April 1970, p. 10.

23. "Attacks of Bus Crews Deplored," *Evening Herald*, 30 April 1970, p. 10.

24. "Terror on Late Night Buses," *Evening Press*, 6 January 1973, p. 1.

25. "Terror on Late Night Buses," *Evening Press*, 6 January 1973, p. 1.

Chapter 13 (p. 262–80)

1.   "The Formidable and Uncompromising Detective Sergeant Jim 'Lugs' Branigan," p. 53.

2.   "I Am No Bullyboy," *Evening Herald*, 23 January 1973, p. 6.

3.   "Detective Gave Man a Few Taps," *Evening Herald*, 20 April 1963, p. 3.

4.   Neary, *Lugs*, p. 71

5.   "Commando Attacks by Guards," *Evening Herald*, 13 September 1954, p. 1.

6.   "He Shouted 'The Russians Will Be Here in 2 Years'," *Evening Press*, 6 June 1955, p. 1.

7.   "The Formidable and Uncompromising Detective Sergeant Jim 'Lugs' Branigan," p. 53.

8.   Quinn, "'Lugs' Branigan," p. 66.

9.   "Man Gets Another Chance," *Evening Herald*, 11 May 1962, p. 1.

10. Quinn, "'Lugs' Branigan," p. 66.

11. "Justice in the Cold, Cold Courts," *Evening Herald*, 4 January 1965, p. 1.

12. "The Formidable and Uncompromising Detective Sergeant Jim 'Lugs' Branigan," p. 53.

13. "I Am No Bullyboy," *Evening Herald*, 23 January 1973, p. 6.

14. "I Am No Bullyboy," *Evening Herald*, 23 January 1973, p. 6.

15. "I Am No Bullyboy," *Evening Herald*, 23 January 1973, p. 6.

16. Neary, *Lugs*, p. 101.

Chapter 14 (p. 281–99)

1.   "The Pavement Hostesses," *Evening Herald*, 25 January 1973, p. 7.

2.   "Why We Girls Held Jim in Such High Esteem," *Evening Herald*, 25 January 1973, p. 7.

3.   "Why We Girls Held Jim in Such High Esteem," *Evening Herald*, 25 January 1973, p. 7.

4.   "The 'Pavement Hostesses'," *Evening Herald*, 25 January 1973, p. 7.

5.   "The 'Pavement Hostesses'," *Evening Herald*, 25 January 1973, p. 7.

6.   "Why We Girls Held Jim in Such High Esteem," *Evening Herald*, 25 January 19 73, p. 7.

7.   "Why We Girls Held Jim in Such High Esteem," *Evening Herald*, 25 January 1973, p. 7.

Chapter 15 (p. 300–30)
1. "Boxing Celebrity," *Evening Herald*, 24 January 1973, p. 7.
2. Cullen, *It's a Long Way from Penny Apples*, p. 90.
3. "Boxing Celebrity," *Evening Herald*, 24 January 1973, p. 7.
4. "He's Dublin's Most Belted Detective," *Evening Press*, 13 March 1972, p. 6.
5. Neary, *Lugs*, p. 81.
6. "He's Dublin's Most Belted Detective," *Evening Press*, 13 March 1972, p. 6.
7. RTE Television tape, 9 September 1985.
8. "Boxing Celebrity," *Evening Herald*, 24 January 1973, p. 7.
9. "Jailed for Assault on Sergeant," *Evening Herald*, 12 July 1968, p. 6.
10. "Month's Jail for Setting Dog on Garda," *Irish Independent*, 19 August 1969, p. 9.
11. "An Irishman's Diary," *Irish Times*, 29 December 1972, p. 11.
12. "Sergeant 'Saw Blow Coming,'" *Irish Independent*, 3 January 1973, p. 5.
13. "Sergeant 'Saw Blow Coming,'" *Irish Independent*, 3 January 1973, p. 5.
14. "Knew No More After Detective Clipped Him," *Evening Herald*, 7 September 1972, p. 8.
15. Neary, *Lugs*, p. 94.
16. "I Am No Bullyboy," *Evening Herald*, 23 January 1973, p. 6.
17. "Dublin Sergeant Will Coach Boxers," *Irish Independent*, 29 December 1972, p. 9.
18. "Dublin Sergeant Will Coach Boxers," *Irish Independent*, 29 December 1972, p. 9.
19. "Bells, Beer Bring in New Year," *Irish Times*, 1 January 1973, p. 1.
20. "Bells, Beer Bring in New Year," *Irish Times*, 1 January.
21. "The 'Pavement Hostesses,'" *Evening Herald*, 25 January 1973, p. 7.
22. "The 'Pavement Hostesses,'" *Evening Herald*, 25 January 1973, p. 7.
23. "Why We Girls Held Jim in Such High Esteem," *Evening Herald*, 25 January 1973, p. 7.
24. "Why We Girls Held Jim in Such High Esteem," *Evening Herald*, 25 January 1973, p. 7.
25. "An Irishman's Diary," *Irish Times*, 29 December 1972, p. 11.
26. "I Am No Bullyboy," *Evening Herald*, 23 January 1973, p. 6.
27. Dalton, *My Own Backyard*, p. 47.
28. "I Am No Bullyboy," *Evening Herald*, 23 January 1973, p. 6.
29. "I Am No Bullyboy," *Evening Herald*, 23 January 1973, p. 6.
30. "Branno's Riot Squad Disbanded," *Evening Herald*, 25 January 1973, p. 1.
31. Liam Ryan, "'Branno' Says a Last Good-Bye," *Irish Independent*, 8 October 1973, p. 24.
32. Liam Ryan, "'Branno' Says a Last Good-Bye," *Irish Independent*, 8 October 1973, p. 24.

Chapter 16 (p. 331–42)
1. "Tough Cop 'Lugs' Dies at 76," *Evening Herald*, 23 May 1986, p. 1.
2. Stephen Dixon, "Tough Lugs Branigan, a Fair Cop," *Irish Independent*, 23 May 1986, p. 1.
3. "The Force Strikes Back and Turns Dublin's Tide of Crime," *Evening Herald*, 21 May 1986, p. 10.
4. Stephen Dixon, "Tough Lugs Branigan, a Fair Cop," *Irish Independent*, 23 May 1986, p. 1.

Chapter 17 (p. 343–6)
1. Neary, *Lugs*, p. 78, 96.
2. "The Formidable and Uncompromising Detective Sergeant Jim 'Lugs' Branigan," p. 53.
3. "The Battle of Baldoyle," *Evening Herald*, 22 January 1973, p. 9.
4. "Boxing Celebrity," *Evening Herald*, 24 January 1973, p. 7.

BIBLIOGRAPHY

BOOKS

Blain, Angeline Kearns, *Stealing Sunlight,* Dublin: A, and A. Farmar, 2000.

Bracken, Pauline, *Light of Other Days: A Dublin Childhood,* Dublin: Mercier Press, 1992.

Breathnach, Séamus, *The Irish Police: From the Earliest Times to the Present Day,* Dublin: Anvil Books, 1974.

Chart, D. A., *The Story of Dublin,* London: Dent, 1932.

Clarke, Desmond, *Dublin,* London: B. T. Batsford, 1977.

Collins, James, *Life in Old Dublin,* Cork: Tower Books, 1978.

Cosgrove, Dillon, *North Dublin: City and Environs,* Dublin: M. H. Gill and Sons, 1909.

Cowan, P., *Report on Dublin Housing,* Dublin: Cahill, 1918.

Cronin, Anthony, *Dead as Doornails,* Dublin: Poolbeg Press, 1976.

Crosbie, Paddy, *Your Dinner's Poured Out!* Dublin: O'Brien Press, 1982.

Crowley, Elaine, *Cowslips and Chainies: A Memoir of Dublin in the 1930s,* Dublin: Lilliput Press, 1996.

Cullen, Bill, *It's a Long Way from Penny Apples,* Cork: Mercier Press, 2001.

Dalton, Greg, *My Own Backyard: Dublin in the Fifties,* Dublin: Wolfhound Press, 1994.

Daly, Mary, *Dublin: The Deposed Capital,* Cork: Cork University Press, 1984.

Davies, Sidney, *Dublin Types,* Dublin: Talbot Press, 1918.

Dickinson, Page L., *The Dublin of Yesterday,* London: Methuen, 1929.

Dunne, John J., *Streets Broad and Narrow,* Dublin: Helicon Press, 1982.

Fagan, Terry, and Savage, Ben, *All Around the Diamond,* Dublin: North City Folklore Project, 1994.

Fitzpatrick, Samuel A. Ossory, *Dublin,* Cork: Tower Books, 1977.

Gillespie, Elgy (ed.), *The Liberties of Dublin,* Dublin: O'Brien Press, 1973.

Johnston, Máirín, *Around the Banks of Pimlico,* Dublin: Attic Press, 1985.

Kearns, Kevin C., *Dublin Pub Life and Lore: An Oral History,* Dublin: Gill & Macmillan, 1996.

Kearns, Kevin C., *Dublin's Lost Heroines,* Dublin: Gill & Macmillan, 2004.

Kearns, Kevin C., *Dublin Tenement Life: An Oral History,* Dublin: Gill & Macmillan, 1994.

Kelly, Bill, *Me Darlin' Dublin's Dead and Gone,* Dublin: Poolbeg Press, 1987.

Lewis, G. C., *Observations on the Habits of the Labouring Classes in Dublin,* Dublin: Miliken and Sons, 1936.

Longford, Christine, *A Biography of Dublin,* London: Methuen, 1936.

MacDonagh, Tom, *My Green Age,* Dublin: Poolbeg Press, 1986.

Mac Thomáis, Éamonn, *Gur Cakes and Coal Blocks,* Dublin: O'Brien Press, 1976.

Mac Thomáis, Éamonn, *Janey Mack, Me Shirt is Black,* Dublin: O'Brien Press, 1982.

Mac Thomáis, Éamonn, *Me Jewel and Darlin' Dublin,* Dublin: O'Brien Press, 1974.

Neary, Bernard, *Lugs: The Life and Times of Garda Jim Branigan,* Dublin: Lenhar Publications, 1985.

Neary, Bernard, *North of the Liffey,* Dublin: Lenhar Publications, 1984.

Newman Devin, Edith, *Speaking Volumes: A Dublin Childhood,* Belfast: Blackstaff Press, 2000.

O'Brien, Joseph V., *Dear, Dirty Dublin: A City in Distress, 1899–1916,* Berkeley: University of California Press, 1982.

O'Connor, Lily, *Can Lily O'Shea Come Out to Play?* Dingle: Brandon Books, 2000.

O'Donovan, John, *Life by the Liffey,* Dublin: Gill & Macmillan, 1986.

O'Keefe, Phil, *Down Cobbled Streets,* Dingle: Brandon Books, 1995.

Peter, A., *Sketches of Old Dublin,* Dublin: Sealy, Bryers and Walker, 1907.

Peter, Ada, *Dublin Fragments: Social and Historic,* Dublin: Hodges, Figgis, 1925.

Quinn, James, "'Lugs' Branigan," *History Ireland,* March–April 2005, p. 66.

Redmond, Lar, *Emerald Square,* Dublin: Glendale Press, 1990.

Redmond, Lar, *Show Us the Moon,* Dingle: Brandon Books, 1995.

Robertson, Olivia, *Dublin Phoenix,* London: Alden Press, 1957.

Sheehan, Ronan, and Walsh, Brendan, *The Heart of the City,* Dingle: Brandon Books, 1988.

Stephens, James, *The Charwoman's Daughter,* London: Macmillan, 1930.

Tobin, Fergal, *The Best of Decades: Ireland in the 1960s,* Dublin: Gill & Macmillan, 1984.

ARTICLES

"17 on Charges Following Dublin Disturbances," *Irish Independent,* 19 April 1969, p. 9.

"27 Moore Street Shopkeepers Summoned: Tables on Street," *Evening Mail,* 26 February 1947, p. 3.

"£1,000 Damage Caused," *Evening Herald,* 19 August 1969, p. 3.

"3,000 Refugees Arrive in Dublin," *Irish Press,* 18 April 1941, p. 1.

"12,000 City Lamps Were Smashed," *Evening Herald,* 23 December 1965, p. 3.

"A Big Night for the City Cats," *Irish Press,* 28 February, 1957, p. 5.

"Accused Men Do Not Give Evidence," *Evening Herald,* 23 June 1942, p. 4.

"'Acted Like Baluba' in Garda Assault," *Evening Herald,* 7 February 1962, p. 3.

"A Final Honour for Lugs," *Evening Herald,* 24 May 1986, p. 4.

"American Offensive Against Japan," *Irish Times,* 21 March 1942, p. 1.

"An Irishman's Diary," *Irish Times,* 29 December 1972, p. 11.

"'Asking for Trouble' to Say 'Trousers Too Narrow'," *Irish Press,* 13 October 1955, p. 4.

"Assaulted Cinema Attendant," *Evening Herald,* 5 January 1965, p. 4.

"Assaulted His Sister—Got Jail," *Evening Herald,* 14 May 1966, p. 3.

"Assaulted Mother: Gets Six Months," *Evening Herald,* 1 January 1965, p. 5.

"Attacks on Bus Crews Deplored," *Evening Herald,* 30 April 1970, p. 10.

"Baldoyle Case: Address to Jury," *Evening Mail,* 23 November 1940, p. 8.

"Baldoyle Case: Men Sentenced," *Evening Herald,* 2 December 1940, p. 1.

"Baldoyle Case Witness 'Hostile and Adverse'," *Evening Herald,* 21 November 1940, p. 6.

"Baldoyle Races Riot," *Irish Times,* 3 December 1940, p. 6.

"Baldoyle Riot Case," *Evening Mail,* 20 November 1940, p. 5.

"Baldoyle Riot Charges," *Irish Times,* 23 November 1940, p. 6.

"Baldoyle Selections," *Irish Independent,* 14 May 1940, p. 10.

"Bars and Bottles in Battle," *Evening Herald,* 18 October 1965, p. 1.

"Batons Drawn at Dublin Football Match," *Irish Press,* 25 March 1940, p. 1.

"'Battle' at Tolka Park Followed 'Invasion' in Commandeered Boats," *Evening Herald,* 23 March 1942, p. 1.

"Battle in Dublin Street," *Evening Herald,* 7 May 1940, p. 1.

"'Battle of Baldoyle' Witness Hostile," *Evening Mail,* 21 November 1940, p. 6.

"Battle of Dolphin's Barn," *Evening Herald,* 6 June 1955, p. 1.

"'Battle' Scenes from the Beatles," *Evening Herald,* 8 November 1963, p. 1.

"Beaten with Belts," *Evening Herald,* 14 May 1966, p. 3.

"Beatles and Bizet," *Evening Herald,* 22 August 1964, p. 4.

"Beatles Leave Quietly as Corporation Cleans Up," *Irish Times,* 9 November 1963, p. 1.

"Beat Up Child, Wife and Mother-in-Law," *Evening Herald,* 27 February 1962, p. 9.

"Be Courteous, Guards Are Told," *Evening Herald,* 4 April 1956, p. 1.

"Bells, Beer Bring in New Year," *Irish Times,* 1 January 1973, p. 1.

"Bill Haley & Co. Well Pleased with Dublin Reception," *Evening Herald*, 1 March 1957, p. 1.

"Bill Haley Flies In: 'Proud of Irish Name,' He Says," *Evening Herald*, 27 February 1957, p. 1.

"Bishop Says Teenagers Are Wrongly Blamed," *Irish Press*, 18 April 1967, p. 1.

"Bit Man in Dance Hall," *Evening Herald*, 23 April 1970, p. 5.

"Black Market Cinema Ticket Vendors," *Evening Herald*, 26 November 1956, p. 3.

"Blackmarket in Tickets," *Evening Herald*, 7 November 1963, p. 12.

"Blizzard Hits Country," *Irish Independent*, 31 December 1962, p. 1.

"Blood All Over the Place," *Evening Herald*, 24 May 1966, p. 5.

"Boasted He Used Knife," *Evening Herald*, 20 January 1965, p. 4.

"Bombed Area Theft Charge," *Irish Press*, 4 June 1941, p. 3.

"Boxing," *Irish Times*, 7 November 1936, p. 13.

"Boxing Celebrity," *Evening Herald*, 24 January 1973, p. 7.

"Boy's Theft from Garda Station," *Evening Mail*, 25 February 1947, p. 3.

"'Branno' Says a Last Good-Bye," *Irish Independent*, 8 October 1973, p. 24.

"'Branno's' Riot Squad Now Disbanded," *Evening Herald*, 25 January 1973, p. 1.

"Bus Conductor Was Kicked in Head," *Evening Herald*, 22 May 1967, p. 3.

"Bus Had No Conductor," *Evening Herald*, 27 December 1965, p. 1.

"Busmen Attacks: Action Call," *Evening Herald*, 11 March 1970, p. 1.

"Camp Youths Hurt in Gang Fight," *Evening Herald*, 11 April 1970, p. 4.

"Charged with Knife Attack on Garda," *Irish Independent*, 18 June 1963, p. 3.

"Christmas Armistice Proposal," *Evening Herald*, 22 November 1940, p. 6.

"Christmas Gifts Sought for Dublin's Poor Children," *Evening Mail*, 2 December 1940, p. 6.

"Churchill's Battle Cry," *Irish Independent*, May 1940, p. 7.

"Cigarettes Expected to Be Scarcer," *Irish Times*, 14 February 1947, p. 1.

"Cinema in State of Chaos," *Evening Herald*, 12 March 1963, p. 6.

"City Manager on Dublin A.R.P. Plans," *Irish Press*, 4 February 1941, p. 1.

"City Riot Squad," *Evening Herald*, 3 August 1964, p. 1.

"Collision with Guards," *Irish Independent*, 20 June 1931, p. 6.

"Combat Crime in Dublin," *Evening Herald*, 28 November 1963, p. 8.

"'Commando Raid' on 'Toss Schools'," *Evening Herald*, 25 June 1942, p. 4.

"Commando Tactics by Guards," *Evening Herald*, 13 September 1954, p. 1.

"Control of Flick Knives," *Evening Herald*, 9 November 1965, p. 1.

"Corporal Punishment the Answer," *Evening Herald*, 2 June 1967, p. 12.

"Costs of Freedom and Neutrality," *Irish Times*, 21 March 1942, p. 1.

"Country Awaits Kennedy," *Irish Independent*, 26 June 1963, p. 1.

"Court Tributes for Det. Sergeant Branigan," *Evening Herald*, 5 January 1973, p. 3.

"Crack-Down on Knifing Crimes," *Evening Herald*, 21 June 1966, p. 4.

"Crime in the Streets," *Evening Herald*, 17 April 1967, p. 10.

"Crippled Ship," *Evening Herald*, 19 November 1940, p. 6.

"Crowd Fought in Street," *Evening Herald*, 1 December 1950, p. 2.

"Crowds Cheer on Route to State Dinner," *Irish Independent*, 28 June 1963, p. 14.

"Crowd Would Side Against Young Garda," *Evening Herald*, 13 August 1964, p. 9.

"Dance Hall Assault Sentence," *Evening Herald*, 24 August 1964, p. 3.

"Dance Hall Owner Tells of Knife Threat," *Irish Press*, 3 October 1955, p. 8.

"Detective Force Ready for Major Crackdown on Crime Gangs," *Evening Herald*, 8 January 1973, p. 3.

"Dig This, You Cats!" *Evening Herald*, 16 June 1956, p. 4.

"Disorderly Scene in Patrick Street," *Evening Herald*, 5 June 1952, p. 7.

"Disorderly Scenes in Dublin," *Irish Independent*, 23 September 1963, p. 9.

"Drama Before Houses Crashed," *Irish Press*, 2 July 1963, p. 4.

"Drunken Cyclists and Pedestrians," *Irish Independent,* 4 October 1963, p. 10.

"Dublin 'A Dangerous City at Night'," *Evening Herald,* 12 May 1967, p. 14.

"Dublin Bombing Victims," *Irish Times,* 4 June 1941, p. 5.

"Dublin 'Bookie' and Henchmen Get Penal Servitude," *Evening Mail,* December 1940, p. 6.

"Dublin Bookmaker Led Gang Story," *Evening Mail,* 19 November 1940, p. 8.

"Dublin Cinema Scenes," *Evening Herald,* 16 November 1956, p. 11.

"Dublin Detective Promotion," *Evening Press,* 4 July 1960, p. 1.

"Dublin Football Venue Onslaught," *Irish Times,* 24 March 1940, p. 1.

"Dublin Gardaí Battle with Beatles Fans," *Irish Independent,* 8 November 1963, p. 1.

"Dublin 'Invasion' Test This Morning," *Sunday Independent,* 29 June 1941, p. 1.

"Dublin 'Rock' Fans in Street Scuffles," *Irish Press,* 1 March 1957, p. 3.

"Dublin Sergt. Will Coach Boxers," *Irish Independent,* 29 December 1972, p. 9.

"Dublin Takes Kennedy to Its Heart," *Irish Press,* 27 June 1963, p. 1.

"Dublin Tenements Collapse," *Irish Independent,* 2 June 1941, p. 3.

"Dublin Vandals on the Loose," *Irish Independent,* 29 November 1963, p. 9.

"Éire Pledges to Defend," *Sunday Independent,* 29 June 1941, p. 1.

"Excitement at Dublin Greyhound Meeting," *Irish Independent,* 15 May 1940, p. 8.

"'Fair Ina' Unbeaten Filly," *Irish Independent,* 14 May 1940, p. 10.

"Family Tells of Attacks," *Evening Herald,* 17 November 1952, p. 1.

"Fashions at the Baldoyle Races," *Irish Independent,* 13 May 1940, p. 11.

"Father and Son on Wounding Charge," *Evening Herald,* 18 November 1952, p. 7.

"Few Raid Casualties," *Evening Mail,* 19 November 1940, p. 8.

"Fierce Fighting round Kharkov," *Irish Times,* 23 March 1942, p. 1.

"Fight Against Diphtheria," *Evening Mail,* 2 June 1941, p. 3.

"Fight at Football Match," *Irish Times,* 23 March 1942, p. 1.

"Fight with Bank Thief," *Evening Herald,* 15 March 1963, p. 1.

"Films," *Evening Herald,* 8 February 1947, p. 4.

"Five Men Sentenced for Tolka Park Assault," *Evening Herald,* 23 June 1942, p. 3.

"Flogging for Men If Law Allowed," *Evening Herald,* 14 August 1964, p. 1.

"Flogging Is Still Lawful in Ireland," *Evening Herald,* 5 December 1963, p. 1.

"Flood Havoc Hits Dublin Suburbs," *Irish Times,* 12 June 1963, p. 11.

"For Assault Man Gets 'the Limit'," *Evening Herald,* 19 August 1964, p. 3.

"Former Boxer Was Assaulted in City Bar," *Evening Herald,* 23 April 1963, p. 3.

"Four Cleared of Dangerous Weapons Charges," *Irish Times,* 6 April 1966, p. 7.

"Four on Ballroom Charges," *Evening Herald,* 28 November 1960, p. 4.

"Four on Wounding Charges," *Evening Herald,* 20 April 1967, p. 4.

"Fracas at Race Meeting," *Irish Independent,* 15 May 1940, p. 11.

"Gangs Fight Nightly," *Evening Herald,* 3 August 1963, p. 5.

"Gangs of Youths at Dolphin's Barn," *Evening Herald,* 23 October 1936, p. 1.

"Gang Terror in Benburb Street," *Evening Herald,* 16 January 1973, p. 1.

"Garda Escort for Buses to Ballyfermot," *Sunday Independent,* 1 March 1970, p. 1.

"Gardaí Hunt Knife Gang," *Evening Herald,* 15 April 1967, p. 3.

"Gardaí Prepare for 'Operation Beatles'," *Evening Herald,* 6 November 1963, p. 1.

"Gardaí Seek the 'Toy Gun' Man," *Evening Herald,* 15 March 1963, p. 1.

"Gardaí Will Pay Tribute to Popular Colleague," *Evening Herald,* 6 October 1973, p. 1.

"Garda Tells of Fight in Dublin Street," *Evening Herald,* 3 August 1963, p. 4.

"Garda Was Hit on Head with Brandy Bottle," *Evening Herald,* 16 January 1973, p. 3.

"'Gardiner Street Gang Used Bottles on Us'," *Dublin Evening Mail,* 22 November 1940, p. 6.

"Germans Continue Fierce Onslaught: Allies Retire," *Irish Independent*, 14 May 1940, p. 7.

"Germans Occupy Greek Islands," *Irish Independent*, 26 April 1941, p. 5.

"German War Scare," *Irish Independent*, 6 January 1910, p. 9.

"Girls Boycott Club over 'Skinheads' Ban," *Sunday Independent*, 19 April 1970, p. 7.

"Girls Convicted of Handbag Thefts," *Evening Herald*, 12 August 1964, p. 1.

"Goods That Were Ordered before Rationing," *Evening Herald*, 23 June 1942, p. 4.

"Guards Sought Piece of Man's Ear," *Evening Herald*, 18 December 1952, p. 1.

"Gunman Gets Six Months," *Evening Herald*, 4 November 1965, p. 9.

"Had Knife Stuck in Head," *Evening Herald*, 20 October 1965, p. 1.

"Hatchets in Howth Bus Riot: Five Held," *Sunday Independent*, 24 October 1965, p. 1.

"He Asked Squad Car Men to Drive Him Home," *Evening Herald*, 3 August 1963, p. 4.

"Heavy Attack on Kiel," *Irish Independent*, 26 April 1941, p. 5.

"Hectic Chase through City Streets," *Evening Herald*, 15 March 1963, p. 1.

"He Has Seen 'Rock' Film 60 Times," *Evening Herald*, 22 August 1957, p. 1.

"Hell's Angels and Skinheads," *Irish Press*, April 1970, p. 11.

"He's Dublin's Most Belted Detective," *Evening Press*, 13 March 1972, p. 6.

"He Shouted 'The Russians Will Be Here in 2 Years!'" *Evening Press*, 6 June 1955, p. 1.

"Hitler Leading His Army," *Evening Herald*, 10 May 1940, p. 1.

"Hold What We Have," *Irish Independent*, 26 April 1941, p. 5.

"Home Rule Question," *Irish Independent*, 6 January 1910, p. 9.

"Hooligan Activities in Dublin," *Saturday Herald*, 7 November 1936, p. 2.

"'Horrified' by Dublin Boy Gangsters," *Evening Herald*, 10 June 1967, p. 3.

"Housebreakers 'Who Frisk About and Do Not Work' Jailed," *Evening Mail*, 14 March 1947, p. 5.

"I Am No Bullyboy," *Evening Herald*, 23 January 1973, p. 6.

"Illegal Money Deals 'In Most Parts of City'," *Irish Press*, 17 March 1970, p. 4.

"Incidents on Bus: 3 Charged," *Evening Herald*, 10 August 1964, p. 2.

"Indictable Crime Rise Last Year," *Irish Times*, 1 May 1963, p. 6.

"'In War Next Year,' U.S. Army Men Believe," *Evening Herald*, 22 December 1940, p. 1.

"Ireland Enters E.E.C. Without Any Fanfare," *Irish Times*, 1 January 1973, p. 1.

"Ireland Is Threatened by Worst Floods in Many Years," *Irish Times*, 17 March 1947, p. 1.

"Irish Citizens in U.S. May Be Called Up," *Irish Times*, 23 March 1942, p. 1.

"Irish Government Makes Protest to Germany," *Irish Press*, 4 January 1941, p. 1.

"Irish Hoodlums on the Loose," *Evening Herald*, 12 November 1963, p. 6.

"Irishmen in Berlin," *Irish Times*, 8 January 1938, p. 18.

Irish Press (no article title), 8 January 1938, p. 12.

"'It's Trash,' Says Bing," *Irish Press*, 24 June 1957, p. 7.

"Jailed 6 Months for Attack," *Evening Herald*, 4 January 1965, p. 1.

"Jailed for Assault on Sergeant," *Evening Herald*, 12 July 1968, p. 6.

"Jailed for Knife Attack," *Evening Herald*, 1 December 1965, p. 3.

"Jailed for Vicious Assault," *Irish Press*, 11 April 1970, p. 3.

"Jail for Son Who Hit Father," *Evening Herald*, 18 December 1965, p. 4.

"Japan's Communication," *Irish Press*, 23 March 1942, p. 2.

"Jim Branigan," *Evening Herald*, 5 December 1963, p. 1.

"Jim Branigan Obituary," *Irish Times*, 23 May 1986, p. 1.

"Jockey Injured: Horse Killed," *Irish Independent*, 15 May 1940, p. 10.

"Justice Aims to Stop Jungle Boys in Dublin," *Evening Herald*, 19 August 1964, p. 3.

"Justice in the Cold, Cold Courts," *Evening Herald*, 4 January 1965, p. 1.

Kenny, Austin, "The Day Rank-and-File Gardaí Rose Up," *Irish Examiner*, 10 November 2011, at www.irishexaminer.com.

"Kevin Street Families Tell of Hardships," *Evening Herald,* 1 September 1954, p. 3.

"Knew No More After Detective Clipped Him," *Evening Herald,* 7 September 1972, p. 6.

"Knifed Man's Escape Dash," *Evening Herald,* 17 January 1966, p. 1.

"Larry Changed His Course of Action," *Evening Herald,* 14 July 1960, p. 4.

"Larry Has Lost All His Fight," *Evening Herald,* 8 December 1960, p. 5.

"Last Passing Out Parade at 121-Year-Old Depot," *Irish Independent,* 20 December 1963, p. 7.

"Lights of Dublin," *Evening Herald,* 6 March 1947, p. 4.

"Lower Tea Ration To-day," *Irish Times,* 19 April 1941, p. 5.

"Magistrate's Comment," *Evening Herald,* 13 August 1964, p. 6.

"Making Fun of Teddy Boys," *Evening Herald,* 8 June 1955, p. 4.

"Man Gets Another Chance," *Evening Herald,* 11 May 1962, p. 1.

"Maniac Stabs Dublin Girls," *Evening Herald,* 17 September 1963, p. 1.

"Man Jailed for Assault on Guard," *Evening Herald,* 13 May 1940, p. 2.

"Man Sank Teeth into Brother's Arm," *Evening Herald,* 23 April 1956, p. 1.

"Man Thought Dead after Park Assault," *Evening Herald,* 23 June 1942, p. 3.

"Man Who Loves to Hear Crash of Glass," *Evening Herald,* 12 August 1954, p. 1.

"Many Arrested as City Crowds Riot," *Irish Times,* 8 November 1963, p. 1.

"Many Bank Holiday Attractions," *Evening Herald,* 13 May 1940, p. 2.

"Many Hurt in Irish Racecourse Clash," *Irish Press,* 15 May 1940, p. 7.

"Many Injured as Beatle Crowds Run Riot in City," *Irish Press,* 8 November 1963, p. 1.

"Marked for Life' Says Sergeant," *Evening Herald,* 19 April 1967, p. 6.

"Masked Gang Rob Dublin Mail Van," *Irish Times,* 4 May 1940, p. 1.

"Men Charged Following Dublin Rows," *Irish Times,* 4 August 1964, p. 5.

"Men Were Found with Long Bayonet," *Evening Herald,* 9 June 1967, p. 3.

"'Men Will Reach the Moon and Mars'," *Irish Independent,* 28 March 1947, p. 4.

"Met by Guard at Night," *Evening Herald,* 17 April 1963, p. 5.

"Microphone Church Thefts," *Evening Herald,* 2 August 1967, p. 1.

"Mods Row with Rockers on Beach," *Evening Herald,* 3 August 1964, p. 5.

"Month's Jail for Setting Dog on Garda," *Irish Independent,* 19 August 1969, p. 9.

"More Court Stories of 'Battle of Baldoyle'," *Evening Herald,* 22 November 1940, p. 6.

"More Women Than Men on Drink Charges," *Evening Herald,* 17 April 1967, p. 4.

"Mother Hits at Youth Gangs," *Evening Herald,* 18 July 1966, p. 5.

"Motorists and Petrol Ban Effects," *Irish Times,* 21 March 1942, p. 1.

"Mr Justice Maguire Sums Up," *Saturday Herald,* 23 November 1940, p. 2.

"Mystery Shots at City Buses," *Evening Herald,* 23 January 1963, p. 1.

"N.B.B.I. Suggests Potato Bread," *Irish Times,* 23 March 1942, p. 1.

"New Type of Vandalism in Inchicore," *Evening Herald,* 29 August 1964, p. 1.

"Night of Horror," *Evening Herald,* 31 May 1941, p. 1.

"Nineteen Held after Youth Gangs Clash," *Irish Independent,* 19 October 1965, p. 7.

"No Ordinary Crisis," *Irish Independent,* 6 September 1946, p. 5.

"Not All Beatles," *Evening Herald,* 14 November 1963, p. 8.

"O'Connell Street Gaming Licence is Refused," *Irish Independent,* 5 September 1963, p. 5.

O'Dwyer, Rory, "On Show to the World: The Eucharistic Congress, 1932," *History Ireland,* November–December.

"One Way to Deal with Blackguardism," *Evening Herald,* 2 June 1967, p. 12.

"Organ Grinders Sent to Jail," *Evening Mail,* 2 June 1941, p. 3.

"Outraged Youth," *Evening Herald,* 22 August 1964, p. 4.

"Pitch and Toss on Roadway," *Evening Herald,* 27 April 1967, p. 7.

"Pitch and Toss 'Schools'," *Irish Times,* 26 June 1942, p. 3.

"Police Have Cap Belonging to Bag Snatcher," *Evening Herald*, 20 April 1963, p. 3.

"Police Officers Unfit to Hold Their Posts," *Irish Times*, 5 June 1941, p. 5.

"Pontiff's Pity for Teddy Boys," *Irish Independent*, 18 August 1964, p. 1.

"Priest Will Correct Hooligan Image," *Irish Independent*, 19 August 1969, p. 9.

"Pub Dart Row: Man Charged," *Evening Herald*, 10 November 1965, p. 5.

"Quake Felt in Dublin," *Irish Press*, 27 January 1947, p. 1.

"Raids on Toss Schools," *Irish Times*, 27 June 1942, p. 3.

"Regarded Lenders as 'Vampires'," *Evening Herald*, 23 March 1970, p. 5.

"Remanded on Assault Charges," *Evening Herald*, 3 August 1964, p. 5.

"Riot Men Check Gangs," *Evening Herald*, 18 August 1964, p. 1.

"Rival Gang Clash Described," *Irish Press*, 23 November 1940, p. 2.

"Rival Gangs Have Fight in Dublin Suburbs," *Irish Press*, 29 March 1940, p. 1.

"Roaming the Streets," *Evening Herald*, 8 October 1955, p. 2.

"Rock-'n'-Rollers" Greet Bill Haley," *Irish Press*, 28 February 1937, p. 1.

Ruane, Tony, "Mickey Edmonds, RIP," *IPA Journal*, spring 2012, p. 21–2.

"Savage Brutal Assault at Ballroom," *Evening Herald*, 8 July 1960, p. 19.

"Saw Busman 'Being Kicked in the Face'," *Evening Herald*, 13 June 1967, p. 5.

"Saw Knife Flash," *Evening Herald*, 5 November 1969, p. 2.

"Scene at Mountjoy Jail," *Evening Herald*, 19 June 1931, p. 1.

"Scene Outside City Ballroom," *Evening Herald*, 3 October 1955, p. 2.

"Sentenced After Row at Club," *Evening Herald*, 10 April 1970, p. 3.

"Sentence May Be Flogging," *Irish Press*, 5 December 1963, p. 1.

"Sequel to Disturbance on City Bus," *Evening Press*, 10 August 1964, p. 7.

"Sergeant Fought Alsatian," *Evening Herald*, 19 August 1969, p. 4.

"Sergeant Getting Treatment," *Evening Herald*, 16 August 1967, p. 3.

"Sergeant in Hospital after City Affray," *Evening Herald*, 5 June 1961, p. 2.

"Sergeant 'Saw Blow Coming'," *Irish Independent*, 3 January 1973, p. 5.

"She Made Punches at Patrol Car," *Evening Press*, 3 August 1964, p. 1.

"Shocked by Teds," *Evening Herald*, 13 August 1964, p. 6.

"Shop Early for Christmas," *Irish Times*, 22 November 1940, p. 6.

"Shop Was Wrecked by Two Boys," *Evening Herald*, 4 January 1963, p. 1.

"Six Jailed Following Dance Row," *Evening Herald*, 27 April 1967, p. 7.

"Six Months for Breaking Window," *Evening Herald*, 30 August 1957, p. 1.

"Skinhead Rampage in City," *Irish Press*, 26 December 1972, p. 1.

"Slapbangs near City Ballroom," *Evening Herald*, 1 January 1955, p. 1.

"Something Must Be Done to Halt Crime Wave," *Evening Herald*, 24 May 1967, p. 10.

"Squib Thrown During 'Rock' Film Showing," *Evening Herald*, 24 October 1956, p. 3.

"Stabbed Man Cross-Examined," *Irish Press*, 22 November 1940, p. 2.

"Stabbed Man—Jailed for 12 Months," *Evening Herald*, 17 November 1965, p. 11.

"Stabbed with Steel Comb," *Evening Herald*, 18 October 1965, p. 3.

"Stab Right Through Man's Body," *Evening Herald*, 20 November 1940, p. 6.

"Story of 'Battle of Baldoyle'," *Evening Herald*, 19 November 1940, p. 6.

"Surgeon Says Men Lucky to Survive," *Irish Press*, 21 November 1940, p. 6.

"Talked His Way out of Danger," *Evening Herald*, 20 January 1965, p. 4.

"Teddy Boy and Girl Gangs," *Evening Herald*, 15 May 1957, p. 2.

"Teddy Boy Attack on Garda," *Evening Herald*, 12 February 1962, p. 1.

"'Teddy Boys' Struck Usher at Theatre," *Irish Press*, 7 October 1955, p. 8.

"Teddy Boy Tactics," *Evening Herald*, 6 August 1964, p. 6.

"Teenagerism," *Evening Herald*, 13 November 1963, p. 5.

"Tempo Goes to the Bill Haley Show," *Evening Herald*, 28 February 1957, p. 5.

"Terror of the Teddy Boys Promoted," *Evening Press*, July 1958, p. 6.

"That Was a Day That Was," *Evening Herald*, 12 June 1963, p. 8.

"Theatre to Bar 'Teddy Boys' from Entering," *Evening Herald*, 6 October 1963, p. 1.

"The Battle of Baldoyle," *Evening Herald*, 22 January 1973, p. 9.

"The Battle of Baldoyle," *Irish Times*, 20 November 1940, p. 1.

"The Beatles Taken to Safety in Evening Herald Van," *Evening Herald*, 8 November 1963, p. 7.

"The Cigarette Lighter Case," *Evening Herald*, 27 January 1973, p. 7.

"The Depot," *Irish Independent*, 20 December 1963, p. 12.

"The Dublin Bombings," *Irish Press*, 2 June 1941, p. 2.

"The Force Strikes Back and Turns Dublin's Tide of Crime," *Evening Herald*, 21 May 1986, p. 10.

"The Formidable and Uncompromising Detective Sergeant Jim 'Lugs' Branigan," *Garda Review*, vol. 1, issue 4, p. 43–53.

"The Passing of the Tramcar," *Irish Independent*, 1 March 1947, p. 6.

"The 'Pavement Hostesses'," *Evening Herald*, 25 January 1973, p. 7.

"The Scene in Abbey Street," *Evening Herald*, 14 November 1963, p. 8.

"The Vandal's Target," *Evening Herald*, 6 August 1964, p. 8.

"They Jeered and Threw Stones at Gardaí," *Evening Herald*, 21 August 1963, p. 3.

"This Blackguardism Should Be Put Down—Now," *Evening Herald*, 25 May 1967, p. 10.

"Three Boys Aged 15 on Break-In Charges," *Evening Herald*, 4 February 1964, p. 5.

"Three Card Trick," *Evening Herald*, 11 September 1954, p. 9.

"Three Held on Stab Charges," *Evening Herald*, 17 April 1967, p. 1.

"Throwback to Tribal Rhythms," *Evening Herald*, 7 March 1957, p. 1.

"Ticker Tape Tribute in O'Connell Street," *Irish Independent*, 27 June 1963, p. 14.

"Tolka Park Case 'a Very Serious One'," *Evening Herald*, 1 April 1942, p. 1.

"Tough Cop 'Lugs' Dies at 76," *Evening Herald*, 23 May 1986, p. 1.

"Tough Lugs Branigan, a Fair Cop," *Irish Independent*, 23 May 1986, p. 1.

"Trousers Width Led to Row," *Evening Herald*, 12 October 1955, p. 1.

"Tuberculosis Ravages in Dublin," *Irish Independent*, 28 February 1947, p. 2.

"Vandalism in City Cinema," *Evening Herald*, 9 December 1960, p. 3.

"Vandalism in Dublin: An Appeal to Parents," *Evening Herald*, 13 May 1940, p. 2.

"Vicious Assault in Teddy Boy Style," *Evening Herald*, 13 October 1955, p. 13.

"Wanted Fight with Garda," *Evening Herald*, 29 June 1959, p. 5,

"Waves of Planes Rain Bombs on Belfast," *Irish Press*, 17 April 1941, p. 1.

"Wife-Beaters in Court," *Irish Press*, 23 December 1972, p. 7.

"Woman Found Lying in Street Sent to Jail," *Evening Mail*, 28 February 1947, p. 6.

"Women Faint as Riot Sentences are Pronounced," *Irish Press*, 3 December 1940, p. 2.

"World's Toughest Cop Dies," *Evening Press*, 17 January 1966, p. 5.

"Young Bus Conductor Savagely Attacked," *Evening Herald*, 9 May 1967, p. 3.

"Young Man Stabbed in Bolton Street," Sunday Independent, 23 January 1966, p. 1.

"Young Men Who Took to Crime," *Evening Herald*, 1 February 1964, p. 4.

"Youth Banned After Dance Hall Row," *Evening Herald*, 29 August 1964, p. 3.

"Youth Gang Attack Garda," *Evening Herald*, 19 August 1963, p. 1.

"Youth Gangs Set Fire to Live Terrier," Evening Herald, 29 March 1962, p. 1.

"Youth Jived in Crumlin Cinema," *Evening Herald*, 24 October 1956, p.1.

"Youth Lost Eye in Club Fracas," *Evening Herald*, 31 August 1964, p. 1.

"Youths Spray Dublin Cinema Audience with Extinguishers," *Irish Times*, 22 June 1963, p. 1.

INDEX

Bold type indicates a photo number.